LIFE IN FEEJEE,

OR,

𝕱𝖎𝖛𝖊 𝖄𝖊𝖆𝖗𝖘 𝖆𝖒𝖔𝖓𝖌 𝖙𝖍𝖊 𝕮𝖆𝖓𝖓𝖎𝖇𝖆𝖑𝖘.

"Truth is strange, stranger than fiction."

BY A LADY.

GREGG PRESS/RIDGEWOOD

First published in 1851, by William Heath.
Republished in 1967.
Copyright © The Gregg Press, Inc.
Ridgewood, N. J.
Library of Congress catalog card #6729607.

This book was printed and bound by McQuiddy Printing Company
of Nashville, Tennessee,
represented by Ray Freiman & Company, New York.

PREFACE.

—◆—

Expecting to embark with my husband on a long voyage to the Pacific Ocean, I was induced to make a record of passing scenes and events, for my own amusement, to beguile the many lonely hours which must be experienced when far away from home and friends, and to afford some little entertainment to my personal friends on my return. Subsequently, however, those whose opinions I respect at home, and the missionaries at the Feejee Islands, with whom I had the happiness of becoming acquainted, advised me to offer my journal to the public, as it contained many facts never before published in America, and some things which have not appeared in any land. This opinion is thus expressed by Rev. James Calvert, Wesleyan Missionary, in a communication addressed to Rev. C. W. Flanders, of Beverly, Mass.

"Vewa, Feejee, Dec. 7, 1849.

" Rev. Sir,

" It has been the happiness of the Wesleyan Mission families who reside in Feejee, to be favored with visits from Mrs. WALLIS, a member of your church. She has been one with us, has labored to promote the cause of missions, and has eagerly availed herself of every opportunity to attend the means of grace with us at the mission stations.

"I have been favored with a peep at her journal, and have been pleased with her account of the state of society in popish Manilla, and with her remarks on tedious and long voyaging, and on the various places she visited. But her journal is peculiarly interesting and instructive, on account of its copious delineations of the condition and practices of the Feejeeans. As far as I have read, I consider her accounts quite correct, and they must have cost her much time and deep application. No account has been given to the public, which details so fully the past and present abominations of cannibal Feejee. This long neglected and deeply degraded people have excited much Christian sympathy, expense, and effort, and the Great Head of the church has been pleased to succeed our labors with his abundant blessing. Long and firmly established principles and precedents are giving way; the entrance of God's word is spreading light, and the chiefs and people are saying in effect, 'We know that the Lord hath given you the land; for the Lord your God, He is God in heaven above, and in earth beneath.'

"The glorious gospel of the blessed God has been attended with a saving energy, so that a goodly number of the most debased of our species have been completely turned from darkness to light; from the power of Satan unto God.

"I think it exceedingly desirable that Mrs. Wallis's journal should be published; and that, too, as speedily as possible. I hope you will coincide in this view, and hasten the publication."

Many others have expressed themselves decidedly in favor of the publication of the journal, believing that it would be both entertaining and useful. Influenced by these opinions, the following pages are submitted to the reading public; and if they contribute to the gratification and entertainment of any; especially, if they are the means of exciting deeper feelings of philanthropy, and of awakening a livelier interest in Christian missions, which aim at the enlightenment and elevation of the benighted and degraded of our race, my most fondly cherished desires will be gratified.

M. D. W.

November, 1850.

INTRODUCTION.

———◆———

ARCHITECTS tell us that the vestibule of a building should correspond with the edifice into which it conducts us. It should correspond in architecture, in proportion and in taste, so that the vestibule should not cause us to anticipate in the building what we do not find when we enter it.

Something of this relation should the introduction of a book bear to the book itself. There should be proportion in length, correctness in statement, appropriateness in imagery, and in all, a scrupulous avoiding of anticipating for the reader, in the body of the volume, what he does not meet when he arrives there.

The work before us possesses some features of unusual merit and interest. It contains an account of a strange and savage people; of whose manners and customs little has been known, until within the last few years; a people whom it has been difficult and dangerous to approach.

The natives of the Feejee Islands have, heretofore, been regarded as the Ishmaelites of the South Pacific Ocean, who would never endure the discipline of civilization, and who, if ever converted to Christianity, would be the last brought into the kingdom of

heaven. Their natural ferocity and habits of cannibalism have discouraged all attempts even to civilize
them, much more to make them the followers of the
meek and lowly Jesus.

Since, however, the residence of Christian missionaries among them, they have been found, in some re-
spects, an interesting people. Beneath their wild and
uncouth exterior, have been found marks of intellec-
tual power and sagacity. Minds have been discovered there, which, under the discipline of refined cul-
ture, might have ranked high upon the scale of men-
tal attainment. The record of their traditions and
wonderful events would, if given in full to the his-
torian, afford him material, unsurpassed in value and
interest.

Their improvement in civilization within the last
ten years has been, to a certain extent, truly wonderful. Many of these islanders have abandoned their
cannibalism, and introduced into their habits of
living, the manners and forms of humanized life.
Their hideous looks and attitudes have been changed
for the decent appearance and deportment of civilized
society.

And no less wonderful has been the change in their
moral natures and condition. Many of these tribes
have not only become civilized, but Christianized.
They have not only abjured cannibalism, but have
embraced the gospel.

These changes, so astonishing in their character,
have been, under God, wrought by the English Wesleyan Methodists, a sect always ready to every good
work, and found wherever the sons of men are to be

enlightened and saved. They have gone to these islands of the sea, planted their missions, and in a measure unexpected by themselves, and surprising to others, have gained access to the minds and hearts of these besotted and ferocious islanders. In some instances whole tribes have abjured their obscene rites and fearful customs, and have worshipped the living and true God. Places, which once witnessed their cruel feasts, have resounded with the voice of prayer; and their habitations of cruelty have been converted into habitations of mercy and love.

The source from which this information comes to us, can be relied upon. This has not always been the case. Occasionally we have been furnished by narrators with brief accounts of the Feejeeans. The medium through which they have received their knowledge, has not, however, always been of the most truthful character. Navigators have sometimes entered upon their journals information imparted to them by those whose policy it was to describe every thing connected with this people, as marvellously as possible. Those who have written upon their manners and customs have not, in many cases, been eye witnesses of what they describe.

But not so has it been with the author of this volume. For five or six years she has been personally acquainted with these strange tribes of the South Pacific, either by residing in the families of missionaries, or living in her floating-house in their harbors. She was the first white female that many of these islanders had ever seen. On this account, they were disposed to regard her with superstitious reverence and fear. Uncivilized and savage as they were, they approached her with a deference and respect which they had not shown to any one else.

She has been a part of the history which she writes, visiting their dwellings, witnessing their scenes, and has been a guest at their entertainments. For these reasons, her opportunity for becoming acquainted with their nature and character, for observing their manners and customs, was what other writers had not been favored with. On account of these superior advantages which she enjoyed, we may safely confide in the contents of this volume, as not exaggerated in statement, or overcolored in drapery. And yet we confess, in reading some sections of the work, one might be half inclined to think the author is dealing in hyperbole; that, forgetting herself, she is reveling in fiction, and not narrating sober facts; that, like the dusky Moor before the Senate of Venice, when speaking

> " Of the cannibals that each other eat,
> The Anthropophagi, and men whose heads
> Do grow beneath their shoulders,"

she has a suit to gain, so marvellously strange are some of the incidents and scenes which she describes. But whatever, in her rare knowledge of this people, has tempted her fruitfully imaginative mind, to write a book exaggerated in statement, or overcolored in drapery, we are sure such a temptation has been disregarded, and that no volume of narration has been before the public more true to the reality, than the one before us.

We have said that the introduction to a book should not anticipate for us in the book itself, what we do not find on perusing it. That we have not departed from this rule, we trust will be found true in our remarks upon the *style* of the author. There is a pleasantry in the manner of narration, which gives increasing interest to the contents of the volume. Its descriptions we regard as unsurpassed. In following our author in her delineations of facts and incidents, we seem to be gazing upon a moving panorama, where all its scenes and shadings are vivid and impressive, or upon a stage, across which, as the actors move, we see all their features and mark all their costume. And, then, there is a change of character, so graphically described, that, while we see a difference in the parts performed, we can hardly persuade ourselves that the different parts are performed by the same persons. Here, the ferocious islander appears with his formidable war-club—and there it is exchanged for the implement of husbandry. Here, descending with savage cries upon a neighboring island to murder its unsuspecting inhabitants—and there assembled with them in the same sanctuary, listening to the words of eternal life. Here, around the burning pile, feasting upon the flesh of their slaughtered captives—and there around the communion-table, celebrating the dying love of Him in whom they have believed.

And here we are disposed to pause and ask, what has wrought such a change in these once barbarous islanders? What has converted them into enlightened and peaceful communities? What has opened their bays and rivers to the quiet entrance of our commerce, and sent them to the sea-shore to welcome us to their confidence and friendship? It is the gospel, the glorious gospel of the blessed God, taught in their dwellings and preached at their mission stations. Surely the gospel has wrought a change here, which is marvellous in our eyes. In has, indeed, been the power of God unto salvation.

To the public, then, we commend this volume of rare information and interest; a volume, unprecedented in its scenes and events; a volume, which should obtain a wide circulation, not only among our communities in general, but especially among those who love to contemplate the wonder-working power of the Holy Spirit upon benighted minds and depraved hearts, and more especially among that religious and devoted sect, who have been successful in winning so many of these degraded tribes to Christ.

C. W. FLANDERS.

CONCORD, N. H.

CONTENTS.

CHAPTER I.

CHAPTER II.

CHAPTER III.

CHAPTER IV.

CHAPTER V.

CHAPTER VI.

CHAPTER VII.

CHAPTER VIII.

CHAPTER IX.

CHAPTER X.

CHAPTER XI.

CHAPTER XII.

CHAPTER XIII.

CHAPTER XIV.

CHAPTER XV.

CHAPTER XVI.

CHAPTER XVII.

CHAPTER XVIII.

CHAPTER XIX.

CHAPTER XX.

CHAPTER XXI.

GLOSSARY OF FEEJEEAN TERMS.

Ba ni valu.—A fence of war.
Beech de mer.—A sea slug.
Buri kalou.—A sacred temple.
Buri bolo.—A house to sleep in.
Bulu.—Another world.
Buka waqa.—Hell fire.
Balawa.—A pine-apple.
Kali.—A native pillar.
Kuru.—An earthen vessel to cook food in.
Kaise.—A poor person.
Kawai.—A kind of potato.
Kalavu.—A rat.
Lotu.—Christianity.
Leku.—A woman's dress.
Lovo.—An oven.
Lovo mbokolo.—Oven for the dead.
Mate ge Mbau.—Messenger to Bau.
Mbokolo.—A dead body.
Mboli mboling.—Thanking.
Mandrai.—Bread.
Mbete.—A priest.
Marama.—A title for the wife and daughter of a chief.
Marama-lavu.—A title for a wife and daughter of a chief of high rank.
Masi.—Native cloth.
Na-mata-ni-vanua.—An owner of the land.
Ndawa—A fruit not unlike a plum.
Ndua, whoa.—A salutation.
Papalagi.—A white person.
Qalova.—A ceremony used on receiving company.
Rara.—An open space of ground, where meetings and feasts are held.

Solavu.—A feast.
Solavu vaka masi.—A feast where native cloth is presented.
Sara sara.—To observe, to explore, to see.
Solanga.—Concubine.
Soro.—To ask pardon for an offence.
Sala.—A head-dress.
Saka.—A term used without reference to gender, as Sir and Madam.
Sanka.—A vessel to hold water.
Tui.—King.
Turaga-lavu.—A chief of high rank.
Turaga.—A chief.
Tambu.—Forbidden.
Tutuvi.—A covering for a bed.
Tufndree.—One who assists in a beech de mer house.
Tombi.—A neck ornament.
Turaga ndena.—A true chief.
Vata.—A shelf of any description.
Vaka lolo.—A pudding.
Venaka.—Good.
Vari.—A plot, a conspiracy.
Vale vatu.—A stone house.
Vale kau.—A house built of wood.
Waqa lavu.—A large vessel.
Waqa vanua.—The same.
Waqa ni lotu.—A vessel where bad conduct is not allowed.
Yandi.—Madam.
Yanggona.—A root producing a stupefying effect upon those who drink it.

LIFE IN FEEJEE.

CHAPTER I.

Arrival at New Zealand—Visit at Pahia—Departure from New Zealand—
Arrival at Feejee—Visits from the Natives—Arrival at Bau—Visit from
Tanoa, the King of Bau, and his son, Thakombau—Departure of the
Zotoff—Vewa and its Missionaries—Its Chiefs—Destruction of Vewa.

Bark Zotoff, July 22, 1844.

I embarked this day on board the abovenamed bark,
to accompany my husband on a voyage to the Pacific,
intending first to stop at New Zealand, and then proceed
to the Feejee Islands to procure a cargo of " *beech de
mer.*" For many years my husband had been accustomed to visit these islands on trading voyages, and had
become familiar with the language and customs of their
inhabitants. On our passage out, nothing occurred worthy of particular note. It is sufficient to say, that we
had the usual complement of squalls, calms and strong
breezes, and I had my full share of sea-sickness.

Nov. 17. We are now in sight of land. How re-
freshing to the eye that had grown weary with gazing
on sky and water for the space of four months !

18. To-day we are riding at anchor in the Bay of
Islands, the entrance to which is not visible from our

2

bark, and we appear to be lying on the bosom of a beautiful basin, so smooth is the water. Directly in front of us is the town of Kororarika, which appears small, consisting of a few houses along the shore, and cottages scattered here and there on the slope of the hills behind. Nothing is to be seen back of the town but lofty hills not particularly verdant.

19. Yesterday Mr. W. called at the house of Capt. Clayton, a gentleman with whom he had formerly been acquainted. He was absent; but Mrs. C. invited us to make her house our home while we remained in the place. We gladly availed ourselves of this invitation, and I soon found myself once more on *terra firma*. We were received by Mrs. C. with a warmth of manner which was truly grateful to our feelings; indeed, one must be deprived of all society of her own sex for at least four months, to be enabled fully to appreciate such a reception. We found Capt C.'s house to be one of the pretty cottages I had admired from the bark. It is situated on the declivity of a hill, and commands a fine view of the harbor. In the afternoon some friends of Mrs. C.'s called, and invited us to walk. We were soon equipped, and sallied forth to climb the rugged acclivities of the hills, which I found rather tedious, having been unaccustomed to such exercise for so long a time. When we reached the hill-top, we came in sight of another harbor. On looking beyond, nothing meets the eye but hills over hills, covered with a kind of fern, of a dark olive green. I am told that there are more than fifty varieties on the island.

20. This morning I received a fine bunch of flowers, with the compliments of Mr. and Mrs. Caflin, and a polite invitation for us to call with Mrs. Clayton and walk in their garden. During the morning I was preparing

letters for home. In the afternoon Mrs. C. and myself called on Mr. and Mrs. Dudley. Mr. D. is settled here as the pastor of the Episcopal Church, for a short time; after which, he is appointed to go somewhere into the interior, as a missionary. I found them warm-hearted and very social. They appeared truly devoted to the great and good cause in which they are engaged. After a long and pleasant visit, we took leave of Mr. and Mrs. D. with reluctance, and departed for the residence of Mr. and Mrs. Caflin. They met us at their gate, and accompanied us around their beautiful garden. We could not admire it enough; it was truly an oasis,—a garden blooming in the desert. We remained here a long time, feasting our eyes upon the rich beauties of nature, which were so nicely arranged by the good taste of the owner that we seemed not to tire, nor take note of time as it passed. Mr. W. soon joined us, and we were reminded, by the departing rays of the sun, that we should be wending our way homeward. We passed from the garden to the house, and after remaining a short time, departed.

21. This morning Mr. W. procured a boat and men, to take Mrs. C. and myself across the harbor to a place called Pahia, where Rev. Mr. Williams, one of the first missionaries to this place, is settled. Mr. W. was absent. Mrs. W., who is a fine, active woman, received us with apparent pleasure, and showed us about their premises. The mission buildings are situated in a little vale, at the foot of a lofty hill. They consist of a few dwelling houses, a chapel, and a printing office. They had gardens also, filled with the useful and orna-mental. We had not been here long when Dr. Ford and his wife came in. They had been to Mrs. C.'s to call upon us, and learning where we were, had followed.

I learned that Mr. W. had been a missionary here about twenty-one years.   As our time was limited, having engaged to meet Mr. W. at Wapoa, I could not learn much of their doings.

It had commenced raining fast when we embarked in our little boat.   We had a distance of three miles to sail, but the men rowed hard, and in due time we arrived at Wapoa, opposite the consulate.   The consul and Mr. W. met us at the landing, and we were conducted to the residence of the former.   This fine mansion is situated on a small elevation, and commands a pleasant view in front.   Roses, geraniums and many other beautiful flowers were blooming there, but no lady was to be found to grace so delightful a home.   Its residents were not Benedicts, and although we found a handsome house, richly furnished, yet there appeared an air of solitariness, a want of something to perfect the whole.   The consul favored us with music, and treated us with refreshments, after which, seeing no signs of pleasant weather, we took our leave, and after a sail of half an hour, arrived home.

23.   It rained immoderately all day.   As I was conversing with Mrs. C. about the mission families, I inquired if there had ever been a family at that place of the name of Myers.   She replied that there had been a merchant of that name, but no missionary.   My husband and myself were visiting, about two years since, in Salem, Mass., when a lady said to my husband, "Is it true, Mr. W., that when you were last at New Zealand, you gave my son a bottle and a dollar, and directed him to go on shore, to the store of a missionary, and purchase a bottle of brandy?"   "It is true," replied he; "I inquired of a man on board, who lived on shore, where brandy was to be bought, and he said of Mr. Myers, the mission-

ary. Your son was directed thither; procured the article and brought it on board." Mrs. C. said that could be easily explained. The natives and loafers, who live along the shore, call every one who is not a heathen, a missionary; and use the word as we use the word, "*Christian.*" We say that England and America are Christian lands, and their inhabitants are Christians, yet many are not, in the real sense of the word. So, they will say of any one here who is not a heathen, "He missionary." This brought to my recollection an incident which I heard Mr. W. relate a short time previous. On a former voyage to Feejee, a "*Kanaka,*" who was in his service, wished to be discharged, giving as a reason, that he had found some relatives on shore, and he wished to go and live with them. "But," said Mr. W., "these persons live with the missionaries, and you cannot live with them." "Oh, yes I can," he replied, "cause I missionary too." These facts will account for many of the unfavorable reports which come to us from the mission stations.

24. To-day Mrs. C. and family, with several other friends, accompanied Mr. W. and myself to our bark. We showed them our vessel, entertained them according to the best of our ability, and enjoyed a pleasant interview. From the vessel we repaired to the shore, when it was proposed, by one of the party, that we should ascend to the top of Flag-Staff Hill. The proposal being agreed to, we commenced our toilsome way. Some of us said, "Oh, dear," while others breathed short, but our journey, like every thing else, came to an end; and we reached the spot where England's proud banner waved. About a month since there were signs of a rebellion here, and this flag-staff was cut down by the natives, but was immediately erected by the agents of the

English Government. There is now a great deal of talk about an insurrection; some fear that there is something wrong, while others laugh at their fears, and regard them as groundless. We seated ourselves around the flag-staff just as the sun was sinking into the west, surmounted by a host of resplendent clouds. A spot was pointed out to us where lived a widow with three children about three years since, who were all murdered by a native. She had employed him to get in some sheep which had strayed away; some dispute arose about the pay, and the savage murdered the whole family. He was tried, condemned and hung for the crime. From our elevation we could see several beautiful valleys and bays; the scenery was bold and grand, but there was a want of verdancy to make it beautiful to me. The bright, round, full moon rose in all her pride and glory, and as she lighted us on our way home, I was asked if America could boast of so beautiful a moon. On our arrival home, poor Mr. W. drew a long breath, and remarked that he would never be caught going up another hill like that again. After tea we felt quite rested, and, for myself, I can truly say that I enjoyed the excursion much.

25. This morning I attended the native service in the chapel. About forty natives were present. It was deeply interesting to see those, who were once cannibals, now engaged in the worship of the true God. Two of the worshippers were chiefs, whose faces were entirely disfigured by being tattooed; the lips of the women were also tattooed. Strange taste this for a woman to imagine that blue lips add to her beauty. At 11 o'clock we attended the English services in the chapel. I was truly glad to join once more with the people of God in prayer and praise. The sermon was plain and practical; the subject, the Christian's hope. After the

services were concluded, Mr. and Mrs. D. spoke to us, and gave us an invitation to dine with them. There are two chapels here; one is a Catholic, and I believe they have as many converts as the Episcopal. The Episcopal chapel is not yet finished, nor does there seem to be any prospect of it at present. It was once supposed that this place would be the seat of government, but the Governor resides at Auckland, and nearly all the wealthy of this place have removed there.

27. We took leave of our kind friends, and came on board for the purpose of sailing for Feejee; but as there was too much wind for us to get under way, we did not attempt it. Our stay at New Zealand was so short, that I had not opportunity to learn much of the place or its inhabitants. It first greets the eye with a long extension of rocky coast, interspersed here and there with woodland hills and sea-beaches. I have been told that the traveller, as he goes inland, finds the country more level, and some spots very fertile. I could not learn that there were any native vegetables or fruits, except the "*kumuru*,"—a kind of sweet potato. The Irish potato was brought here by Capt. Cook, and is now quite abundant. The climate is between the extremes of heat and cold. The inhabitants are a robust people, with straight, black hair, a broad forehead, and thick lips. The countenances of the men are much disfigured by their practice of tattooing, the females tattoo their lips only. They are an exceedingly impulsive people, seldom, if ever, deliberate, but are governed by the impulse of the moment, regardless of consequences; hence their cruelties are without warning. The gospel is doing something among them; for cannibalism is vanishing, or is practised only in secret.

Dec. 5. After a pleasant passage of ten days we ar-

rived in Feejee, and anchored at an island called Ovalau.　It is a beautiful island, mountainous, and covered
with verdure.　Several canoes are along side, and many
natives are on board.　They are nearly in a state of
nudity; they are of a dark brown color, and appear
quite active; hair, when short, resembles the hair of an
African, but unlike that of the Africans, it grows quite
long, is often dyed yellow, or brown, and dressed in
a variety of fashions.　We have a chief on board of the
name of Verani, or France.　About nine years ago there
was a French vessel here for the purpose of trade.　Verani was on terms of intimacy with the captain, and was
on board nearly all the time.　The chiefs of Bau compelled him to murder the captain and take the vessel,
which he did.　The seamen escaped; the natives not
knowing how to manage a vessel, soon got it on a reef,
and it was broken up.　Several white men have for many
years been living on the island of Ovalau, but they have
been lately driven from their home by the supreme ruler
of Bau, and are now settled at a place called Solavu.

6.　We sailed round Ovalau and anchored at a small
island called Motureke.　The schooner Warwick, Capt.
Cheever, of Salem, is at this place, and we have been
favored with a visit from Capt. C. and Mr. Saunders.

7.　We weighed anchor and sailed for Bau, which
may with propriety be called the capital of Feejee.　The
island is small, being only two miles in circumference.
A king and many chiefs reside there.　The ruling chief
is named Thakombau, although Tanoa, his father, is the
nominal king, and has been a very powerful one in his
time, but is now quite aged and his son bears rule.　In
the afternoon we received a visit from Thakombau.　His
Majesty was saluted by the firing of three large guns.
He is tall, rather good looking, appears fully aware of

his consequence, and is not destitute of dignity. He wore an enormous quantity of hair on his head, and several yards of native cloth around his body; he was attended by a crowd of his officers of state. He came on board in a very angry mood, from the following causes:— Bau, it seems, is at enmity with the king of Rewa. Capt. Hartwell, commander of the brig Gambia, of Salem, came to Rewa, engaged some Rewa men, and a white man, who has made himself particularly obnoxious to Bau, to fish for him. He then came to Bau, keeping it secret from him that he had any thing to do with Rewa, and obtained some Vewa men to go to Ba in his service. After he went, the white man from Rewa persuaded Capt. H. to send the Vewa people home, which was an imprudent act, as Vewa is one with Bau, and if the latter is insulted, they possess the power to ruin Capt. H.'s voyage. Thakombau said that Capt. H. had come here and made a fool of him, and that Capt. Wallis would do the same; he wished them both to go to Rewa for their cargo, for he would have nothing to do with either; they were both one concern. Mr. W. told him that he had nothing to do with Capt. Hartwell's conduct, nor should he have any thing to do with the enemies of Bau. At length, after a long conversation and many presents, he became pacified; but declared that he would go to Ba, kill the Rewa men, and burn the " beech de mer " houses. After this declaration he sent a messenger on shore to tell his people to prepare for the hostile expedition. When the conversation was ended, His Majesty condescended to notice my humble self. He took a seat on the sofa, gazed at me, then took my hand and held it up, that his people might see how white it was (by contrast, I presume). He left the vessel about dark.

8. Rev. J. Hunt, missionary at Vewa, called on us,

and invited us to visit him. A missionary station was established in Vewa in 1839, by Rev. Wm. Cross. Mr. Hunt came here in 1842, and has labored since that time in the gospel, with much success. His manners were so easy, that we felt acquainted with him at first; he remained with us to dinner, and we had a delightful interview. Thakombau and suite made us another visit to-day.

10. To-day we visited Vewa. There are three missionary families residing at the place:—Mr. and Mrs. Jaggar, and Mr. and Mrs. Watsford, with their families, besides Mr. and Mrs. Hunt, who have one child. Messrs. Jaggar and Watsford were stationed at Rewa, but have been obliged to leave on account of the war.

17. Thakombau has gone to Ba with a fleet of thirty canoes, well filled with warriors. After the fleet had sailed, Samonunu, the principal wife of Thakombau, with several of her women, came off to the vessel to visit us. When she saw me, she caught both of my hands in hers, and exclaimed, " *Venaka, venaka,*"—"good, good." She is of quite a light color, as were several that were with her; rather fleshy, but has a fine eye and handsome features; her hair was nicely dressed, and powdered with the ashes of the burnt bread-fruit leaves. She expressed a strong desire that I should go to Bau and live; after begging all that they could obtain, and stealing my best scissors, they departed. Our visitors had not reached Bau, when we were honored with a visit from the old King Tanoa. I must confess that his personal appearance is not very imposing; he is small of stature, and now rather deaf; his beard, however, *was* rather imposing, being about half a yard in length, and very white, though I am told that he usually has it dyed black. He has the reputation of being one of the greatest cannibals

in Feejee. Owing to his age and infirmities, he seldom visits the vessels that come to Bau, but as Mr. W. is an old and particular friend of His Highness, we are specially honored.

18. Mr. W., intending to visit the Mathuata coast, and the season being unfavorable for me to accompany him, arrangements have been made for me to remain at Vewa for the present, Mr. and Mrs. Hunt having kindly consented to receive me into their family. The Zotoff sails to-morrow.

21. The warriors have returned without doing much harm. When the hostile fleet first made their appearance at Ba, the Rewa men fled, and the white man ran to the mast-head of the Gambia, and tried to hide himself. The warriors destroyed all the canoes they could find, and then went on board the Gambia. Thakombau soon espied the white man, and said, " Do you think that we cannot reach you where you are ? It is a very small thing to shoot you if we wish." Capt. H promised to send all the Rewa men home; and Thakombau, that he would trouble them no more; and thus ended the affair. Vewa is a small island, about three miles in circumference, and one mile from Bau. There is not a level spot comprising one acre of land on the island. Between the hills, there is here and there a little dale. The island is covered with a variety of beautiful trees, shrubs and creeping plants. There are two towns, containing about 300 inhabitants. Each town is governed by a chief; the younger chief, however, is in subjection to the elder. The principal, or head chief, is named Namosimalua; his nephew, the second chief, is our friend Verani. The houses are built of thatch. Mr. Hunt has commenced a building of stone ; the mission families, however, now

occupy native houses, with the added conveniences of wooden doors and glass windows.

22.   Attended Divine service in the native chapel. About 200 natives were assembled to worship the true God.   It was truly a pleasant thing to see so many of the cannibal race engage with such apparent devotion in the religious exercises of the Sabbath.   One thing amused me much.   The chief had provided a man to keep the drowsy ones awake, and the children in order. The natives were seated on mats, and the anti-sleeper was continually threading his way between them, with a small stick in his hand, which he never failed to use as occasion required.   The Sabbath begins with a prayer meeting at sunrise; at nine o'clock the native service commences; at twelve, there is preaching in English; at four, P. M., preaching in native, and at seven, preaching in Touguese.   During the intervals between the public services, the sounds of prayer and praise are heard from almost every dwelling.   I understand that from the following causes, may be dated the introduction of the gospel at Vewa.   About two years after the murder of the French captain, two French men-of-war came and destroyed the houses and plantations on Vewa.   When the vessels first came in sight, the inhabitants suspected who they were, but the priest said to the chief, " Do not fear, no harm will come to you; the things that you see are animals that I have ordered to come here."   Whatever may have formerly been their confidence in their priest, they did not believe this story, and hastened their preparations for escaping to the main land, which is quite near. After all had been prepared, and the frightened natives were crowding on board the canoes, there was the priest, as anxious as any one, to flee for his life.   " What are you here for?" said the chief; " Stay, and entertain the

huge animals that you have ordered to come." The
wise man declined the honor, and departed with the rest.
After the departure of the vessels, the two chiefs, with
their people, returned to Vewa, where all was desolation,
which they had richly deserved. Namosimalua had now
no confidence in the gods of Feejee, since they could not
save their temple from being burnt. About this time, a
man who had been in the service of Rev. Mr. Cross, told
one of the Vewa men, that if Namosimalua would become
a Christian, the French would never seek to harm him.
The speech was carried to the chief, who immediately
sent to Mr. Cross to know if it was true. Mr. Cross replied, that if he became a Christian, he thought that neither French nor English would give him any farther
trouble. As soon as the messenger returned, Namosimalua, and a few of his people, immediately renounced
heathenism, and a teacher was sent to the place. Verani
still continues a heathen; and Namosimalua has never
yet been admitted as a member of the church, but is
merely a nominal Christian.

24. Vatai, the head wife of Namosimalua, with several of her attendants and myself, ascended and descended
some of the hills of Vewa. Truly, I thought, nature has
abundantly clothed every thing here. How stupid of
man not to learn! The bread-fruit tree is very abundant
on this island; also the eva, which, when in blossom,
emits a delightful odor. Arrow-root, ginger and cotton,
grow here in small quantities.

25. Christmas day. This morning my slumbers were
broken by a little band of choristers, singing the songs
of Zion. The missionaries have taught the little tawnies
this beautiful custom, which is still extant in many parts
of England. At sunrise, I listened to the sweet voice of
Mrs. Hunt, as she sung, "Christian, Awake!" In the

evening, Mrs. Hunt invited the singers to partake of some tea and cake. They prayed and sung, ate their cake, drank their tea, and went home.

27. Thakombau has honored Vewa with a visit. He went into the school, and seemed pleased; said "it was good to learn to read." He has acquired more influence in Feejee, than any other chief.

Several years ago, a dissatisfaction arose in Bau, among some of the chieftains of the place, on account of the arbitrary proceedings of Tanoa. They rose in rebellion, stripped the king of his authority, and would have killed him, had he not fled. Thakombau was then a mere lad, and the rebels thought him quite too young to cause them any trouble. He did not appear to sympathize at all with his father in his troubles, but mingled freely with the rebel party. During this time, however, he was forming plans for his father's restoration. He gathered privately a party to favor his cause, who secretly procured materials, and in one night built a fence around that part of the island where they resided. He then ordered his people to fasten pieces of native cloth on the ends of their spears and arrows, and discharge them at the thatch of the houses of their enemies. In a few moments the dwellings were all in flames, and reduced to ashes. The surprised rebels were not prepared for this sudden attack; some were killed, while others sought safety in flight. Thakombau immediately sent to his father, who was then residing in Rewa. Tanoa returned to Bau, and united his efforts with those of his son in securing the advantages already gained. Bau is near one of the largest islands of the group;—many of the rebels fled thither for safety, but the chiefs, whose protection they sought, either through treachery or fear, betrayed them into the hands of their relentless enemies.

An indiscriminating slaughter ensued; very few escaped
the vigilance of Tanoa and his son. The bodies of the
slaughtered were cooked and eaten. The Rev. Mr.
Cross visited Bau at this time, and found the king feasting upon a dead body, and two more were being cooked
for the next meal. On one occasion, he ordered a chief
to be brought before him; he then commanded his tongue
to be cut out, which he devoured raw, talking and joking
with the mutilated chief at the same time. It is said that
Thakombau has all the cruelty of his father, and is far
superior in his warlike abilities. His influence in Feejee
is now almost unbounded. For the last year he has been
engaged in a war with Rewa. I think that he may truly
be called the Napoleon of Feejee.

29. A few days since, twenty-five Rewa men were
brought to Bau, where they were placed alive on coals
of fire, roasted, and then devoured by fiends in human
shape. The town of Rewa is situated on the large island
about twenty miles from Bau. It is said that the town is
large, and contains many inhabitants. Its chiefs are of
equal rank with the Bau chiefs, being near relatives.

About seven years ago, a prophecy was delivered in
Feejee by a blind man, well known to Namosimalua, and
many others in Vewa. The prophet resided in a distant
part of the group, which had no political connection with
Bau, or Rewa, and he knew but little about either place.
At the time the prophecy was delivered, Bau and Rewa
were on the best of terms; but he declared that in a few
years, there would be war between these two powers.
At that time the King of Rewa had four brothers. The
prophet declared "that one would die a natural death,
another would float away, two would be killed, the most
diminutive of the whole would be made king, and the
principal chief of Bau would be shot during a war with

Rewa." One of the brothers has died a natural death; another has been taken to America, and died; therefore the natives are confidently expecting the fulfilment of the whole prophecy.

Respecting the Feejeean prophets and prophecies, Mr. Hunt says, "Among many other things which clearly show that the Feejeeans have derived their religious ideas from the same source as the Jews, one is remarkable, viz. : the existence of prophets, properly so called, as well as priests. Priests are generally prophets, one part of their work being to predict the success that will attend warlike expeditions, &c.; but there are others, who are more particularly prophets, who foretell distant events, which appear very improbable to any but themselves. The name of this class of persons is ' *Rairai*,' (seer,) from ' *Rai*,' to see. This word has a very similar sound to the ancient name of the prophets, who, we are told, ' were called seers at the first.'—1 Sam. 9 : 9. The resemblance is to be found in the sense, as well as the sound, and is certainly remarkable. The Hebrew word for seer is ' *roeh*,' which is the participle of ' *raah*,' which is certainly much like ' *rai*,' and means precisely the same. ' *Rairai* ' is the same word reduplicated, and means the same as *roeh;* both designate a person who sees preternatural things, yet not always by means of the bodily senses, but in a preternatural way; that is, by means of inspiration. Sometimes the Feejeean seers describe what they predict, in a way exactly similar to the ancient heathen Sybil, expressed in the following lines—

' Wars, horrid wars I foresee,
And Tiber, foaming with a deluge of blood.'

The Feejeean seers profess to see the town whose destruction they predict, in flames; and sometimes declare that they feel the clubs of the successful warriors on their heads."

30. It appears that the occasion of the late visit of Thakombau to Vewa, was to tell the people to take all the riches they possess to Bau to-day, for a *solavu*, or gift to the people of Somosomo. This people protected Tanoa a part of the time during his exile when he fled from Bau. All the towns that are subject to Bau, have been required to carry their gifts to Tanoa, and he presents them to the Somosomo people. The Feejeeans, it seems, are not very prompt in the payment of their national obligations, any more than some civilized countries which could be named. All the male inhabitants, and some of the fairer portion, too, have gone to Bau with all the property they possess; the town is so quiet, it seems like all the boys having "gone to training."

31. The meeting held at Bau yesterday, was attended with quite a romantic affair in high life. There are three different tribes who live on the island of Bau, namely, the Bau, Lasakau and Soso. About three years since, the Lasakau tribe rejected their ruling chief, being in favor of another. Nalela fled to Vewa, and has been protected by the chiefs of this place. Bau could not injure the chief without declaring war with Vewa. One of the youngest of the wives of the exiled chief, is a woman of some rank, a relative of Namosimalua, and an adopted daughter. At the conclusion of the meeting, Namosi and his party were observed to linger behind; and soon after were accosted by a handsome young man, a brother of Thakombau, who took the young lady by the hand, and walked away with her to his house. The rejected chief is very angry at the insult. Revelete, the young Bau chief, was here a few days since, and passed the

3

day with Namosi;* a pig was killed, yanggona drank, and the chiefs, without doubt, then planned the affair.

Jan. 1. According to Feejeean custom, Namosi is going to offer a present to Nalela, and ask his pardon; if the pardon is received, the affair is settled, and the parties are friends. The Vewa people are afraid to leave their homes during the present state of things.

3. The Lasakau tribe, who, for three years past, have kept Nalela a prisoner on this island, and sought every opportunity to kill him if he attempted to leave it, now pretend to take his part, and have been near Vewa the last two nights, challenging this people to come and fight them in their canoes.

4. Mr. Hunt's house containing but three rooms, and one of them being occupied by Mr. Jaggar and family, I have had a house built within the mission premises. It is constructed of thatch, like the other native buildings, but has been made far more comfortable. The interior, which consists of one apartment, is lined with mats; the floor is boarded, and covered with mats; and it is furnished with a looking-glass, wash-stand, table, chairs and writing-desk. There are three glass windows, prettily ornamented with white fringed curtains; my bed also has white curtains. There is no house in Feejee half so pretty. Mr. Hunt thinks it must be very warm, being lined. I had rather have it so, than to have centipedes and other like insects falling from the thatch upon me. To-day I have taken possession of the little domicil, but shall continue to occupy my seat at Mr. Hunt's table.

---

* " *Namosi*," abbreviation of *Namosimalua*.

CHAPTER II.

Lasakau Procession—Murder—Massacre at Vewa—Islands of Feejee—
Storm—Rebellion at Bau.

Jan. 5. A long procession of the Lasakau tribe, headed by their young chief, Navinda, has just passed, on
their way to the house of Nalela. Their bodies were
painted and ornamented as if for war, or a feast. All
were armed with clubs, spears and muskets. The Vewa
people are somewhat troubled, for Nalela has not yet received the peace offering of Namosimalua. It is said
that it would be quite like Feejeeans, to set to and massacre the inhabitants of Vewa. I think this might happen, if Nalela had been on good terms with his tribe previous to the late affair. I am of the opinion, however,
that this visit denotes treachery towards Nalela. Navinde and his people have for three years expressed the
most inveterate hatred towards Nalela; now, they say
that they are sorry for him, and will avenge the late insult that has been offered him by Namosi.

6. Yesterday, the Lasakau people all assembled in
the house of Nalela. Navinde told him that they had
come to make peace with him, and invite him back to
Bau; that they would then avenge the ill-treatment received from Namosimalua, but if he continued to live
here, they could do nothing for him. They drank yanggona together, and parted, apparently the best of friends.
In the afternoon Navinde called to see me, accompanied
by Vataie, who is his half sister. I asked her if she
thought her brother was sincere in his professions to
Nalela. She replied, "It is hard to say; he may be sincere, and he may only wish to get Nalela back to Bau

that he may kill him by and by; for he has long been seeking his life." Navinde duly admired my house, became smitten with a handsome pearl handled pen-knife, which he happened to see, begged it, and departed.

Navinde and a part of his men accompanied the chief of Bau in his late expedition to Ba. When they returned, they saw nine men coming from Bau in a canoe, which they immediately attacked, and killed them, just for a frolic.

It is, or has been, the custom of the Feejeeans, when canoes go to fight, to kill all the natives they may find; but when a war expedition is fitting out, messengers are sent to all the towns in the way, to give the inhabitants timely notice, that all may keep in their houses. The Lasakaus, in this instance, had not killed any one at Ba, and were unwilling to return without dead bodies to feast upon. They were disappointed, however, for the Bau and Vewa chiefs were angry about it, and made them burn the bodies. This appears like a dawning of civilization. A short time since, these chiefs would have joined in the massacre and the feasting.

7. It is now midsummer. There is a good deal of rain, and the weather is rather hot; the thermometer is at 95° in the shade. Centipedes, flies, musquitoes and rats in great abundance. I am obliged to get beneath the bed-curtains as soon as I leave the supper table, and there, with my lantern, I read till I feel sleepy.

At the dinner table to-day, Mr. Hunt related some anecdotes respecting Verani. The first was as follows : "About three months ago, some evil disposed person reported that criminal connection was being held between the wife of Verani and a young man who had professed Christianity. They both declared their innocence. A woman who was accused of aiding in the intercourse, was murdered, cooked and eaten, and Verani sought the young man's life; he fled to the missionaries for protection. Mr. Hunt sought Verani, and asked him if he fully believed the man and woman to be guilty. Verani said, 'No; he believed the report to be false; but he was disgraced by it, and nothing but the death of the young man would satisfy him.' For three months the man remained safe within the mission premises, and the angry chief could get no opportunity to execute his fell purpose. At length he thought of the following expedient. He told his cousin, the son of Namosimalua, that he would leave the island for a short time, and when he returned, he should expect to find the heart of the young man ready to eat. When he had been gone a few days, Masapai, the cousin, said to the man, 'You have been a prisoner a long time; your enemy is now away; come, let us go and gather nuts, and roast them.' The man asked Mr. Hunt what he should do, saying that Masapai and himself had always been true friends. Mr. Hunt said, 'You had better stay; the Feejeeans are treacherous.' But the young man greatly desired to wander among his native wilds again—to pluck the ripe fruit from the trees, and again enjoy the sweet breath of heaven. They walked off, apparently in high glee, the victim wholly unconscious that his doom was so near. About two hours after they left the mission house, a native came running to Mr. Hunt, exclaiming, 'They've clubbed him! they've clubbed him!' Mr. Hunt asked where; for he quickly surmised who was clubbed, and hastened to the spot. The man yet breathed, although his skull was cleft nearly in twain. He was carried to the mission house, where he soon breathed his last. Masapai sent for the dead body, as they wished to feast upon it; this, of course, was refused. He then sent word that he must have the heart. Mr. Hunt said, 'Tell Masapai that he made it easy to kill the man, but it would be difficult to get his heart.' The man was interred, and a watch kept over his grave. The murder was accomplished in the following manner : The young men rambled about in the woods, talked of past scenes (for they had been friends from early childhood), and related stories, as is their custom. After spending some time in this manner, and having gathered a quantity of nuts, Masapai said, 'Let us now make a fire and roast them; you strike the fire, while I gather the wood.' The man was stooping down, engaged in rubbing sticks to procure fire, when a signal was given by the treacherous Masapai; a man sprung from the thicket, struck his victim on the head, and the devoted one knew no more." To see Verani, one could scarcely believe him capable of such wickedness, for there is nothing savage in his appearance. He told Mr. Wallis, on our first arrival, that he was a Christian a little, and by and by he intended to be a great and a good one. When we sat at table, he said, "Why do you not ask a blessing? you are like the pigs to eat, and not ask God to bless your food."

8.   The Feejeeans appear to delight in war, yet they are not inspired with manly force; they have but little true courage. They are not an impulsive race; but when they conquer, it is usually done by deliberate treachery. The following account of a massacre which was committed at this place about three years ago, as found in the journal of Mr. Cross, missionary to these islands, illustrates this trait of their character.

" In the year 1840, a war commenced between Somo-somo and a town on the same island called Vuna. The Bau people took the part of Vuna, which eventually caused a war between Somosomo and Bau. The elder

brother, or rather cousin, of Thakombau, disgraced himself, fled to Somosomo, and assisted the king of that place
against Bau. By means of this chief, and a son of the
principal officer of Tanoa, who had also espoused the
cause of the King of Somosomo, a considerable party of
the allies of Bau joined Somosomo. Among these, the
principal was a powerful town called Namena. Private
messengers were sent to Vewa from this place to engage
Verani and Namosimalua on their side. Verani received
the messengers with kindness, and promised them his
support, stating that all the people of Vewa were of the
same mind. He immediately communicated what he had
done to Thakombau, and assured him that by this means
he should place the Namena people at his entire disposal.
Thakombau had attempted in vain to subdue the inhabitants of Namena, and was, of course, exceedingly glad
that Verani had undertaken to effect the object in another way. He sent Verani a large present, promised
him one of his daughters for a wife, and said, ' My house
and its riches are yours; only effect the destruction of
the people of Namena.'

Verani, thus encouraged, began to think of the means
by which his object should be accomplished. In order
to secure the coöperation of Namosimalua, he circulated
a report that the Bau chiefs were exceedingly angry with
the Vewa people, and had determined utterly to destroy
them. This report failed in producing the desired effect.

Shortly after, an event occurred which Verani had
skill enough to press into his service. The principal
wife of Namosimalua had displeased him, and in his rage
he had beaten her most unmercifully. Being a niece of
Tanoa's, she ran away to her friends (a common practice
by which the ladies of Feejee revenge themselves on
their husbands), and declared that she would never re-

turn.   After much persuasion, however, she was induced
to go back; but she had only been in Vewa a few days,
when a report was brought to Namosimalua that was calculated more than any thing to make him the enemy of
Bau.   The report was, that a young chief of Bau had
committed adultery with the Queen of Vewa during her
absence from her husband.   Verani on hearing this, appeared much enraged, and urged the propriety of making
immediate preparations for war, in order that they might
be revenged on Bau for the insult; and proposed that
they should at once decide in favor of Namena and Somosomo.   Namosimalua said that he would not join
Somosomo against Bau, wishing to make war upon that
tribe only which had insulted him.   His nephew, however, prevailed upon him to fall in with his proposition,
and the preparations for war commenced.

Mr. Cross now interposed, and reasoned with the
chiefs and people on the impropriety of involving many
tribes in war on account of an injury they had suffered
from one tribe only; and assured the Christian party,
that it would be much more consistent with their character and profession 'to suffer wrong,' rather than avenge
themselves in this manner.   Afterward several feared to
proceed, and the speech of the missionary bade fair to
keep the country in peace.

Verani, however, was indefatigable.   He caused reports to be taken to Namosimalua, of plots that had
been discovered against his life; and declared that the
Bau people had actually collected a number of yams to
be offered to their gods, but had neglected, as was usual,
to collect pigs to be presented with them, as they intended the bodies of the Vewa people to serve instead of that
animal.

Namosimalua could hesitate no longer; and as the

war appeared to be strictly defensive, the Christians joined them heartily in fortifying the town.

Verani now sent to the Namena people to request their aid in defending Vewa, and twelve canoes, with about one hundred and forty men, were sent from a place called Mathoé. This exactly met the wishes of the Bau chiefs. One hundred and forty men could not be formidable to them, and yet they were sufficient to gratify their revenge and intimidate their enemies. The poor Mathoé people were in the net, and Verani and Thakombau formed the plan of securing them as quickly as possible. It was arranged that Thakombau should attack Vewa with a large force, which was to be divided into three companies. The strongest, with Thakombau at its head, was to land at a part of the island most distant from the town, and the others to be posted so as to cut off those who might attempt to escape. Verani met the party that was to attack the town, and pretended to oppose their landing. After a few muskets had been fired on both sides, Verani explained his whole design to his men, many of whom had known nothing of it till that moment. Thakombau did the same to his warriors, warning them not to kill any Vewa men, as they were their friends, nor to touch any thing belonging to the missionary, but to assist Verani to kill the Mathoé warriors.

During the firing, some of the Bau people pretended to be shot, and the news was immediately taken to the town that an enemy had fallen; the Mathoé people, who were to die in a few moments, clapped their hands and rattled their spears for joy. The drum was beating, to indicate success on the Vewa side, and all was joy in the town, when Verani and his party rushed in with the Bau people close after them, and fell on their surprised

victims like so many wolves. In the space of a few minutes about one hundred of them were massacred. A few
were shot, others were cut to pieces with hatchets, others
had their brains dashed out with the fearful clubs of ' these
horrible dogs of war.' Many of them fell within a few
paces of the mission house, and some close by the door.

Notwithstanding they were so hotly pursued, the Christian party succeeded in saving several of them, by hiding
them in their houses, and sending them home in the
night. The rest were taken to Bau, cooked and eaten.

Mr. Cross with his family and the native teachers had
shut themselves up in the middle room of the mission
house, and piled chests, cases, &c., one upon another,
as a barricade."

The above is a fair specimen of Feejeean warfare.

9. As I shall probably have occasion to allude, during the progress of my journal, to the different islands of
this group, I will give some account of them as furnished
by the kindness of Mr. Hunt.

The Feejee Islands were discovered by Tasman, in
the year 1643. The group lies between 16° and 21°
south latitude, and between 177° east longitude and 178°
west longitude, occupying an area of about 40,000 square
miles. The group is divided into three parts; namely,
the large, the windward, and the leeward islands. The
large islands are two in number. One is called Vetelavu, the other Vanualavu. These two stretch, north-
east and south-west, nearly through the whole breadth
of the group. They are each about three hundred miles
in circumference, and about thirty miles distant from
each other. The south-western island, Vetelavu, is
more populous, containing about one hundred thousand
inhabitants. The windward islands lay east of the larger
group, and to the leeward of the west. There are, prob-

ably, one hundred inhabited islands, besides the two large ones, and many which are uninhabited. They are of various dimensions, from two to sixty miles in circumference. The windward islands are not more in number than the leeward; but, when taken as a whole, are much larger, and possess a greater population. Kandavu is the principal island towards the south. It is a fine, well-populated island, and admirably situated for shipping. Near it are the following smaller islands:— Dravuni, Yankuvir, Bulia and Ono. These form an insignificant group to themselves, and are the most southerly of all the leeward islands. Bengga, Vatulele and Yanutha are near Vetelavu. Malolo is the principal of the most westerly group, which form a small cluster, called Natuyasawa, or Sau Islands. Mathuata, Jekombia, and others, are near Vanualavu. The names of the principal windward islands are as follows:—those connected with Lakemba are strictly the windward islands, as Vatoa, or Turtle Island, Ono, Ongaa, Vulange, Namuka, Oneata, Mothe, Kambara, Vanuavatu, Nayau, and some smaller ones, which constitute the kingdom of Tuinayau, king of Lakemba. Thethea, Tuvutha, Munea and Vanuabalavu, form a kind of separate kingdom. The chiefs of the Thakandrove and Lakemba have, however, considerable influence over them. Taveune, often called Somosomo, from the name of the principal town, is the residence of the chiefs of Thakandrove, Lauthala, Nggamea, Naitaube, and Rambe, are near Vanualavu, and, with a number of towns on that island, form the kingdom of Thakandrove. Koro, Nairai, Ngau, Bateke, Wakaya, Makouyai, Naingane, Ovalau, Yanutha, Motureke and Vewa, are subject to Bau. It is supposed that there are about three hundred thousand inhabitants in this group; fifteen thousand are subject to

Bau, and the other great chiefs possess perhaps from five to ten thousand each. Several of these, however, are tributary to Bau. There are many independent tribes in the interior of the large islands, of which but little is known.

12. I find my residence in Feejee very pleasant. My little house is cool and comfortable, and is very much admired.

The mission families are social, and lovely in their deportment. Our meals are peculiarly pleasant. The conversation is lively and intelligent; indeed, it is almost the only time that the gentlemen allow themselves any relaxation from their arduous labors. This is the time when I inquire all about Feejee and Feejeeans, and Mr. Hunt (who always delights to impart information,) never seems weary of answering my inquiries; nor does he merely answer quickly, and dismiss the subject, (as the manner of some is,) but appears interested to have me fully understand the subject of my inquiries. It is a time, too, when we do not feel as though every word that we stopped to speak cost a dollar, although I have listened to some that are worth that money.

13. A storm commenced yesterday and still continues. The thatch which covers the top of the mission house, having shown some disposition to leave its present location, has been securely lashed with cinnet and boards.

The tropical storms are sometimes very severe, prostrating every thing in their course. A fine orange tree which stood in the yard, loaded with unripe fruit, now lies prostrate. The occupants of all canoes which are driven ashore, or wrecked among these islands, are invariably killed and devoured.

There is a man now at Vewa who had a narrow escape a short time since. He is an Englishman, and was out in his boat with a native woman and their child. A storm drove them near the island of Geer; the natives swam off to them and killed their child; but when the man told them that he could mend their muskets, they agreed to spare his life and that of the woman till their work should be done. Every day the natives would tell them that on the next day they were to be eaten. Capt. Osborne was fishing at Mathuata at the time, and hearing of their situation, obtained their release.

A few months ago another Englishman, of the name of Wilson, was murdered at one of the Sau Islands. His murder was occasioned by the following circumstances.

A young American went to live at a place called Rabatu, near Ragerage. Here he was treated with kindness by the natives, and the chiefs, it is said, made quite a pet of him. Being, however, of a passionate temper, he became angry one day with the chief, and threw a hot yam at him. This was a great insult, and the natives wished to kill and eat him at once; this the insulted chief would not permit, preferring, no doubt, some other way of satisfying his vengeance, for vengeance he would have had at some time, if it had been in his power. A young chief of the place took pity upon the offending and thoughtless man, removed him to another town, and would not leave him lest harm should come to him.

At length a boat came to the place, commanded by the white man of Rewa, who was alluded to in Capt. Hartwell's case. This fiend in human shape took the American on board his boat, and invited the kind chief to go on board that he might receive a reward for his protection of the American. The chief complied with his request, but was no sooner on board than he was made a prisoner, and threatened with death unless every thing belonging to the American was restored.

This was soon done. He was then told to order his people to bring to the boat, mats, pigs and several other articles. The command was obeyed, but this was not enough; and he was told that they must have a certain girl, who was betrothed to him, which was more than all. He had consented to be despoiled of what little property he owned, but how could he part with this girl, whom he had loved from childhood! She was as " the face of the sun " to him. He hesitated at this demand; but the fiend with whom he had to deal, said, " If you hesitate, I will kill you, and then it will be easy to get the girl " He sent word to his loved one that he was to be killed, and he wished her to come and be strangled with him. Pleased with this token of his love, she hastened to him that they might die and go to " bulu " together, where she would be his only wife. She came; the white fiend took her on board, liberated her lover and set sail, exulting in his villany. But know, oh man, that there is a day of reckoning at hand!

The young chief returned to his town, vowing vengeance on the first white man that came in his way. He had saved the life of one, and his heart had known compassion, but it should know it no more; he had been despoiled of his little property, and the object of his affections had been torn from him; nothing was now left him but revenge.

A few months after this affair, the injured chief was at one of the Sau Islands with some of his people. Wilson, with his native woman, her sister, and their child, were in the boat. The natives swam off to the boat, clubbed Wilson and the woman, while the sister, a girl of ten years of age, took the child, a boy of two years of age, on her back and swam to the shore. The body of Wilson and his woman were taken ashore, where they were cooked and eaten; the lives of the children were spared that they might be fattened before they should be killed. Some part of the cooked bodies were offered them to eat.

Mr. Hunt heard of the affair soon after it was perpetrated, and lost no time in procuring their release. They have been brought here, and now live in his family.

14. The storm still continues violent, but my little house stands it bravely. I am somewhat lonely, however, as I cannot go to the mission house, and am obliged to take my meals alone, or rather with company I do not fancy. The flies and musquitoes are very social, and in the evening the mice are not at all bashful. I wish that the musquitoes were homœopathists, for then they would not be drawing blood from me so freely.

16. The storm has abated, and I am again at liberty. A tribe of natives are here from the main land, building a small house within the mission fence; the natives are very noisy. My house and myself attract a great deal of notice; the last, quite a new thing to me. If you wish to be noticed, you must come to Feejee, where many pretty things will be said of you, such as, "She is like the face of the sun,"—"She is the root of all that is good," and even, "She is a god." It is truly surprising that one could reside in a civilized land for the space of forty years, among intelligent people, too, and yet such beauty and so many excellencies never be discovered.

The chief of this tribe is called Ko Mai Namara. He is an exceedingly smooth-spoken man, and one would think that he would not harm even a fly; yet only a few weeks since, he killed one of his women and sent her to

Bau to be eaten.   She had offended him by running away to Bau several times.

This morning, at day light, Masapai was at my door to beg paint, as he was going to Bau to attend a feast. I gave him some to prevent any more teazing, but I never like to see the treacherous fellow.

18.   Mrs. Jaggar, Mrs. Watsford, Vatai, with several of her attendants and myself, took a long and pleasant walk to-day over the hills of Vewa.   A man (a stranger,) joined our company.   He walked before us, warning us of all the difficult places in our way, would climb trees, or descend ravines to gather specimens of plants, and was as attentive as though it had always been his business to wait upon the ladies.   I believe the Feejeeans, when not excited, are very kind.

On our return I found a bunch of nice bananas on the steps of my door,—a present from Verani.   The other day he sent me a large bunch of bread-fruit.   I feel a deep interest in this very wicked man.   While we were on board the vessel, he would keep the Feejeeans out of the cabin as much as possible, saying they were not suitable company for me.   I think he is about the only one in Vewa who has not been to see my house, or to beg something.

Mr. Hunt thinks that he would renounce heathenism were it not for his intimacy with Thakombau.   With his talents, he would be very useful in the cause of Christianity.

19.   Vatai with her attendants, and myself with the lad, Whippy, visited Verani's town this afternoon.   It is not so large or so pleasant as that of Namosimalua. The Lasakau chief occupies the largest house in it.   As we passed it, there appeared to be many people inside; we were invited to enter, but declined.

David showed me the precipice where so many of the Namena people were dashed during the massacre; another spot where the woman was killed, who, it was said, favored the intimacy between the wife of Verani and the young man who was murdered by Masapai ; another spot where her body was cooked, and also the place where they partook of the horrible feast. Indeed, there seemed scarcely a place which had not its tale.

20. Attended the native service in the morning as usual. Six natives have to-day lotued (renounced heathenism). The principal wife of Verani and two of his people were among the number.

21. Namosimalua, who has been living in a very common house, has now commenced building a large one on one of the highest hills of Vewa, which faces the sea. He called to see me to-day, and observing that I was making a fancy bed-quilt, he wished me to make him a flag like it, that he might raise it on a staff near his new house, so that when vessels came in sight, it might be said, '' Namosimalua lives there.''

Namosimalua is a tall, powerful-looking chief. He is well known throughout Feejee, and feared in many parts of the group. It was surprising to many that his life was spared when Tanoa was restored; but all the circumstances of the case were not known at the time.

When Tanoa fled from Bau, he stopped at an island called Nairai, about sixty miles from Bau. The rebel party offered Namosimalua a young woman of high rank (a niece of Tanoa), and six whale's teeth, to follow and kill the king. Namosimalua accepted the present, and started to overtake the exile. He knew the town where Tanoa was residing; but he refused to land there and take him by surprise, saying that his people were weary, and must have rest and food before they proceeded farther. During the night a messenger was privately despatched to inform Tanoa of all that had taken place, and urging him to escape to some place of safety. The king, on hearing this, immediately put to sea with his followers; but the wind proving contrary, he did not get far from land before daylight.

Namosimalua fearing that the king might not have believed his messengers, still determined to be cautious. In the morning he ordered his people to follow, instead of preceding him, as is their usual custom, into the town. When they arrived, they saw Tanoa's canoe out at sea. Namosi said, "Never mind, he is not going far; he will soon return to some other town on the island, and we can then accomplish our purpose." He amused his people in this manner till he saw the king make sail for Somosomo, and then he said, "Let us return to Bau, it will be useless to follow him to Somosomo with our present force."

The rebel chiefs never suspected his duplicity, although they were not pleased with the result of his voyage. Namosimalua seldom failed in what he engaged to do, and no doubt that was the reason he was employed to kill the king. They confidently expected him to return with their object accomplished. He had ever appeared to be one with the rebels in purpose, and some said that he was the originator of the rebellion.

But Namosi had an "eye to the windward." He knew that all the inhabitants of Bau were not engaged in the rebellion; the Lasakau tribe still adhered to Tanoa. He would gain nothing by the death of the king, as his party might yet gain the ascendancy. He had also received his reward, and would get nothing more if he murdered the king; but by sparing his life he would gain the favor of both parties.

To satisfy the rebel party, he proposed that a large fleet should be sent to Somosomo, and demand the king from the chiefs of that place. The fleet was sent; but the chiefs and people insulted them, refused to give up Tanoa, and they returned to Bau leaving the king in safety.

After the restoration of Tanoa, a great meeting was held in Bau for the consolidation of peace. Vatai was the young woman that was presented to Namosimalua, with the whale's teeth; her father was a brother of Tanoa, and was the one who was brought before him and had his tongue cut out and devoured, as before related. He was one of the first who fell before the vengeance of the angry king. Tanoa had another brother named Tuiveikoso; he had been compelled by the rebels to be crowned king. He was a man of small abilities, wholly incapable of ruling, or of exerting any influence, either good or bad. Tuiveikoso thus addressed his brother at the meeting. "I only am one with you. You and I are two. I knew not the design of your enemies. They brought your title to me; but I desired it not, nor did I take any part against you; therefore, be gracious to me, that I may live." Tanoa rose and said, "Fear not; what should I do to you? you are not as I am, strong, and able to go to other lands. I am as a god,—I cannot be killed; but you can do nothing; for you are like a large pig, which has grown too fat to walk about; you can only sit, and sleep, and wake, and take your food" (which was literally the case). They then both laughed; Tanoa kissed his brother and sat down. Namosimalua, who was one of this company, then went out, and the inquiry arose as to who originated the rebellion. Tanoa said, "The man who caused it has retired; no doubt he has gone to contrive something else that is evil; to-morrow we will have him tried."

The next day the meeting again assembled, and Namosimalua was brought before them and charged with being the originator of the late rebellion: this he denied. He was then charged with having engaged to kill Tanoa, which he acknowledged, and stated that he received from the rebels a niece of Tanoa for a wife, and six whale's teeth, as an inducement to accomplish this object. Tanoa then said, "You engaged to kill me for six whale's teeth and a woman." He replied, "Yes, sir." Tanoa said, "That is good, and I like you for speaking the truth. You shall not die, but live, though you have done me much evil."

The king of Somosomo, who was present, then addressed Namosi, charging him with all the late troubles, and said, "If the king will allow us, we will kill you at once." A tumult ensued, which was stopped by the king of Rewa, who addressed the people in a conciliatory speech, and the meeting broke up.

Tanoa, no doubt, understood the motives which had actuated Namosi, in not complying with the wishes of the rebel party to kill him, and had no confidence in him; still, as he had spared him, it seemed to suit his present purpose to let him live.

Namosimalua is proud of Vatai, and she holds the highest rank of the ten wives that he possesses; but he is jealous and tyrannical, besides being some forty years her senior. She has never loved him, and has several times run away to Bau. Of late, however, she appears to endure with more patience. She is a handsome woman, of good natural abilities, has learned to read and write, and was one of the first on the island who renounced heathenism.

It is of consequence to a Feejeean to possess a woman of high rank, as the children rank from the mother. Vatai's mother, after her husband was killed, was taken by the chief of Lasakau to wife; consequently, Vatai is nearly connected with that tribe, as has been related. Navinde, the present chief, is her brother by the same mother; therefore Vatai's children are "*vasus*" to Bau and to Lasakau. They can go to these places at any time, and take whatever they wish, and even if there should be war between Vewa and Bau, no person would dare to molest them.

Chief women are never to be obtained by poor men. If a poor man takes a wife from another town or tribe, her children are "*vasus*" to her family only; but the children of a chief woman are "*vasus*" to all of her tribe. The queen of Bau is the daughter of the king of Somosomo; consequently her child is a "*vasu*" not only to the town of Somosomo, but to all the towns and tribes who are subject to its king.

CHAPTER III.

Gods of Feejee—The faithfulness of a Feejeean—Temples of Feejee— Verani renounces Heathenism—Murder of a Lasakau Chief—Strangling of Women.

Jan. 23. The Bau people have a set day, which comes about once in two weeks, to go to Rewa to fight. Each town that is subject to Bau takes its turn in leading the battle. The last week it was the turn of the Namara people to lead; three of them were shot, and the rest fled. The Spartan dame would never have owned these for her sons!

24. Namosimalua has had a feast prepared to-day for the people who are building his house. There were about two hundred to partake of it. Bread-fruit, fish, and native puddings, had been prepared in great abundance. About noon the old men commenced arranging the food. They would take a roast pig (of which they had several very large ones roasted whole), and put in one place, and then change it to another; the same of the rest of the food, and then they would appear at a loss to know where to place it to the best advantage. I really felt a strong desire to go and take the management of the affair. Many times the managers would clap their hands slowly, and thank the chief (who was seated on the ground under the mission fence), for his provisions. In this ceremony Namosi joined in thanking himself. About four o'clock all was prepared, thanks were again offered, and the multitude, consisting only of the Matais (carpenters,) partook of the feast, and took what was left, as is their custom on such occasions.

25. Navinde has again visited Vewa. Nalela came to Mr. Hunt's with him, and they drank yanggona together. Mr. Hunt thinks the reconciliation is sincere. They chatted a long time, apparently in the greatest harmony, and then visited me. They thought I was very extravagant to have my house lined with mats. Nalela is a wicked-looking man, about forty-five years of age.

28. Navinde has again visited Nalela. He seems to take much pains to convince him that he is sincere in his wish that the reconciliation between them should be perfect. Navinde calls me his friend, and brought me four orange cowrie shells, as a present. Nalela and Namosi do not speak, and when they go out, are armed with a club. This is the custom in Feejee, but in Vewa the Christian party have laid aside their arms. Nalela has

not yet ventured to visit Bau. The girl that Revelete took, was not his principal wife, but one of his solangas. The household of the chiefs is composed of three classes of women:—First, the Marama lavu, which is their highest title; second, a solanga, which answers to our word for concubine; and lastly the kaises, which means a poor person; these are the servants. Nalela's household is composed of ten females. The Marama lavu is a sister of Verani. Nalela's mother was a sister of Namosimalua, consequently, he is a vasu to Vewa, and can appropriate whatever he chooses to himself.

Feb. 1. Mr. Hunt has been sent for to visit Bau, and prescribe some medicine for the stolen Miss of Revelete. She has been sick for several days. Vatai says that an offering has been made to the gods, to know why she is sick. The priest had a shaking fit, and then said that the god was angry because Revelete had taken her to the house intended for the king of Rewa's daughter, to whom he is betrothed. The offering was a large canoe. Mr. Hunt has furnished me with the following account of the gods of Feejee.

"Their gods, though numerous, may be arranged under two classes. First, those who were gods in their origin, which are called ' na kalou vu;' and, secondly, those which are acknowledged to be the spirits of departed chiefs, or other persons. Some of their gods had a disgusting origin, some as ridiculous as any of the gods of the ancient heathen.

Many of the natives believe in the existence of a deity called 'Ovē,' who is considered the maker of all men, and is supposed to reside in the heavens; some say in the moon. He is not worshipped, to my knowledge, by any of the Feejeeans. Though he is the supposed creator of all men, yet different parts of the group as-

cribe their origin to other gods.   A certain female deity
is said to have created the Vewa people;   and yet if a
child is born malformed, it is attributed to an oversight
of Ovē.   The god most generally known, next to Ovē,
is Dengei.   He resides in a cave near Ragerage, on the
northern coast of Vetelavu.   He is supposed to be en-
shrined in a serpent, on which account the Christian natives say he is the devil.   All the gods have shrines,
when they are supposed to visit this world,—some a fish,
others vegetables, others birds, and some even men.   It
is unlawful to eat the shrine of their gods; so that some
of the natives dare not partake of certain fish, birds, vegetables, &c.;   and a few, on this account, abstain even
from feeding on human flesh.   They have no idols, properly so called, though these shrines may be considered
as such ;   and, like all other idolators, the ignorant
make scarcely any distinction between the shrine and the
god; so that we frequently hear them say of the former,
' That is my god.'

The principal residence of the gods, and of all separate spirits, is called ' bulu.'   Of this place there are
various accounts.   Some suppose it to be a place of rest
and quiet; others think it is much the same as the present world.

As to the nature of their gods, they consider them
very much like themselves, only more expert in evil.
All kinds of human passions and vices are attributed
to them.   If a handsome woman dies, they say some
god has fallen in love with her, and taken her for his
wife.   As they consider their gods are possessed of like
passions with themselves, they employ the same means
to frighten or appease them as succeed among themselves.   In times of affliction, or any other calamity,
they sometimes challenge them to fight, and demand an

explanation of their conduct in thus afflicting them. If the gods are supposed to be angry, they present an offering similar to those presented to an angry chief. The gift has the same name, and is presented in the same way.

The number of their deities is prodigious. Every tribe has its god, while some are acknowledged by all. They profess to multiply them at pleasure, as the departed spirits of their friends are all eligible to the same office; the only difficulty is in finding some person who has impudence and hypocrisy enough to declare that the spirit of a certain person has visited him in the character of a god, and selected him for his priest.

The priest is the connecting link between the people and their gods. He is the living interpreter of their will, and receives, in their names, the offerings of the people.

These offerings are of two kinds;—the *sais*, or atonement for sin, and the *mandrale*, or thank-offering; both are often called *mandrale*, which is a general name for religious offerings.

The power of their gods is confined to the present life, with the following exception:—When a person dies, he is furnished with a club, or other instrument of war, that he may contend successfully with a deity called ravuyalo, ' soul-killer,' who is posted some where in the passage between this world and ' bulu,' for the purpose of clubbing the souls of the dead. If they escape this evil, they become the companions of the divinities in ' *bulu*.' All their offerings refer to the present life. They propitiate their gods for favorable winds, fruitful seasons, success in war, deliverance from sickness, &c., &c.; but their religious ideas neither extend to the soul, nor to another world. They prepare for death just as for a feast, and the wives of chiefs are strangled under the consideration that they will be as necessary and useful in the next world as in the present.

2.   Mr. Hunt found the Miss of Revelete convalescent. He observed that the Turaga-lavus of Bau were mostly engaged in the harmless amusement of flying kites.   A much better employment than eating men!

Another storm has commenced more violent than the last.   I have been advised to have every thing as snug and secure as possible, as all may be unsheltered before morning.

5.   The storm is now abating.   It has exceeded in violence any that I have before witnessed.   The last two nights have been almost sleepless ones, as I was constantly expecting my house would be blown away.   Not many buildings, however, have blown down, as they are somewhat sheltered by the surrounding hills.   The trees look as though they had been seared by fire.

6.   This morning a Tonga man came to my door, and said, "Good morning, ma'am; you sewing, sir?" "Where did you learn your English?" said I.   "Oh, me live with one mission in Tonga; I learn English, I wash, my wife, he iron; suppose you want wash, me wash."   Mr. Jaggar has a Rotumah servant who amuses us much.   To-day he asked for some *peter-salt*, to put into the pork-barrel.   He cannot think that he speaks respectfully unless he says " sir," when addressing a lady.   Mrs. Hunt told him one day that he should say " ma'am," to a lady, and " sir," to a gentleman.   Now, he always says, " yes ma'am, sir—no ma'am, sir."

7.   I believe that human nature is the same the world over.   To-day some Bau ladies were praising my house, and thinking probably to say something pleasing to me, they pointed to Namosimalua's new house, and said,

"Vatai's house is a bad one; this is a good one." I
replied, "They are both good. My house is very small,
and is only for one person to live in; Vatai's is large,
and many people can live there." But they still said,
"No, no, it is not a good house." The civilized lady
continued, "Have you seen Mrs. Smith's new house?"

"Yes."

"How do you like her furniture?"

"Some of it is in good taste."

"I think there is no taste displayed there. What horrid colors her curtains and carpets are!"

7. To-day I was told that a canoe had arrived from
Mathuata. As I had reason to suppose they had brought
letters from my husband, I waited rather impatiently
several hours, and as they were not forthcoming, I took
the lad, David, with me, and went to Verani's town in
quest of them. I found a box had been sent to me by
my husband, but I could not get possession of it. It had
been committed to the care of a chief named Ndury, who
was to deliver it to Verani for me. Verani was in Bau,
and Ndury had gone to see him there, committing the
box in the meantime to the care of one of his men, who
was strictly charged not to lose sight of it till his return.
The man knew that it belonged to me, yet he would not
allow me to open or take it, and appeared exceedingly
alarmed lest I should remove it. David said that it might
cost the man his head if I should take it away. I returned without my letters, provoked at their detention,
yet admiring the faithfulness of the Feejeean.

It was not long after I returned, before Verani, Ndury,
and the faithful man came, bearing the box, which really
appeared of as much importance as the mysterious box
which contained the crown of Scotland, in the days of
our valiant namesake.

8.   We have learned that a chief with his tribe, who reside at Ovalau, have renounced heathenism, and wish to be instructed in the Christian religion.

The brig Columbine, Capt. Stratton, has arrived, and he has his lady with him.

The following item of news is in circulation :—Some little time since, the Rewa people destroyed a town that belonged to Bau.   Thakombau has been collecting a force under the pretence of going to rebuild it.   He commanded the warriors of Namata to go and assist.   It is said that his object is to get the Namata people in his power, to destroy them.   They heard of the plot, and refused to go.

9.   The conversation at table to-day, turned upon America.   One remarked that "if America had to fight now for her liberties, she would not gain her object." "Why?" I asked.   "There are several reasons," he replied; "one is, if we may judge by their political papers, that there is not unity enough among them."   I found that he had been reading some of the productions of the "glorious liberty of our press," newspaper slang, and papers that are filled with the lowest abuse of their opponents.   I will never again endure this annoyance from the dissemination of them among foreigners.   I replied, "We are now at peace, and no alarm is felt at present that the liberties of our nation are in danger. You know the old adage,

> ' Satan always finds some work
> For idle hands to do '—

His Majesty (although we profess not to be subject to kings) is now exercising his talents in the way of abuse; but should our liberties be invaded, I think that they would unite to a man in repelling their invaders."

"Should that ever be the case," remarked one, "they have not the courage that was possessed by former generations." "England has tried our courage twice," I replied, "if she doubts it now, let her try again."

12. The weather is very hot. Natives, musquitoes and flies are swarming my house. I take a stick and drive the children away, lock the door to keep out the grown people, shut my mouth to keep the flies from going down my throat, bear the stings of the musquitoes as well as possible, and try to look amiable, but do not feel so.

13. Received a visit from the Queen of Bau, or the Marama-lavu, as she is called. The title of Marama is given to all females of high rank, and Marama-lavu is the title of the highest rank, as Tui and Turaga-lavu are the titles of great chiefs. Tui is their word for king—Lavu is their word for great. I do not learn that the females have more than two titles—Marama and Yande—the latter of which answers to our word for madam. My visitor is the principal wife of Tanoa, although he has many others of equal rank. After her departure, the following interesting tale was related respecting her ladyship.

Not long since, she cast her eyes upon a young man, as did the Queen of Egypt upon Joseph; but the young man in this case, having no garment to leave in her hands, and not possessing the virtue of Joseph, after some time yielded to her entreaties, though he had no love for the woman, and great fear of the king. The Marama, fearing that the story of her love would get to the ears of the king, told him that she had been insulted by the man, and had him clubbed to death at once. These are the facts, though not given in the words of the narrator.

14. Mr. Hunt visited Capt. Stratton and lady, on on board the Columbine. Thakombau was there, and seemed quite disposed to tease Mr. Hunt, saying to him, "If I am the first to '*lotu*' among my people, I shall be first in heaven, shall I not?" "If you love God the most, and serve him the best, you may have a higher place in heaven," replied Mr. Hunt. "But," said he, "Namosimalua has '*lotued*.' Have you given him glass windows for his new house, and English carpets for his floors, and have you sent to England for a vessel for him?" "He gets no riches because he has renounced heathenism. We do not come here to give riches to those who '*lotu*,' but to tell you about God and Jesus Christ, that you may love Him, and your souls be saved," said Mr. H. "Then I will not '*lotu*,'" he replied. He then inquired about the resurrection. Mr. H. told him that his body, and the bodies of all those he had eaten, would be raised at the day of judgment, and if he did not repent, they would all be sentenced to the "*buka-waqa*" together. "Well," replied he, "it is a fine thing to have a fire in cold weather." Mr. Hunt said, "I shall still pray for you with a good mind, although you treat the subject so lightly." To which he replied, "Go on with that."

15. Visited by a Bau lady, who brought me a present of a mat. She said that was her love to me, and that her husband, who was a great chief of Bau, but was now dead, had loved my husband very much; on this account she loved my husband and me very much. She informed us that two men were eaten in Bau yesterday, and a woman the day before.

18. Mr. Hunt received a visit from the great high priest of Bau. He looks as though he was well fed.

19. Received a visit from another of the wives of Ta-

noa. Not long since this woman came to Vewa to receive medical treatment. While here she renounced
heathenism, but when she recovered and returned to
Bau, Thakombau said that she had " *lotued*," that she
might not be strangled when his father died; and he
compelled her to return to heathenism again.

21. Mrs. Stratton passed the day with us. In the afternoon we walked to the heathen temple, of which there
is but one in the place. Being situated on the brow of a
hill, and surrounded by trees, its appearance from the
sea is quite picturesque and beautiful.

The temples of Feejee are called "*buris*," of which
there are three classes. Two of them are sacred to their
gods, and no woman is allowed to enter them. At the
time of the destruction of Vewa by the French, the temples were also destroyed. In 1843, the present one was
built, but the priest dying about the same time, no one
could be found to sustain the office, both of the sons of
the old priest having become Christians.

22. Mrs. Jaggar and myself called this afternoon on
the Marama at her new house. Namosimalua saw us go
into his house, from his garden, and soon came to tell us
how glad he was to see us. We noticed among his women one who was dumb. Vatai said that about two
years since, she was married, and very soon after sick-
ened, and as her friends thought, died. Her body was
prepared for the grave, and as they were bearing it out
of the house, her mother said, " No, she shall not be
buried yet; lay her here, by the door." They left the
body by the door, and departed. Some time after, signs
of life were perceived, which soon increased to a cer-
tainty. She recovered her health, but has never spoken
since. Namosi asked Mrs. Jaggar if her speech would
not be restored if she turned Christian. Mrs. J. told her

that it would be well for her to become a Christian, that
her soul might be saved, but she could not say that her
power of speech would be restored.

There are many strangers here as the day is fine. My
windows are surrounded with admirers. I receive nearly
as many compliments as my house. Being nearly overpowered by the delightful odor of my room, as the *copper-
colored blinds* prevented the pure breezes of heaven from
passing through, I left, and passed the most of the day
with my pleasant neighbors.

23. We learn that a town belonging to Rewa has
been destroyed by Bau. Six men were killed, who were
taken to Bau and eaten.

Mrs. Jaggar, Mrs. Watsford and myself, have commenced teaching a class of girls to sew; one teaching
one week, and the other the next, and so on. Mrs.
Hunt does not join us at present, on account of ill health.

24. Namosimalua has beaten two of his women most
unmercifully, for some trifling fault. None seem to like
him or respect his character. Many of his women are
pious, but cannot enjoy the privileges of the church while
living in a state of concubinage, and this they are compelled to do, as he will not release them. He is neither
Christian nor heathen. He has renounced many of his
heathen practices, given up cannibalism, has no confidence in heathen gods, believes in the only true God, but
neither loves nor serves Him.

March 8. The solemn notes of a bell are now sound-
ing in my ears. Some one is about to be laid in his
last resting-place on earth. How many times has the
bell of my own church tolled since I left my native land!
Many of my own loved friends, from whom I parted in
the full glow of health, may be resting in the cold grave.
I am 15,000 miles from home.

16. Capt. Stratton has sailed for Sydney, and taken letters to forward to England and America. The white men living at this place, of whom there are several, procured rum from Capt. S., and had a grand time last night. They sent for Verani, and invited him to join them; this he refused, telling them that he did not wish to get drunk, that it was bad to do so. They told him that the drink they offered him was not rum, but wine, which the missionaries had given to a sick woman, wife of one of the tempters. Verani thought it no harm to drink wine, and soon they all became drunk together.

21. Verani came to Mr. Jaggar, and inquired why religious services were to be held on this day. He was told that it was " Good Friday," the day on which it was supposed that Jesus Christ died. " Then this shall be the day on which I will lotu," said Verani; and in accordance with this resolution, he attended the morning prayer meeting, and on his knees, publicly renounced heathenism. It appears that the mind of this chief has been much exercised upon the subject of religion for some two or three months past, but he has had much to struggle against. He has fully believed, that unless he repented of his sins, and loved God, he could not be happy in another world. If he became a Christian, however, he must not only brave the resentment of Thakombau, which is no slight thing, but he must give up all which is dear to a heathen; and in return he sees in prospect no earthly reward. He knows that those who become Christians, gain no riches from the missionaries; but are taught how to gain the " pearl of great price," and that is all. He could not expect to gain any thing from the masters of trading vessels, either, for these, with but very few exceptions, prefer to have nothing to do with Christianity, or Christians. It may be seen from

5

this, that he is now willing to give up all for the salvation of his soul. He has learned to read, and has many times of late sat up all night with a teacher, talking about religion.

The Lasakaus have at length accomplished their purpose. Nalela was killed last night in Bau. Navinde has been here very often since the pretended reconciliation, and used every means to convince Nalela of his sincerity. Nalela has, however, declined going to Bau to live, but occasionally visited there. Last night, as he was sitting in the "*buri*," he was shot. The Marama and others of his women have gone to Bau, where it is most likely that some of them will be strangled. Namosimalua looks dark, and says that Bau is determined to kill off the old chiefs, and his turn will soon come. He has sent to Bau to ask if this is intended as an insult to Vewa. If so, they may come on; Vewa is ready to meet them.

Last evening Vewa received a present of several muskets and kegs of powder from Thakombau. This was, that he might receive the news of the morning with "a good mind." Bau has as much to do with the affair as Lasakau.

22. Nalela went to Bau the day before he was killed, to see Navinde, who, they pretended, was sick. He spent his first night there safely, and avowed his intention of remaining the second. During the day, some friend secretly warned him of his danger, and advised his return to Vewa immediately. He disregarded the friendly warning and decided to remain, thinking, perhaps, if they were determined to kill him, they might as well accomplish their purpose at once. He had been a prisoner for three years, and had now tasted again the sweets of liberty, rendered doubly dear, no doubt, by being so long

deprived of them. In the evening, Nalela, with his father, Navinde, and others, were seated in the great "*buri*" of Bau, drinking yanggona, and enjoying a social chat, when suddenly the report of a musket was heard, and Nalela fell. Navinde sprung to his feet, and struck the fallen chief several blows with his club. The poor old father of Nalela said to him, "Oh, do not do that, he will die with the shot." With the fury of a demon, Navinde turned, and struck the old man so violently that he fell to the ground a corpse. In the morning Tanoa was told of the death of Nalela. "Very good," said the king, "send to Vewa that his wife may come and kiss the body of her husband." She found his body exceedingly mutilated—the heart, liver and tongue had been devoured.

23. The chiefs of Bau would not consent to strangle any of the women that had belonged to Nalela, as they wished to have him feel the effects of their hatred in the next world. After having shot and clubbed him out of this world, they mean to starve him in the next, by not allowing any woman to go with him to do his cooking. The Marama, after returning from Bau, went to Namosimalua, and said, "Come, strangle me quick, that my spirit may go with the spirit of Nalela, and comfort him; he is even now faint for food." Namosi is Christian enough to refuse her request. She then applied to Verani, who said, "No, you must not be strangled, for you can do no good to Nalela where he is; you must live and repent of your sins, that when you die, you may go to heaven." "Ah!" she exclaimed, in accents of the deepest woe, "it is true that no one loves me. There was one that loved me, but they have killed him, and there is not one left that loves me enough to send me to

him. You are my brother, but you do not love me. I
will starve myself."

The manner of strangling the females when a chief
dies, is as follows :—The woman first kisses the corpse,
then hastens to the house of her nearest male relative, or
in his absence, to the chief, and says, " I wish to die,
that I may go where my husband is. Love me, and
make haste to strangle me, that I may hasten and overtake him." The relatives applaud her resolution, and
direct her to bathe herself. Her ablutions being accomplished, her female friends accompany her to the house
of the deceased with all despatch, and dress and decorate
her for the journey which she is about to undertake.
Her mother, if alive, spreads a mat for her to sit upon.
All, then, give her their parting salutation. While some
rejoice at, and commend her heroism, occasionally there
are some whose feelings recoil at the apparatus of death,
and by such persons (but the number is comparatively
few), the murderous cord is touched with a trembling
hand, or seized with the grasp of a maniac. The widow
summons all her energy, and surrenders herself to her
murderers. The willing victim is placed in the lap of a
female, and a piece of native cloth is folded so as to make
a strong cord, which is placed round her neck. A knot
is tied on each side of the windpipe, and the two ends
are made to pass each other in opposite directions; and
while one woman is pressing down her head, and another
holding her hand over her mouth and nostrils, five or six
men take hold of each end of the cord, and pull it till the
two ends meet, or pass each other. The work of death
is violent, brief and certain. The body is soon stretched
on the mat a breathless corpse. The cord is left about
her neck, the ends unfolded and tied in a knot. The
body is then rubbed over with tumeric, and placed by

the side of the dead chief. The friends of the chief then present a whale's tooth to her nearest male relative, and say, "*A kenai sere, ni wa ni kuna.*"—"This is the untying of the cord of strangling." The cord is then untied, and left loose about her neck. She is buried in the same grave with her husband. If the chief is of very high rank, several women are thus sacrificed.

24. Mr. Hunt has visited at the house of the murdered chief. He did not see the widow, but found the other women making a great noise. It is the custom to burn the houses of deceased chiefs, with every thing they contain; but Verani would not allow it in this case. The widow has, however, burned and broken many articles, and the last accounts stated that she was hard at work in accomplishing the ruin of a pair of strong scissors.

Nalela was a very wicked, blood-thirsty tyrant. Although while a prisoner at Vewa, in constant fear and real danger, yet he omitted no opportunity of showing his *amiable character*. He was a "*vasu*" to Vewa, and exercised his power with the younger portion of the population, in the most despotic manner.

Not long since, Masapai told one of his men to take a pig belonging to himself, to another island, which he named. Nalela heard of it, and determined to kill the man who had executed the orders of Masapai. Mr. Hunt heard of the affair, and "*soroed*" to the chief in time to save the life of the young man. "*To soro*," is to take a present to the offended party, and say "*Au soro*," "I ask pardon."

25. Last evening being fine, and lighted by the full, unclouded moon, Mr. and Mrs. Watsford and myself walked to the spacious mansion of the Turaga-lavu. The prospect from the elevation where this mansion is located, is extensive and beautiful, either by sunlight or moon-

light. I love beautiful prospects, rich and charming scenery, but fail in any attempt to describe it. As we reached the dwelling of the chief, we heard the sound of prayer. When it was ended, Namosi and Vatai came forth. We remarked that we had come to look at the bright moon, the sparkling waters, and the lands of Feejee. Namosi said, "The sun is true, the moon is true and the stars are true, for they were made by the true God." Vatai said, "Many have been the days of my foolishness, when I did not know the true God. I believed in the gods of Feejee. When the lands trembled, I believed that the god Dengai turned over in his cave, and that caused the earth to shake."

26. Received a nice basket and a pair of chickens, as a present from Verani. He appears quite like a young convert. He says that his past life has been one of wickedness, that he prays a great deal that God will pardon him, and he appears very anxious for instruction, that he may know what is right, and sin no more. He says, also, that he has served the gods of Feejee long enough, and he has learned that they are false; that there is one true God, and Him will he serve.

27. Thakombau has been told that Verani has "lotued." "Have you seen him 'lotu?'" asked the angry chief. "Yes," was the reply. "Tell him, then, to go to his God for his food; he shall have none from my lands. He has not hearkened to my speech. I told him to wait a little, and then we would 'lotu' together. Tell him to stay at Vewa. He is not to come to Bau any more, or receive riches from me." When the message was delivered to Verani, he replied, "I do not want riches. I want to go to heaven more than to receive riches, and go to the 'buku waqa.' The lands are the Lord's. If He sees fit, I shall not want food. If I am

hungry, it will be but a little time before I shall die, and go to heaven, and I shall never be hungry there."

A message came to Namosimalua at the same time, saying, "Verani has '*lotued*,' therefore you must give it up, as I wish one of you to serve as a 'Namatanevanua.'" This is the name of one of the principal officers of state, or "eyes of the land." One or more of these are always near the person of the king, and are the connecting link between him and his people. They receive messengers, report their business to him, and communicate his orders to them. Many of them are special messengers to different towns, the name of which, with the word "mata" prefixed, constitutes their title, as "Mata ki Bau," "Mata ki Vewa," &c.

CHAPTER IV.

An instance of Feejeean Justice—Visit to the Lasakau Widow—A Sabbath in Vewa—A Feejeean Princess—Arrival of the Zotoff—Meeting of the Chiefs on board—Polygamy—Departure from Vewa—Treachery of a Chief—Arrival at Bua—Its King—Introduction of Fire-arms.

March 28. To-day another message from Bau has been received, saying, "Verani, send us the riches that you have obtained by '*lotuing*.' They belong to us. Why have you '*lotued*?' What have we done, that you have become angry with us, and left us?" Verani sent back the following answer:—"You well know that I receive no riches by '*lotuing*.'" You ask, "why I have '*lotued*?'" My reply is, "To save my soul. It is not because I am angry with you, but I was afraid to wait longer, lest I should die and lose my soul. Some time ago you wished me to build a '*buri kalou*.' I did as you wished. After the '*buri*' was built, my child died. I cut the posts for another '*buri*;' and another child died; my intimate friend was killed also. I then began to think that the gods of Feejee were lying gods, and thought I would see what the '*lotu*' books said about the '*popalagi's*' God. The teachers sent to me, and told me about the true God. I believed that *He* would not lie. I did not dare to wait for you, and now I have promised to serve Him."

29. A Bau chief visited Mr. Hunt and related the following little incident. A man was suspected of having stolen some yams from a plantation belonging to Tanoa. No one could prove his guilt; therefore, they tried him by the following ordeal. A native took a stick, and muttered over it some words, then handed it to one of their "*seers*." If the suspected one is guilty, the "*seer*" feels a peculiar pain in his arm. In this case the pain came, and the man was pronounced guilty, and condemned to die. But the man had taken himself out of the way. When this was told Tanoa, the *humane monarch* said, "Ah, well, take his father and kill him; it makes no difference." The innocent father was killed for the fault, real or supposed, of the son.

Namosimalua has been in, and says that he has received private information from Bau that its chiefs, or a part of them, have repeatedly tried to get Nalela to kill him; and he thinks that Nalela would have done so, had he not have kept himself out of the way.

30. Verani has married one of his four wives, and disposed of the others as follows:—One is to be the wife of a cousin, another of a nephew, and the third is living at Bua with her father, the king of that place. It is not improbable that Tuimbua will be greatly offended that his daughter is rejected.

In the afternoon Mrs. Jaggar and myself called on Verani. He said that when Mr. Wallis was here on his former voyage, he told him, "That unless they both became good men, they would go to the ' *buku waqa* ' when they died." He told him in reply, that when he came back to Feejee, he would become a Christian, and they would go to church together.

From the house of Verani, we went to the house of the widow of Nalela. As we stooped to enter the door, we observed eight fingers on the ends of sticks, just over our heads. At the right hand of the entrance stood the block, stained with the blood of the mutilated hands. The mourning widow was seated near the door, and two women near her, engaged in burning her back. A few sticks of sandal wood were burning near, and one of the women was employed in rolling up pieces of native cloth, which she would light at the fire and hand it to the other women, who applied it to the back of the mourner, who sat perfectly quiet under the operation. The widow and all the rest of the women had their heads shaved, and all but her were minus a finger. The house was darkened, and every one was still; but they had been howling most dreadfully. The Marama has adhered, thus far, to her resolution of starvation, and no entreaties had prevailed upon her to take food till our visit. Mrs. Jaggar said to her in the tenderest manner,—"You cannot help Nalela now. It is true that he does not need your company. Do not starve yourself, but live, take some food, and become a good woman that you may go to heaven when you die." She replied, very sadly, "I do not wish to do that. I only wish to die, that I may see my murdered husband again." After a pause, she asked, "Shall I ever see Nalela again?" "Yes," was the reply, "you will." After some more conversation, she

consented to take some arrow-root. On our return, some
was prepared. I took it to her, but she made many ex-
cuses, saying "That she could not eat, it was so long
since she had taken any." I told her that she had promised, and I should remain by her till I had seen her promise performed. "It will do you no good that I eat," she
said; "No," replied I, (through David, my interpreter,)
"but it is my love for you." "Why do you love me?"
asked she. "Because God made you, and I wish you
to go to heaven," I replied. "I will eat," she said,
"and live." As she had touched the dead body of her
husband, her hands were "*tambued*" for forty days; but
one of her servants was called, who fed her. The poor
creature suffered a great deal in swallowing at first.

31. The old men and the wise men of Vewa were
called together, to consult with its chief upon a matter
of vast importance. When all were assembled, Namosi
made known the fact that a pig had been stolen from
him, and he had assembled them together to ask if it
would not be well to strangle the thief. "What!" says
an old man, "kill a man for a pig! In the days of our
foolishness we did these things; but now we know better.
Have we not been taught that a man is worth more
than a pig?" Another said, "Are you a lotu chief, and
talk of taking the life of a man for a pig?" Another remarked, that "They were ashamed of their chief; he
was such a bad man that they did not go to see him, but
kept away from his house." Verani said, "Let the
man work for you, or restore two pigs for the one he has
stolen."

Before Namosi renounced heathenism, if a man had
offended him, even in the most trifling manner, he
would have had the offender killed at once. He might
have done the same in this case, for there is no law to

punish him for it, and his not doing it shows that he is somewhat under the restraints of Christianity. The independence and fearlessness which his subjects have manifested in the expression of their feelings, are much to be admired. They show that they cannot respect evil even in their chief. The wisdom of Verani's counsel, too, coming from one so late a heathen, shows that the Spirit of the Lord is the best teacher.

April 1. Received a visit from Namosi and the old chief who killed one of his women the other day, and sent her to Bau to be eaten. He is a great cannibal himself. He told Mr. Hunt the other day that he had killed and eaten a great many people, and that he expected to be killed himself, when his body would be eaten by Feejeeans, and his soul would go to the " *buku waqa*," and burn forever. " Ah, *Marama*," he exclaimed, as they came into the house, " you are a god!— Truly, you are a god !"

2. Sabbath. Several of the heathen have renounced their gods to-day, and several couples have been married. Mr. Watsford usually preaches on some of the adjacent islands. He has been here but a short time, but has advanced rapidly in his knowledge of the language, and appears desirous to do good among this degraded race.

All who renounce heathenism are required to attend the day schools to be instructed in reading. A school is held each day for adults, and one for children. Two hours are devoted, on Monday afternoons, to the examination of the natives upon what they may have heard on the Sabbath. Mr. Hunt is preparing an interesting class of young men to become teachers to their own people. Preaching in native every Wednesday afternoon. A prayer meeting is held on Saturday afternoons, and at sunrise on Sabbath mornings.

No idle time is spent by these devoted missionaries;—
no indolence of a tropical clime is suffered to steal away
the moments which they feel belong to the Master whom
they have come here to serve. No one, who sees life as
it is in Feejee, can doubt that intelligent men and women, who are willing to renounce the comforts of home
and come here to bring the gospel, are actuated by any
other motive than true love to God. Here is no ro-
mance, no poetry, but heathenism in its lowest state of
degradation.

3. A message has been received from Bau, commanding the men of Vewa to go and assist in building the
town of Suva, in place of the one that has been destroyed
by Rewa. I received by the messenger a present of a
Feejeean basket and a wig, from the daughter of Thakombau. My head may now be abundantly supplied if I
should lose my hair; but I should hardly dare avail myself of the beautiful appendage in this climate, lest I
should have to mourn the loss of brains as well as hair.

I visited my "*protegé*," as is my daily custom, and
carried her bread and arrow-root, which Mrs. Hunt
kindly allows me to have prepared for her. She smiles
when she sees me, but her countenance is one of deep
sadness, and she talks much about Nalela. David Whippy generally goes with me and acts as interpreter. I
often remain a long time with her.

4. Attended a wedding at the chapel. A daughter
of Mr. Whippy was married to a young man named
Christy.

I have been troubled all day with company from Bau.
Samonunu made me a present of ten mats.

6. My sewing class brought me a fine boquet of wild
flowers. The children of the place having learned my
fondness for flowers, seldom allow my table to remain

without them. I have received a visit from the chief of Kamba, who brought me a basket of fine " *ndawas*," a fruit not unlike a plum.

9. Received a visit from Samonunu and the little princess, daughter of Thakombau. It is the custom of the great ones of these lands to confide their children of high rank to the care of one of their officers. In this case the little " *Kagua* " was given in charge to a " *Matavanua* " of Bau, named Vakambua, who, with his wife, has the sole care of her; and their authority appears to supersede that of the parents. About a year ago the child was taken sick with an intermittent fever. Thakombau said it would be good for her to go to Vewa, " *lotu*," and receive medical aid from the missionaries. Vakambua, however, was of the opinion that the Feejean gods could cure her as well. She has now been suffering under a similar attack ; but the Feejean gods proving deaf or obstinate, they have brought the child to Vewa, and she has renounced heathenism. Medicines are dispensed to all who apply, whether heathen or Christian; but the heathen appear to think that the white man's God would not heal a worshipper of a heathen god. I cannot learn where they got this idea, but perhaps it is not a bad one, since it brings more people under religious instruction.

10. As I was returning to my house, after breakfast, I found the steps covered with ripe bananas, which had been brought by the chief of Kamba, who came with four of his women to see me and my good house. I asked him if the women were his wives. He said they were, and asked how many Mr. Wallis had. When I told him that he had but one, he exclaimed, " What a bad man to have but one wife!" " No," I replied. " You are a very bad man to have so many wives." At this

the old man laughed most heartily. It is not customary for chiefs to be accompanied any where by their women. This is the first instance I have known. The old man, however, is only a petty chief.

14. The bark Zotoff has arrived from Mathuata, and I am now on board. Retova, with his priest and several of his attendants, came up in the vessel. Tuimathuata formerly governed the lands and waters which are now governed by Retova. The king is an uncle of the present chief, who has driven him from his dominions, and he now lives in exile at a place called Muta. The manners of Retova are even courteous. I am surprised at the mild and affable behavior of all these cannibals.

15. This morning Thakombau came on board early, and soon after, Namosimalua and Retova came. Thakombau was seated on the sofa (a privilege granted to him and his father only,) when the two chiefs entered the cabin. The chiefs, with their Matavanuas and other officers, seated themselves on the floor. No one spoke when they entered, nor for some time after. It was with some effort that I was able to look grave and sober on this eventful occasion; for if ever I feel an inclination to laugh, it is when a large company are assembled, and silence reigns. At length the Matavanua of Vewa said that "It was good that Retova had come to see them." To which they all responded, "*Mana, ndina*," and slowly clapped their hands. Retova then ordered a box containing whale's teeth to be brought forward. His Matavanua took the teeth and made a speech, declaring the friendship of Retova for Bau, and his wish to live in peace with the powers that be. The chief officer of Thakombau accepted the offering, and made a speech quite as friendly in return. It was some time after the speeches were ended before the chiefs spoke; but at

length they became quite social. Retova's visit is at
Vewa, where he has come to obtain mats for his "*buri.*"
He is afraid to go to Bau, as Tanoa does not like his
conduct to the king, his uncle, who is a friend of Tanoa's.

After dinner Thakombau and Namosimalua held a long
conversation. Thakombau told the latter that he was
trying to have him killed. Namosi said, "No; you are
a great chief, and I could not kill you; but I am a
"*kaise*" (a poor person,) and am continually afraid of
my life." Thakombau went on charging him with de-
ceit, treachery, &c., till the old man cried out, "It is
enough, it is enough." "No," said the angry chief,
"we are here. You are not on my land, nor am I on
yours. This is the place to tell you my mind, and I will
do it." Namosi had to listen and be still. After the
conversation was ended, Namosi, feeling the need of
consolation, applied to Mr. W. for some rum. This was
refused, as there was but little on board, and that was
kept for medicinal purposes. The refusal made him angry, and he took Retova aside and said, "Do not let
your people fish for Mr. Wallis. I have looked, and he
has no riches in his vessel; he will not pay you, for he
is a '*kaise sara*' (a poor man indeed)."

16. Mr. W. invited the old king to breakfast with us,
but forgot the invitation; and when His Majesty came,
no food was prepared for him. Such forgetfulness, however, is pardonable in an American. How should they
know how to treat kings! The favorite companions of
the king are old men and boys (children in both stages).
He brought a large number with him. The boys performed several amusing dances on deck, the evolutions
of which were not ungraceful. Tanoa asked if I was the
only wife of my husband. On being told that I was, he
said, "That is bad, Mr. Wallis, you should have more."

He then became quite animated while enumerating the advantages of polygamy, said that he had one hundred wives, and ended by advising my husband to get an immediate supply. I asked him if his hundred women were not jealous, and if they did not quarrel. He said "That they did sometimes, but when that was the case he had them clubbed, and the matter was ended." After the departure of the king and his suite, Thakombau, with many other chiefs, came and spent the remainder of the day.

17. Revelete, Navinde and Verani made us a visit. Revelete, it will be recollected, is the son of Tanoa, who stole the girl from Nalela. I presume she did not much regret leaving that wicked-looking Nalela for the gay Lothario. The mother of Revelete is a sister of the king of Rewa; therefore he is a " vasu " to the kingdom of Rewa, and can go there at any time with perfect safety. She has no love for her husband, and is residing at Rewa among her kindred. Verani talked long and faithfully with Navinde about religion. The chief said that the " lotu " was very good, but he dared not embrace it, as he feared the anger of Thakombau. " I once feared his anger," said Verani, " but what is his anger in comparison with the value of our souls? His anger cannot reach us in another world, but can only hurt us in this, and it is but a little thing to suffer here, if we may go to heaven when we die. Oh, we have been very bad men! May the true God save all our souls."

18. It being arranged that I should accompany my husband to Mathuata, we visited Vewa for the purpose of taking leave of our very kind friends,—the missionaries. I went also to visit the Lasakau widow. She promised me that she would " lotu " as soon as the days of her mourn-

ing had expired, which were seventy from the day that her husband was murdered. "Ah!" said she, "the friend who has loved me is going away, and I shall not see her for a long time, but after she has departed I will learn to love the God that she loves. She kissed my hands several times, and said, "Will you not love me when you are far away?" I answered, "Yes," and left her, feeling that she would become a good woman.

When I returned to Mr. Hunt's, Amelia, a pretty Tongu girl, who had served me during my residence in V——, stood folding some clothes that she had been washing for me, and said, "Ah! I can wash no more clothes for Marama;—these are the last! Why can she not continue to live at Vewa?"

After taking leave of the dear families with whom I had spent so many happy hours, we repaired to the shore, where our boat waited. Here we found the servants belonging to the three mission families, our sewing class, Vatai with her household, and many of the inhabitants of Vewa assembled to bid me farewell. All came forward to shake hands, and said in tones of sadness, "*Marama sa lako,*"—Marama is going. They would, probably, have manifested the same affection and interest in any white female who had resided among them the same length of time.

It is my wish to show the Feejeeans as I found them, and to record truly their several traits of character as they came under my own observation. Little has been known of this people except that they are cannibals. It is said that there is not one of the natives of Vewa, over five years of age, that has not eaten human flesh. The hands of the slain are given to the children to eat; and a common amusement of the young is to lash a string about a log of wood, when they had no little bodies, and

6

drag them about, crying, "Here is my dead body, here is my dead body." They will then play cut it up and bake it.

18. On our return to the bark we found the little princess, with her guardians, on board. She brought me a present of a large hog and an orange cowrie shell. They call her Mary Wallis, and me, Kagua, which I am told is a great compliment.

19. The weather is not suitable for sailing to-day. Thakombau has been to visit us, and brought us the following item of news. It appears that the inhabitants of a town near here, on Vetelavu, possessed a knowledge of poisonous herbs. A short time since, they tried their skill upon ten men belonging to another town; six of them died and four recovered. The chief reported the case to Thakombau, and asked permission to kill the natives of the offending town. They were told to do as he liked. All were massacred save one. We asked if the bodies were brought to Bau and eaten. He said, "No, they were not my enemies."

20. The weather is still unpleasant. Another visit from Thakombau. His mind seems disturbed about the "*lotu.*" He tells Mr. W. that if he "*lotues,*" he will burn his "*beech de mer*" houses, and forbid the natives to fish. He says that the "*lotu*" is well enough for the white people, but Feejeeans are better as they are. He seems both provoked and grieved about Verani. One day he said to Retova, "*Verani sa lotu.*" His tone and manner were the same as our own would be were we saying, "Our friend is dead!"

21. Verani came on board to take leave of us. He gave Retova many charges respecting my safety, should any thing happen to the vessel. At eleven, A. M., we sailed for Ovalau. Besides Retova and his personal at-

tendants, we have six or eight others that we take to
Mathuata on his account. Not content with this, the
humble chief had ordered several more to come, which the
captain very unostentatiously sent back. On our arrival
at Ovalau, we received a visit from Capt. Hartwell,
whom we found here.

Retova was offended about something, and did not
come to tea. On inquiry, it was found that the fatted
hogs had not been killed in sufficient number for his
people. The poor creatures scarcely ever get any thing
more than vegetables to eat on shore, but when on board
of vessels they cry out for meat. And whose fault is it ?
Did not the captains begin it, and shall they not carry
it on?

Capt. Hartwell says that just before Nalela was killed, he sent a native dress belonging to the girl who was
stolen at Bau, to a place near where he had been fishing, and had it poisoned, intending to send it to her at
Bau. A Vewa man heard about it, procured it, and
carried it to Bau the day before the chief was murdered.
This, no doubt, hastened his fate.

In the afternoon the chief of Verata came on board.
When he saw me, he actually screamed, and called his
followers to see the " *Marama ni Papalagi.*" We have
bought pigs, yams, tarro, bread-fruit and oranges.

22. We are still at Ovalau waiting for a fair wind.
A few miles distant from us there is a small island
called Ngau, the inhabitants of which the Bau people
tried some years ago to conquer, but in vain. At length
they gained by treachery what they could not by valor.
Several canoes filled with warriors approached the
island, and sent their " *Matavanua* " to say that if they
wished to " *soro*," the soro would be received, and they
would be at peace. The natives of Ngau then took with

them some whale's teeth, a young girl of rank, and a
basket of earth; their "*Matavanua*" then approached
the chiefs of Bau on his knees, presented the "*soro*,"
which was accepted, and peace was declared. After all
was settled, the natives proceeded to prepare food for
their quondam enemies, but now their guests. While
they were thus employed, the Bau people set to and
massacred the men and women, tied the children by
their heels to the masts of their canoes, and having set
fire to the houses, departed for Bau. On their arrival
they were greeted with the sound of the drum and yells
of savage joy.

A town was depopulated on Motureke some time since
in the following manner:—Namosimalua had fought, or
rather harassed it for a long time without gaining any
advantage. At length he assembled together a large
number of men, with several of their largest canoes, and
sailed for Motureke. On arriving at the place, he fear-
lessly went on shore, carrying a white flag. He appeared exceedingly friendly, complimented the natives, telling them that they were a strong and brave people, but
added, "The chiefs of Bau are great chiefs. They do
not like to have it said that they cannot subdue you;
therefore, remove on the island of Ovalau. Let us burn
your town, that we may say we have conquered, and
then we will assist you to erect buildings on Ovalau,
will be your friends, and we shall be at peace." The
besieged hesitated; their present situation was any thing
but comfortable. Some of their enemies were continually on the watch, so that if any of their number went
from the town they were sure to be killed; they could
obtain no fish from the reefs, and had long suffered serious inconveniences. They said, "We have not canoes
enough to remove." "We will remove you on our

canoes," said the treacherous chief. After deliberating
for some time they concluded to accept the terms which
had been offered, and they embarked with their little
ones and their goods and chattels. The sails were set
to the breeze, and the canoes with their victims were
skimming lightly over the placid waters, when, at a given
signal from Namosimalua, his warriors massacred all but
the children, who, as in the case before related, were
strung to the masts and carried to Bau; those who died
from their bruises were fried (they usually fry the
young,) and the others were given over to the tender
mercies of their own children, to torment them to death.

Such is the *innocence* of heathenism. Many times have
I heard sentiments expressed like the following:—" It
is useless and unnecessary to send missionaries to the
heathen; they are innocent and happy as they are, and
why disturb them? It is *cruel*,—let them enjoy their own
customs." Is it *cruel*, I would ask, to come and tell
this people that it is not good to eat each other, and
that it is good to love the Lord Jesus Christ, of whom
they cannot hear without a preacher, and he cannot
preach unless he is sent? But now we come to the *cruelty* of the thing. It requires money from our pockets to
send a preacher; and this is *cruel*. Did it cost us nothing, we should never hear of the *cruelty* of saving men's
souls.

21. We sailed and arrived at Bua. We anchored
here for the purpose of taking " *beech de mer* " on board,
and breaking up the house. Bua is situated on Vanualavu and is governed by Tuimbua, who is now quite
aged. He came on board, but would not come below.
He is mourning the death of a grandchild, who was a
son of Verani. He is angry that his daughter has been
rejected by Verani, and says that she shall be the wife

of no other man. His head was shaved and his hands were "*tambued*," so that he must be fed by some one else for a long time.

25. We got under way and anchored at Yanganga about 5 P. M. We are not far from the Vanualavu, and can plainly see the rock where a man, named Charles Savage, was killed by the natives. It is said that sail needles were afterwards made of his bones. He was cast away, and the vessel that he came in was wrecked some where near Bau. I think it was a Swedish vessel, which contained a profusion of arms and ammunition, that was saved, and Savage taught the Bau people their use. He accompanied the Bau warriors to their battles, where hundreds, who were ignorant of the use and effect of fire-arms, were shot at a time. It is said that at one place a fortification, breast high, was built around a part of their town, of the dead bodies of those who were shot by the inhuman Savage and the Bau warriors. He was rightly named, exceeding as he did these cannibals in every act of cruelty. One cannot feel much sympathy for his ultimate fate.

CHAPTER V.

Mathuata and its Chiefs—Funeral Ceremonies—Conversation with a Priest—Wreck of the Ship Glide, of Salem—Jekombea—The Exiled Chief—Visit to Vesongo—A Feast.

April 26. At ten o'clock we set sail for Raverave, but owing to a contrary wind, we could only go within five miles of the place. On our way we saw a canoe containing ten natives. Four of them were painted red, and were engaged in performing some sort of a dance, while one was blowing a conch most lustily. Retova said that some chief was dead; and when we came within hailing distance, we were told that it was the Turaga-lavu Beraga. It appears that Tuimbua, Beraga and Tuimathuata, were the Turaga-lavus of this side of Vanualavu with the adjacent islands. The kingdom of Tuimbua is the first, and where his authority ends, Beraga's commences, and where his ends, that of Tuimathuata commences. As has been shown, the latter has been driven into exile, and Retova has usurped his authority. Beraga has left no successor; therefore his dominions will have no ruler of rank, but several petty chiefs, who will probably exercise their authority in harassing each other.

The ceremonies which are performed after the death of a chief of high rank, are exceedingly numerous. When death is approaching, his friends present him with whales' teeth, that he may be furnished with missiles to throw at a certain tree which is supposed to stand in the centre of the way between this world and " *bulu.*" Want of skill to hit the tree is considered an evil omen, and it is asserted that the souls of the wives of the deceased, who are so unfortunate as to miss the tree, are prevented from following them. Immediately after life is extinct, messengers are sent with a whale's tooth to all the tribes who were subject to him, informing them of the decease of their chief, and begging them to be of " a good mind." The canoe that we saw was bearing messages of this character. For some time after the breath has left the body, (and in many instances they do not wait for them to die, but if they are insensible, or incapable of helping themselves, they say the person is dead, his soul is gone, he knows nothing, and go on with all their ceremonies, burying them alive,) a profound stillness reigns throughout the town, which is at length broken by the loudest

outcries, as though they would rend the air with their
shouts.   The grave-diggers are then sent for, whose
duty it is to wash the corpse, dig the ground and inter
the bodies.   The body, after being washed, is decorated
in the same manner as it would be were he about to attend a feast.   It is then anointed with oil; the face,
neck and arms, as far as the elbow, are daubed with a
jet black, greasy substance; a bandage of white native
cloth is wound round the head, and tied in a graceful
knot above the temples; a club is put in each hand, and
one is placed on the breast, that he may retain his
rank in the next world as a chief and warrior.   The
body is then laid on a kind of bier, where it is usually
kept till various personages from the tribes under the dominion of the departed, assemble.   On their arrival, the
chief of each tribe presents a whale's tooth suspended by
a string.   He holds it in his hand, while the Matavanua,
or some other officer, delivers the following oration:—

"This is an offering to the dead.   We are poor, and
cannot find riches.   This is the length of my speech."
After this eloquent oration, one replied, "*Ai mumudai ni
mati.*"   (A wish that death may not visit them.)   All
who are assembled then respond, "*Mana ndena.*"   (Let
it be so.)

The grave-diggers then proceed to their business of
digging a resting place for the dead.   This is done in a
sitting posture, as it is not lawful or respectful to perform the labor standing.   Long sticks, sharpened to a
point, are used as substitutes for spades.   Before any of
the earth is removed, one of the grave-diggers takes a
stick in his hands, and places himself in an attitude of
digging, but does not bring the stick in contact with the
earth.   This is done three times, and the fourth time he
thrusts the stick into the ground, and the first handful of

earth which he digs up is called the earth of the god, and is carefully preserved in a leaf till the bodies are interred, when it is placed under a stone on the surface of the grave near the centre.   After the grave is dug, which is scarcely three feet deep, four large green leaves are placed on the bottom of it, and the sides are lined with mats and cloth.

When only two females are buried with the chief, one is placed on each side; but when more are strangled, their bodies are placed on the bottom, on each side, and on the top of the corpse, and are covered with the ends of the cloth and mats with which the grave is lined.   After this, a small quantity of earth is put into the grave four times with all possible despatch, and then four more leaves are put in, and the grave digger says, "*A kila na kala ma kua sa na mate*," which is a petition to his god that they may live.   While the grave diggers are filling the grave, the house of the deceased chief, with its contents, is burned, and when the dead are buried, and the house burned, all the natives disperse to bathe.

The grave diggers are obliged to pass under the branch of a certain tree, which two men hold over the foot-path.   As they pass, they are smartly whipped with something resembling the nettles of our own land.   This is to prevent contamination from the effluvia of the dead bodies.   After this they bathe, and rub themselves with some fragrant herb.

A little building is erected where the grave diggers live for one hundred nights, during which they daily bathe in fresh water, taking a club with them, which had been deposited in the grave of the dead.   They say that the spirit of the club went with the departed, and the club was not wanted.   They are not at liberty to return or visit their homes until the hundred nights have expired;

but they are plentifully supplied with food, and at the termination of the time are sent home with many presents.

After four days from the time of interment, a neat and substantial house is erected over the grave of the dead. The hands of all persons who have touched the dead are "*tambued*," and they must receive their food, and be fed by others.

After the death of a chief there are great times, amputating fingers, shaving heads and beards, circumcising boys, burning faces, arms, backs, necks, &c. Nor is this all :—A grand frolic is held for the space of ten days by all who choose to join in it. The men arm themselves with an instrument formed of pieces of bamboo tied together, which are about a foot in length, and with these they throw mud and clay at the women, seldom missing their mark. The women retaliate by severely lashing their assailants with the supple roots of trees, or the tough stems of creeping shrubs. Those who can procure them, often furnish themselves with a bunch of cords, with shells attached to the ends. They wield these weapons with great efficiency, and frequently produce deep gashes on the backs of their antagonists. The females are so ardent and intrepid in the celebration of this part of the funeral obsequies, that one is apt to think they are determined, during this reign of anarchy, to redress all former grievances, and avenge all the wrongs to which they have been obliged to submit. This ceremony is called Vainara.

Thus, at the death of a great chief, all are employed in mourning or rejoicing. Some of the near relatives fast all day, and feast at night. Some are forbidden to eat pork, others to eat yams, &c. They can, however, kill and eat each other. Such are the inconsistencies of heathenism!

27. We sailed for, and arrived at Raverave. Its chief dared not go on shore till he had received some intelligence from the town. A canoe came off, and said that all was right, when he ventured to revisit his home.

28. Retova, with his " *Bete* " (priest), and many others, came to get their mats, which they brought for a " *buri*," which has been recently erected. We asked the " *Bete* " how many people they intended to kill when the mats were placed in the " *buri*." He said he did not know. He was then asked how many had been killed during its erection. He replied, " only five;" and said, " One night when the ' *buri* ' was nearly completed, I went in and slept. During my sleep, the god came, and said, ' Go to a town on the mountains, and club three men for my house.' This was done. In a few days I went again to sleep in the ' *buri*,' but this time I did not mean that the god should enter, and I fastened all the doors and openings that he might not come in and tell me to kill more men. I slept till the god found some way to enter, and said, ' Go again to the mountains, and bring me two more men.' This order was also executed." Mr. W. told the priest that there was a great and true God, who made the isles and the waters, the white men and the Feejeeans, the sun, moon and stars, and that He made their food to grow. He would not lie like the Feejeean gods, and was the God to worship. " Yes," said the priest, " I know that Jehovah is a very great God. If the Feejeeans saw him coming here, they would all run, and hide in the bushes." He was told that he had heard about the true God at Vewa, and asked why he did not worship Him. He replied that he would if Retova told him to do so.

29. We got under way, and reached Kandavu, a town about two miles above Raverave, where our

schooner is tending a "*beech de mer*" house. Ratonga, a brother of Retova, is one of our number, and has just related to us the following little incident.

On the arrival of Retova, one of his people complained that his wife had broken the seventh commandment. "She shall be killed," said the chief. When the husband heard the sentence, he relented, but it was too late. The chief had company, and was probably glad to have the body for them to eat with their yams. The woman was killed and devoured. Ratonga says that none but "*kaises*" eat human flesh, and they say that none but the Turagas eat it. This shows that the people are becoming somewhat ashamed of the practice.

Ratonga wishes me to take the name of Tuikana, for his sister, who bears that name. "Tui," means king; "kana," is to eat. But what is a name! The word Tanoa, means a wooden bowl; it is also the name of the King of Bau.

Kandavu is where the ship Glide, of Salem, was cast away some years ago. We have the murderer of the Raverave woman on board. He requested to-day to have his hatchet ground. Mr. W. asked how it became so much injured. He said it struck against the skull of the woman that he killed at Raverave. He was asked how he committed the deed. He said that she did not know she was to be killed, and was on her way to a pond to bathe; he stood in the pathway, and after she had passed him, wholly unconscious of evil, he struck her in the back of her head, and killed her instantly. "Did you not feel sorry?" I asked. "*Sega au mbasa.*"— "No, I would not," was the reply. He says that her husband did not complain to Retova, and did not know any thing of the affair till he was told that the body of his wife was being cooked. The man cried very loud when he heard this. The *amiable* Retova heard him, and said, "If you do not stop that, you shall soon be cooked, too."

May 6. We sailed for, and arrived at Ndury, after a passage of three hours. A canoe has arrived from Jekombea. Harry, our pilot, does not express much delight at their visit. On the voyage preceding this, my husband sent a boat containing Harry, a man named Tom, four natives, and some trade to buy tortoise shell. They were instructed to visit the islands in this vicinity for that purpose. On arriving at Jekombea, they anchored the boat, and all went to sleep. The natives quietly went off to the boat, killed all but Harry, and took possession of the boat and trade. The *gentle* natives supposed at the time that they had killed all on board, but as morning advanced, they discovered Harry rolled up in a mat. The chief said, "Let him live;" and he lived, perhaps, to meet a worse fate from the ruthless cannibals of Feejee. Retova is acknowledged as the Turaga-lavu of Jekombea; therefore, he received his part of the plunder of the boat, and in due time the *honest* chief brought shell, which had been previously bought with trade, from the vessel to Mr. W. to buy of him. My husband told him that the shell was his, and he should not buy it again.

8. After getting a house under way, and leaving two white men to collect cargo, we again set sail for Vesonga. I listened, last evening, to the following tale, showing how the Jekombearites were outwitted by white men.

Soon after the escape of Harry, a little boat anchored near the island. One native came to the shore, and invited them to land, telling them that he was a Christian teacher that had been sent from Vewa. The white men landed, and inquired the name of the island. On being told, they said, "Ah, we have a root of *yanggona*, and

some sugar cane for the chief; we will return on board
for it." Several natives followed to help draw the boat
nearer the shore. When they had got safely on board
of their own little craft, they requested a part of the natives to return to the shore, and get a large stone that
they might fasten the boat to it. After they had departed, the men succeeded in clearing their boat of the rest.
This being done, they set sail, and were soon in a place
of safety.

9.   We are still pursuing our way to Vesonga by day,
and anchoring at night. The reefs and shoals are too
numerous to "run" at night. The whole coast this side
of Vanua lavu, beginning at Kutu and ending at Natawa,
belongs to Retova and his uncle. I learn that although
the king has been driven into exile, he is not deprived of
all his lands. Many towns still adhere to him, though
such is the treachery of Feejeeans that none can be
trusted long at a time. A town belonging to one party
one day, may turn to the other the next, and thus they
are continually harassing each other for years.

10.   This sailing along through placid lagoons, formed
by the reefs on one side and the Vanua lavu on the other,
is very delightful. We can look at golden sunsets,
sparkling waters, fleecy clouds and dusky natives.

Nearly every island and reef that we pass, has its incident. While Mr. W. commanded the Gambia, on the
voyage preceding this, Retova pretended that he was
exceedingly anxious to make peace with his uncle. Accordingly, he collected a number of men and canoes, with
the usual presents, and visited him to offer the "soro."
The offerings were accepted, and peace was declared.
Retova was entertained for some days like a great chief,
and then suffered to depart in safety. While Retova
was returning to Mathuata, he saw people fishing "beech

de mer " from a reef, near which we are passing. The ruthless being had them all murdered. This affair put an end to the reconciliation which had so recently taken place, as several of them belonged to the exiled king.

11. We anchored between the Vanua lavu and a small isle, called Navu. We perceived several canoes and natives on the beach; our hostage called to them to come on board, but they gave no heed to the invitation. They were probably afraid, as a Salem schooner chased some canoes here, and fired upon them a short time since.

The little island of Navu, too, has its tale of recent occurrence. This isle is not inhabited permanently, but canoes often stop here and pass the night. Our hostage, with some other natives, and two or three white heathen, came here in a canoe. Soon after their arrival, which was at night, they perceived a light on Navu. They went to the island, where they found two canoes. The natives belonging to them being asleep, our worthy hostage, and a man named Carter, fired upon them, and killed several, but not all; some escaped by flight. I told him that by and by he would go to the " *buku waqa,*" and would there receive his reward for all this. "No," he said, "the ' *buku waqa* ' was made for white people; the Feejeeans would not be allowed there. Carter has subsequently been murdered by three Oahu natives.

12. We arrived at Vesonga. This place is where Tomarau resides, the hero of the late murder at Rave-rave. He is the Matavanua from Vesonga to Raverave.

My husband's purpose in visiting this place, being to get a house and fish " *beech de mer,*" Tomarau went on shore, and delivered the speech of Retova to the chief, who, it seems, bears rule here, though there are several petty chiefs residing in the town.

13. This morning, a canoe filled with natives came off to see the *lioness;* a white one never having been seen by the natives of this part of Feejee. The wonder was gazed at, and every motion watched with the most intense interest.

14. We were visited last night by a tribe called Namu. They were all armed with a short, sharp instrument, and attacked us most furiously. Their numbers were so numerous that we found it impossible to defend ourselves, and we suffered exceedingly from their poisoned instruments. The English name of this hostile tribe, is "Musquitoes."

15. The chief, Masella, came off to the vessel, and wished Mr. W. to send a boat for his wife, as she wished to visit me. The boat was sent, and the *Marama* came, bringing us a present of some bread-fruit. She admired me very much, but failed to excite a corresponding sentiment. She asked Mr. W. why he did not bring more of his wives. When he told her he had no more, she exclaimed with surprise, "Why! you are a ' *Turagalavu.*'"

20. We visited the reefs. It being perfectly calm, the waters were like one vast sheet of glass. As we were borne along over the beautiful marine productions which every where met the eye, it appeared like some enchanted scene. There are times, and places, and scenery even in Feejee. In connection with this, I am reminded of the following wish expressed by some writer: —"I sometimes desire to be far away on the deep blue ocean, with nothing but the heavens above, and the waters beneath, that I may give utterance to thoughts that have dwelt in the depths of my heart from childhood, and which it would be profanation for the gross ears of mortals to hear." Could the same lady have been here in

her little boat, she might have "freed her mind." Here
she could have looked upon splendid beds of coral, and
admired the beauty of their various hues, and their arrangement amid the sparkling sands. Here, too, she
would have for listeners blithe little beings, gaily decked,
some in gold and purple, and others in azure and silver,
instead of the uncouth tenants of the great deep, clad in
sombre grey. But, whoever the lady may be, I think
she would find no poetry in being alone on the deep blue
ocean, and would have to search a long time for those
thoughts which she deems too refined for the gross ears
of mortals.

21. Mr. W., believing that nearly all the male inhabitants of Vesonga were fishing on the reefs, proposed
going on shore to see the " beech de mer " house. When
the boat was ready, I expressed a wish to accompany
him. " Perhaps it is not safe," said he. " If it is safe
for you, it is for me," I replied, and we started with only
two rowers and ourselves in the boat. When we reached
the shore we were surprised to see Masella and twenty
other men upon the beach. I observed that Masella held
a hatchet behind him, as if trying to hide it. On looking
around, I perceived the men were all armed; some with
clubs, and others with muskets. Truly, thought I, we
are not so formidable as to require such strength of arms.
Mr. W. told Masella that we would go to the " beech de
mer " house first, and then to his house. Some of the
natives preceded, and others followed us to the building
where the " beech de mer " was drying. A deep trench
is usually dug the whole length of one of the houses,
which is filled with burning logs of wood. The glare and
heat from such an immense fire, and surrounded as we
were by nearly naked savages, numbering perhaps fifty
in all, including women who had joined us, reminded me

7

of the "*buka waqa,*" and sent a strange sort of thrill through my frame.

Many of the faces of the men were painted a shiny black upon one side, and a bright vermillion on the other. Others had the forehead, nose, and the upper part of their cheeks daubed with one color, and the lower part of their faces with another. An endless variety of tastes was displayed, which did not in my view add to their beauty, although the house was well lighted from the deep red flames issuing from the trench, and well calculated to show their personal decorations to the greatest possible advantage. When we came from the house, Mr. W. suddenly altered his mind about visiting Masella's house, and we immediately returned to the bark.

22. We received a visit from the "*Bete*" of the town. Mr. W. asked him how it was that he did not "*tambu*" the fish for him as he had promised. He replied that he did, and the fish were all lying still on the reefs, but Capt. Cheever came, then the god got mad with himself, and Capt. C. got the fish; but not long after, Masella got mad with Capt. Cheever, then the god was pleased with his priest, and said, "Let no one but Capt. Wallis have the fish that are on the reefs." Soon after this, another came to get the fish, but the god caused a strong wind to blow, and prevented him from collecting any, and now he had come, and the god had promised fine weather.

26. The wind last night blew almost a hurricane. As several canoes were fishing, some anxiety was felt on their account. At sunrise, the out-rigger of a canoe was discovered at some distance with people on it; a boat was sent, which took up five. Four women swam for the shore, a distance of two miles, which they reached in

safety. In the afternoon, the priest came on board again. He was asked why his god sent such a wind after promising fine weather. "My god was angry because you did not give me a knife when I was here last," was the reply.

June 1. Retova has visited us on his way to Navu, a place two miles above this. A boat accompanied him from the bark, for the purpose of establishing a "beech de mer" house at that place.

3. Yesterday a grand Solavu was held at Vesonga. The Geer people brought sail mats, which were exchanged for yams. When the natives hold a Solavu, they take great pains in decorating their persons. A necklace of whale's teeth is the favorite ornament for the neck, but all are not able to procure them; therefore some wear one of shells, others of human teeth, and some wear beads. The barbers have full employment for several days previous, in dressing heads, which are ornamented according to their different tastes. Bone bracelets are worn on the arms, and their faces are usually painted black, or so disguised that one is not known from another. This is probably done that they may not be recognized, should there be any treachery going on at the time, as is often the case. When the parties meet, which is generally in some open space called the "rara," the riches belonging to each are deposited in huge piles on two sides of the "rara," food is placed in the centre, and the visitors are feasted with great abundance, and carry away with them what is left. The entertainers do not partake of the feast with their guests. When the riches are exchanged, a great many fine speeches are made by the officers of both parties. A great deal of love is expressed, and one would suppose that no enmity could ever find a place in such affectionate hearts. After the feasting and speeches are ended, dancing commen-

ces. Each party engage in their several dances by themselves. Their fears of each other, form a barrier between them. It is not always that riches are exchanged at " *Solavus*." Sometimes presents are made, and the people are feasted to discharge some former obligation, as was the case with Bau and Somosomo, and sometimes one tribe visit another, and carry riches, but receive no return at the time, although they are always feasted, and, some time after, the visit is returned in the same manner. A feast of any description is called a " *Solavu*."

7. One of our crew inquired if I would purchase a servant, a native woman that was to be killed at Vesonga to-night. On inquiry, I learned the following particulars: —A man who belonged to the Charles Wirgman, of Salem, had brought the woman from some distant coast, and while the brig lay here, she ran away from her keeper to Vesonga, where she had remained ever since. Yesterday the Marama became angry with her for some offence, and threatened punishment. The girl attempted to run away, but was caught and brought to the town. The " *Marama* " attempted to take off her dress, or " *leku*." When this is done, it is like passing sentence of death upon the victim; but the man who had returned the offender, caught her away, saying, " Do not do that." The angry " *Marama* " replied, " Tie her, and to-night she shall die." A musket was sent on shore with an order for Harry to buy the offending woman, and send her on board, where she might serve me till I had an opportunity to send her home.

8. Harry came off, and said that he had made it all right with the " *Marama*," and the woman was safe. In the afternoon, a large double canoe came alongside, with at least two hundred men in it. It was commanded by

Korovakaturaga, a chief of some note in these parts. I thought I saw a little expression of anxiety on the countenance of my husband, and a manifest relief when they departed.

10. I learn that Harry told the " *Marama* " on shore, that the Marama-lavu on board the " *waqa lavu*" had heard that she had given orders to club a woman, and that she was very much ashamed for her. " Go and tell the Marama-lavu that my anger is over now, and the woman shall receive no harm," she replied. He then told the girl that Capt. Wallis had sent a musket to buy her for one of his people. She told him that he did not say what was true, for no Feejeean women were allowed on board the " *waqa lavu.*" He showed her the musket, and said, " What I tell you is true; therefore go not near the vessel, or you will be detained for one of his men." The girl appeared to dread this more than death. Her experience while a captive on board the brig, must have been a painful one. I know not what are the motives of Harry, unless they are to restore her to her keeper, who is now living at Solavu. The woman who accompanies him, would not have been allowed, had not he and a companion named Valentine, positively declared that they were married. We have since learned, however, that they are not. They do not live on board, but stay at some " *beech de mer* " house.

We were told before we came to this place, that the natives were exceedingly treacherous, and we must keep a look out for them. I do not perceive but that they are as civil as any that we have seen. One day a woman who came on board, said, " Ah! the white men make gods of their wives." " Yes," said her husband, " the white women are wise, but Feejeean women are foolish." The man could not perceive any foolishness in himself. Thus it is, I thought, you are true to your kind, and had you your periodicals, we should see chapter after chapter headed, "Advice to women," as with us. We are told that we must always meet our husband at the door with a smile, take his hat and cane, and see that the best chair is ready for him (although it may be occupied by an aged or infirm parent), with his slippers near it. If he is cold, we must have a good fire to warm him; if he is warm, a fan to cool him; if he frowns, we must smile; if he is angry, we must look pleased; if he is in a passion, we must look delighted; and sundry other wise suggestions to strengthen and fortify our minds, that we may be good, and bear all the infirmities of our "lords" with patience. For all this I am truly grateful, and, with all due humility, would confess that we need "line upon line, and precept upon precept." But why, I would ask, is the one thing done and the other left undone? Does perfection dwell with man? or is his mind rendered impervious to improvement by his own sense of superiority? I believe that man has his part to act in the domestic relations of life, independent of his duty of supplying the means for support.

CHAPTER VI.

Intelligence from Bau—The Frolic of the White Men—Burning of the "beech de mer" House—Murder of the King of Mathuata—A Story—Ingratitude—The Rescue.

Aug. 7. Tommy brings us accounts from the city, that Revelete has been killed by his brother Thakombau. When we left Vewa, or very soon after we left, Revelete went to Somosomo, where he remained about three months. During his absence, Thakombau received intelligence that his brother had for a long time been engaged in a "vere* " against himself. He informed his father of the reports, who said, " When he returns from Somosomo, let him be killed." Thakombau was well convinced that the report was true. Verani was one of the informants, through a man that he had engaged to watch and protect the life of Thakombau. He became acquainted with the "vere," in the following manner:— When the expedition went to Ba on Capt. Hartwell's account, he overheard Revelete and Navinde talking over the affair; he did not listen long, but went on the deck of the Gambia (on board of which vessel they were at the time), and sent a man whom he could trust, to listen to their words. I cannot learn whether Navinde was one of the party of Revelete, or whether the latter was telling the former his plans, and inviting Navinde to join him. The subsequent conduct of the Lasakau chief, however, appears to evince his innocence. The man who had been employed by Verani to listen to the conversation of the conspirators, returned to the deck, and said that the " vere " was to murder Thakombau, Verani and one other, when Revelete was to be king of Bau.

On their return to Bau, Verani sent his trusty man to watch Thakombau, and see that no harm came to him. The inhabitants of the city greatly wondered why that Vewa man was always in attendance upon Thakombau. The chief, too, was surprised, and at length the man told him that there was a " vere " to kill him, and Verani had sent him to watch for his safety. The chief did not believe the story, and the informant was dismissed.

After Revelete's departure, Navinde told Thakombau all about it, and the chief promised the Lasakau his sister for a wife. After this, he received information from

* A plot.

another authentic source, and he was then fully convinced of his brother's guilt, told his father, and the sentence had gone forth that the offending son and brother must die.

Revelete received warning of his approaching fate, and was advised to remain in Somosomo or go to Rewa. He persisted in returning to Bau. On his arrival he went first to see his father, who received him pleasantly and said, "Stop, my son, and drink yanggona with me." "No," said the son, "I am hungry, and will go to my own house and get food." He was always accompanied by a young man named Salem. They had been companions from childhood, and loved each other much. When Revelete and Salem left the house of the king, they met Thakombau, who immediately caught his brother by both arms, and held him, saying to Salem, "Kill him." Salem refused to obey. "Ah," said Thakombau, "I know where you are." Revelete affectionately leaned his head on his brother's bosom, and said, "Do not kill me, my brother." "I must, I cannot save you; you intended to kill me," said the chief. "No," said Revelete, "I never did intend harm to you; my enemies have told you lies. Let me live, I am your friend."

Just as the above words were uttered, the voice of the old king was heard, crying, "Kill him, why do you not kill him at once?" Thakombau then gave the order, and one standing near quickly obeyed. Revelete was clubbed, but not killed with the blows, and was thrown into a hole still breathing, and some earth was thrown over the throbbing body. The feet were unburied, and were seen to move for some time after.

Salem went to his house and said, "My friend is killed, and soon they will come to choke me; therefore,

make haste and prepare my body, that I may be ready
when they come and that no time may be lost, for I am
in haste to rejoin the friend I love." His friends painted and decorated his body for the grave, prepared the
" *wa 'ni kuna,*" and then sent word to Thakombau that
all was ready. On the arrival of the chief, Salem said,
" Is it true that my friend sought to kill you?" " How
many were in the *vere,* and who are they?" inquired
Thakombau. " Namosimalua and his son, Masapai, the
chief of Namara, the two Lasakau chiefs, and two chiefs
of Soso," was the reply; " and you are not safe till they
are killed." The conference ended, the fatal cord was
tightened, and the spirits of the friends were reunited,—
who shall say where?

Thakombau passed a house that had belonged to his
brother on his return to his own, and the voice of the
girl that had been stolen from Nalela was heard lament-
ing the death of Revelete. " Ah," he exclaimed, " you
had better save your tears for your father, who will go
soon." It will be remembered that she was the adopted
child of Namosimalua.

8. Another item of news brought by Tommy was
that a schooner had been sent to the island from Tahiti,
loaded with rum, and the white men of Vewa (of course
I do not include missionaries, even when I say white
men. I mean a different class of persons, and always
speak of missionaries with their distinctive title,) had a
grand " drunken frolic." It commenced on Saturday
evening, and they were in a bad trim for the Sabbath.
When the bell rung, they went staggering off to meeting, filled with unholy *spiritual* influences. After they
had entered the room, it was some time before they
could get seated to their minds; one tipped his neighbor
from the end of the seat to the floor; and another, not

readily perceiving a chair, yet having some indistinct notion that he could find a seat some where near, pitched over it. At length they were all seated after a fashion, and sat reeling to and fro, with their heads nodding, not like the plume of the warrior, nor like the graceful willow which is gently swayed by the breezes of heaven; Oh, no, not like these; but like one of those images that is placed sometimes in our open fields at home, to frighten mischievous birds from the new planted grain. During the prayer they behaved tolerably well, with the exception of uttering a loud groan now and then. But when the sermon commenced—then was the time! As the preacher went on, each seemed moved to say something. One said, "Ah, yes, sir, we all deserve to go to hell;"—another, "Oh, yes, we must go to hell;"— a third, "Sir, you tell us the truth;"—a fourth, "No, we shall never get to heaven unless we repent," and so on through the whole. At length one rose from his seat, and staggering towards the table where the preacher stood, and moving his hands one over the other, as we sometimes see a boy who is about to strike another, he stammered, "Now,—now,—sir,—I,—I,—think,—that, —that." When he had got thus far in his speech, one of his two nether limbs became lighter than its companion, tipped up, and causing the speaker to lose his balance, he was laid sprawling on the floor. This ceremony ended the meeting, and the congregation was dismissed.

Such are some of the scenes enacted by the white heathen of the South Seas. Every means is used by this class of persons to destroy the influence of missionaries. Some person comes along, perhaps, who is capable of preparing a book. He avoids all intercourse with the missionaries, collects all his information from "prison birds" and deserters, then goes home and publishes to

the world how little good is accomplished by the missionary among the heathen, giving long accounts of what he
witnessed among those who had become degraded by
their intercourse with Christians. There is such an art-
ful mingling in these narratives, of the two classes,—the
missionary and the white residents,—that the general
and unreflecting reader sees no difference; and feels almost insulted when he is asked to contribute something
for the support of a mission.

After the drunkards were dismissed, they resumed
their potations, and became so uproarious and dangerous
that the chiefs commanded some of the natives to tie
them, which was done, and they were kept in that situation till they became sober.

11. About ten o'clock last night a bright light was
seen in the direction of the *" beech de mer "* house at
Kutu. A boat was immediately sent to the place, which
returned with the intelligence that several native houses
had been burned; but the *" beech de mer "* house was
safe. It seems that two natives had a quarrel yesterday.
The one who struck the other with an axe first, was soon
after taken to the town and shot. The friends of the
murdered man revenged themselves by burning houses.
The cause of the affray was jealousy.

21. As Mr. W. and myself were quietly seated in the
cabin last evening, we were suddenly startled by a
noise resembling the discharge of a large volley of mus-
ketry. We rushed to the deck, Mr. W. exclaiming,
" The ' beech de mer ' house is on fire." On reaching
the deck, a truly splendid sight met our eyes, but grieved our hearts. Fires of this kind have become exceedingly common,—this being the sixth house that has been
burned during this voyage.

22. A boat was sent to Kutu with orders to take all

on board which belonged to the bark, and set fire to the house. Another boat was sent to Yanganga with similar orders. As soon as the blaze of the Kutu house was seen at Tavea, Natemba came off to inquire about it. Mr. W. said, "You have burned my house here. You have made a fool of me, and I am very angry. I sent to have the Kutu house burned, and soon you will see the fires of the Yanganga house. I shall leave the place when the boats return." Natemba replied that he was very angry about the burning of the house, and that he had told the people on shore that no vessels would come here to trade if they conducted in this way. He did not know who burned the house, but supposed it was done by the orders of a jealous chief at Tavea. He begged that his canoe, with his brother, might be sent at once to Yanganga to countermand the orders for burning the house, and said that he would go there and fish. The anger of Mr. W. was somewhat appeased, and he consented.

26. Namosimalua is yet among the living, and has called to see us on his return from Raverave to Bau, where he has been to take whales' teeth from the chiefs of Bau to induce Retova to join them in a contemplated hostile attack upon Natawa.

Namosimalua gave us the following history of the doings at Raverave:—It appears that for some months past Retova has frequently sent messages to his uncle, the exiled king, urging him to make peace, saying, "You are an old man, my father. Let our enmity be ended. I will be as a loving son to you. Return to your own lands. I will build you houses. Bring your wives and all your riches, and we will live in peace; and when your days are ended, you shall be buried on the island that you love." The king was in reality sin-

cerely desirous of peace. He was an exile from the land
of his birth, and his heart was ever turning towards it;
but his past experience of the treacherous character of
Retova rendered him fearful, and for a long time very
cautious. At length he yielded to the affectionate importunities of his relative, and taking twelve of his old
and trusty friends, he left Muta for Raverave. On his
way he stopped at Kandavu, and sent its chief to Raverave to see how the " wind blew," and whether its
breezes appeared favorable or not. Tomorau-ni-waqa,
the chief, returned, and said that Retova appeared to be
sincere, and he thought the king could go in safety.
The party then proceeded to Raverave, where its chief
received them with delight, and feasted them abundantly.
They remained there two days, and all the ceremonies
appertaining to the ratification of peace between the
chiefs had been performed. Retova had shown his uncle
the preparations which he had made for his house, to be
built on the island of Mathuata, which pleased the old
man much. " In two moons your house shall be ready,"
said Retova. " In two moons I will come with my women and live in it," said the happy king.

All was joy and hilarity in Raverave at the reconciliation of the Turaga-lavus. The old people looked
pleased and happy, and the young chanted their songs
in gleeful mirth.

On the morning of the third day of this delightful visit,
the sun shone brightly over the hills, and the king said
that he must depart early, that he might rest at noon.
The yanggona was already prepared in the " buri," and
Tuimathuata, Retova and Koravakaturaga entered to par
take of the parting " cup," while the followers of the
king remained without, in company with Ratanga and
many others. They had not been long in the " buri,"

when Koravakaturaga was seen advancing towards the king, with a raised club in his hand. The king observed him and said, "What are you about to do?" "To murder the king," was the reply; and in a few moments the king was a breathless corpse.

Ratanga was on the watch, and as soon as the first blow was struck in the "*buri*," he gave the signal, and all the followers of the king were inhumanly butchered except one, who fled and hid himself till night, then walked to Kandavu, and entering the house of the chief, awoke him, and while the tears rolled over his face, related the sad occurrences of the morning. "Remain not here," said the chief; "I cannot save your life; fly while it is yet dark, and no one can see you." The old man did not heed the advice, probably knowing that if he attempted flight, he would be discovered and murdered before he could reach a friendly town. He went to a "*buri*," where he was discovered the next morning by Retova's barber, murdered, and sent to Raverave by noon, where his body was cooked with those of his companions, and portions of it sent round to different towns as choice bits.

Thus Retova has accomplished his desires without improving the political condition of this coast. The king has left a son, called Mbata, a favorite child, as he has always been faithful to his father. He is of no rank, as his mother is a poor woman; but the king having no other son, and Mbata being one possessing superior abilities, he has made himself something.

The treacherous murder of the king will arouse all he revengeful feelings of his party, and headed by the son, they will continually harass their enemy, till Retova or Mbata dies.

It is highly probable, too, that Retova will gain an enemy in the person of Koravakaturaga. They have been great friends for some time, but their participation in the murder is likely to cause fear in both parties, and that will probably lead to enmity.

27. Harry, the man whom Mr. W. dismissed a short time since, has arrived in his boat, accompanied by three others, who are on their way round the land to buy tortoise shell.

A man, named William Russell, was discharged from the bark to join the boat, and a black man, named Johnson, was received in his room. After the boat had departed, Mr. W. was informed that Harry and George Runnells, who accompanied him, intended to go to Vesonga, and put the chief in irons, and keep him confined until the girl, whom I had wished to liberate while we were there, should be restored to her purchaser and master.

If such are their intentions, Harry had better not sleep on his watch, as he did at Jekombea. If he had been faithful at that time, when taking his turn to watch for the safety of the boat, no lives or property would have been lost. He is generally disliked by the natives, and it becomes him to "keep a bright eye to the windward."

28. "He that diggeth a pit for another, shall surely fall therein." These are the words of my text, and if I do not preach a sermon to illustrate it, I will tell a story that will show its truth.

I have learned to-day from Mr. W. the following history of the origin of the war between Tuimathuata and his nephew. The king had from his birth lived on a small island, called Mathuata, situated quite near the main land. His son, Mbata, who is exceedingly ambitious, gained a great influence over the mind of the king as the latter became old. Retova, and a brother of equal rank with himself, resided on the main land quite near his uncle. As the king advanced in years, his son having no rank by birth, the young chiefs, Retova and Ngenge, acquired influence among their tribes, and almost entirely monopolized the trade with foreign vessels. This raised the jealousy of the king and his son. Mbata told his father that his cousins treated him like a " *kaise,*" and urged him to have them killed, saying, "Then, my father, you will be the only Turaga-lavu of these lands, and I shall be the second chief." Mbata well knew that if he could accomplish this design, in the absence of any other chiefs, he would be head, as he already ruled his father.

It is sometimes the case in Feejee that, like the victorious chanticleer of the barn-yard, the strongest will bear rule in spite of all the disadvantages of low birth. Tuimathuata hearkened to his son, and orders were given to murder the young chiefs. Ngenge was killed, and Retova fled to Raverave, where he was protected.

For some time previous to these events, Bau had tried in vain to make Mathuata tributary to its chiefs; but the Mathuata chiefs, when united, were strong; divided, they fell. The king was old, his son not acknowledged as a chief, Ngenge was killed, and Retova imprisoned, or what amounted to the same.

Soon after the murder of Ngenge, Verani came to Lekutu, and Retova sent to request his assistance. Verani immediately departed for Bau, and collected a fleet of canoes, well manned. As they came down the coast they were joined by many of the subjects of the old king, as well as those who were favorable to Retova.

On their arrival at Raverave, Retova joined the fleet, and sailed for the island of Mathuata, intending to set fire to the town and massacre the inhabitants. They were, however, hindered by a head wind, and did not reach the islands in time, as the birds, both old and young, had forsaken their nests, and flown to more genial climes. As Raverave is in sight of Mathuata, the canoes had been seen in time for the islanders to make their escape during the night, and they reached Muta, an inland town on Vanualavu, in safety, where they have resided ever since.

The disappointed warriors set fire to the town, and passed on, carrying desolation and death, for the space of sixty miles, to all who refused to join them. Thus, taking advantage of the times, the people of Bau accomplished their long desired purposes, and this coast has since paid tribute to its haughty chiefs.

29. I have been informed to-day that Namosimalua appeared to be retracing his steps to heathenism. The following story shows that he is not advancing in Christianity.

In the year 1843, a brother of Verani was murdered by some of the murder-loving men of Feejee. Soon after I left Vewa, intelligence was received there, that nine men belonging to the tribe who committed the murder, were at Ovalau. A younger brother of Verani said, "Who will go and revenge the death of our brother? Verani has 'lotued,'—he will not; there is none but me left, and I must perform the deed." Namosimalua gave him canoes and men, with which he sailed for Ovalau, where he executed his fell purpose, and returned, bringing with him the dead bodies.

The whole affair had been kept secret from the missionaries till the arrival of the canoes bearing the dead. Namosi had given strict orders for the canoes to go to Bau, that the missionaries might not know that he had any

8

hand in the murder. When he perceived the refractory canoes sailing direct for Vewa, he appeared greatly troubled, and was seen on the hill, waving his hand to them in the direction of Bau, but all to no purpose. On,—on they would and did come, till they arrived at Vewa's shores, where they were greeted with every demonstration of joy by the Lasakau widow. She waved on high an ornament that had belonged to the deceased relative, then burning it on one of the bodies, said, " Now is our brother revenged." As soon as the missionaries heard of the affair, they sent them away. They carried the dead men to Bau, where, as is their custom, they were devoured. What a record are the annals of Feejee!

30. The boat, Star, belonging to the bark, has just returned from Raverave, by which we learn that Retova is going to carry a *blessing* to his cousin, Mbata, in the shape of muskets and powder ; or, in other words, he is going to fight the inhabitants of Muta. Andrew asked Retova why he killed the king. "Oh," he replied, " I had him killed Feejee fashion. It will be my turn next. Bau has sent for me to go to Natawa;' perhaps that is a ' *vere* ' to kill me." If this people feared death, they would never enjoy life.

Sept. 6. Our schooner arrived from the windward isles with forty peculs of fish and a sick man,—an American sailor,—who was injured some four years since by a whale, and has been a cripple ever since. The schooner brought him from Lakemba, where he had been taken care of by Rev. Messrs. Lyth and Calvert, English Wesleyan missionaries, who had supplied him with food, clothing, medicines and gospel instruction. The Wesleyans, who are stationed at Feejee, never make any distinctions of country,—an Englishman is never favored by them because he is an Englishman.

While I resided at Vewa there came to the place a deserter, who was prowling about for some time, to the terror of the native women, whom he continually insulted. At length he was taken sick with the dysentery, and there was no one to take him in. Mr. Hunt provided a house for him, with some one to be with him, sent or carried him suitable nourishment, and attended himself to preparing and administering his medicines. For many days the man was not expected to live. Unexpectedly, however, the disorder took a favorable turn, and he slowly recovered. During his convalescence he was constantly supplied with suitable food from the table of the missionary. While he was sick, he appeared very humble and grateful. On his recovery, he came to thank Mr. and Mrs. Hunt for their kindness. I was present, and witnessed the grateful outpourings of his *heart*,—no, not his *heart*, for sin had consumed that before his sickness ;—but I listened to his grateful words. "You have saved my life, sir. You have served me like a brother. I can never pay you. I think I shall be a better man in future. May God forever bless you!" As he conversed, a flock of little hot crocodiles jumped from his eyes, and tumbled over his thin, pale face, to the floor. I began to think that I would cry a little, but I looked at Mr. Hunt, and found that he was not in a crying mood, (he had seen too many such scenes,) so I concluded to defer it, fearing that I might cry in the wrong place.

Three or four days after this scene took place, a fine brood of eight English ducks were missing from the premises of Mr. Hunt. There was a vessel at anchor off Vewa at the time, and Mr. Hunt was informed that the grateful man and the ducks were both on board.

Mr. H. wrote a note to the captain, who, in reply, said that the man brought the ducks to him to sell, saying that they belonged to him, that he had paid for them; and he engaged the man, as a sailor, to serve on board his vessel.

" Such instances of ingratitude are enough to discourage any one," I said to Mr. Hunt, when I heard about the stolen ducks. "Ah!" he replied, "with that we have nothing to do. If he was again in the same situation in which I found him, I should act towards him as I did before. His ingratitude cannot destroy our peace of mind, flowing from a consciousness of having done our duty." He then related the following little incident, which occurred soon after he came to Vewa. A white man was brought to this place as sick as the one you saw, but he was a long time recovering. We paid him every needed attention, and on his recovery he appeared exceedingly grateful, but said he had nothing to pay me for the attention which he had received. His language was so affecting that I wept. As the man left me he said, " You have a teacher near the place where I live; and when the yams come in, I have a great many due me, and will give your teacher two thousand." "Very well," I said, "do so if you have enough." In due time the yams were presented, and in about a year a bill was sent, requesting me to pay for the two thousand yams. I sent word that he had adopted a good plan,—that of keeping accounts of debt and credit,—and as soon as I had time to make out his bill, for board and medical attendance, we would settle our little affair. Nothing more was heard of it.

7. We are now lying at anchor off the island of Yanganga, which has its tale of interest, to my mind at least. But to relate it, I must " begin at the beginning,"

and go as far back as the year 1835, when Mr. W. visited this coast as chief mate and trading officer of a Salem
brig. On their arrival at Mathuata, they were joined by
another brig from the same place. On board the latter
was a man of age and experience, one who possessed the confidence of his employers and associates,
and acted as trading officer for the vessel. Mr. W. had
had two years' experience in the Feejee trade, but he and
his counsel were set at nought by the trio; viz., the two
captains and the trading master. One, if not both of the
captains, had never been here before, consequently, they
were entirely ignorant of the business, and gave its management to the elder trading master, deeming the younger quite too ignorant to take any part in their affairs.
When the vessels joined company, Mr. W. remarked
that if they kept separate, and fished at different places,
it would be better for both. The remark was treated
with contempt.

While the vessels were at Mathuata, the chiefs talked about holding a great " *Solavu.*" If this was done,
it would greatly hinder the voyage, and the trio consulted how to prevent it at that time, and how to keep
the natives from leaving the fishing. " I will tell you
how it can be done," said the trading master. " Take
Retova and Ngenge and put them in irons on board the
vessels; they will not hold their feast without their chiefs,
and our business will not be interrupted." When Mr.
W. heard of the plan, he said, " If you proceed thus, it
will be the ruin of your voyages." "When we want
your advice, we will ask it," replied his captain.
" Thank you, sir," was the answer. In pursuance of
the foregoing plan, the chiefs were put in irons; one on
board each vessel. This did not greatly offend the king
and his son, who had even then become jealous of the

influence of his nephews. The plan of imprisoning the chiefs, however, proved a failure. The natives all left off fishing and held their " *Solavu.* " When this terminated, they left off fishing. "Why do you not make your people fish?" the prisoners were asked. "Because they are now their own masters. They know that we are prisoners, and we have no authority over them until we gain our liberty," they replied. The trio were now in a dilemma. They dared not set their prisoners at liberty, as they feared their revenge, yet they gained nothing by their detention. Thus they were idle for about six weeks, hoping that the natives would be induced to go on. The king exerted no authority, as he had been displeased with the previous arrangements.

On the arrival of the second vessel at Mathuata, the king said, "Ngenge and Retova are fishing for the other brig; my son and myself will go up the coast with the last arrived vessel, and load her in a short time. This plan, it has been seen, was not executed, as the trading master would not consent to the separation of the vessels, —being actuated, no doubt, either by fear or jealousy. At last the natives declared that there was no fish on the reefs (although many cargoes have been collected from the same since,) and the vessels left Mathuata for Yanganga. The king followed with canoes and men. There were at that time no inhabitants on the island, and the king erected temporary dwellings, where he lived with his people, and engaged in fishing. Retova and Ngenge, although chiefs, were subjects of the king, and so were their tribes; and the king, having a purpose to execute, exerted his authority in commanding all whom he chose, to go and fish. "*Beech de mer*" was plenty, and affairs went on prosperously for a time.

We will now reveal the plans of the king. He desired to accomplish the death of the two chiefs, whom he considered as his rivals. He knew that they had an enemy in the person of a chief, named Logi,—a relative of Tuimbua. By removing to Yanganga he could communicate without suspicion with Logi, and they might devise together some means for the destruction of his nephews.

After they had fished for awhile, Logi came to visit the king, and they had a long conference together; after which, the king went home to Mathuata. After his departure, several natives came to the " beech de mer " house, and sold to Mr. W. (who had charge of the house, and lived there with one other white man,) wood, mats, and several articles for a trifle,—much less than they had been in the habit of doing, and then left the island. This excited some suspicion at first, but they finally concluded that the natives were tired of work, and had gone to rest a little. In the afternoon natives came in from the reefs, sold their fish, and instead of dispersing, as usual, remained in little companies, whispering together. It was observed that they were armed. All these appearances foretold evil doings. It was nearly dark when a native came and told Mr. W. and his companion that during the evening the trade house was to be set on fire, and they were both to be killed. What was to be done! It was then near the time set for their destruction. It was true, there was another " beech de mer " house on the other side of the island, in view of the vessels, but how were they to reach it unobserved? Numbers of armed natives were collected even then. Mr. W. took a pistol in his hand, and went into the " beech de mer " house. About fifty were assembled there with clubs and spears. On his return to the trade house, a native followed him with a heavy club in his hand; he turned, and showing the loaded pistol, threatened to blow the man's brains out, if he did not leave him. He looked around and observed natives stationed about in such a manner as rendered it impossible for them to escape. He returned in despair to the trade house, and told his companion that they must die; for there was no possible way of escaping the vigilance of their murderers. They sat a moment, when Mr. W. said "No; these cursed cannibals shall never feed upon this body. Here are two kegs of powder,—here is fire,—and here is a shovel. As soon as they set fire to the house, —which will be at the end opposite,—I will throw fire out of the door and powder after it; we must lie flat till the explosion; we may be saved, and we may be blown to atoms,—better the latter than to be eaten. They knocked the heads from the powder kegs, and placed them near the door. Mr. W. sat holding the shovel in his hand, feeling a desire, like Samson, that many should die with him, if such was to be his fate. They had not sat long after their few preparations were completed, before they heard the sound of oars. "'Tis the boat! 'tis the boat!" they both exclaimed. " *Sa lako mai ni vals, ni kai papalagi sagela ni vere,*" shouted the flying Feejeeans. "The boat is coming, and the white men understand our plot."

Mr. W. and his companion sprung from the house, leaped over several wood-piles some five feet high, and reached the boat in safety. Here we see a grand exhibition of Feejeean bravery! There were on the island some two hundred natives, who had assembled to kill two men. When the boat came in sight, they knew that it could scarcely contain more than four or five, and nothing could have been easier than for a part of their number to have placed themselves in ambush, and, on the arrival of the boat, to have despatched its crew, while the others could have murdered those in the house. But thanks to an overruling Providence and the native cowardice for the preservation of my husband's life !

It seems that when Logi visited Tuimathuata, they formed the following plan:—On a given night the natives were to set the *"beech de mer"* house on fire that was situated in view of the vessels; and when the light of the fire was seen by the natives on the other side of the island, they were to set fire to the opposite end of the trade house from the door, and as Mr. W. and his companion rushed out, they were to be murdered, and the other *"beech de mer"* house set on fire. By this means they were, as they thought, to secure their ends; namely, have Retova and Ngenge killed. As soon as the blaze of the burning house was seen on board the vessels, a boat was sent to the island, which took the white man and some natives to the vessel where Retova was confined, and where the trio had assembled for a social smoke and chat.

The natives were questioned as to their purpose in burning the house. They said it was to serve as a signal for burning the other house and killing Mr. Wallis, which would probably have been done. As nothing was said by the trio about sending a boat to ascertain the fate of Mr. W., a man named Rogers, who was then a sailor, and is now a respectable resident at Feejee, inquired whether a boat was not to be sent round the island to ascertain the truth, saying that it was possible Mr. W. and his companion might be saved. " Send a boat!" exclaimed the *worthy* trading master, " No; what is the use of sending for dead men? who would go?" "I," said the undaunted Rogers; "and I," said another,—" and I,"—" and I,"—" and I," said others.

" Well, go and be d——d," replied the trading master. The intrepid sailors sailed to the island in time to rescue two human beings from their perilous situation. The life of one is exceedingly precious to the writer of these pages, and she will ever be grateful to the sailors who were instrumental in saving it.

The natives, from some unknown cause, did not perceive the light from the burning house, which was to have been their signal; hence their delay till the arrival of the boat.

It appears to have been the design of the king at this time, only to compass the destruction of his nephews, but, failing in this, his canoes and men were withdrawn, and the fishing again stopped. At length the trio liberated Retova, who procured a chief, named Ndury, to take his place. Retova went to Mathuata, and soon returned with a few canoes, but it was mere play, and evident that they did not mean to do much for the vessels. While they were thus hesitating, some Bau canoes came to the coast. The chiefs of Bau had heard of the detention of the young chiefs, and determined to liberate them. On their arrival they told the trio that they had better set the chiefs at liberty, that they would look out for the safety of the vessels, and would send for the Lasakau people, that all would join in fishing, and soon load both vessels. The chiefs were liberated, and they commenced building houses with a prospect of procuring a cargo or cargoes. Mr. W. went to a house on Vanualavu, at a place called Tamburua. Here the natives worked well for a little time, when Mr. W. and Mr. Brotherton, who was with him, received information that that house was to be burned. He informed his captain, and asked if the fish had not better be taken to the vessel. The gentleman laughed at his fears, as he was pleased to term

them, assured Mr. W. that there was no danger, and
added, "We still have a hostage on board; if they kill
you, we should kill him." There was in this assurance
enough to nerve any man with courage, but Mr. W. was
probably too "*ignorant*" to benefit by it, for he answered, "A Feejeean head will not suit my shoulders." The
captain did not think of this I presume, nor the consolation that it would impart to mourning relatives at home
on being told that a couple of cannibals had lost their
heads, as a retaliation for the loss of their friends. But to
return to my story. Mr. W. returned to the shore feeling provoked that so little regard was paid to their safety,
and scarcely caring whether he lived or not, feeling sick
and tired of the doings and mismanagement which had
been so evident during the whole voyage.

In the evening, Mr. W., Mr. Brotherton, and a native
were seated in the trade house, when they perceived the
"*beech de mer*" house on fire, and on turning their
heads, they found the end of the trade house opposite the
door also in flames. They were about to make their escape through the door, when a friendly native pulled
them back, and rushed through the thatch at the other
end. The two followed, and reached the boat, which
was very near. The houses are usually built quite near
the shore, and when on board the boat, they looked
towards the burning house and saw several natives at
the door with raised clubs, ready to strike when they
should appear. This ended their business on the coast.
The Bau and Vewa people having accomplished their
purpose of liberating the chiefs, went home, having advanced by this means one step more towards subjecting
Mathuata to Bau. The two vessels went about seeking
fish, and finding none. Wherever they went, the story
of the chiefs in irons preceded them, and the natives

feared to have any thing to do with them. After being among the group for fifteen months, they left; one with six hundred peculs of fish, and the other with four hundred.

———

CHAPTER VII.

Missionary Intelligence—Murder of Four White Men at Navu—An Amusing Occurrence—Retova's Barber—Manufacture of Cloth—Productions of the Islands.

Sept. 8. The Star has arrived from Raverave, and brings word that Retova went to Muta, but did no fighting. The braves were frightened, and ran home.

18. The natives have done fishing at Yanganga, and we remove to Nivaka to-morrow, where there is a house belonging to the bark. The schooner sailed to-day for Natawa.

28. After remaining at Nivaka a short time, and making things straight, we left for Kandavu, and arrived here to-day. Received a letter from Mrs. Hunt, who writes that religion appears to be progressing at Vewa. Verani has been baptized, and received the name of Elijah. The Lasakau widow had renounced heathenism, and received by baptism the name of Mary Wallis.

Oct. 1. The Nivaka people have burnt their "*beech de mer*" house, stolen several articles, and retired from business.

4. Capt. Hartwell has arrived here, and brought our letters from home that Capt. King detained for us four months. At the close of a note received by Mr. W. from Capt. K., he remarks, "When I bring a wife to Feejee,

she shall be blind and dumb." He should have added, " and deaf too."

6. Capt. Hartwell has sailed for Bau. Korovakaturanga honored us with a visit. As the chiefs usually eat at the table with us, he was invited to take a seat at the dinner table. A seat was placed for him, and he seated himself very properly on it at first, but not liking his position, he first drew up one foot on the seat, and then the other, which placed him in a most ludicrous position.

10. We have just received the news that Harry, who left our vessel at Tavea, has been murdered, and three men, also, who were with him. The accounts are as follows :—They proceeded to Vesonga, and put the young chief, Otima, in irons, telling him that they should not liberate him till the girl belonging to Runnells was restored to him. The natives at Vesonga, on hearing of the affair, manned three canoes and started for the boat, which was anchored off some distance from the town. Tomorau, the murderer of the Raverave woman, took the girl on board his canoe, and preceding the other two, arrived first to the boat, when several of the natives suddenly jumped on board, and disarmed Harry and his men. " Now," said Tomorau, " here are men enough to kill you all, and if you attempt any resistance we will do it. There is the girl, but you shall not have her. We will take Otima and the girl, too, back to the town. Leave this place, and if ever you come here again, we will eat you. If you fire at us when we leave the boat, we will kill and eat you now." He then set the captive at liberty, and they departed.

Harry then sailed for Navu, about two miles distant, where he anchored for the night, quite near the shore. It was Harry's first watch, and he slept. The natives came, waded off, and dragged the boat still nearer the shore; this awaked the men, who fought for their lives, but were overpowered by numbers, and all but Harry were killed immediately. He was wounded in the leg, and taken ashore with the bodies of his companions. The next day he was obliged to witness the horrible feast, and listen to the praises bestowed upon the flesh of his friends. The next day they took off his leg, and obliged him to sit and see that devoured also. On the third day they finished him. My heart sickens while I record these horrible truths.

Many think that Retova seeing the boat pass, sent orders by land for the murder. He hated Harry, and the natives generally appeared to have a strong feeling of hatred towards him. Retova has received some of the property that was in the boat, and his late absence up the coast, from which he has just returned, bringing the accounts of Harry's murder with him, looks as though he was guilty.

The names of the killed are as follows :—Harry Gavet, England; Wm. Russell, England; Lorenzo Hamilton, New York; George Runnells, New York.

11. The Star has arrived from Fofo, a town on Vanua lavu, where it had been sent to procure provisions. Tommy and a native of Tavea composed her crew, the craft being commanded by Andrew, as usual. On their arrival at Fofo, which is situated some distance up a river, Tommy and the Feejeean went on shore, while Andrew remained to take care of the boat. Capt. Andrew is a great lover of yanggona, or native grog, but never wishing to have the trouble of preparing it with his own distillery, he always employs the natives whenever it is possible. On this occasion, Andrew sat smoking his pipe on the quarter deck, when a company of gay young Feejeeans, of the rougher sort, appeared on the beach

near the boat. Andrew invited them to come on board, and "*chaw*" some grog for him. The young men cheerfully complied with his request, and were soon quietly seated in the boat, when each distillery was set in motion. Andrew smoked on, anticipating the delights of soon quaffing the delicious beverage. Ah! these were happy moments in Andrew's chequered life, when he sat on the deck of that nice little craft, with his pipe in his mouth, watching the smoke that so "gracefully curled," —he had no troubles then!

When the grog was "*chawed*" and prepared, the pipe was laid aside, the lips were wiped and smacked, and the head of the man was thrust into the flowing bowl (for such is the custom of these happy lands). He drank, and drank—determined never to raise his head again, while there was one drop in the bowl. There he lay, scarcely knowing whether he was in the body or out of it, when the young men raised him and threw him overboard. What an awakening! He was surprised out of all his happiness, for but a moment before, he was prostrate before the "flowing bowl," and now where was he? why, prostrate in flowing *mud*, which need not have surprised him; it was a natural consequence. Not being satisfied, however, with his present position, he climbed on board, when he was immediately secured to the mast, while the young sparks rewarded themselves for "*chawing*" the grog by robbing the boat. This being done, they departed, leaving Andrew "alone in his glory." When all was still, he found means to liberate himself; the tide had risen, and he departed from the frolic-loving land. He arrived alone at the bark, looking pale and frightened, and we trust that he will not soon forget the "*chawing* of the grog."

12. The boat has gone to Fofo to see about Tommy,

and if he is a prisoner, to liberate him if possible. Retova has not visited us since his return from Vesonga. He says that he is ashamed to come, because his people have killed the white men. Navu belongs to Korovaka-turanga.

P. M. Retova has been on board and dined. He brought a Somosomo chief and his priest with him. He tells the following story of the murdered Harry. He says that Harry went to Muta, and Mbata agreed to pay him three hundred pounds of tortoise shell if he would get Retova to Muta; this he promised to do by decoying the chief on board a whaler, when it would be easy to deliver him into the hands of his enemy. This story is only another evidence to our minds of the guilt of Retova.

13. The Star has arrived, bringing Tommy and the trade that had been stolen by the " grog *chawers*." The following is Tommy's account of his adventures, as related by himself:—" Come, Tommy," I said, " I wish to hear what happened to you at Fofo." " Yes ma'am, sir," he replied. Tommy was the servant at Vewa, who had been told to say " Yes ma'am," to ladies, and " Yes sir," to gentlemen. He never forgot his instructions, but applied them in his own way.

" Well, you see ma'am sir," said Tommy, " that when I go shore to buy yams, the chief, he no be at the town. I send boy tell a chief to come home; Capt. Wallis he send boat here to buy yams and pig. Tavea man and I go in house, where we wait long time for chief. By and by man come in house, he all scared, he say Andrew killed. Feejeean got a boat. I feel scared too. I think—well, Feejee man kill Andrew, they kill me too; but I no let Feejee man see me fraid. I say, I go see. No, no, said all Feejee woman; spose you go, they kill you; spose you stay here, they no kill. Then woman go on hill, come back and say, Andrew no kill, he go away in boat. Then chief come—me hear great cry— we all go out—see chief cry ver much. He say, me go live to nother town. You all dead man (a Feejeean curse), me no live with you. Mr. Wallis be angry—all white man be angry—no send boat to bring us riches for our pigs and yams. He then cry more, then load musket and walk away, saying, I go, I no live with you. Then all the men and womens all make great cry, and say, no, no, no, don't leave us; we will ' soro,' take our ' soro.' Then chief he set down, man he get all whale's teeth in the town to ' soro.' The chief then he no cry, but tell 'em get all he take out the boat, put it in canoe. Tavea man and Tom go too, and tell captain he shamed. So they get all the things put in canoe, tell the Fofo man take us Tavea. When we get Tavea we see boat coming after us, so we put all the thing in the boat, and come here."

15. The schooner arrived, bringing ten peculs of fish. Mr. Smith states that they were doing well, when several canoes came from Somosomo, and commenced hostilities with the Natawans, and put a stop to all farther trade.

20. Last night, about eleven o'clock, we witnessed the burning of the " beech de mer " house at this place. A boat was sent to receive all that could be saved. About two hundred dollars worth of " beech de mer " was destroyed.

21. We have removed our station to the island of Mathuata. This island was the home of the king, but it is now uninhabited. Houses are to be built here, and it is pretended that Retova will do great things in the " beech de mer " way. Canoes are coming from Geer and Raverave to fish for the vessel. The chief of Kan-

9

davu is building another house so near his town that if
one burns, the other must.

22.   Received a visit from Retova's barber, the man
who murdered the man from Raverave at the time of the
late slaughter at that place.   He is an ugly looking,
petty chief, of the name of Tuvutuvu.   He is a great
thief, and we are obliged to watch when he *honors* the
vessel with his presence.   Although it is said that the
natives are very thievish, we have suffered but little from
their depredations.   While I was at Vewa, Mrs. Jaggar
informed me that when they lived at Lakemba, two large
tubs of clothes were stolen from them.   When they complained to the king, he said, "I will make that all right."
The next day they were expecting the lost clothes to be
restored, knowing that the king possessed the power.
About noon, the king was seen to approach with several
attendants.   He came into the house, bearing—not the
clothes, but as a "*soro*," six nice looking fingers which
he had had taken from the hands of the thieves.   As the
missionaries needed their clothing, and could not wear
the fingers, this was poor consolation; yet poor as it was,
they received no other.

23.   A petty chief, named Ndury (the same who
was for a little while held in "durance vile" by the trio),
is on board, and lately from Vewa, where he has a niece
of Elijah's for a wife.   He says that Elijah has lately
had a "*Solavu*" for Mr. Hunt.   I inquired why he had
one for him.   He said that Elijah had formerly stolen
many pigs and chickens from the mission; he was now
sorry and ashamed, and wished to make all the restoration in his power.   This was not required by the missionaries, who told him that as they hoped God had forgiven
the past, so would they.   He would not be satisfied till
he had done what he could.

24. As I have often alluded to the "*masi*," or native cloth used by the natives, I will describe its manufacture. The natives cultivate a tree, called in native, "*masi-kau*" (a kind of papyrus), from which their cloth is made. The trees are set out about one foot apart. When they have reached maturity they are about five feet high, and six inches in circumference. The natives then peel off the outside bark, which is thrown away, and carefully stripping the inner bark from the tree, they put it in water and let it remain for twelve hours; it is then spread, and pounded with instruments made of iron wood till it is thin as muslin and looks very white. Some of the cloth is retained in this state, and worn for head-dresses. All that is required for other purposes, such as bed-screens, and men's wear, is made stouter by placing several thicknesses of muslin one upon another, while in its damp state. A part of the cloth is retained in its native color, and some of it displays the native ingenuity in painting. Cloth is mostly manufactured at Somosomo. It is only worn by men, and in very small quantities. The women wear "*lekus*," made also from the bark of some tree, but not resembling cloth at all.

25. The principal and most loved article of food in Feejee, is yams, which are to a Feejeean what bread is to us. The bread-fruit, tarro and carwais are next in value to the yams. Of the three latter, the natives prepare what they call "*mandrai*," which they live upon when other food fails. It often occurs that a "*Solavu*" takes all the vegetables and fruits from a town, or an enemy destroys their plantations; and they are then obliged to live upon the *mandrai* till their next harvest.

At the windward part of the group, only one crop of vams is gathered in a year; but on the Ba coast of Vete-lavu, it is said that two crops are gathered in one year.

The bread-fruit tree yields its ripe fruits in great abundance semi-annually. I know of no tree in Feejee more beautiful than this. It is ever green, presenting to the eye no decay. Its aged leaves change so gradually that they are scarcely ever observed, being mostly hidden by the verdant branches, from which is ever springing the beautifully scalloped leaf. There are a great many of these trees in Vewa. I was one day remarking upon their form and beauty to Mr. Hunt, who joined in my praises, but, after a pause, said, " Sometimes, however, I tire of this evergreen, and would like to see the changing hues of autumn. Are not your American forests more beautiful with all their autumnal tints?" " Our forests," I replied, " have their admirers, but I am not one of them. I do not love all that is loveable, nor do I admire all that is admirable. I do not love winter with its cold sterility—I do not love autumn with its chilly nights; the rustling of its dried and shrivelled leaves is not music to my ears—I cannot look upon our forests with pleasure, for they tell me of snow, and wind, hail and storm. Oh no; I could as soon admire the elegant dress of one who came to tell me that my dearest friend was buried in the ocean." But to return to edibles. During the seasons of tarro and bread-fruit, they are gathered, and the rind of the one, and the skin of the other are taken from the outside, holes are dug in the ground, and lined with fresh leaves. Into these holes the tarro, bread-fruit or carwais—whichever may be in its season—is placed, and covered with leaves; several layers of stones are then piled over the whole, where it remains for years if not wanted for use. When it is needed, portions of it are taken from the hole, and kneaded in a tray; small portions are then carefully wrapped in the bread-fruit leaf and boiled, when they consider it fit for eating.

Among their luxuries, they consider *vaka-lololes* one of the greatest; hence, no feast or Solavu is held without them, if they can possibly be procured. They are made of tarro, or bread-fruit, and grated cocoa-nut. The vegetable, or fruit, is boiled or roasted, then thoroughly washed in a tray, and made into balls about the size of a small hen's egg, from twenty to thirty of which are laid in a large green leaf. The milk of the grated cocoa-nut is then sweetened with the compressed juice from the *ti* root, and poured over them; they are then tied up in the leaf till wanted, when they make a delicious dessert.

Among the fruits of Feejee, are to be found the orange, lemon, pine-apple, banana and shaddoc, all of which are well known at home. Besides these is a fruit called *ndawa*, which is about the size of a peach, and resembles a plum inside, but lacks its delicious flavor. There is another fruit called "*kaveka*," which is very beautiful to the eye; the form is like that of the pear, and the color is a beautiful red and white. A basket of this elegant fruit was brought here yesterday, and was the first I had seen. "How beautiful!" I exclaimed. "Are they to eat?" "Yes," was the answer. I took of the fruit and ate, but not finding it sweet to the taste, did not hand it to my husband. It is neither sour, bitter, palatable nor unpalatable, but appears to be composed of wind and water. What a fine essay might the moralist write from the "*kaveka!*"

I must give a description of it, for although its component parts resemble two of the elements, there is a good deal of character about the beautiful "*kaveka*." It possesses great beauty, but has no sweetness, and is very cold; it is subject to an early decay, and is never fit to be eaten after it has been gathered twelve hours.

There is another fruit in this favored land, called the "*wi.*" This tree resembles the pear tree in size and foliage; the fruit is formed like the egg of a turkey, and is about as large. It is of a deep golden color when ripe, and emits an odor precisely like that of a quince. It is filled with fibrous substances, which make it necessary to grate them before they are cooked; when stewed, they make a nice sauce, not unlike a green apple-sauce. One could scarcely tell them from apples, when made into tarts and puddings. Ginger, arrow-root, tumeric and tobacco are found here in great abundance. Cotton is found in small quantities along the coasts, but is supposed to abound in the interior. On the mountains of Ovalau are a few wild nutmeg trees, or shrubs. It is said that they abound in the interior of Vete-lavu. It has been shown that the natives are not backward in the use of *manimal* food; but that of other species is seldom used, except at their *Solavus*, when pigs are cooked by hundreds. They are sometimes "*tambued*" for a year previous to the time of a feast. Chickens are raised, but seldom eaten by the natives, being mostly sold to white residents, vessels and missionaries. The sugar-cane, too, should be numbered among the sweet things of Feejee. Fruitful and beautiful are these lands! But oh! what a moral waste! reminding one of the language of the excellent Heber,

> "In vain, with lavish kindness,
>   The gifts of God are strewn;
> The heathen in his blindness,
>   Bows down to wood and stone."

29. The people have begun to fish to-day at the Mathuata house, and are coming for their pay.

When a vessel lays near a " *beech de mer* " house, the natives often receive orders to come to the bark, when muskets, or any large articles are due. The following is a pretty good illustration of the manner in which this try-patience people trouble those who answer their orders. This morning a man came, bringing an order for a musket. One was given him, with which he appeared satisfied. He remained about deck awhile, when he found the spring too tight; this was set right. After a little while something else was wrong, and he wished to have several more muskets brought, that he might select for himself; this was done. An hour or more was spent in handling and selecting. After he had suited himself, and the muskets were returned to the chest, he discovered some flaw, or was not satisfied with the color of the barrel, and wished to select from the chest. After handling and examining them all as long as he wished, he departed with the one that was first offered. Thus he was from ten in the morning till four in the afternoon deciding about his musket, which was really a good one in the first place. This is not a solitary case. I always dread to see a canoe filled with natives coming to be paid from the bark. One will want cloth, and when it is measured off, he will alter his mind and take beads; the cloth is returned and beads are given, and after a while these are not wanted, but something else, and so on. If any one wishes to increase in patience, let them come to Feejee for " *beech de mer.*"

30. Mr. W. has sent an ambassador to Raverave with a whale's tooth, inviting His Majesty to come, according to promise, to Mathuata, to keep his subjects from idling away their time. The schooner is fishing at Tavea.

Nov. 3. The Star has arrived from Tavea and Raverave. Retova has sent word that he will be here in two days.

While the Star lay at Tavea, a canoe came from Ndama with two men, who offered shell to Mr. Smith, wishing him to buy it. As they asked too much for it, Mr. S. did not trade with them, and they left the schooner to return to Ndama. On their way, the men, canoe, and tortoise shell were taken by a Tavea canoe (containing superior numbers of men) and carried to Tavea. The shell was again offered to Mr. Smith for sale, by Tavear men. The fate of the captives is not known. " Might makes right," here.

Ndury tells me that a man died of repletion at Rave-rave the day after the cannibal feast.

———

CHAPTER VIII.

The Plot—The Unwelcome Guests—The Flight—False Statements.

Nov. 5. A Solavu vessel has arrived, bringing a load of yams for the bark, and very important information from Capt. Hartwell. The Gambia went from Bau to a place called Nivatu, for the purpose of fishing " *beech de mer.*" Capt. H. received on board at Bau, a young native named Tatave, a nephew of the murdered Lasakau chief, to go with him as a hostage, and a kind of messenger from Bau. It is always desirable to have some one on board the vessels belonging to Bau when fishing in the dominions of its chiefs. In this instance, however, the man had better have been left behind. On their arrival at Nivatu, Tatave went to several towns near, and told them that it was the wish of the Bau chiefs for them to join the Nivatu people, and fish for Capt. H. It was very well so far; but he did not stop there. He told them that after they had fished a little, it was the command of the chief for them to take the vessel. One day several natives assembled on board with their faces painted black. Other indications of mischief being visible, the suspicions of the captain were excited, when he resorted to such measures as insured his safety at that time. The captain did not learn then the plans of the natives, or what Tatave had been doing. He only knew that they had assembled for mischief of some kind, and as the Nivatu people did not appear to be concerned in the affair, he kept on fishing with redoubled vigilance.

Nivatu is a small island about twelve miles distant from Solavu, which is the residence of the white people who formerly lived at Levuka. It so happened that on a certain night a woman of Solavu went out to draw water, and as she was returning from the pond, she heard voices in conversation; and some words reaching her ears that excited her suspicion, she listened. The voices proceeded from two native men who had just returned from Nivatu. They were in a little "buri," nor knew they that one hearkened to their speech. They were heard to say that on the following day a canoe was to go off to the Gambia to offer several articles for sale. There were to be just double the number of natives that there were on board the Gambia. Half were to go on board first, unarmed, and engage the people in barter; while thus engaged, the other half were to follow, one at a time, armed, and gradually mingle with the rest. On a given signal, each of the two natives were to attack and kill their man, and take possession of the brig. Their first step, however, was to kill the trading officer on shore. The woman, having listened to the whole plan, returned to her house and related the same to her husband. The next morning, as soon as there was light enough for them to see their way over the reefs, several of the white men took a vessel and started, greatly fearing that they would not reach Nivatu in time to save the vessel. The wind favored them, however, and on their arrival they found all safe. The captain was informed of his danger, and boats were immediately manned, armed, and sent to the relief of the trading master on shore. When the boats reached the shore, they observed many natives, with their clubs and painted faces, walking about as though they were in waiting for something. Tatave was found and secured; but Mr. Goodrich, the trading officer, was no where to be found. Tatave said that he was not killed, but he supposed that he had fled and hid himself in the bush. After half a day's search, he was found half dead with terror. He said that he perceived danger from the natives, and knowing that his single arm would not avail him any thing with such a host, and seeing no other way of escape, he had fled and concealed himself.

I think that this affair originated entirely with Navinde when they were at Ba, where, as it will be recollected, an expedition was sent on Capt. Hartwell's account. Navinde and several of his people, with Verani, were on board the Gambia. A fine opportunity occurred at the time for taking possession of the vessel. Navinde proposed that the opportunity should be improved, but Verani prevented him.

After Mr. Goodrich was found, the boats returned to the vessel, where Tatave confessed that they intended to do as had been stated at Solavu; but he would not tell who employed him. Soon after the captivity of Tatave, Elijah came to the vessel. Capt. Hartwell informed him of the facts that have been made known, and asked him what he should do with the prisoner. "Kill, hang him, or any thing," said Elijah, who was very angry at what he had heard. Capt. H. then ordered him to be tied to the mainmast, and receive thirty-nine lashes; this was done, and his feet were confined in irons, that he may do no more harm for the present.

We have heard that one of Capt. King's trading men, on the Ba coast, has just had a narrow escape of his life, as there was a plan laid to kill him.

As at home, when thieves are about, every means are used to secure our property, so these things cause us to redouble our vigilance. Our big guns have been fired off and reloaded, and are now looking saucily out of the ports, seeming to say, "Come here if you dare." The arm chests, in the fore and main top, are all ready to fight. A loaded musket stands near our bed, several loaded pistols are quietly lying in our state-room, and orders have been issued that the bell should be struck every half hour, that the natives on shore may learn that there are some on board who are not napping.

6. Retova still delays coming; it is said through fear, on account of Harry's murder. We learn that he reached Navu in time to devour the heart of the man he hated. The Navu people must have been expecting him, or the heart would not have been saved for his cannibal Majesty.

9. Retova has come at last. He remained on board but a few moments, and then departed for the shore. He has lost much flesh, and looks quite dejected and ill.

10. The chief has passed the day on board. Seeing him look sad, I proceeded to comfort him in the following manner. "When Thakombau killed his brother," I said, "you thought it very bad, and said that

you could not do such a thing, that Bau was bad, and its chiefs were always engaged in '*veres*.' Now what do you think of the Mathuata chiefs? Are they learning '*veres*' of Bau? Did the Bau chiefs '*vere*' to kill your uncle?" "No," he replied, "that was Korova-katuranga's '*vere*,' in revenge for the murder of his own father, who was killed by the king." "But," I replied, "he could not have killed so great a chief without your consent, which shows that you are as bad as the Bau chiefs. The God of heaven is angry when we commit murder, and will punish you for it, perhaps in this life. Korovakaturanga is your friend now; but you see he is strong, and has taken the life of the king to please you. By and by he may take your life to please himself." He looked very sober, and I added, "You know now about the '*lotu*,' and you are ashamed to have your bad deeds known, because you know that they are wrong." "*Ndena, Marama*," he replied. "Truly Marama."

11.   This morning His Majesty asked me for a razor. I handed him one, and he requested me to shave him. I declined the honor with one of my best courtsies, while Mr. W. sat almost convulsed with laughter at the scene.

12.   We are obliged, while lying here, to send a long distance for water. To-day the boat was sent with four men, which left us rather short, as some of our people are with the schooner, and some at the houses on shore. Three men only, besides the captain, were on board after the boat had left. No sooner had it disappeared behind the island, than we observed two canoes put off, and sail for the bark; they were well filled with men. When we saw this *goodly* company approaching, we felt in our very hearts that we would rather defer the reception of so many visitors in the absence of our crew.

The captain told the few that were on board to leave their work, and each have some weapon at hand, without seeming to be armed, and to let no one come on board but the chiefs. He then put a small pistol in his pocket, while I, not caring to wield a broom-stick, took a pair of large scissors in my hand. When the chief came on board, he presented an order for an axe; another presented one for a hatchet, and another for a musket, and so on. This looked suspicious. It is sometimes the case that when it is intended to take a vessel, they go without arms, and provide themselves in this manner from the vessel, in order that no suspicion may be excited on board. Retova came into the cabin, and the captain brought him an axe from the trade room. After examining it some time he called for another, which was brought, and soon after he requested a third; this was all that the box contained. The captain had contrived to keep one axe in his hand the most of the time, but the chief put one under his seat, laid another in his lap, and held a third in his hand. I was standing near, playing awkwardly with my scissors, when observing that he had possession of all the axes, I took one from his lap, and after remarking upon its goodness and beauty, handed it to my husband. He was a long time selecting one of the three instruments, but at last succeeded, and prepared to depart. As he rose to go, he held the gleaming axe over my head and said, "Now, Marama, I will kill you with this hatchet." "It is very good for you to do it, and I will kill you with these scissors," I answered, pointing them to his heart. "Saga, sara; iko Marama venaka." "No, indeed; you are a good Marama," he said, laughing, and left the cabin. When he returned to the deck, he appeared surprised that the natives were all in their canoes. I followed the chief and my husband to the deck, knowing that a Feejeean would seldom injure a man, if watched. Such is his cowardice.

13. Yesterday Retova ordered some of his people to put in their fish for him to pay for some articles of his own that were on board the bark. The *obedient* subjects brought in their fish and received their pay. His Majesty heard of it, and repaired to the "*beech de mer*" house in a great rage. Here he found the chief of the offending party, and hurled his spear at him, which missed its aim. The offender set off at full speed, followed by several of his people, who were followed by the *tufundres;* these were followed by a white man, who was followed by an African, and the whole were followed by the king himself. The party were racing at the top of their speed, tumbling over each other, logs of wood, stones and various other obstructions, (for the party had been formed so suddenly that the race-ground had not been prepared,) while the angry chief was close upon them, his head-dress and *masi* standing out straight about a yard, giving him the appearance of an animal with two tails. At length he gave up the chase, and calling to the black and white men who belonged to the house, he told them that he was not angry with them, and desired them to return. The offending chief sent a whale's tooth as "*a soro,*" and his people approached His Majesty on their hands and knees, their bodies covered with ashes, and exclaiming, "*Sa soro ko au.*" "I ask pardon." The king received the "*soro,*" and pardoned his disobedient subjects.

14. Retova came on board to-day, and acted over the scene of yesterday with great glee. He said that Johnson, our black man, turned nearly white, and his face could scarcely be seen for lips. Some of the Feejeeans are grand mimics. I have seen them hand my

husband an order, and walk behind him imitating his manner exactly when he is vexed.

15. Two Geer canoes that are fishing here came alongside, while Thouthou, their chief, paid us a visit. Geer is about twelve miles from Mathuata, is owned by Retova, and its inhabitants are subject to his power. When vessels are here, he often sends for them to come and fish for them. As Mr. W. did not choose to give him all he wanted, he became quite impudent, saying, "Capt. —— said you were a 'kaise,' and it is true indeed. You are a 'kaise.'" Mr. W. said, "Yes, it is true. I am a 'kaise,' and if you knew it, why did you come to beg of me? It is not your custom to beg of such." "Well," he returned, "I want you to have the sail mended for my canoe, or I will not fish." "Very well," said Mr. W., "do as you please. I shall not have your sail mended, as you had time enough to repair it before you came." "Then give my people some yams to eat; they are hungry," said he. "I can scarcely get yams enough for my own people," replied Mr. W. "Then I will go home," was his reply. "Go home if you choose," said Mr. W., who had given presents, and tried every method but indifference. He now thought that he would try a little of that. Thouthou thought that he might play Retova, who, it is said, has received from some masters of vessels whatever he chose to ask for. If he was refused, he would return to his home, and there remain till a "soro" was sent in the shape of a musket, a whale's tooth, or some other article, when he would return and set his people to work again.

When Thouthou left, Mr. W. told him that he had doubled his prices for fish, and paid well. If he chose to fish, well, and if he chose to go home it was just as well. It is very probable that the chief had taken a lesson from his superior before he visited the bark.

16. The boat was again sent for water, and, as before, two canoes came to the bark, with a large number of men in them. Retova has never brought so many people to the vessel since the boat went last for water. The captain gave the same orders that he did on a previous visit. Retova came into the cabin while Ratanga remained on deck; no others were allowed to leave the canoes. While the chief remained below, he happened to observe a part of the little pistol which had been stowed snugly away in a certain pocket. "What is that in your pocket for? are you afraid?" said he. "No, I am not afraid," was the reply; "but it is best to keep some weapon about one. You know that there are many strangers here at present. The Geer people are bad. Do you not remember that they killed the white man's child, and would have murdered its parents if Capt. Osborne had not sent and liberated them?" "Ah, it is true," he replied. After remaining below a while, he repaired to the deck, followed by Mr. W. and myself. He appeared quite surprised to see all his people in the canoes, and turning to Mr. W., said, "Why are not the people allowed to come on board? what are you afraid of?" "Do you not see," said the captain, "that several of my men are absent? Why should all these men come on board?—you could not see that they did not steal, and how could I recover articles thus stolen?" "Ah, you do not fear that," replied he; "you think, perhaps, that we are engaged in a 'vere' to take your vessel." "We are prepared for that; Feejeeans would gain nothing by a 'vere.' You know where our powder is, and you see that Mrs. W. is always watching; if she sees any thing wrong, she knows how to send

fire to the powder, and away we go all together." "We are good men, and would do you no harm." "Yes," said Mr. W., "I know what a good man you are; but some of your people may not be as good as your Majesty; therefore it is best to look out for them." When the boat appeared in sight our visitors departed.

17. The Star brings word from Kandavu that their canoes have been fired into by the Mathuata people, and they were afraid to go to the reefs again for fish. Retova, too, had sent for the Kandavuns to come here and fight. Mr. W. inquired the meaning of all this. Retova replied, by saying that a Mathuata canoe ran across the bows of a Kandavu canoe in play, but the Kandavuns took it in earnest, and were angry. He sent word to them, therefore, that they might come here in sight of the two Turaga-lavus and fight it out. He immediately sent a messenger to his frightened subjects to tell them to go on with their fishing, and no one should harm them.

In the afternoon Retova went on shore, and soon after an order was sent off for a hatchet,—as it was not marked black fish, the hatchet was refused, not knowing who had sent for it. Retova had sent the man, and when he returned and said the hatchet had been refused, the testy chief flew into a rage, and sent word that Mr. W. might send for the fish as soon as he pleased, as he should burn the house to-night. The hatchet was sent with a suitable apology, and the affair was settled.

18. The schooner arrived from Tavea. Mr. Smith left the natives delicately feeding upon the bodies of five men whom they had surprised and taken from an inland town.

I find that I have been mistaken about Muta. It is not an inland town, but is situated about half a mile from the seashore, on Vanualavu, and is approached from seaward by a river that leads from the shore to the town.

Some of the friends of the late king are now saying that Capt. Osborne joined Retova in the "*vere*" to kill the king. This we believe to be false, though, as the affair terminated, we are not surprised that the natives should think so. Capt. O. probably believed that Retova sincerely desired to make peace, which was truly desirable on many accounts. It would be advantageous to himself, and to others who were engaged in the same business, as the whole coast could engage in fishing without fear of each other. He, therefore, did all in his power to bring about a reconciliation, and establish a permanent peace along this coast. The failure was not owing to any thing wrong on his part, but to the deception and treachery of Retova.

While we were breakfasting this morning, Mr. W. sneezed when pouring out a cup of coffee for the Turagalavu. He refused the coffee, saying if he should drink it, he would be clubbed. They never drink yanggona if a person sneezes when preparing it.

19. I overheard Cunningham tell the captain that he fully believed Retova was planning some mischief, and advised his being closely watched. Jack has been off from the house, and says that he is certain the natives intend to try to take the vessel, and that when the canoes came off with all those men, when the boat had gone for water, the natives armed themselves and assembled on the beach, watching intently the vessel and the canoes. We are not sorry that the people are somewhat frightened, as they have been feeling so secure that they have been found napping when they should have been watching. It is said that a Feejeean is too much of a coward ever to strike any one when facing him. I

make it a part of my business, therefore, to watch, that
Mr. W. may not get a blow on his back. Retova and
Ratanga have been on board all day. Mr. W. does not
think that mischief is intended us, but thinks that there
may be trouble among themselves; however, he is watching for the safety of all.

20. The Turaga-lavu came on board, and said that
the Tavea people, with others, were coming to kill him,
and he wished Mr. W. to look out for the appearance of
the war canoes, that he might have time to come on
board the bark for safety. Our men on shore hear the
natives talking about the affair, and understanding the
language but imperfectly, think that they are about to
be eaten.

21. Ratanga came off to the bark in high glee, stating that a dead man had been brought to them, and
they should feast upon his body. I tried to talk with
him about it, but he was too much elated to hearken to
my speech. The dead man, about ten years ago, had
stolen a woman from a town called Nagumu, and fled to
the interior with her, where they had lived since that
time. The man, supposing that his offence had been
forgotten, ventured to revisit his native place. He had
no sooner arrived than he was killed, and as the Turaga-
lavu was at Mathuata, the body was sent to him without
delay. When natives are killed at any of the "kaise"
towns, the bodies are sent to the Turaga-lavu, who de-
vours the choice bits, such as the heart and tongue, and
has the rest divided among his people. If he has several bodies, he sends them to different towns, as little
tokens of his love for, and remembrance of them. How
delightful such affectionate remembrances from their
chief! What a pity that any one should interfere with
such innocent and simple customs!

22. We learn that the body of the murdered man was yesterday carried to the "*beech de mer*" house, where it was prepared for the oven. It was then taken away to some place out of sight of the vessel, where it was cooked and eaten. A piece of the disgusting food was offered to our men at the house, who set to and chased the man with a large stick. Another man came with a piece of the flesh and sat down by the trade house and enjoyed his treat, after which he threw the bones behind some bushes.

23. We are exceedingly amused at the little tales often told us by Retova and Ndury. They will beg something of Mr. W. which he thinks proper to refuse, making them feel a little irritated; when His Majesty will relate some interesting tale which has been told him by Capt. ———. The following is a record of the conversation which took place to-day. The chief, addressing Mr. W., said, " Capt. ——— says that you are a '*kaise*' in America, that no Turagas talk with you, that you do not own any part of the vessel that you come in, nor any of the riches it contains; but he owns the vessel that was here with all that it contained, besides another vessel in America that is coming out the next time he comes ; and he owns two houses filled with riches in America." "Indeed!" said Mr. W., "what a great man he is. He can well afford to give you all you ask of him, if he owns so much property. How is it that you ask me for riches, when you know that I have none? Suppose that you should send a canoe to Bau in charge of one of your '*kaises*',—you load the canoe with riches, such as cloth, sail mats, &c., for which you are to receive an equivalent. What would you say if your '*kaise*' gave your riches away, and brought you nothing back?" The chief was not prepared for this kind of rea-

soning. It is a great insult to call a chief a "*kaise*,"
and he supposed that Mr. W. would argue in favor of
his own respectability. It has been the custom for many
of the trading masters who come to Feejee, to tell the
chiefs and natives what great men they are at home.
The chief paused a moment, and then said, "Capt. ——
says that you belong to a poor little town, where they
have nothing but beans to eat." At this we laughed
loud, long and merrily. At length I said, "Do you not
think that the food is good? Look at Mr. W. and see
how large he is (weighing about two hundred and thirty).
If you should ever see Capt. —— again, do advise him
to feed awhile upon the same." The chief paused again,
but soon rallied, and resumed, "Capt. —— has a great
many colors on board his vessel; and he says that none
but sons of the king of America are allowed so many
colors,——that if you were to bring so many you would be
killed. He says, too, that you are a foolish man to
bring your wife here, and that she is old and ugly." At
this another merry peal rang through the cabin, which
interrupted the chief for a moment, when he went on to
say, "Capt. —— says that his wife is young and handsome, and rides on a beautiful horse." How should a
report be circulated in Feejee so near the truth! I am
not young,—I am not handsome,—I never rode a beautiful horse in my life; and I am not wedded to a
donkey for a husband. The chief, however, felt better
after awhile, and remained on board all night. When it
was time to retire, I told the steward to bring the tele-
graphic signals, the national flag, the signal of the bark,
and every other that could be found, into the cabin.
This being done, he was farther ordered to unfold and
place them, one by one, on the floor of the cabin for the
chief's bed. Retova watched the doings with surprise;

for his bed was becoming soft and yielding.   At length
he exclaimed, "*A lavu ni lasu.*"   Capt. ——, a great
liar is Capt. ——.   When the colors were all placed, I
inquired, quietly, if he would like any more.   "*Sagai
sara; a lavu,*" he replied.   No, indeed; enough.

———

CHAPTER IX.

Destruction of Rewa—The Prisoner—Return to Bau—A Mistake—Arri-
val of the American Consul—The Lazy Boy—The Escape—Return to
Bau—Vatai—The Tonga Chief—Queen of Rewa—Captives at Bau—
Origin of the War with Rewa.

Dec. 8.   Capt. Hartwell has arrived, and brings intelligence of the destruction of Rewa.   The town was
burnt, and about four hundred inhabitants massacred.
The following are the particulars of the affair:—It appears that a party in Rewa favored Bau.   A petty chief
of this party went to Bau, and had an interview with Thakombau, its master spirit, when he promised to betray
Rewa into his hands.   The messenger was instructed to
return to Rewa, and tell its king that Thakombau would
come and fight Rewa on a given day, and after the battle
he would receive their "*soro,*" and they would be at
peace.   When the day arrived, Thakombau, accompanied by his warriors and butchers (Lasakaus), sailed for
Rewa, and appeared before the town about daylight.   A
message was sent to the principal wife of the king, who
is a near relative of the king of Bau, commanding her,
with her children and all the Bau women, to come on
board his canoe for safety, as they were about to engage
in battle, and the town was to be burned.   As the women were preparing to obey the message, the king

awoke, and surprised at what he saw, he inquired where
the women were going. When his wife told him, he
said, "I shall go with you." When they had assembled
at the river side, two canoes were in waiting. Thakombau, with some of his followers, were in one, and the
other was empty. Thakombau ordered the king to come
to the one that he occupied, and the women and children
to embark on board the other. "No," said the king,
"I will not leave my women and children,—where they
go, I will go." He thought, probably, that while he remained with his queen his life was safe, as she was a
Bau woman of high rank. Such has heretofore been
their custom, and its violation has never been known
previous to the present instance. Thakombau ordered a
man to fire at the king. This being done, he fell, exclaiming, "Has it come to this?" The king was wounded, not killed; and Thakombau perceiving this, ordered
several warriors to step to the other canoe, and despatch
him with their clubs.

The Marama had appeared as one stunned from the
moment she had embarked in the canoe. She did not
suspect that her husband's life was in danger from his
enemies while she was with him. Such a thing had
never been known in the annals of her country. The
order to club her husband, however, roused her from
her stupor, and she hastily stepped on to the other canoe, and knelt at the feet of her cousin, and in a voice
of agony said, "Oh! my brother, my brother, (cousins
are called brothers and sisters, as they have no word in
their language which expresses uncle, aunt, or cousin,)
save the life of my husband. Do not kill him, but let
him be 'bulu' (well), and he will bring wood to cook
your food, or do any thing for you. Oh! brother, hear

my speech!" "He has greatly injured me and shall die," was the reply.

While the half distracted wife was vainly pleading with her inhuman cousin for the life of her husband, two warriors were pounding him with their clubs, but it seemed as though the victim bore a charmed life. They did not kill him, and he was at last strangled. The wife and children witnessed the whole scene.

While the above was being enacted on board the canoes, the town had been fired by its betrayer, and the butchers had commenced their slaughter. The brother of the king fled to the mountains, and the strong men of Rewa mostly fled, leaving their aged, and women and children, to meet the murderous club, and supply the cannibal feasts. Thakombau returned immediately to the capitol, bearing his captives, among whom was the mother of Revelete, who was an own sister of the king of Rewa.

Thus another victory has been gained by treachery; and it is said that Thakombau has stepped upon the top round of the ladder, from which some prophecy that he will soon begin to descend. He may be hurled from its top, but I do not think he will ever descend by its rounds.

The natives say that the prophecy is still fulfilling respecting the five brothers of Rewa. Two are left; and to accomplish the whole, it is only necessary to kill Garenggeo, make "Ko-mai-ni-mana," or Phillips, as he is generally called, king, and shoot Thakombau.

Capt. H. has his prisoner on board the Gambia, being undetermined, as yet, what to do with him. He found means to loose his irons last night, intending to swim to the shore. His intentions, however, were frustrated, and he was obliged to sleep without the benefit of a salt water bath.

11. The king came on board with an old musket,
and desired a new one for it. Mr. W. was busy at the
time attending to the weight of some fish, and sent him
word that the old musket was not worth a fish-hook.
The message greatly offended His Majesty, and he took
the hostage in his canoe and departed for the island.
As soon as Mr. W. heard how he had offended the chief,
he sent a whale's tooth as a " *soro,*" which was received,
and the hostage returned.

12. The Nagumu people leave Mathuata and fishing
to-day, to return home, declaring that they are afraid on
account of the man in irons on board the Gambia. Our
hostage is also afflicted in the same way. He says that
he has not slept for two nights. He has been allowed to
leave, and we shall have one of higher rank in his room.

13. The Gambia sailed away in fine style. A parting salute was fired by both vessels.

15. Retova says that Tatave told him that it was by
the direction of the Bau chiefs that they were about to
take the Gambia. He said Bau was angry because
Capt. H. went to Rewa, and supplied their enemies with
ammunition. I presume that Capt. H. did not do this,
but their jealousy was such that they accused him of it.
Tatave said that many angry messages had been sent to
Vewa, and Thakombau was intending soon to attack the
place, as he was very angry with the missionary for con-
verting Verani.

Mr. Hunt writes us that the gospel progresses, and
the heathen rage. But their trust is in God, who has
hitherto kept them from harm.

16. The Star brings word from Kandavu that Retova
is angry with that people, because they attended a
" *Solavu* " in a neighboring town without his permission.
He has sent them word that four men must be brought

him to eat, as payment for their offence. Since the message, the people are afraid to go to the reefs. Thus he has sent the Geer and Nagumu people home, and prevented the Kandavu people from fishing. He promised Mr. W. that if he would take him to Bau, on his return the vessel should be loaded in four months. His object, however, is evidently to enrich himself without working, which is very well for him, but does not load the bark. Ndury came off to-day in a very ill-humor, and talked in the most impudent manner. He inquired what would be done with Tatave. Mr. W. told him that he did not know. "I know," he answered. "He will be carried to America and brought back again ; for there is no one to punish him there. It is a poor place, and the sons of its king have to come here for " *beech de mer* ". "What son of its king has ever been here?" was asked. "Capt. ——, who wore a red sash," was the reply. "He said that none but the sons of kings were allowed to wear a red sash." "His Man-Friday wears a red sash, too. Is he also the king's son?" "Yes," was the reply. "He married Capt. ——'s sister." "The Malolo people," said I, "do not think that America is a little place." "The vessels that come here," he replied, "are now all rotten, and the king is too poor to have any more made. The Turaga-lavu said that vessels of war would be sent here in four years; they do not come, though many white men have been killed. If Capt. Hartwell's vessel had been taken, no one would come to see about it." What could be said to this? During the four years succeeding the squadron's visit, no murders were committed upon white men; but since the expiration of that term some fifteen persons have been killed. It is a pity that a promise of that kind should have been made, as since its non-fulfilment, the

natives have become more daring. When Ndury had
"freed his mind," he departed.

17. Johnson, from the house on shore, relates
that after the cannibal dinner, which took place the
other day, all who shared in these delights were very
particular in their ablutions afterwards. Not one of them
are willing to visit the spot after dark where their meal
was taken. The young man who threw a bone behind
the house, will not go out after dark, declaring that the
bone had whistled to him as he left the house one evening. This shows that there must be a little monitor
within which tells them that it is wrong to eat each other.
Ratanga once said to me, "Do the Americans never eat
each other?" "No," I replied, "we know better. Our
pigs and cats sometimes devour their young, but we are
not like pigs and cats. Do you not see how superior
men and women are to these animals? You would think
it very strange, if, instead of talking, we were to grunt
and mew like them, and it would be equally strange did
we learn of them to eat each other. We do not wish to
learn the habits of these animals." He looked exceedingly ashamed, and after a pause said, "The Feejeeans
are then like pigs!" "No," I replied; "they are
worse than pigs, for they do not eat great pigs that live
with them ; only their little ones, and seldom these.
They know no better. It is many years since Feejeeans
have been told that it is horrible to eat each other, and
they are now becoming ashamed of the practice. You
told me that you did not eat any of that man the other
day. Why did you tell me so? It was because you
were ashamed; and why were you ashamed? It was because you knew it to be wrong." "*Ko eko sa ngase*,"—
"You are wise." And thus the conversation ended with
a compliment to myself. I have never found a native,

chief, priest, or poor man, who would say any thing in favor of their customs, but will usually say, "Yes, we are a foolish people, and our customs are foolish." This is not said because they believe it to be the case, but out of courtesy.

18. Broke up the fishing establishment at this place, and set sail for Raverave in more than half a gale of wind, which carried away the maintop gallant yard, and split the mainsail. As the sails and yards were wanted for farther use, the captain thought best to anchor at Kandavu till the gale subsided.

20. The boat was sent into the town for water, and the natives on seeing it approach, armed themselves, and waited on the beach for its arrival. The men, however, went and filled their casks without any trouble.

About ten o'clock we sailed for Raverave, where we soon arrived and anchored.

21. Mr. W. made his final settlement with Retova, who brought me a present of two pigs and a valuable war-club.

22. We anchored last night at Nivaka. The boat was sent ashore to buy bananas and cocoa-nuts, but stopped about twenty yards from the shore. There were four natives to be seen on the beach, who stood and looked at the men in the boat, and the men in the boat looked at the men on the shore. As there were no bananas or cocoa-nuts in the water, and the men showed no inclination to go any nearer the shore for them, the captain ordered a musket to be fired for their return.

23. The morning being bright and fair, our sails were spread to the breeze, and we started for Bua. We had not advanced far, however, when the sun became obscured by heavy masses of clouds, and the rain poured in torrents. Our situation was rather dangerous for sev-

eral hours, from the many sunken rocks, besides shoals
and reefs which abound in our course. We arrived at
Bua in safety, and the anchor was cast in its bay. In
the afternoon the weather became clear, and we received
several native visitors, who brought some very acceptable eatables for sale. We have seldom had any thing
offered for sale during our late sojourn on the Mathuata
coast, which may be truly termed a land of dearth. The
towns which belonged to Tuimathuata, and those of its
present chief, were so intermixed that they are continually destroying each other's food, and are often nearly
starving themselves.

While we were bartering with the natives, I asked if
there were any *kalavus* on the land (meaning *balawas*, or
pine-apples). "Yes," they replied, "there are a great
many there." "Ah, it is very good. I wish you would
bring me some," I said. "Bring you *kalavus*, marama!
What for?" "To eat," I replied. "To eat! How
many?" "Oh, a hundred," I said. "A hundred! well,
we did not know that white people ate *kalavus*." "Yes
we do, and we love them very much. I love them, Mr.
W. loves them, and the sailors, and all love them."
"*Na kalavu marama, vaka ogo?*" "*A rat, marama?*"
and he set his fingers crawling along on the table. "Oh,
no, no, no!" I exclaimed, for I found that I had been
engaging them to bring me a hundred rats.

The old Turaga does not come off, as he is getting to
feel a grasshopper to be a burden. His son, Batenamu
(Putnam), took tea with us.

26. We are now anchored at Bua point. Four sail-
boats of various sizes, and double that number of canoes
are about us. The visit is principally from the white
residents at Solavu. Among them, however, is a boat
measuring three fathoms in length and nine in breadth.

This little craft has just arrived from New Zealand, commanded by Capt. Walker, late of Salem, Mass. We learn by him that the United States Consul for the South Pacific will be here soon. A young man accompanies the Consul, and brings letters for us from home, which I presume will not be detained as our last were.

We are here favored with an abundance of fruits, vegetables and pure water, which I have learned to appreciate. I think it is almost a miracle that we are not all sick from the effects of the vile liquid misnamed water, that we have sometimes used. While our vessel was at Mathuata, we learned that the natives bathed in the place where our water casks were filled. The casks were then sent to Kandavu, where one of our crew and a Salem boy were stationed. Orders were sent for the boy always to go with the natives, and see that clean water was sent to the vessel. For two weeks, however, the stuff that came instead of water was exceedingly filthy. At length the Star put in at the place one day for water, and Tommy repaired to the pond to dip and fill his "*saka*." As he approached a certain mud-puddle whose dimensions were somewhat extensive, he observed some ten or twelve little urchins in it, tossing about two water casks, and engaging in all sorts of pretty antics, while a woman was washing a child, whose flesh was not perfectly pure ; and another was cleaning yams. How useful such ponds are in Feejee!

"How is this?" inquired Tom. "Do you fill the casks for the vessel from this place?" "Yes," was the reply. "Why, do you not go to a clean place?" said Tom. "Because it is farther," he answered. Tommy (bless him for it!) made the boys take the casks to a pure running rivulet, where he washed and filled them with water. When he returned to the "*beech de mer*" house, he asked the boy, who was about seventeen years of age, why he did not go and see to the water. "Oh, it is some distance to go," said the boy. In justice to the lad, however, it should be stated that he was somewhat inclined to corpulency, and had never been remarkable for his activity; besides, he was there merely for company for the man at the house, and the exertion of going to the spring once in two days was too much for him. When Tommy told Mr. W. about the water, he wrote to the lad, and sent him a bottle of the filth that we had on hand. The answer received in reply, was, "I did not know, sir, that the natives washed in the place where the casks were filled, but I knew that they washed above and below it."

27. The Star anchored last night at a place called Bau-lailai. About midnight Tommy observed several natives swimming off to visit them. Not being prepared to receive and entertain so large a company, he awoke Andrew, and as there was no wind, they used their oars to some effect till they had well distanced their unwelcome visitors, who no doubt would have bitten them the next day, had they have reached the boat and found the men asleep. It is very important that all should watch in these cannibal lands.

Jan. 2. We anchored at Bau after an absence of nine months. As soon as the tide suited, I paid a visit to my friends at Vewa, and found them all well. Several conversions have taken place since I left, and they have also had many anxious hours on account of the anger of the Bau chief, but for the last few weeks, affairs have been more quiet. It was forbidden that food should be sold to the Vewa people.

A few days since, Thakombau visited Vewa and passed nearly a day with the missionaries, but did not go near either of the chiefs, and made many suspicious inquiries, such as, where do the *lotu* people live? where do you and your families sleep? where do your servants sleep? &c. Mr. Hunt told him the various reports in circulation. He neither affirmed nor denied them.

Vatai came to him, and addressed him in the following manner:—" I know, '*saka*,'* that it is a very great ' *tambu* ' for a woman to approach so great a chief and talk with him, but my love to you is so great that I am constrained to do it. I must tell you that you must give up your sins and love the true God, or you will go to the ' *buku waqa.*' God is now very angry with you, but He will forgive you if you will repent and forsake your sins. Believe me, the Feejeean gods are false, lying gods, and they cannot assist or help you." The chief heard her patiently, but vouchsafed no reply. On his return to Bau, the conversation was repeated at court. Much was said about it and the Maramas showed their contempt for the doctrine which usually finds but little favor in courts.

5. Returned to the bark, and found His Majesty and a Tonga chief on board. The chief observed to Mr. W. that I looked very thin. " Yes," was the reply. " I could procure no pigs or chickens for her food while we were absent, and now she lives at Vewa, where you have forbidden your people to sell food, so she must continue to look poor and thin." He asked me to give him some small beads, which I did, but he returned them, saying, " Take them to Vewa, and the Marama will go there and see you; she will bring you a pig and some chickens, and you may then give her the beads." The Tonga chief, whose name is Tubou Toutai, is a fine looking man, and very dignified. He informed me that he had

---

* Sir.

spent some time in Sydney, where he had picked up some knowledge of the English language. The following is a specimen:—"Mrs. Wallis, I got one nice mat in Bau for you; spose you come Bau, I give him to you; spose you no come Bau, I come Vewa, I fetch him you."

After their departure, a canoe came from Bau loaded with damsels. Among them were two of the daughters of the late King of Rewa. We were truly glad when night came, and they departed.

6. Returned to Vewa, and again took possession of my little domicil. There is one custom of the *papalagis* which Feejeeans really love; namely, the shaking of hands. I think there is not a man, woman or child over seven years of age, that I have not been obliged to shake hands with. On the Sabbath, the congregation formed a line after the morning service to shake hands with me. I thought the ceremony had been duly passed on the shore, when I first landed. My namesake, whom I left mourning the death of her husband, is full of love for me. Elijah has thus far lived an honor to religion since his profession.

7. Yesterday the Queen of Rewa and several other captives came to visit Mr. and Mrs. Jaggar, who were stationed at that place till the commencement of the war. Vatai came in to see them, accompanied by an old man, who has professed Christianity for some time past. "You have," said the man (addressing the Marama), "had the gospel preached to you, but your hearts were proud. You believed it to be true, yet you rejected it. God is very angry with you about it, and He has allowed your town to be destroyed. There is now no King of Rewa. There is now no Rewa." "I love you," said Vatai, "and what but the love that I bear to my relatives would have caused me to brave the anger of Thakombau,

11

and beg of him to ' *lotu?*' Your husband was killed, and
my heart was full of pity and love for you, and I begged
that he might ' *lotu,*' that you might ' *lotu,*' and that all
might be happy. Once I did not know how to love, but
the gospel teaches us to love. But now your hearts are
proud. You laughed at my speech to the chief, which
was made from love for you, and all my relatives in Bau
ridiculed me, and would not speak to me; but I do not
mind it, and I will still pray to God for you all ' with a
very good mind.' " The visitors looked sober, but made
no reply.

Samonunu came with the pig and fowls, as was promised. Several attendants came with her, both men and
women The men brought the presents, or they would
not have been in attendance.

8. Received a visit from the widowed queen. She is
a good looking woman (for Feejee,) of about thirty-five
years of age. She appeared rather sad. I presented
her with a basket and a few little notions, which pleased
her much. On her departure, she took a tortoise shell
ring from her finger, and presenting it to me, said, " This
was my husband's love to me. He is dead; but I have
others which he gave me, and this is my love to you."

We learn that the principal wife of Garenggeo, with
her children, are among the captives at Bau. The mother of Revelete declares, that, although she is compelled
to live in Bau, she will not be strangled when the king
(her husband) dies, for she hates him, and wishes she
could stick sharp pointed sticks through his flesh.

9. Being curious to learn the origin of the late war
which terminated in the destruction of Rewa, on inquiry
I received the following account.

In 1841, Garenggeo, the younger brother of the king,
was detected in a love affair with the queen. The con-

sequence was, that he fled to Bau and attempted to engage the Bau chiefs in a war with Rewa in his favor. This they refused to do, but tried every means in their power to pacify the offended king and reconcile the brothers. The king, however, would accept of no " soro " from the capitol. At length Garenggeo, seeing that all his influence failed to excite the chiefs against Rewa, determined to return and risk the anger of his offended brother. Contrary, however, to his expectations, the king received him with favor, and Bau soon heard of the reconciliation instead of the civil war, which they expected in consequence of the return of the offender to Rewa. This led the ruling powers of Bau to suppose that the " soro " which had been offered by them for the offence of Garenggeo, had been refused out of ill-will to them.

Soon after the reconciliation of the brothers, a story was circulated that a town belonging to Bau was menaced by Garenggeo. Thakombau informed the inhabitants of their danger, and advised them to build a fence round their town, and to keep quiet. Soon after this, the Rewa chiefs were somewhat insulted by the chief of a town called Suva, belonging to Bau. This town had long been a favorite place with the king of Bau and his son; its chief, too, enjoyed their confidence. This town was attacked by Garenggeo and his warriors, but they gained no advantage. The chief retired from the place to collect a larger force, being determined to destroy Suva. Thakombau now thought it time to notice the affair. He sent a messenger, therefore, to inquire why these things were so, and to tell the chiefs of Rewa, what they already knew,—that it had always been the custom of Bau and Rewa, when a town belonging to one party had offended the other, to ask leave before engaging in hostilities with the offenders. The messenger was received by the king and his brother with but little ceremony, and told that their preparations for war were to attack Kandavu, a place belonging to themselves, and it was not their purpose to trouble Suva. This was a mere pretence. The chiefs did not wish their intentions to be known lest Suva should receive aid from Bau. The messenger remained at Rewa till they were ready to sail, when he was informed that Suva was to be destroyed. He then returned to Bau, stating what he had seen and heard, and ended by advising the rulers at Bau to do as Christians did,—forgive.

Bau and Rewa were nearly related. The queen of the latter was the child of the king of Bau's sister. Many Bau women of high rank were wives of the chiefs of Rewa, and many Rewa women were wives of some of the principal chiefs of Bau, and the two places had, for many years, lived on the most friendly terms. Offences would sometimes occur, but they were speedily settled, and Bau appeared determined at this time to endure, rather than be at enmity, or engage in hostilities with those so nearly related. Suva was burned, many of its inhabitants were killed at the time, and those who escaped were pursued on the next day with a barbarity not always evinced even by cannibal savages. This made a deep impression on the minds of the chiefs of Bau; but they kept still. "Let them destroy another town before we notice this, or insult us in some other way," said the king of Bau. Thakombau went on a visit to the windward about this time, declaring that he did not wish to fight with Rewa. Bau was never known to show so much forbearance in any other affair. None could ever insult its haughty chiefs with impunity. But Rewa seemed determined to go on with the same insulting conduct, which has resulted in its destruction.

About this time a serious misunderstanding took place between the king of Bau and one of his principal wives, the king of Rewa's sister. She left him and repaired to Rewa, with all her household, consisting of many of the concubines of the king, who were Rewa women. This was a serious loss to the king, who possessed only one hundred wives. The loss, however, might have been endured, had it not been followed by insult of the most aggravating kind to a Feejeean. The king gave his sister to a Rewa chief for a wife, and disposed of the other women as he pleased. The most bitter hatred now took entire possession of the heart of the old king, and he declared that Rewa should be destroyed.

On the return of Thakombau, Tanoa called his sons together, and thus addressed them:—" My sons, I have been deeply insulted by my relatives. I am old, and am not able to avenge my wrongs. Oh, that I had some one to love me, and avenge them for me! Alas! I have no son to punish my enemies!" Thakombau deeply sympathized with his father, and determined to accomplish his wishes. The sympathies of Revelete, no doubt, were enlisted on the side of his mother and her relatives, but he dared not show them. Besides, he would be but little, if any, affected by the war; being " vasu " to Rewa, he could go and come when he chose; no one would dare harm him at Rewa, although he should engage on the side of Bau.

War was now declared in its worst form. A war of the chiefs, which was not to end till the kings of one party or the other were destroyed. Messengers were sent to Rewa to take leave of its chiefs, and terminate all friendly intercourse, as is their custom on such occasions. The Rewa chiefs now desired to " soro " to Bau, but it was too late; the Rubicon was passed, and nothing would answer but the blotting out of Rewa as an independent state. When wars are declared in Feejee, even among those who may have lived on the most friendly terms, kind feelings are laid aside, and the worst degree of enmity is exhibited. Every means is considered lawful to effect the destruction of each other. The Rewa chiefs did not suppose that Bau ever intended its destruction. They were not aware of the enmity which they had excited, and supposed that after a little skirmishing they could " soro ' to Bau, receive their pardon, and live on the same friendly terms as before. In this they were mistaken, as has been shown. Preparations were now commenced for the war in Bau with great spirit. Men and arms were collected, the gods were supplicated, and the war commenced by the burning of several towns belonging to Rewa. The latter made but a faint resistance, and such was the success of Thakombau, that, had he known how to have followed it up, the war might have been ended in six months.

At one time he, with his warriors, approached quite near the town of Rewa, which threw the inhabitants into such a fright, that had an attack then been made, he would have conquered. But having been so near the place was glory enough for that time, and they returned to Bau to thank their gods and honor those who had been so successful as to kill any of the enemy during the expedition. The consequences of these delays were murders, treachery and cannibalism on both sides. For the space of two years, scarcely a week passed without a cannibal feast at Bau. A large party of Bau warriors located themselves near Rewa, and were continually harassing the town and its dependencies. If women went to fish, or men went to their plantations, they were sure to become food for their relentless foes. Rewa could do

but little except to act upon the defensive; neither was
it in its full strength, having been weakened by civil dissensions. This state had been governed by three brothers, the eldest of whom bore the title of king; the second was Garenggeo, and the third has, of late, been
called Phillips. The mother of the latter was a Bau
woman of high rank, and his favorite wife was a niece of
Tanoa, and sister of Vatai of Vewa.

At the commencement of the war, Phillips took part
with neither party; but, subsequently, having discovered that his eldest brother, the king, had been holding
criminal intercourse with his favorite wife, he nearly
killed her and joined Bau. He resided at a town called
Nuque, quite near Rewa, where he had a fine opportunity to assist Bau. Thakombau promised Phillips that
when Rewa was destroyed, he would rebuild it and make
him its king. Thus the war was prosecuted with vigor
on the part of Bau, and with marked success, too, though
with the loss of some men, a great expense for food,
presents to warriors and offerings to their deities. Some
of the towns connected with Rewa displayed some courage. There was one called Toketoke that resisted and
defended itself nobly, till wearied by watching, and exhausted by hunger, the people turned to Bau. Several other towns joined Bau in the same manner, while
others remained faithful to Rewa till the last. There is
a district called Nakalu, that belonged to Rewa. Its
chief is of high rank, and governed about ten towns.
Thakombau sent to this chief, promising that if he would
join Bau, when Rewa was destroyed he would give his
sister to his son for a wife. This brilliant offer was not
to be rejected. The chief joined his forces with Bau, and
such was now its strength, that it could at any time have
conquered its enemies, had it not lacked one important

quality, namely, courage.   The war has now terminated,
as has been shown, by treachery.   As it is the practice
of warriors to disguise their faces with paint, it is difficult to recognize one from another.   Of the four hundred inhabitants that were massacred when Rewa was
destroyed, two hundred were supposed to have been
murdered by Rewa men.

After Bau had accomplished its designs, Phillips reminded its chiefs of their promise to rebuild Rewa and
make him king.   " By and by," they replied.   " Wait
a little."   Phillips sent to several towns, saying, " Come
to me and ' soro.'   Your ' soro ' shall be received and
your pardon granted."   Many came, and their " soro "
was accepted; after which they were murdered and their
bodies sent to Bau.   So great was their supply of *manimal* food, they were obliged to send to Somosomo for a
reinforcement of cannibals to partake with them.

Thus the famous war between these two powerful districts, which has been prosecuted for three years, is now,
to all appearance, ended, and Thakombau has shown to
his father that he loved him, and has avenged his insults.
It is said that the old king cannot consume the quantity
of his favorite food that he would like, on account of
poor teeth.   This must be a great annoyance to him.

10.   Mrs. Jaggar has related to me the following
speech of my namesake, which shows that she has improved some during my absence.   " I once hated the
' *lotu*,' and I said in my heart, I never will join the ' *lotu*.'
When the missionaries passed my house, I would tell
the big dog to bark at them.   The chief killed Nalela at
Bau, and then I wished to be killed too.   I knew that his
spirit had gone to the ' *buka-waqa*,' and I wished to go
there with him.   I was very angry that no one would
kill me, and I said in my heart, I will kill myself.   I will

not ' *lotu* ' and go to heaven, where I cannot see Nalela.
I thought about my husband all the time, and for many
days I would not take food.   At length I ate some food,
and promised that I would ' *lotu* ' when my days of
mourning had ended, but still I hated it.   After they had
ended, however, I ' *lotued* ' because I had promised, and
then I prayed to Jesus, not because I loved to pray to
Him, but I knew it was the fashion for ' *lotus* ' to
pray.   After a little while, I began to love prayer.
When I prayed I felt less unhappy, and I began to think
more about Jesus Christ than of Nalela, and then I
prayed very often that Jesus would make me good, that
I might go to heaven and be forever happy.   Jesus has
made me see how foolish my former doings were, and
I now hate my wicked conduct.   I pray now with ' a
good mind,' that I may always love Jesus Christ and be
good."   This Marama has been a very wicked woman.
Having rank and influence, she was always ready to assist in the wicked customs of her people.   She has assisted in strangling many women, and it has been shown
with what savage delight she exulted in the vengeance
which had been taken of those who had murdered her
relative.   The tigress has now changed to a lamb.
What has effected this change?—the gospel.   Oh! ye
enemies of missions, look at this woman as she was, and
as she now is, in the full exhibition of the peaceful and
lovely graces of the Christian, and shut your mouths!
Put your hands in your purses, and contribute of your
abundance.   Dismiss all your fears about disturbing the
minds of the heathen with the gospel.   Believe me; the
Saviour never would have employed missionaries if
there had been no necessity for them.   Send them the
gospel, and civilization follows in its train.   As soon as
the natives of these isles renounce heathenism, they are

anxious to obtain cloth to cover their persons,—their horrible feasts are looked upon with disgust,—they forgive their enemies,—become industrious, &c.

It is very well to sit at home in our parlors and talk about the heathen; their very few wants; their happiness in the enjoyment of their rites; their freedom from the cares and perplexities of civilized life; the waste of property expended in sending the gospel to them; the beautiful country they enjoy (many of them). There is poetry in this; but go and see them in their degradation, and your language, if you love the truth, will be changed,—I say if you are *lovers* of the truth. We know its enemies have always written in praise of heathenism, and endeavored (those that have been eye-witnesses,) to lay upon the shoulders of the missionaries the vices which they themselves have so abundantly dispensed among the heathen that have been cursed by their visits. I do not mean to say that there are none among the ministers of the gospel who are bad men. I believe there are such ; but their sins are not long concealed, and, on discovery, the good cast out from among them those who are unworthy. It should always be remembered, that among the twelve disciples of our Lord, there was one deceiver. There always were deceivers walking to and fro throughout the whole habitable globe;—those in religion, politics, love, friendship, &c.

CHAPTER X.

Visit to Bau—A Feejeean House—A Temple—Visit to a " *Buri*,"—Departure from Bau—Mock Piety of Namosimalua—Departure from the Islands—Arrival at Manicola—Loss of Two French Ships—A Dangerous Situation—The Island Flower-vase—Young Williams's Group—Straits of Bernardino.

Jan. 11. Mr. and Mrs. Watsford, Mr. Hunt and myself, made a visit to the capitol. On our arrival at the house of Thakombau, Samonunu called to us to come in. Her Highness was seated on several fine mats, and she invited us to be seated beside her. Thakombau soon joined the party, seating himself familiarly on the same. I was surprised at this, knowing that the Turaga-lavu usually occupies a place at some distance from the females of the household. Mr. H. observed that he was very fond of Samonunu, and was often seen occupying a seat near her, and sometimes they have been known to eat together. Thakombau appears to possess sufficient independence to please himself, whether it is in accordance with their customs or not. His house is the largest in Bau, measuring seventy-eight feet in length, thirty-six in width, and forty in height. Its posts, of which there are twelve inside, measure six feet in circumference; the rafters are of bamboo; the sides are thatched with leaves, and the roof with a kind of long, tough grass. The house is all tied together; no hammer or nails are used in the building of a Feejeean dwelling. In the interior are two "*vatas*," extending along the two ends and one side of the house, which are used as store houses. Several *tutuves* of native cloth were thrown over bamboos which are placed crosswise from the posts. These are let down at night, and form sleeping apartments. Each bed was composed of soft, dried grass, and formed with mathematical precision. They were elevated about one foot from the level of the floor, and covered with mats. I should never wish to occupy a better bed in a climate like this. Near the centre of the house, on one side, a trench about two feet in depth, contained their cooking utensils, which consisted of a whaler's try-pot, and several native " *kurus* " of different sizes. Every house has a similar trench, where the cooking is done; nor is the inconvenience from the smoke so great as one would think, for there are so many doors to their houses that the smoke escapes without inconvenience to the inmates. The house of the chief contained several Canton trunks, some dozens of muskets and kegs of powder, large rolls of cinnet and native cloth, a large looking-glass, with many other articles valuable to a Feejeean. The dwelling was perfectly neat, every thing appeared to be in its place, and the floor was entirely covered with new mats. When we departed, His Majesty presented me with a valuable and curious war club to show the Americans.

Bau is a small place, but well filled with people. The Bau tribe occupy one portion of the place,—the Lasakau another,—and the Soso tribe a third. There is a small elevation on the island where they bury their dead. In or near the central part of the isle is an open, level space, called the " *rara*." Here they meet to transact public business, to hold solavus, to prepare the slaughtered for the ovens, to carve the bodies after they have been cooked, to hold their festive pastimes, &c. Near the " *rara* " is the public hotel. This is a large building where strangers are entertained, of whom there are large numbers usually in Bau. At present it is occupied by the Tonguese visitors from Lakemba. The Tonga chief, however, with his wives and their personal attendants, occupy a new house near the hotel. We called on him, and I received the promised mat, which is really a fine one, measuring four fathoms in length and one in breadth.

Having gained permission of Thakombau to enter the great "*buri*" of the city, we repaired thither. When we reached it, several of the aristocracy were about the place, and seeing that we were going to enter, looked quite displeased, and said that no woman had ever been inside of a "*buri*," and it was a very great "*tambu.*" Mr. Hunt stopped to talk with them, and try to gain permission for us to go in, as was proper for him to do, knowing as he did the rank of the parties. While this was going on, I quietly slipped my arm from that of Mr. H., and thinking my offenee might be attributed to my ignorance, I hastened into the sacred building. On seeing this, the natives left talking, and looked astonished at so unheard of a thing in Feejee. Mr. and Mrs. Watsford and Mr. Hunt followed. We met, however, with but little to reward our perseverance. If we may judge of the devotion of the people by their offerings, their religion is certainly at a very low ebb. The temple contained nothing save one solitary roll of cinnet, and a small quantity of native cloth. One breadth of white "*masi*" was suspended from the ridge-pole of the temple to the floor. The spirit remains between that and the thatching of the house, and when the priest wishes to consult it, he seats himself in front of the "*masi*," where he commences a regular set of convulsions, which he declares is occasioned by the spirit entering into his worthy self. The spirit is consulted chiefly about their wars and in cases of sickness. A short time since, Samonunu was sick. Thakombau attended at the "*buri*," and desired the priest to inquire of his god-ship whether she would recover. The answer was, that she would if her husband would give him a horse (there are two in Bau). Thakombau said, "We are quite near Vewa. It is very easy to send the Marama there to be cured by the missionaries. Why did not the god ask something less difficult? I shall not give him a horse." The abashed god, frightened at the bold speech of the chief, withdrew his demand, and cured the Marama with some inferior gift. I don't think that Thakombau is very pious. It is said that the gods were never denied their requests before.

10. As we came out of the temple, we met Rokotuimbau, a great chief of this town of great chiefs. He had been informed of the important fact that two females had entered the sacred edifice, and was very angry about it. He is a heathen "of the first water," ardently devoted to his gods, and I presume would not have denied them two horses, had he possessed them, and they had been required. The angry chief looked as though he would like to bite us, and remarked that no women were allowed to go inside the "*buri*." We happened to know that, but we had violated the *tambu* in spite of him, and there was no help for him. I *tried* to look very sweetly at him, and Mrs. Watsford did look so, for she possesses a lovely countenance; but he still appeared displeased. Mr. Hunt toid him that we had received free permission from Thakombau, but his looks seemed to say, "Who is he to give leave that our temple should be desecrated in such a manner?" We left him to his own cogitations on the steps of the "*buri*," and repaired to the dwelling of Vakambua, one of the lords of the court, who has the charge of the princess—my little namesake. We found

her pined almost to a skeleton, and evidently near the grave. Before leaving, we called at the house of Tanoa; he had gone to attend a ceremony on the spot where Rewa stood, called quenching the fires of Rewa. There we saw the mother of the murdered king; she is very aged, quite deaf, and nearly blind. On being informed who I was, she showed the most extravagant fondness, saying that she had never thought to see the wife of Mr. Wallis, whom she had known so long. We saw, too, the mother of Revelete, the wife of Garenggeo, and two of his children. Several of his children had been murdered. We saw, also, several daughters and one son of the late king. The husband of one of the daughters had been killed during the war. These all occupied the largest of the king's houses. His queen, with her children and their attendants, dwelt in the same building, but the captives kept by themselves. Some were reclining on mats, some were cooking and others were making "*lekus.*" None looked very happy. The women of rank, however, are not degraded. They are treated with all the ceremony of their station, and still served by numerous attendants. After seeing every thing to be seen, we left the cannibal city, and visited the bark. The commander invited us to remain and dine; after this we returned to Vewa.

12. Mary Wallis presented me with a fine, large pig, saying, "that was her love to me;" also a handsome "*kale*" (pillow), which had been her husband's. I have been honored with visitors all day, who came to express their love to me, and last, not least, to indulge their begging propensities.

13. Messrs. Hunt and Watsford have left this place to visit some of the out-stations, expecting to be absent one month. The Tonga chief came to see me, expecting

a present in return for the one he made me. I gave him a full equivalent. He did not appear satisfied, and went on begging. I told him that I was greatly ashamed that I was not better acquainted with their customs,— that when he gave me a mat, I should have begged a pig too. Samonunu came, and presented me with some mats, saying she had ordered others to be made, but we should sail too soon to receive them. I told her they would be just as acceptable when we returned.

In the afternoon we visited at Elijah's, and also called on Mary Wallis. While at Elijah's, I said, taking hold of a Feejeean umbrella, " This is a very nice umbrella." " If you think so, will you take it?" said the Marama. " No," I replied. " You have already presented me with one quite as good, and that is enough." " I know that we are poor, and have nothing worthy to offer you; but why should the umbrella hang in my house, when you have said that it is good." I accepted it, feeling that I gratified the donor. As I expected to sail in the morning for Manilla, I took leave of them. We were followed home by servants, bearing large bunches of bananas, which were left on my door-steps.

In the evening my husband came for me, and we were accompanied to the boat by the mission families, Vatai, Mary Wallis, and many others. I had received some little token of remembrance from them all, and we parted with mutual assurances of friendship. I can scarcely express my feelings towards those dear families of the mission who took me into their dwellings, and allowed me so good a share of their affections. My intercourse with them has been truly delightful. The religion which they profess, and teach, and practise, renders them lovely in their whole deportment. During a residence of ten years in this group, they have ever maintained love and harmony among themselves.

16. We anchored at Ovalau; Elijah took leave of us here, and on the seventeenth we sailed for Raverave.

20. Anchored at Raverave, in sight of the brig Elizabeth, of Salem. In the evening, we were surprised and pleased to receive a visit from Messrs. Hunt and Watsford, accompanied by Capt. King. The former had arrived here the day previous.

Namosimalua has been on board the Elizabeth for some time past.

21. Mr. W. dined on board the Elizabeth, and on his return to the bark was accompanied by Capt. King, and Messrs. Hunt and Watsford, who took tea, and passed the evening with us. It is a very rare thing in Feejee to have *company* to tea.

21. We are informed that a large canoe belonging to Elijah is here from Vewa, with several of the Vewa Christians on board, and a special message came in it to the chief of Bunda, from Thakombau, requesting him to kill Namosimalua and all the Vewa Christians he could come at; then take possession of the canoe, and load it with riches that had belonged to Revelete, and come to Bau, where they should be suitably rewarded. The Bunda chief replied, "that Thakombau might do his own work." The messenger then requested Namosi to visit Ba, and receive some pigs for Bau. Namosi declined going, feeling, probably, that the invitation was like that of the spider, when he said to the fly, " Will you walk into my parlor?" He has heard of the whole affair, and is exceedingly alarmed. He says that Bau will never be satisfied till he is killed.

As usual, when danger threatens, he is very pious, prays a great deal, and leads a most devotional life. He con-

12

ducts precisely as the Jews did in the wilderness. I was much amused once, on witnessing one of his devotional acts at Vewa. He has always been desirous of joining the church, as he has a particular fondness for one of the elements of the communion; namely, the wine. One sacramental day I was walking in front of Mr. Hunt's dwelling, and observed Namosi pacing to and fro, and often casting a glance towards the chapel. At length one appeared, bringing the bread and wine which had been left from the communion. Namosi darted forward, snatched the goblet, and swallowing its contents, returned the empty vessel, smacked his lips, and walked off.

22. We took leave of our friends, and sailed for Ba, where we arrived about noon, and anchored, hoping to procure yams, but no canoes came off.

There is a little tale connected with this place, which shows why the natives would not visit us. It appears that the vessel to which Mr. W. belonged in the year 1835, visited this coast. On their arrival at Ba, a chief, accompanied by several natives, came to the vessel to dispose of shell. His price was more than the captain thought it worth, who told him that he must send to the shore, and have more of the article brought, when he would trade for the whole. The captain no doubt thought that there was a large quantity of shell on shore, and he was desirous to obtain it. The chief declared that he had no more, and the captain said that he should be detained till more was brought. Some of the natives were now frightened, and jumped into their canoes. The chief was about to follow, but was prevented by the captain, who placed one of his men with a loaded musket over him, with orders to shoot him if he attempted to escape. Mr. W. thinking there would be trouble, went below for his pistols; while there, he heard the report of a musket, which was followed by others. He hastened on deck, and saw the bleeding chief in the water; he had been shot. The captain now ordered his men to fire upon the natives. They had, however, left their canoes, and by diving escaped the fire, and only one beside the chief was killed. The captain next ordered the boat to be lowered, and his crew to go and kill as many of the natives as possible. Mr. W. remarked that there were natives enough to upset the boat and kill all hands. The next order issued by the captain, was, to get the brig under way, which was obeyed with alacrity. As they were going out among the reefs, a canoe passed, and the captain ordered his people to fire into it. Mr. W. was at mast head, looking out for the reefs. He heard the order, and sung out, "Hard down your helm!" The order was obeyed, and the canoe escaped.

The captain has not, hitherto, been blamed for this affair among the natives of this coast, who, it is said, all believe that Mr. W. was the captain of the aforesaid vessel, and that it was by his order the chief was shot, although the several commanders who have since visited the coast, have endeavored to inform them correctly how the affair occurred. This people have been called the most barbarous of Feejee. It is difficult to determine how they have acquired the name, as it is almost the only place where no white people have been murdered. Feejeeans usually avenge their wrongs upon the first who come in their way, who belong to the class that has wronged them, as has been shown in the account of the murder of Wilson. In this case, however, it is said that, contrary to their usual custom, they are waiting to get possession of Mr. W., or some of his people if they cannot get him, which they would much prefer, to wreak their long pent-up vengeance upon. We have been told that soon after the murder of the chief, a "*buri*" was built, which has not been opened on account of their inability to procure the proper subject for its dedication, which is no less a personage than my husband. Don't think they'll get him—can't conveniently let him be used for such a purpose.

23. Sailed for, and anchored at Bunda. Collected yams along the coast.

27. An order was given to man the windlass, which was received by the crew with three cheers; and cheerily the order was obeyed, our sails were spread, the wind favored our departure, and the lands of Feejee, with all their man-eating savages, were soon lost in the distance. Our number was whole; none had suffered from contact with cannibal ivory.

Feb. 1. The ocean is cross—I feel cross—the vessel rolls—I roll, and every thing rolls that is not tied. That tormenting, vexing, fretting sea-monster—sea-sickness, is prowling about, preventing me from working, reading, writing, sitting, sleeping, and every other known "ing," except hanging, which I have not yet tried. Besides all this, it makes horrible faces at me when there is food in sight. However, although I can have no comfort, I am not prostrated, as on the passage out.

2. Arrived off the island of Manicola. This island is the largest in the group in Charlotte's Archipelago. In or about the year 1804, two French surveying ships were lost on a reef which surrounds Manicola. The name of one ship was Astrolabe, and nothing was for many years heard from the missing vessels. At length a man named Dillon (the same who visited Feejee and had a battle with the natives when Charles Savage was killed) was sailing about these seas, and picked up a native from

some island near Manicola. From him he received some
hints, which led him to think that the vessels were lost at
that island. A large reward had been offered to any who
would bring intelligence of the lost ships. Dillon went
to Bombay in the year 1826 and succeeded in obtaining
command of a suitable vessel from some merchants, then
sailed for Manicola. He stopped at the island, and took
the native before mentioned on board, and arrived at
Manicola. The man on board appeared well known at
the island, and through him Capt. D. held communication
with the natives. The inhabitants of Manicola treated
Capt. D. and his people in the most civil manner. They
showed him some iron spikes, which they said had belonged to the lost vessels, and a part of a ship's bell, and
several other articles, which evinced the fact that the
ships had been lost somewhere in this region. The natives stated that the vessels struck on the reef and went
to pieces; that a small craft was built from the wreck,
and the people sailed away in it. The latter may be
true, and it may not; no one has lived to tell the tale.
Capt. Dillon sailed for France, where he made known
the fate of the vessels, of which nothing had been heard
for twenty-two years. He received the promised reward,
and the title of Chevalier, besides many costly presents,
and was made a rich man at once.

Within the barrier reef are to be seen numerous smaller ones, and shoals. As we were running for the isle
with a fair wind, Mr. W. came below for a few moments,
telling the mate to look out sharp till he returned. On
his return to the deck, I heard him exclaim, "By
heavens! Mr. Jones, we are inside this dangerous reef."
There we were, sure enough; and how should we get
out again? There was but one opening to be seen, and
we had entered by that which was very narrow; the wind

was fair for our entrance, and of course it was directly
against our returning by the same passage, and there
was no room to beat. Is the fate of the missing vessels
to be ours? I thought, as I looked over the side into the
clear waters beneath, and observed several sunken rocks,
which threatened every moment to make some large holes
in the bottom of the vessel. For a moment all appeared
paralyzed; the stillness of death reigned; but it was for
a moment only, and was soon broken by the voice of the
captain, saying, "There is one little spot where the
water appears somewhat deeper on the reef than any
where else. Down with the boat and sound it!" The
boat was lowered, the mate and four hands sprung into
it, and rowed for the place. Two fathoms of water were
found upon it, and we passed over in safety. The wind
had died away nearly calm, and the waters were so still
and smooth that all their hidden dangers were plainly re-
vealed to the eye, as we passed on our dangerous way.
Each one appeared to hold his breath, that he might
catch the first sound of the grating keel. But that kind
Providence that has preserved us from harm during our
voyage, saved us from this danger also.

After the vessel had cleared the reef, we sailed in
what is marked on the chart as "Dillon's track," and
went into a small bay, where, it is said, Dillon anchored.
We sailed within ten rods of the shore, but could find no
anchorage. Mr. W. remarked that the bottom must have
dropped out since Capt. D.'s visit. Our bark was too
unwieldy, and our cargo was deemed too valuable to risk
its safety among these unknown waters, and we left them
without making any discovery in the "beech de mer"
line. The island of Manicola is of volcanic formation,
and its inhabitants are of a dark brown color, and have
coarse woolly hair, like the Feejeeans. We approached

on the south side, which, evidently, was not inhabited. Hill, mountain and glen presented to the eye a dense forest of trees.

3. We came in sight of a small cluster of islands called Duff's group, in the same archipelago as the group that we passed yesterday. There are seven, which are also of volcanic origin. They present to the eye solid masses of verdure. On one of the isles, a column is seen, of perhaps fifty or sixty feet in height, but appears from the vessel of small circumference. This column is covered with verdure, probably creeping plants, and on its top are some half dozen trees, which seem to say, "Come and repose under my shade if you can."

I have seen nothing so pretty as that island flower-vase, since I became a sailor. It was too beautiful ever to be forgotten. On one island several houses were to be seen that appeared like Feejeean architecture. No inhabitants or canoes were visible. My curiosity was greater than my prudence, and I begged Mr. W. to send a boat ashore, and let me go and "*sara sara.*" He made me no answer, but smiled, and raised his hand to the wind. "Oh, there is just wind enough," I said. "Get out the fore-topmast studding-sail!" shouted the captain. "Get out the fore-topmast studding-sail!" echoed the mate. "Aye, aye, sir," responded the crew, and away we went, leaving Duff's group, its unknown inhabitants, its elegant flower-vase—all to disappear in the distance.

27. We arrived at a group of islands called the Young Williams's group. We counted eighteen in number, all of coral formation, and appearing scarcely above the level of the sea. Those that were near us were covered with cocoa-nut trees. We sailed by one of the largest isles, and soon observed some of its tawnies, men, women and children, all racing along the sand beach,

shouting to us at the top of their voices, while some were showing a white flag to induce us, as we supposed, to anchor and honor them with a visit. We soon saw several canoes approaching, filled with natives. The bark was hove to, and two of the natives came on board. They were shown some " *beech de mer* " and they signified by signs that there was a plenty of the article on the reefs. Weapons were shown to them, both savage and civilized (if there are such things as civilized weapons; I believe there is but one—a broomstick), but they did not seem to understand their uses. They exhibited much astonishment at sight of the pigs, and appeared to have had but little, if any, intercourse with vessels. They brought cocoa-nuts, and received in return fish-hooks.

These islanders are a very handsome race, light colored, no beards, and fine black hair, which they wore long; a few wore it hanging loosely down behind, but the most of them had it twisted and brought to the top of the head, where it was confined, and a small wreath of flowers was worn over it. The young men resembled, at a little distance, very pretty girls, and such we at first thought them. Several wore flowers in their ears, and all had pieces of native cloth, but were not particular in its arrangement till I appeared on deck, when all who were in the canoes proceeded to cover their persons in a proper manner. Those who had come on board had previously done so. Their cloth resembled coarse canvass, and was about half a yard in width. Two breadths were fastened together, and an opening left in the centre ; the head was passed through the opening, and the cloth falling loosely before and behind, gave the wearers a very decent appearance. Their features were regular,—their teeth beautiful,—their eyes very bright, but mild in their expression. The arms of some were tattooed in delicate parallel lines, from the shoulders to the elbows. They were decidedly the handsomest race of men that I have seen in the South Seas. No women came off,—a sure evidence that they have not yet been cursed by intercourse with whaling vessels.

March 8. We are in sight of the Philippine Islands. Farewell to sea-sickness for one month. This disagreeable sensation has accompanied me in some degree ever since I left Feejee. At no time have I been free from it for one day.

Hail! ye green isles of the ocean! How many verses would I write in your praise, if I could!

9. Last evening, at seven o'clock, we entered the straits of St. Bernardino. How delightful the prospect! How glorious appeared the rising sun! Ah! I thought, I must sing, but I suddenly recollected that the sound of my voice would destroy all the harmony of the scene.

Soon after sunrise we passed a volcanic mountain. Smoke was issuing from its top, and as there was no wind, it descended to its base, and the mount appeared to be resting on a heavy mass of clouds. It is about six years since its fires have been seen.

CHAPTER XI.

Arrival at Manilla—Its Inhabitants—Its Buildings—Bazars—Visit to the Pina Factory—The Escolta—Departure from Manilla—Return to the Young Williams's Group—Its Inhabitants—Our Departure—The Greenwich Islands—The Dangerous Reef—Pleasant Island.

March 10. Arrived at Manilla.

11. Having received an invitation from the gentlemen of the well-known firm of Peel, Hubbell & Co., we have

to-day removed to their spacious dwelling. The house
is one of the largest, if not the largest in Manilla, and
built, I presume, like all Spanish houses in warm climates. Not understanding the art, or even the techni-
cal terms of architecture, I will not attempt a description. I perceive, however, that the building is situated
on the margin of a river, opposite the city, and the river
is well filled with vessels of different kinds, from whence
issue sounds of all sorts. I have learned that it is not
the fashion for foreign ladies to make much use of their
feet. Carriages and servants are provided.

12. Yesterday Mr. W. having engaged a carriage
and coachman for the time that we remain here, we
started, after dinner, for a drive into the country. We
first passed through several crowded streets in the suburbs, and then came into the open country. The land
is perfectly level, the roads smooth, our carriage easy,
and we enjoyed a most delightful ride. It was far more
agreeable than riding o'er the mountain wave.

13. During our afternoon drive, we took a view of
the city of Manilla. It is enclosed by a massive wall,
outside of which are several draw-bridges, which afford
entrance to the city. I believe that no foreigners reside
within the walls,—the place being mostly occupied by
the Governor and those connected with Government.
In the evening we received a call from Capt. Doane and
his wife, of ship Congaree, of Boston.

14. Last evening we rode into the city, to listen to
music played by four different bands belonging to the
army. These bands are composed of native musicians,
who play each a quarter of an hour in the square opposite the Governor's palace, and then repair to the Calsada and play another hour. Marches and martial tunes
are played during half the time, and the other half, waltz-

es, songs, &c. As near as I could judge, they played with taste and skill. These musical banquets are given semi-weekly.

15. The inhabitants of the suburbs are exceedingly numerous, and I am always glad when we have passed their crowded thoroughfares. The bazars are extensive and numerous, and are held by the natives. Besides these, nearly every native house that is situated on the roads leading into the open country, has its booth in front containing provisions. Spirituous liquors are observed for sale in great abundance; yet among all the crowds of Manilla, I have not seen one intoxicated person. The suburbs are divided into towns, or rather districts, each one having its church, its padres and spies, and all other things appertaining to Popery. Of the Spanish government I know nothing, therefore can write nothing; but will leave the subject to others.

16. During our afternoon drives I have observed that the dwelling-houses of Manilla appear to consist of three classes. First, the heavy stone edifices, with their red tiled roofs, which are occupied by Spanish and European residents of distinction; second, those of wood and bamboo, or such appear to be the materials, with a roof of thatch; a little veranda runs along the front, which is often prettily ornamented. Owing to the occurrence of earthquakes, no glass is used for windows, but small panes of pearl shell instead. This class of buildings appears to be inhabited by the better or richer sort of Indians. Then comes the third and lowest class; these are built of bamboo and grass, and the most of them are in the most dilapidated condition. Their inhabitants appear to care far less about their personal comfort than the savages we so lately left on the islands of the South Pacific. These dwellings, however, are not uncom-

fortable at this season of the year, when their occupants
live mostly in the open air; but how they contrive to
keep dry during the rainy season, is more than I can determine. Owing to the miasma arising from the humid-
ity of the country, the churches and stone buildings
present an ancient appearance ; indeed, some of the
churches are of ancient date, having been built some
two hundred and fifty years. Opposite the front of the
house of which I am now an inmate, stands an ancient
building that was used as an Inquisition about sixty
years ago, when Inquisitors and Inquisitions were tole-
rated. I often gaze on the small apertures which once
afforded their little quantum of light to the dungeons of the
prisoners, and fancy what must have been their emotions.
The young and the lovely have no doubt been immured
within its walls for the vilest of purposes, and their end
was death. Who shall describe the manner of it?

In the evening we called at the mansion of Mr. Sturgis, United States' Consul, to see Capt. Doane and his
wife, but they had left for their vessel, expecting to sail
in the morning. Mrs. D. has accompanied her husband
in his sea voyages for eleven years past.

17. Mr. W. called on board the Congaree. Mrs. D.
sent me a dear little lap-dog, with a black nose and two
bright black eyes. As I have no pet, I expect to love it
very much. At noon Mr. Edwards sent to my room a
ripe pomegranate, which was quite a curiosity to me.
The fruit was full of seeds, which reminded me of one of
the Arabian tales.

20. It is the custom of the Spanish, as well as Indian ladies, to smoke cigars, and sometimes, though not
frequently, I have seen well-dressed ladies in their carriages indulging in this highly *delicate* and *refined* luxury. The native Indians all use the odorous herb, and

to-day, as we spoke of visiting the Pina establishment, one of the gentlemen of the house remarked that if a cigar was offered me, I must not decline the civility.

At the manufactory we were shown some most beautifully embroidered articles, consisting of mantles, shawls, handkerchiefs, collars, capes and coifs,—all of which are done with the sewing needle by native women. It is not known from whence they acquired this beautiful art; some suppose from the Japanese. Before our departure, we were offered chocolate and cigars from a silver tray. I remembered the advice heretofore given; consequently, I took a cup of chocolate, while Mr. W. helped himself to a cigar.

21. During our pleasant rides, I have often observed negroes mingling, here and there, amidst this dense population. I am told that they are from the interior of the island, and that the original inhabitants of these isles are of that race. They have been driven from the coasts, no one knows where, but have not become extinct. Manilla is situated on the largest of the Philippines. The Spanish took possession of the place some three hundred years ago. Since then, for a time, it was in the hands of the English, from whom it was ransomed in 1809. The native population is estimated at two hundred thousand, and the white residents are about four thousand. An army of fifteen thousand natives, commanded mostly by Spanish officers, is maintained by the Government for the safety of the whole. To prevent conspiracies and revolt in the army, it is composed of natives from the different provinces, who, speaking a different dialect, can hold but little communication with each other. Frequent changes are also made from one division to another.

About nine o'clock in the evening, which is the fashionable hour for making calls, Mr. Sturgis and lady called to see us. We regretted much that we were away. I presume that this journal would scarcely be recognized as having been penned by a female, unless there should be a word, now and then, about dress. The Spanish and European ladies wear dresses of white muslin, made after the Parisian and London fashions, with the exception of the sleeves, which are worn short. The Spanish ladies wear no bonnets or caps, but the English wear both. There are not more than half a dozen of the latter in the place. The elderly Spanish ladies wear their hair combed straight back from the forehead, over the top of the head,—a most unbecoming fashion. The younger ones dress their hair plainly, as many do with us at home. No curls are worn, nor is a stray hair allowed to wander from the fold. It is said that the Spanish ladies wear no stockings. This may be slander. I had no opportunity for personal observation.

The costume of the Mestizoes consists of a full skirt of a bright plaid gingham or silk, and a short jacket of some thin material; a handkerchief is often worn over the shoulders. These are of various descriptions; some are pina, and others are of muslin or lace, which are embroidered; their raven tresses shining and beautiful, are confined by golden ornaments. The Indian women wear a plain piece of cloth, without plait or fold, fastened to the waist and falling to the feet; a jacket and handkerchief, as above described, cover the upper parts of their persons. Many wear their beautiful hair hanging loosely behind. Four of their toes are thrust into a beautifully embroidered slipper without heels.

23. On our arrival at this place, I was informed that ladies did not go a shopping, but purchased all that was wanted at their own dwellings, where the articles were

brought by the shopmen. After my informant had left the room, I exclaimed, " Not go a shopping! A lady not go a shopping! Who originated so barbarous a custom? Some bachelors I —— ; oh, no, not any of that class; but some cross, miserly, money-loving Benedict must have instituted a custom so savage. Not go a shopping!" I muttered in a loud tone. I then remained silent for a time, deeply cogitating; the result of my cogitations I will record for the benefit of those who may be similarly situated. I am a stranger, I thought, a sojourner for a short time. I expect to become acquainted with no one out of this house. I would do nothing to disgrace its honorable occupants, but I must be convinced that going a shopping will do so before I can deprive myself of the indulgence. I have no particular caste to lose, and I will go a shopping.

There is a certain street in Manilla called the Escolta. On each side of the street are rows of low, mean-looking buildings; but one scarcely notices these, for inside are all sorts of fine things kept for sale by Chinese shopmen. Accordingly, in pursuance of my determination, we sometimes visited these Chinese repositories. On entering one of these shops, we admired the neatness with which their goods were arranged. Each building is precisely of the same form and dimensions, consequently, there is no variety. A small apartment fronts the street, and one supposes, on entering the shop, they see all it contains; but this is not the case. Opposite the entrance, a very narrow door is perceived. One day we asked to look at some crape shawls. We saw the man squeeze through a narrow door; we did the same, and I found that we had entered an apartment of equal dimensions with the front. As Mr. W. was engaged in conversation with the shopman, I slipped through another door, and continued my way till I had passed through five or six similar apartments, filled with rich goods. We found English piece goods a little cheaper than they can be obtained at our stores. There is an abundance of Chinese curiosities and toys, no doubt, for sale in Manilla, but I can never learn where; therefore, the numerous nephews and nieces will be none the richer for aunt Mary's visit to the Eastern city.

24. Called at the mansion of Mr. Sturgis; but we were too early, for they had not returned from their ride. We left our cards with the porter at the gate.

Whatever streets we pass, and wherever we go, we meet an abundance of "Holy Fathers." Some are clad in white gowns, others in black, blue and gray. They wear enormous black hats, with less than a yard of brim rolled up at the sides. These gowned persons, I presume, keep the natives more in awe than the army; they are like flies,—in every body's mess. Some of them are very corpulent, and rather roguish looking. They generally reside in monasteries connected with the churches.

There were, in times past, numerous holidays during the year, in which ceremonies were performed relating to Popery, but they are now reduced to about twenty-five; six being held at Christmas.

The amusements of the lower orders are cock-fighting and kite-flying, which usually occur on Sundays and holidays. The fowls are trained with the greatest tenderness and care. A short time since, the dwelling of a poor man was discovered in flames. One of his children (a babe) and his chanticleer were its only occupants; and as the man could save but one, the fowl was saved and the babe perished. A neighbor asked why he did not save his child, instead of the fowl. "The fowl," replied the *affectionate* parent, " earns me bread, and my

child only consumes it." The doors of the churches are
surrounded by natives, each with a noble looking crower
in his arms, waiting the appearance of its owner from
their confessions and prayers. It is too bad that the
fowls are not allowed to enter the churches and receive
absolution with their masters.

25. An account of one day in Manilla is a history
of the whole. We rise at any hour we choose, and ring
for a cup of coffee, tea, or chocolate; breakfast at ten,
partake of a lunch at one, dine at four, and ride till
dark, if we choose. On our return repair to the piazza,
sip a cup of tea, after which, if there is music, go and
listen to it; if not, go and ride on the Calsada, or remain at home, just as we choose. The gentlemen of the
firm of Peel, Hubbell & Co., have shown every attention
to our convenience and personal comfort, for which we
owe them many thanks.

April 1. Mr. W. having completed the sale of his
cargo to some profit, and brought his affairs to a close,
we took leave of our hospitable entertainers and embarked on board the Zotoff. Here I found that some
changes had been made. The chief mate had been discharged, and the second mate had been promoted to fill
the vacancy. A foreigner had been chosen from the
forecastle to act as second mate. Mr. Smith, the mate,
and one or two of the crew objected to going on the next
voyage, unless one of the sailors (an American) who
was shipped in Salem, and who had been the cause of
exciting a great deal of ill-feeling during the voyage,
should be discharged. Many complaints of the man had
been entered to the captain, but he was so fair to the
face, and so smart and active, that a deaf ear had been
turned to them all. On our arrival at Manilla, how-

13

ever, he was fully convinced of the fellow's mischief-making propensities, and he was discharged forthwith. On going ashore, he asserted that he was the son-in-law of one of our most respectable Salem merchants, having married his daughter. The truth was, he had married a servant of the same. On our passage to the bark, we had been told by the Government officer who accompanied us, that two sailors, deserters from the United States ship Columbus, who had left Manilla a few days previous, were secreted on board the bark. On our arrival, inquiry was made, but no one had seen them. The Columbus remained in Manilla but a few days, as the cholera appeared on board in its most malignant form. Several died and many new cases occurred.

Our land comforts are ended for the present,—our carriage is dismissed,—white dresses and all finery are laid aside,—our anchor is again raised, and we depart to visit unknown lands and sail o'er lonely seas. Should I not shed a tear at this place?

> " Life's an ever changing scene,
> Ever onward, ne'er at rest."

8. We are now clear of shoals, rocks and islands, and are once more upon the open sea, with the pleasing variety of ocean and sky one day, and sky and ocean the next. We left Manilla by the Bashee passage. As we entered the bay of Manilla by the Straits of St. Bernardino, we have now made the entire circuit of Luzon. The island is about one thousand and fifty miles in circumference. The second day out, the two deserters from the United States ship Columbus appeared on the deck of our vessel. I presume that they had become hungry. They stated that they succeeded

in secreting themselves on board the day before the vessel sailed from M. One of the men is an Italian, and had been on board the Columbus nearly three years, which was the time he enlisted for. In a few months he would have been entitled to his discharge, and received his pay. Now he has forfeited the whole, and owns only the clothes that he is wearing. He does not complain of ill-treatment, but gives as a reason for his desertion his desire of change. Truly, a sailor is like the sea, "ever restless, ever changing." The other deserter is a stupid looking fellow, of no particular nation, I believe.

June 7. We passed a group of islands of coral formation, called Hasmy's Group. We have been chased by two enormous sharks. They were hungry, and we gave them no food. During our passage thus far, we have had continual head winds with very light breezes. We have lost by death several turkeys, and a number of the long-faced gentry. Their change of life, probably, did not agree with their constitutions. A monkey lies very ill with ill usage from his master, (one of the sailors,) who beats him every day to make him love him. I think the man must have taken lessons of some Irish husbands of the lower order; but the poor little monkey's affections are not to be gained by "the bating."

10. We anchored in a fine little lagoon at the Young Williams's group, after a passage of sixty-seven days from Manilla. We run the distance from here to Manilla in fourteen days. We have on board numerous visitors, who signified by signs that they had recognized our vessel. A boat has gone to "sara sara,"—the reefs.

11. The boat returned last evening, and reported that but little "beech de mer" was to be seen on the reefs. The men visited a small uninhabited island, but report nothing worthy of note. Several natives slept on

board last night, and there are now from twenty-five
to thirty canoes alongside.   Some have a quantity of
cooked fish and bread-fruit on board.   I can discover no
weapons, and the persons of the natives are so free from
scars, I am inclined to think they have never learned the
art of war.   Mr. W.'s talk to them is like Mosaic work.
His sentences are a mingling of English, Feejeean and
Spanish ; but they understand gesticulation the best.
We learn that a chief is called Samola.   As a party
came on board this morning, we observed that one of
the number appeared of superior rank to the rest.   They
approached Mr. W. with an offering of cocoa-nuts, and
two boxes resembling in form infants' coffins.   An officer of royalty, no doubt, then pointed to Mr. W. and to
the vessel, seeming to say, "You are the chief of this
vessel."   He then pointed to his superior and to the
land, signifying that he was the chief of the land.   He
then called Mr. W. "Samola," and his own chief by the
same name, which made the whole plain to us.   His
presents were accepted, and others returned.   They appeared highly delighted with knives, scissors and razors.

Fish-hooks were prized next.   They call a fish "eek,"
very like eka, which word is used for fish in nearly
every known isle of the South Seas.   They have brought
some fowls for sale, which they call "malek."   In the
morning I showed them a hen's egg, and signified to
them that I would like to have some brought.   In the
afternoon two little trembling chicks were brought, looking as though they had burst their shell on their passage
to the bark, and half a dozen eggs; on breaking which, I
found them inhabited.

Several canoes that were here in the morning, sailed
to a distant part of the group ;—another evidence that
the inhabitants are at peace.   One native presented me

with a dozen of delicious fruit, unlike any that I have seen. It was about the size of an orange, but of an irregular form. The rind is like that of the bread-fruit, and there is a core inside like it; the core is surrounded by kernels of the size and form of the hazel nut; the pulp is of bright yellow, emitting a delightful odor, and of a delicious taste; the kernels are strung upon a stick, roasted and then eaten.

12. Some of the natives yesterday brought a small quantity of " *beech de mer*," and the mate, with four men accompanying him, explored the reefs again, but reported the fish as not being sufficiently plentiful to induce our stay at the place. Our exploring expedition also visited an island that they supposed inhabited. Several natives accompanied them. They only saw a few natives, however, and one house (the Astor of the island, probably). The building was of rather extensive dimensions, and kept by a blind man. This did not appear to be the season for company, as the house was not full. Two females were seen peeping at the strangers, but on being observed by their lords, boys were sent to stone the ladies from the premises.

As the order was given this morning to man the windlass, an application was made to the captain by one of the crew to be discharged. This man had been shipped in Manilla from a whaling vessel, and now the sight of land induced him to wish for another change. Mr. W. inquired why he wished for a discharge so soon. He replied, that he did not like the " *beech de mer* " trade. The reason not being deemed sufficient, his request was not granted.

21. We sighted a group of islands called the Greenwich Islands. We counted about twenty in number, and from one of them an extensive reef stretched out

several miles directly in our track.   This was not looked
for, as the group was merely designated on the chart by
one little dot.   The reef runs west north-west from the
isle, and is some eight miles in extent.   Daylight appeared in the morning just in time to show us our dangerous
proximity to this dangerous place.   In one half hour
more our destruction would have been sure.

The bark was hove to, and a boat manned and sent
to examine the reefs around the isles that lay the nearest to the vessel.   The article that is so highly prized
by the Chinese epicure was not found to inhabit this portion of the seas, and our exploring expedition seemed
likely to turn out a deploring one.   A canoe was seen at
one time, which seemed in a hurry to escape from our
observation, and was soon hidden from view.   With
a glass we observed several houses on one island, but no
inhabitant appeared in sight.   Being curious to see the
natives, I regretted their timidity.   The group, like the
Young Williams's, was of coral formation, appearing
scarcely above the level of the ocean, and apparently
covered with the cocoa-nut trees.

29.   While engaged at my morning toilet, I heard
a sudden rush to the quarter deck, followed by the rattling of ropes and other confused sounds.   I felt alarmed, thinking that some one had fallen into the briny element; but I was soon undeceived, and from the tremen-
dous flapping was led to suppose that we had received a
visitor of distinction from the same element.   I hastened
to "sara sara," and perceived Mr. Shark, from "blue
ocean."   He was a dancing master, I presume, as he
continued for a long time exhibiting his knowledge of
that beautiful accomplishment for our amusement.   When
the people had become satiated with the exhibition, they
dragged the visitor very unceremoniously to the main

deck, and, horrible to relate, cut him in two parts. This cruel act, however, did not prevent him from continuing his favorite pastime for the space of an hour.

This reminds me of a well authenticated shark story, which I will record. While we were at Mathuata, I observed that the man, Harry, of whose horrid death at Navu I have previously given an account, had lost two of his fingers. I inquired where he had deposited them. "In the jaws of a shark," he replied. He then related the following story, to which I scarcely gave credence at the time. Afterwards, however, I heard the fact affirmed by two eye-witnesses of respectable character. He stated that while a sailor on board a brig lying at one of the islands, they caught a shark one day just before the dinner hour. Immediately after he was taken, the head was severed from the body, and both parts were left on the deck till the men had dined, smoked and talked their hour of noon; after which, their attention was again turned to the shark, not supposing that any life remained in the dissevered parts, after so long a time had elapsed since it was taken and separated. Harry, with another, first took the head and raised it to the rail of the vessel to throw it overboard. As they were about to plunge it into the deep, Harry cried out, "Stop! let us have prayers over the head, and bury it Christian fashion." At that moment the jaws opened and snapped off two of his fingers. The head was dropped, and notwithstanding the lesson, the lips of the profane Harry did not cease to utter impious oaths.

30. The two past nights the centipedes have been exercising their vocal powers to please us; but strange beings that we are, we are not amused by Mr. Shark's dancing, nor by the music of the vocalists from Feejee. The latter were discovered to-day, and immediately ex-

ecuted.   We have now been trying to sail towards Feejee for three months; but calms, light airs and head
winds appear to have formed a combination against us.
"An surely," in Irish phrase, "we are advancing in re-
trograde motion."   About once in six or seven days we
are favored with copious showers, which we deem a
great blessing, as they supply us with an abundance of
pure water, which the sailor and the traveller of the
sandy desert alone know how to appreciate.   The time
would be somewhat tedious to me, were it not beguiled
by the perusal of books.

July 12.   At eight o'clock, A. M., we discovered a
group of low islands, not mentioned on our charts.
Twenty-two were counted.   Owing to a contrary current we could not conveniently visit them.

Aug. 9.   We arrived at Pleasant Island, or the whaler's depot, I think it should be called.   No anchorage
being found, the bark lay to, and we were visited by
the inhabitants in great numbers.   An African negro,
as black as Africans ever are, came off in one of the
first canoes.   He was asked if there were any white
men on the island.   "Oh, yes, sir, there be *three* besides myself," was his reply.   The white men soon came
off, bringing a sick pig and a well one for sale.   One of
the men, called Bob, was the captain, I presume, as he
appeared a very confident, bold, business sort of a fellow.   They are all deserters from whalers.   He informed me that there were about fifteen hundred inhabitants on the island,—that they were divided into tribes,
each tribe having a petty chief, and the whole being
governed by a queen.   They perform no religious ceremonies, but believe in the immortality of the soul.
When a chief dies, they believe he becomes a star,

(a poor material, I should judge, to make such brilliants
of,) and when a poor man dies, his spirit has to wander about on the island in dark and unfrequented places.
There are often wars among them, but they seldom kill
their enemies,—they only kind o' play fight. With regard to the white men, Capt. Bob coolly stated that not
more than three or four could agree to remain on the
island at a time, as they usually got to fighting and killed each other; but three years had now elapsed since
the last white man was killed.

None of the vegetables or fruits usually found in
tropical climates are found here, except the cocoa-nut.
These, with fish, are the food of the natives. They
raise pigs and fowls for the supply of their whaling visitors. Capt. Bob, however, does not allow the natives to
sell the pigs themselves. He kindly takes possession of
any long face that happens to be brought for sale by
other than his own clan, sells it at sixpence a pound,
and indemnifies the owner with such a quantity of tobacco as he thinks best. He allowed the natives to sell
their fowls, which they did for one negro head of tobacco
apiece. The black man did not belong to Bob's clan,
and lived at another part of the island. He appeared
much better than the trio composing Bob's company.
He asked me if I could give him a Bible or a Testament, or even a few leaves of a Bible. I felt happy that
it was in my power to comply with his request. Capt.
Bob regretted our short stay at the isle, as I was the
first white lady that he had ever seen at the place, although he had been here seven years. He would have
been happy to have had Mr. W. and myself visit the
queen, and to have shown us the island. The sick pig
he. brought was of very large dimensions. It appeared feeble, but Mr. W. was assured that it was only

exhaustion occasioned by his journey from the land to
the vessel, not being accustomed to travel by water.
As we had long been without fresh provisions, Mr. W.
paid eleven dollars in cash for long face.

Our decks were completely filled with native men and
young girls, who stole every thing they could lay their
hands upon.   I saw them handing shirts, trowsers, sailors' knives and various other articles over the sides of
the vessel; but supposing that palm-leaf hats, of which
great numbers were brought for sale, had been bought
by the seamen with them, I said nothing about it.   They
brought a quantity of lines to sell.   Mr. W. stood on
the quarter deck, buying them, and had them passed
into the house, which was filled with natives; and as the
lines and cocoa-nuts were passed in on one side, the
honest natives dexterously passed them out on the other,
selling them again.   This was continued for some time
before they were discovered.   All that they brought was
sold for tobacco, and I was almost stunned by the vocife-
rous cry of the girls, of " Captain's woman, give me
chaw tobacco."   They placed no value upon cloth,
which was offered them, although they wore nothing but
a " *leku*," made of grass.   The whole conduct of this
people was boisterous, rude, and immodest in the ex-
treme.   The girls came on board for the vilest of purposes, but stated that their purposes were not accomplished, as the sailors were afraid of " Captain's
woman."

This little island, which is only six miles in circumference, was discovered by Capt. Fearn in 1798.   Its inhabitants then resembled in character those that I have
before described as belonging to the Young Williams's
group.   Whaling vessels have been in the habit of visiting this place for many years, and here are shown the

effects of a heathen intercourse with white (I can scarcely say civilized) men from civilized lands. It is true that at home this class appear like civilized beings, but it is too often the case that when men visit foreign climes, their conduct shows that they have left their souls at home.

Here is a practical illustration that civilization does not follow intercourse with civilized people, unless accompanied with the gospel. I believe that the state of society at Tahiti and the Sandwich Islands would have been no better than this, had not the gospel been close upon the white man's track. Such in a few years would Feejee become, were not the gospel there to counteract in some measure the baneful consequences of intercourse with trading vessels. The reason why it has not already become so, is, that the dangerous character of the natives has hitherto prevented a free intercourse with them. I presume that there is no class of beings to be found upon this mundane world (Chinese excepted), whose minds would be found more impervious to gospel influences than the inhabitants of Pleasant Island.

CHAPTER XII.

Return to Manicola—Supposed Treachery of the Natives—Arrival at Feejee—A Delicious Feast—Arrival at Bau—Visit of Tanoa—Destruction of Two Whaling Vessels—Natawa War—Ceremony of Anointing a Warrior.

Aug. 15. It is said that we must live slowly to be good. How very good we should be, for we have lived slowly enough since the first of last April! It is now the middle of the fifth month since we have been traversing the ocean. Really, it would seem sometimes that sky, ocean, and every visible object had come to an anchor, so slowly do we advance. Were it not that I have enjoyments called employments, I might long since have died of ennui, and been buried in the deep blue ocean; and although poets may write about its coral beds, I have no wish to try one, believing them to be hard and cold. If all the poets were condemned to live on oceans for the space of five months in succession, we should not read as much from their pens in their praise. We should not hear of a beautiful sunset at sea, for it is not what the poet so often describes it, but is more like the character of an old bachelor—there is an incompleteness about it. The clouds appear to lack variety and beauty, and there is a frigid, stony sameness of scenery, that often tires the eye. I cannot subscribe to the sentiment expressed in the following lines of the poet:—

" Though beauty every where is strewn
    To glad the weary soul—
Upon the burning, torrid zone,
    Around the frozen pole—
Though dark the forest shadows fall,
    Though fair the valley be,
The noblest sight among them all
    Is sunset on the sea."

I think the poet who traced these lines must have been seated on some verdant mound, on a bright summer eve, with hat and cane thrown carelessly by his side, and the gentle zephyrs fanning his cheeks. It seems to me he could not have been floating about on the ocean, amid opposing currents, baffling winds, and try-patience calms, with rice and molasses for breakfast, dinner and supper—if so, the pretty sonnet entitled " Sunset at Sea," would never have graced the pages of a periodical. Believe me, when I say that a completely finished, beautifully glorious sunset can never be witnessed without the diversified scenery of land and water.

23. We made the island of Manicola, and approaching it in a different direction from our last visit, we observed several huts and inhabitants. The boat was lowered, manned, and a superficial examination was made on a part of the reef for "*beech de mer.*" A strong breeze prevented a more thorough search. We suspect that Capt. Osborne had some trouble with the same natives on his way to Manilla, as Mr. O., of Manilla, spoke of an occurrence of the kind, but gave no hint of the name or place. We were so near the isle that we could distinctly see the natives. They seemed exceedingly shy, appearing only at intervals from among the trees, and at the doors of their dwellings. They were dark colored, like the Feejeeans. No canoes were observed. We were only five days from Feejee to this place.

Sept. 16. Since we left Manicola, we have been tumbling about in cross seas, with strong, contrary winds. I am exceedingly wearied in body, but not discouraged in mind. "Hope on, hope ever," is my motto. We are not doomed like the flying Dutchman to wander o'er these seas forever.

Last evening, about eight o'clock, I said to Mr. W., "Are we not about on the centre of Charlotte's Bank?" He had scarcely replied in the affirmative, when the shout of "breakers! breakers!" saluted our ears. We hastened on deck, and the captain cried out, "Hard down your helm!" The order was instantly obeyed, and the bark came round. This bank is marked on the chart as doubtful. Mr. W. had passed the spot, or very near to it, several times without discovering any bank or shoal; but he had given orders for the watch to be vigilant. None were satisfied that the alarm was not occasioned by a shoal of whales.

17. Feejee is in sight! Feejee is in sight! The land of pigs and yams. Shall I sing and dance, and clap my hands for joy? Oh no, that would never do for one of my years. I must remember that I have passed the gleeful age of fifteen, and should have nothing to do with the exercise of such feelings, but should manifest a sober and grave deportment. Such are the suggestions of Dame Propriety. My heart, however, is actually dancing for joy, and the green isles of Feejee were never hailed with greater delight by a weary daughter of the ocean.

18. A mantle of dark gray is thrown over the face of the sun, and veils the sky. We all passed an anxious and sleepless night, fearing our dangerous proximity to shoals and reefs. The past night has been exceedingly dark, but the bark must be kept on her way, as there was no anchorage. The wind blew half a gale, and they "wore ship" every two hours. We were running between the islands of Kandavu and Ngau. May we feel grateful to Him who has saved us from the dangers of the night, and the many perils of a protracted voyage!

19. We arrived at Motureke about noon, and anchored in a snug little bay. Our vessel is still, and we are at rest, after being tossed hither and thither for six months. I never knew the delight of rest before. I was never before truly weary, and such only as are, can enjoy perfect rest. The natives brought us pigs, fowls, yams, sweet potatoes, bananas and pine-apples. Our people eagerly devoured raw yams, not being willing to wait for them to be cooked. The scurvy had begun to appear among them, and had our passage been prolonged a week

or two longer, I fear that none would have had sufficient strength to have managed the vessel. Our voyage from Feejee to Manilla was performed in forty-four days. Mr. W. knew that the prevailing winds would not favor our return here, but he never supposed that our passage would exceed three months, and he supplied the vessel with suitable provisions for that time. Several of the pigs and fowls died. The flour soon grew wormy and musty. Our bread was occupied by living tenants when we left home (this was not the fault of the gentlemanly owners of the bark, who supposed the bread was good). I could not feel an appetite for the salt beef and sandwiches, and my sustenance for the last three months had been rice and molasses. During the last month, while our vessel was being continually tossed about, the winds blowing almost a gale, I could take but little of that. I never felt any disposition, however, to complain of our bill of fare. We had a good supply of coffee and tea, the clouds of heaven supplied us with pure water, and our rice was of the very best kind. We were never threatened with starvation, and we never knew thirst. How many a poor mariner would gladly have exchanged situations with us! How grateful, too, should we be, that we did not suffer!

But did'nt we enjoy the bountiful, delicious feast, that was spread upon our table on the afternoon of the 19th of September! It was at the hour of five. I could not have eaten before, had the food been prepared. I did not feel hungry for some hours, but at length the emotions of my joyful heart became more quiet, and the table, unaccustomed to the load of luxuries, seemed to say, "Come, and lighten my burden!" What a good supper we did have! Roast fowls, boiled yams, tarro, baked sweet potatoes, bananas, &c.

20. Received a visit from a chief of Bau. We learn from him that the bark Samos, Capt. Archer, is here from Salem, Mass.; the bark Catherine, Capt. Pratt, of Boston, Mass., and the schooner Sir John Franklin, of New Zealand; the latter has brought Mr. J. B. Williams, the United States Consul and general agent for the Pacific.

Namosimalua is still numbered among the living; Bau has allowed him to continue here a little longer. Perhaps, as they deem him neither Christian nor heathen, they think that his spirit would not gain admittance to any habitation in the spirit land, and thus be left to wander about here to their annoyance. It is certain that his life has not been spared through love to him.

21. Our anchor was raised, and with a fair wind we sailed for Bau, where we arrived at two P. M. A canoe soon came off from Vewa. The mission families sent their compliments, and an invitation to visit them as soon as the tide would allow us. The reefs are so extensive, that Vewa can only be visited at the very top of the tide; consequently, only four hours out of the twenty-four will suit. This may sound strange to those who have read what Ellis, in his Polynesian Researches, says about the tides in the South Pacific Ocean. His remarks appear to apply only to Tahiti. Here the tide is full at six o'clock only, at the full and change of the moon, after which it varies forty minutes daily. At Tonga, Rotumah, and many other islands, the tides are the same as they are here.

At five, P. M., we started for Vewa. The mission families with their servants, the queen with her household, Mary Wallis and many others, awaited our arrival at the landing. Our meeting was any thing but cold or ceremonious. It was most delightfully heart-cheering. "How dreadfully you look!" said one. "Are you

sick?" inquired another. "Have you been sick?" said
a third. "Let me have a seat at your tables, and you'll
see how sick I am," was my answer. We then informed
our friends that we had been on a *deploring* expedition
for the last six months, and it had been found to disagree
with my constitution. We found that some alterations
had taken place during our absence. Mr. Watsford and
family had removed to Ono. A stone house had been
completed, and Mr. Jaggar and family had removed into
it, using a part of it as a printing office. Mrs. Wilson,
the widow of the late Francis Wilson, who died in Tonga
about three months since, is here, waiting the return of
the mission schooner from Lakemba, when she will depart for New Zealand. As Mrs. Wilson occupies my
little domicil, I shall pass the nights on board the bark
for the present.

22. Passed the day at Vewa. I was deeply interested
in listening to Mrs. Wilson's account of a revival of religion at Vavau, a Tonga island where she had resided.
She told me of the sickness and happy death of her beloved husband. She is a most interesting woman.

23. Just as the boat was ready to take me to Vewa,
I was hindered by the arrival of the old king and suite.
He had come dressed for the occasion, I presume. A
glazed cap, somewhat the worse for wear, and decorated
with a faded garland of flowers, had formed a resting
place somewhere on the top of his head, where it appeared ready to fall at the feet of royalty upon the slight-
est hint. His arms were decorated with several circlets
of beads. His beard, which was about ten inches in
length, has been recently dyed black. Several yards of
clean, white *masi* were worn around his person in neat
folds. He was accompanied, as usual, by old men and
children. Thakombau, with a large company of war-

14

riors, has gone to assist Somosomo in the war with Natawa. After the departure of the king and suite, Navinde came to visit us. He wished to beg five axes of Mr. W., which being refused, he departed, very much displeased. Since this chief has been betrothed to the daughter of the king, he appears to be looking up, and begs in a wholesale manner.

24. Again I have lost the tide, and cannot visit Vewa, being prevented by a call from the Queen of Bau, with her ladies and maidens. My royal visitors are a poor substitute for the loss of the society of my Vewa friends.

Before we left this place for Manilla, Mr. W. gave the schooner Perseverance in charge of two men with trade, and instructions to fish " *beech de mer* " during our absence. One of the men died, and the other, not being capable of taking the lead of business of any description, the schooner was laid by to rest, and was condemned as unseaworthy by all who had vessels out of employ. Mr. W., however, not being converted to their opinion, has sent for the vessel to prepare it for farther service; consequently, as we shall probably remain here some little time, several " *beech de mer* " houses have been commenced in this vicinity.

Verani, the chief, who is now called Elijah, still lives, an honor to his calling. He has built a fine new chapel, and is becoming very useful to the missionaries. The chiefs of Bau have become reconciled to him, and all has been peaceful between the two little islands. Namosimalua is with Thakombau. During our absence, two whaling vessels have been destroyed at Ovalau. They were set on fire by their crews. Both were American vessels; one was named the Elizabeth, and the other the Canton Packet. We learn that a few weeks since, a mountain tribe of Ovalau made a sudden descent upon the coast of that island, murdering many of the natives, and robbing all the white inhabitants, besides killing the native women.

29. Samonunu came on board with a dozen others. They had not been here long when some one told them that the Turaga-lavu was coming on board. The ladies appeared frightened, drew themselves into the smallest possible compass, and occupied every nook and cranny that they could find below. As soon as the king was seated on the sofa, they crawled from their hiding places on their hands and knees, and ascended to the deck. Many of these women were of high rank, yet none would dare to assume an upright position in the presence of any chief of rank. The women of Feejee are always seen in parties by themselves, and the men the same. Parties of chiefs, however, do not associate. We should never see Thakombau visit at any place with his father, or any chiefs of high rank in the company of either. If one chief came on board the vessel, he would retire to some remote part, and remain till the first had left. The women never eat with the men, and there is but little social intercourse among them. When a woman meets a chief in a common pathway, she steps from the path, and kneels till he has passed, whatever her rank may be.

We are informed that the chief of Nakalo, finding that Thakombau has violated his promise respecting his sister, who has been given to Navinde, sent word to Garenggeo that if he would return to Rewa, he would assist him to rebuild the town, and defend it. The exiled chief embraced the proposal, returned, and they have rebuilt the place; consequently, hostilities have again commenced between the powers that be. Phillips is still at Nuque.

Oct. 2. Thakombau has returned from the war with Natawa. As the Rev. Mr. Williams has forwarded a full account of this celebrated affair to the mission station at Vewa, I shall transcribe it, that the heroism of the Feejeeans may be truly appreciated. He commences his narrative in June, 1846, with the following observations:—"Our soldiers have done no fighting for the last five months. Besides being otherwise employed, it is possible that they think the splendid feats of the former part of the year should suffice for the latter; namely, the capture and entire demolition of two defenceless women, the slaughter of a young lad, and their complete victory over a poor, stray idiot boy. This was the crowning triumph of the year. With reason then, they may now rest upon their illustrious deeds. The Somosomo people have long been waiting for the promised assistance from Bau against their enemies. About the 12th of June, Tuilili, the chief, received certain intelligence of the near approach of his friends and allies, and the following preparations were made for them. Five of the best " *buris* " were first built, and then five " *bolo buris* " were added to them, and several other large houses are to be vacated for their use. Thirty-eight thousand yams, besides large quantities of arrow-root, are interspersed among the buildings, and many thousands more of yams are in store for their use. Sixty large turtles are secured, and fishers are continually adding to them. On the opposite land, many pigs are in reserve.

About forty huge bales of native cloth, and hundreds of head-dresses are ready to excite the strangers to deeds of valor, also a completely equipped new canoe, a lot of *yanggona* brought from Ramba in five canoes, which, when piled, formed a wall thirty-five feet long and seven high.

June 18. It was reported that all the warriors had assembled at Vuna. On the 13th, Tuilili with forty of his chief men, joined the Bau party at Vuna to perform the ceremony, when the chiefs were presented with one large bale of *masi*, forty dresses, and fifty large whales' teeth. The Vuna people prepared food, danced, and presented a quantity of native cloth that excited the surprise of the receivers. Thakombau told Tuilili that he should remain at Vuna during the Sabbath, and on Monday proceed to Somosomo. Tuilili returned to Somosomo with his people on Saturday, and on Monday Thakombau arrived with a fleet of sixty-six large double canoes, and sixteen single ones.

The canoes had scarcely reached the shore, when a succession of shouts from behind the settlement announced the arrival of hundreds who came inland from Vuna. We are informed that the Lasakau people burned several towns on their way to this place, and some natives were killed at the lowering of the masts of some of the Bau canoes. When the Bau chiefs had landed, the ceremony of *Qalova* was performed, when they received about one hundred dresses, twenty whales' teeth, and a quantity of baked yams, tarro and pigs. On Monday night, the inhabitants of Somosomo, with those of many other towns, were employed in preparing food. On Tuesday, two hundred people were employed till noon in piling food. The warriors passed their time in shouting and in blacking themselves.

The accumulated labors of the cooks were seen in the shape of one large heap of ground tarro puddings, four heaps of baked tarro, and yams covered with arrow-root puddings, and turtles. Seventy turtles were placed by themselves in another heap. These hills of food were flanked on the left with a wall of yanggona, thirty-five feet long and seven high. On the right was a fence of uncooked yams, numbering thirty-eight thousand.

After the food was set in order, a large bale of cloth was brought and placed opposite, leaving a space of two hundred yards between. This was followed by twenty others laid side by side, which elicited from the warriors a shout truly deafening. After a space, a Somosomo chief came to the fence with a train of "*masi*" sixty yards in length. A stout man had brought a marked dress thus far for him, and then assisted in placing it upon his shoulders. After being thus equipped, the lad marched manfully across the open space to the place where the Bau chiefs sat, when he tossed off his dress, and marched back again amid the shouts of the multitude. He repeated this ceremony five times, leaving a dress each time.

After this, the warriors retired to form themselves into a procession, which entered [the western avenue to the arena. Two young chiefs, sons of Tuilili, came running from the town by different ways, raising their fans on high, and kicking up a great dust with their trains of sixty yards in length. They were followed by their father, whose train measured one hundred fathoms. His squire came behind him, bearing an immense dress, and was followed by two hundred men, each bearing a dress hanging in immense folds. Two men came next, with bamboos on their shoulders, from which were suspended four large dresses hanging in bunches. These were followed by one hundred men bearing bales of cloth, who took their seats on and about the cloth, and were joined by one hundred and fifty men, all bearing cloth. The sons of Tuilili, commenced running again, shortening their distance, however, each time as the procession of warriors approached the arena by the easterly entrance. They came in the following order:—

Thakombau and Tuilili, bearing beautiful spears and clubs.
One hundred men bearing spears and clubs.
Five with two muskets each.
Ten with one musket each.
Five with one musket each.
Ten with two muskets each.
Sixty-eight with one musket each.
Six with two muskets each.
Fifty-one with one musket each.
Two with two muskets each.
Thirteen with one musket each.
Two with two muskets each.
Sixty with one musket each.
Twenty carpenters with American axes.
Sixty men with clubs and spears.
One man with bow and arrow.
Twenty-eight with muskets.
Sixty with spears and arrows.
One bearing bows, and a large bundle of arrows.
Thirty with clubs, spears and hatchets.
Sixty-one with muskets.
Forty with clubs, spears and hatchets.
Twenty with muskets.
One hundred with clubs, spears and battle-axes.
Eighty-five with muskets.
Twenty with spears and clubs.
Six with two muskets each.
Twenty-one with muskets.
One old man with a large bundle of spears closed the procession.

The warriors of Bau formed a line four deep in front
of the provisions, the musket bearers forming the right,
and the club and spear men the left wings. These had
scarcely formed in order, when our ears were saluted
with the most frightful yells, with clanking of arms and
axes. On looking in the direction from whence the
sounds proceeded, we observed a large company of the

common fighting men, who, after shaking their spears awhile, rushed "*en masse*" into the open space, some through it, and others over the fence. After these had run, capered and shouted till they were tired, they retired to the seaside, behind the Bau chiefs, waving a white banner whereon were painted several marvellous figures. The enormous bales of cloth were then removed and the shouting again commenced. Tuilili took a hundred whales' teeth upon his shoulders, (he is almost a giant in size, and quite one in strength,) and approaching Thakombau, stooped and made a speech. When he had finished, he arose and returned to his place, bearing the teeth with him. Thakombau then commenced the "*mbole, mboling,*" (thanking) and was followed by many of the chiefs singly,—then by companies of eight and ten each. As the respectability of the company decreased, the numbers increased, all endeavoring by their gestures and words to evince their valor. A Bau chief now took the whales' teeth from Tuilili, and other Bau men took about twenty bunches of spears, and laid them at the feet of Thakombau. Several ceremonies connected with welcoming the Bau warriors to Somosomo were then performed, after which the multitude dispersed with yells, and shouts, and firing of muskets. Thakombau is accompanied by Tubo, the Tonga chief, and his tribe. It is said that the army of Thakombau numbers about three thousand, including the Tonguese.

July 1. The warriors depart to-morrow for their scene of action. Thakombau has observed the Sabbaths, and tried to have his people do the same; but he complains that the Tonguese make it difficult for his commands to be obeyed, by their habitual negligence and disregard of them. The very lowest of the heathen complain of the vicious conduct and indecent dances of

Tubo's party. When any thing is said to him, he has
an excuse ready, and makes himself appear very good.
A new temple has been built to propitiate the god who
has been invoked, and he is so pleased with his new
" *buri*," that his godship has promised them entire success in the coming conflict. Tanoa's little boy, who is
" *vasu* " to Somosomo, has taken one double canoe and
twenty-one single ones; this " *vasuing* " is a great affair.
It is said that it is mostly done while they are children,
as when the " *vasu* " becomes older, they are ashamed
to help themselves in this way.

24. The warriors having returned, we are able to proceed in our narrative. It appears that the Natawa people were determined to give their enemies battle; and
some of their bravest men singled out Thakombau as
their victim. The warriors approached so near the
fighting fence as to converse with each other. "Where
is Thakombau?" asked some. "Here I am," he replied, "I have brought these warriors here." The
Natawa people had sheltered themselves in a place difficult of access. The roads are represented as being less
than three feet in width, with frightful precipices on
either side. When our warriors had gained the small flat
on which the town was built, they erected a fence to
serve as a guard against the shot of the besieged. Then
a brisk, but slightly effective fire, was kept up for some
time.

The Somosomo people were desirous to assist in the
skirmish, but Thakombau told them not to interfere, for
the war was his, and he should manage it. After some
firing, the besieged made a sally, and a fine young man,
named Mai Vatarovo, was killed. Thakombau shot a
man that was in the act of darting a spear at him. This
appears to have been the heat of the battle. The be-

seiged retired into their town, which the warriors assail-
ed, and succeeded in making a small breach in the fence,
when Thakombua stopped all farther proceedings for the
day, saying, "We will take the town tomorrow." Whether he intended to give the inhabitants an opportunity to
escape, or whether he felt that they had achieved glory
enough for one day, is not known ; probably the first,
as there is reason to suppose that the Bau chiefs had determined that Natawa should not be destroyed, and they
engaged in the affair that they might gratify the old king
of Somosomo and increase their own powers, by bringing
the Somosomo people under an obligation to them, and
by bringing the Natawa people to submit to the dominion
of Bau. Thus Somosomo has to bear all the expense of
the war, while Bau gains all the glory and advantage.

To-morrow came, and the warriors entered the town,
where they found the houses standing, and ready to be
destroyed, the inmates having fled. The body of a Bau
man, who had been killed the day before, was baking in
an oven, and the body of another was cut up, ready for
cooking. Several towns, which had been vacated during
the night, were burned. The spoil collected consisted
of four bars of soap, some fishing nets, and a small quantity of cinnet.

The forces next moved to Oro ni Yasatha; against
which place Tuilili was very bitter. A fence was built,
as before, and a ceaseless fire was kept up for several
hours, to the alarm of the women and children. During
the night a man stole from the town, and early in the
morning was conducted to Thakombau. His business
was to inform the chief that the inhabitants wished to
"soro" to Bau. He was told that it was good for them
to do so. Soon persons appointed were seen approaching, bearing whales' teeth and baskets of earth. The

men approached Thakombau, as is their custom, on their knees; first presenting the teeth as their " *soro*," and then the baskets of earth, to signify their full surrender of their lands to Bau. The " *soro* " was accepted, and notice sent to Tuilili, who replied, " If it is good to you, it is well." After the " *soro* " was accepted, the Somosomo people amused themselves by throwing stones, and even firing at the Oro ni Yasatha fence, which, coming to the ears of Thakombau, caused him to send to know who it was that continued hostilities after he had said "Let there be peace. The people have submitted to Bau ; and had they not have done so, I should have finished them. I have said that they shall live;—they *shall* live."

The Natawa people did not " *soro* " so readily, but fled from one fastness to another, till at length a Bau chief, well known to them, was sent to inquire why they conducted in this manner. They replied, " We mean to ' *soro*.' Will you be of a good mind, and present our ' *soro* ' to Bau? not to Somosomo, for they will be sure to kill us." The Bau chiefs could not agree to their proposal, and the Natawa chiefs were afraid to go themselves to offer their " *soro*." At length they concluded to send six youths, with the teeth and earth, as representatives. The " *soro* " was accepted, peace was declared, and the war ended.

Tuilili, with his company, returned very quietly. A few days after, about fifty canoes returned with shouting, beating of drums, firing of muskets, blowing of conch shells, &c. Several of the warriors left for Bau on the Thakandrove side, where they amused themselves by destroying plantations, placing traps for the destruction of the unwary, &c.

In the course of a few days, the Somosomo people danced before the Bau people, and left large quantities of native cloth for Bau. Hundreds of musquito curtains and marked cloths have been presented since the return of the warriors. The people complain that there is nothing left. The Bau people are complaining of their bill of fare since their return, having nothing to subsist upon but tarro and land crabs. They indulge in observations like the following:—"How many men are there in Somosomo,—a hundred, or not?"—"Natawa has nothing to fear."—"This is a land for pork, but where are the pigs?"—"This is a land of plenty," said Thakombau, "a plenty of water, and a plenty of impudence." The Somosomo people make the following remarks:— "This has been a bad war, a useless war. Bau hates us, and we will be revenged." The Natawa people say: —"We shall know Bau only. We have long been tired of 'soroing' to a people that are never satisfied. We do not always wish to be hearing of clubs and ovens. Why should they ever be baking our people?"

Somosomo is just as much at enmity with Natawa as ever, but their hands are tied; they can do nothing now unless they brave the displeasure of Bau, which they are not in a condition to do. The bodies of the slain were all presented to 'Tuilili, who, with his people, devoured them. A part of one was sent to Thakombau after it was cooked, but he sent it away untouched.

Aug. 6. The warriors have departed, and quiet is again restored. Their time has been mostly spent, since their return, in teaching and learning dances."

Oct. 3. I have now given a fair specimen of Feejeean wars, how their battles are fought and their victories won. It is well for the population of Feejee, that its warriors do not possess the skill and tact of the warriors of civilized lands.

The following ceremony of anointing a successful warrior, was furnished me by Mr. Hunt, who was an eye-
witness of the same.

"The ceremony commenced by several old men
chanting a piece to the following effect. 'Let us attend
to the ceremony of the chiefs who have killed our enemies.' After this had been repeated several times, the
king called out for the warriors in a most unnatural tone,
using words that appear to be kept for such occasions
only. He asks who they are, and gives them a new
name. This being done, some very curious chanting
followed, accompanied by the blowing of conch shells,
the effect of which is utterly indescribable; the tones
were most unnatural, and the words ridiculous. The
art of blowing the conch appeared to be to make as short
a sound as possible, resembling the short base notes in a
quick march, and was about as harmonious as such
sounds usually are, without the combination of other
sounds necessary to constitute music. Those who responded, made a noise resembling the creaking of a
door that needed oiling. This performance was continued for a very long time, the actors appearing to at-
tach great importance to it. At its conclusion, five men
took a large banana leaf each, and a person poured water
in them. They held these in their hands a short time,
and then stood so as to form a diameter of the circle of
actors. After exchanging places several times, they
poured the water on the ground. This appeared to represent the pouring out of the blood of the rest of their
enemies, as the actors chanted, 'Pour it out,—pour it
out,—amen,—amen.' This finished the introductory
part of the ceremony.

The heroes were now introduced. One of them had

never killed a person in war before, and was, consequently, introduced first. He was accompanied by a person bearing a large new dress, and others with mats. The latter were placed on the ground for the honored one to stand upon. An old man disrobed the hero, and arrayed him in his new dress. The dress was of native cloth, folded lengthwise. A part of it was folded around the person of the warrior, and the remainder placed so as to form a large bunch on the back, and the hero now appeared like a soldier with a knapsack on. While this was taking place, three parties of females appeared in different parts of the 'rara,' each holding a wooden bowl containing an ointment composed of the stock of the banana, oil and tumeric. These ointment bearers approached slowly, repeating words that I did not understand, and after placing the bowls on the mats, retired. The other heroes now advanced, but as they had killed men in war before, they came dressed. Each hero bore a club on his shoulders, which was removed by the attendants, and others placed in their stead. These again were replaced by others, and so on, till about twenty were handled in this manner. It seemed to be considered a great privilege to possess a club that had been handled by the heroes.

After this came the anointing. The king's house steward divided the ointment, and persons appointed for the occasion, daubed the heroes from head to feet, which being concluded, the whole party repaired to the seaside, and the ceremonies ended. The heroes are required to remain in the 'rara' four days. A shed is erected for their shelter at night, and to screen them from the noon-day sun; but they are not allowed to lie down, or take their clubs from their shoulders. During these four days no drum is allowed to be beaten, or any noise to be made, and the heroes are treated, in every respect, like great chiefs. At the expiration of this time, the warriors doff all their honors but their new name, (which is usually the one that was borne by the person whom they had killed,) and become ordinary men again."

Thakombau visited the bark to-day, and was received with a salute of three large guns. Of course we felt exceedingly honored by the visit of this Napoleon of Feejee,—this illustrious conqueror. He has not returned ladened with the spoils of the conquered,—the soap and cinnet having been sold to the mission for a trifle ; but what of that ?—he killed a man himself, and his braves, consisting of an army of three thousand, besides killing ten or twelve men, set fire to as many as three hundred straw houses with nothing in them. To be serious, however, he has been a conqueror in the late war, and in the very best way he obtained the victory with comparatively little bloodshed. He had no enmity towards Natawa, but was actuated only by the desire of conquest. In this he is unlike the former chiefs of Feejee, who only fought to revenge some real or fancied injury, and have ever delighted more in butchering and devouring their kind than any thing else.

CHAPTER XIII.

Visit at Bau—The Fancy Ball—The Ride—Arrival of the Mission Schooner, Triton—A Perilous Adventure—A Novel Mode of Punishment—Execution at Bau—The Bachelor.

Oct. 4. Mr. Hunt preached on board the bark. All but the cook attended the services. This is the first time that preaching has ever been held on board a trading vessel at Feejee.

10.   Mr. Hunt, Mrs. Wilson and myself visited at Bau. We found all the ladies busily employed in preparing for a fancy ball, which was to be held in the evening.   Two barbers were dressing the head of Samonunu.   Thakombau was amusing himself with a little pop-gun, by slyly hitting the several ladies of the court.   There was as much finery about as would be found in any lady's dressing room who was preparing for a fancy ball at home. A profusion of wild flowers and aromatic shrubs were being arranged into very pretty wreaths.   I was truly surprised at the taste displayed by these untutored savages.   Some were cutting little ornaments from bright-colored cloth or paper, for the head; others were preparing cocoa-nut oil, scented with sandal wood, to anoint their persons ;   and several were giving the finishing touch to their best " *lekus*."   While this was going on, some one would receive the contents of Thakombau's pop-gun (which was usually a piece of uncooked yam,) upon the top of her nose, lip, or cheek; she would spring and look towards His Majesty, but his attention would be fixed upon some distant object with the most innocent look imaginable.

We called at several other houses, and found all the females similarly employed.   At last we called at the house of Tanoa.   Here we found the royal captives of Rewa, except the wife of Garenggeo, who had made her escape and joined her husband.   The widow of the murdered king was mourning the death of her only son, whom she declares has been poisoned.   They were not preparing to engage in the festivities of the coming evening; but the queen and her court were making preparations like the rest.   We here partook of some refreshments, consisting of baked tarro and little boiled fish. The natives manufacture a kind of pottery which they call "*kurus*," in which they cook their food. Their fish is carefully wrapped in fresh green leaves, and boiled in the "*kuru*." When sufficiently cooked, they are taken from the leaf and placed in order on a large banana leaf, and the water in which they are boiled is served hot in a cocoa-nut shell. After our banana leaf was spread, Mr. H. asked a blessing, and we proceeded to satisfy our hunger with no other knife or fork except what nature had provided. Our meal was really very nice. At its conclusion, water was brought to wash our hands, and we used our handkerchiefs for napkins. We then visited the king in his little "*buri*" and departed. The tide being considerably on the ebb, we rode the distance of a quarter of a mile on chairs made of human arms,—our own arms encircling the necks of our carriers. I laughed at Mrs. Wilson, she laughed at me, and Mr. Hunt, who was travelling on the back of a native, laughed at both of us.

11. Rev. Mr. Jaggar held divine service on board the bark. I spent the Sabbath at Vewa. The natives of this region do not visit the vessel on the Sabbath, as formerly. The gospel appears to be exerting its influence, and a very perceptible change is visible since our first arrival at this place.

14. Some of Phillips's warriors have killed two of Garenggeo's people, who were brought to Bau yesterday and devoured. In the afternoon Thakombau came on board. He appeared highly displeased that the Consul had located himself at Nuque, under the protection of Phillips. "Well, Mr. Wallis," he said, "they say that the king of America has come here." "Surely he must be much poorer than myself, to come so far for oil for

15

his lamps." "How is it," said Thakombau, "that you do not call yourself a king, or the son of a king? such is the fashion of the captains." "I am the master of this vessel, and hold no other rank. Why should I tell you lies? The great and rich men of America are never to be seen in Feejee after oil and '*beech de mer*,'" said Mr. W. "Ah! these men take us for fools, but we laugh at them when they tell us such stories. Mr. Williams has sent for me to collect a cargo of oil, but I sent word that he must come himself, if he wished me to do any thing for him, as I do not trade with '*kaises*.'" He appears to understand human nature, and to appreciate character as well as any one I have seen. One day when we had first arrived at the group, the man Harry was in the cabin with Thakombau and Mr. W. As they were conversing, he made some remarks. The chief turned to him, exhibiting in his whole bearing the utmost "*hauteur*," and said, "Who are you?—nothing but a runaway sailor, who has no riches but what he earns. You are not to say your own words. When Mr. Wallis tells you to speak, then you may speak." "You black rascal!" muttered Harry in English, "I wish I had you in Virginia, I think the tables would be turned." The man was hushed; he dared not open his mouth again to speak his own words.

A canoe from Ovalau has just passed with the body of a mountaineer lashed to it, which they are taking to Bau to be eaten,—the natives of the coast having killed five of their enemies,—the mountaineers.

23. The mission schooner, Triton, has arrived from Lakemba. As this vessel was absent four weeks longer than was expected, some anxiety had been felt on her account. Rev. Dr. Lyth and family have arrived to take the place of Mr. Watsford.

24. The day being unpleasant, I remained on board the bark. In the afternoon Mr. W. went to Bau in the Star. As the day closed, the wind increased to half a gale. When the steward was preparing the tea-table, I asked if he had not better show a light on deck. He said, "Capt. W. is just here,—only a few rods from the vessel." Relieved from my anxiety, and supposing that all was right, I continued reading till the expiration of some fifteen or twenty minutes, when I called to inquire if Mr. W. was on deck. I was told that he was not there, and the boat was not to be seen. I hastened to the deck, but could discern only the dim outlines of the surrounding isles. There was one hope that sustained me,—the wind, though strong, was fair for the boat to go to Vewa; and as our schooner lay there, I thought perhaps Mr. W. had suddenly altered his mind and gone there. I remained standing on the quarter deck from seven o'clock till nine. I then felt that there had been time for them to have returned, or some messenger to have been sent, as Mr. W. would know that I should be alarmed. I told the second mate that the boat must be sent to Vewa without another moment's delay. "De men is all turned in, ma'am," was the quiet reply. "Turned in!" I exclaimed. "Is it possible that there is no more interest or feeling in this case? Well, turn them out, and send the boat at once." "But de men could not fetch de boat back against de wind an tide,—she be too heavy." "There is a surf boat at Vewa," I replied, "ours can be left and that taken." "But ma'am, suppose de wind should come a gale, who will take care of de bark?" "Both anchors are out, and a hundred men could not save her from the reefs, if the wind should be strong enough to drive her there," I answered. "Call all hands,—send four in the boat, and let the rest watch

till we hear from Vewa; and if no intelligence is gained
from the Star, let them bring Mr. Smith from our schooner! Let all Vewa be alarmed, and canoes sent out in
every direction!" The men were called, the boat lowered, and they started. Ten o'clock came and no intelligence,—eleven, and I hear between the fitful gusts of
wind, the sound of oars. The sounds come nearer. I
hear voices, too, hark! I hear the voice of my husband,
—yes, I am certain 'tis he. Then I wept. I could not
weep before; my head seemed to be on fire, and my
throat filled to suffocation. It seems that when the
Star neared the bark, a squall very nearly capsized her,
and finding that they could not reach the bark with the
wind so strong ahead, they made for Vewa as their only
mode of safety. They had, however, various difficulties to encounter, owing to the darkness of the night and
the violence of the wind; but about nine o'clock they
gained the shore in safety, and Mr. W. had just procured a boat and men to bring him on board as our boat
arrived at Vewa. Our people left their boat, and they
all came off in a surf boat.

Nov. 4. Passed the last week at Vewa. On the Sabbath Mr. Hunt preached on board the Triton in the
morning, and then came, accompanied by Capt. Lilliwall, and preached on board the bark. Mrs. Wilson
passed the day with me on board the vessel.

8. Mr. Williams has arrived from Rewa, and at present is our visitor. He has just returned from a tour to
the interior of Vetelavu. He was accompanied by the
Vice Consul, Mr. Whippy, and several others. They
penetrated into the wilds to a distance of thirty miles.
They report the inhabitants as being civil and honest.
The distance across that part of Vetelavu where they
travelled, is about sixty miles; consequently, they visit-

ed the central part of the island. Mr. Whippy is the only white man who has ever been honored with a Feejeean office. He sustains that of Matta ge Mbau. Mr. W. has resided in Feejee for many years, and is truly respected by all who are acquainted with him. There are several white men now residing at Solavu, who have been lately married, and are becoming industrious and respectable. The missionaries have ever labored for their benefit, have treated them like men, and they now begin to conduct like men.

12. The Consul, Mr. Wallis and myself, were invited to breakfast on board the Triton, where we met Mrs. Wilson, Messrs. Hunt, Lyth and Jaggar. We found the Triton a nice little vessel, well fitted for passengers. In the cabin, directly opposite the entrance, hung a likeness of the founder of the Wesleyan order, and underneath was a brass plate, on which were the words, "God is with us." After breakfast and prayers, we took leave of Mrs. Wilson and Capt. Lilliwall, and departed for Vewa. The anchor of the Triton was raised, the sails unfurled, and the vessel was soon lost to our view.

16. Mr. W. hearing that the Bau and Lasakau people had stopped fishing for the bark, went to inquire about it. The chiefs said that they had been informed that " *beech de mer* " was sold in Manilla for large quantities of gold, and that the Feejeeans were not paid enough for it,—that Capt. Wallis would pay any price rather than not obtain it,—that they had been advised to stop fishing, demand higher prices for their fish, and they would obtain them. Mr. W. replied, " I came here a lad; now my hair is becoming gray. Why am I here now? Rich men do not come here. Should I not remain at home if " *beech de mer* " brought so great

riches? Do you not see that lies have been told you?"
"Yes; you talk wisely," they replied. "We see it
now, and we were fools to listen to the lying '*kaise.*'"

Mr. W. learned that this had been the work of John
Johnson, the survivor of the two with whom the schooner
had been left in charge on our departure for Manilla.
A written agreement had been signed by those men, that
the vessel should be delivered to Mr. W. on his return
from M. in good repair, and he was to buy what fish
they procured at a handsome profit to themselves. They
were to have no other reward. As has been shown, the
vessel had been laid up during our eight months' absence, not a fish had been procured, and the schooner
had not only been found in the worst possible order, but
several things missing; and the crowning of the whole
affair was, that Johnson was very angry that Mr. W.
would not pay him for doing nothing the past eight
months, saying that he could not afford to lose so much
time, and threatened vengeance. The above is his first
attempt. He seems to forget that Mr. W.'s hair is gray,
and that he has visited Feejee previous to the present time.
Mr. Williams has written to him, warning him as to his
future conduct. Johnson left Salem with us as a sailor,
and continued as such till the bark left for Manilla. On
our return Mr. W. offered Johnson employment, but he
refused it.

24. The Consul has to-day taken his departure for
his residence at Nukulau. This is a small island near
Rewa. Mr. Williams told Phillips when he left the isle,
(which he has purchased,) that he would rather not have
any Feejeeans visit at the place during his absence.
The Consul had not been absent long, when Phillips saw
a canoe sailing towards Nukulau. He immediately despatched two canoes, with orders to kill all on board.

Two were killed, and the rest escaped by jumping overboard and swimming away. Mr. Williams had not a
thought that his wishes would have been so strictly obeyed, and regretted that he had said any thing about it.
The canoe belonged to Phillips, and was manned by his
own people, who would have obeyed him at once, had he
sent word for them not to go to the isle. Phillips is a
great coward, but delights in bloodshed and murder.
Mr. Wallis once presented him with a large demijohn,
which he passed into his canoe, and gave it in charge to
two of his people; while they were putting it in a place
of safety, they broke it. Phillips immediately made the
men chew a quantity of broken glass, which killed them.
He then begged for another demijohn. Mr. W. told
him that he should give him no more glass to use for
such a purpose. He thought, probably, that Mr. W.
ought to reward him for the loss he had sustained.

The Feejeeans, in all their transactions with white
people, expect payment. The following instances will
illustrate my meaning:—A Feejeean at one time had a
very troublesome eruption on his arm. He went on
board a trading vessel that was here at the time, and requested medical aid. The captain told him that he
might remain on board, and he would see what he could
do for him. Accordingly the man remained till his arm
was cured, and then requested the captain to pay him,
that he might return to his home. "For what?" asked
the captain. "For staying on board your vessel," was
the reply. "What work have you done?" "Nothing."
"Who has given you food and cured your arm?" "You
have." "Then who should receive pay?" "Myself,"
was the reply of the *grateful* native. The man went
ashore and set fire to the "*beech de mer*" house, and
destroyed some four or five hundred dollars worth of fish.

The second instance came under my own observation. A canoe broke adrift that had been slightly fastened to our bark. Mr. W. let the natives have the jolly boat to go and pick up their own craft. They soon secured the canoe, and returned to the vessel, leaving two natives to bring the boat back. The wind was strong, and the rain poured in torrents. The boat drifted about for some time, when the canoe went to its assistance, and brought it safely to the vessel. The whole party, numbering about twelve, then asked to be paid for bringing the boat back, stating that it would have been lost had they not saved it.

30.   Mr. Williams writes us that on his arrival at Nukulau, a canoe with five dead bodies on board arrived at the isle at the same time. They were Garenggeo's men, who had been killed, and were being taken to Phillips. The war between Rewa and Bau appears to be renewed with all its former vigor.

Dec. 7.   Three women belonging to Navinde attempted last week to escape to Rewa, but, losing their way, they were returned to Bau. They had, for sometime past, caused him trouble by their bad conduct. They told him that they intended to run away the first opportunity, and he said that if they attempted it, and did not succeed, he should have them shot. Accordingly their dresses were taken off, and they were fastened to stakes on a shoal near Bau, where they remained for marks, to receive the shots of any who chose to fire at them,—the marksmen being stationed on the island. It is said that one of the victims received twelve musket shot in her body before a fatal one.

Females of Bau, who are condemned to death, are usually obliged to suffer a punishment before they are killed that is too horrible to be recorded. The above execution took place on the Sabbath. Mr. Jaggar started that morning to preach at Bau before he went to the bark, but the wind was strong ahead, their canoe was upset, and they were obliged to relinquish the attempt to reach Bau. He states that he heard the firing of muskets, and had he known of the affair, he should have made another attempt to have reached Bau, when he thinks that he could have saved the lives of the women. It is said that Navinde shut himself up in a little "*buri,*" and no one dared to approach him; and when he appeared, after the women were shot, his face was very pale, and he was exceedingly agitated. Does this not show that there is a monitor within the breast of even a cannibal savage?

8. Mr. Hunt went to Bau, and talked to the Lasakau chief about the murdered women. He said that if he had pardoned them, it would have excited the jealousy of Bau at once, and they would have accused him of getting up a "*vari*" with Rewa against Bau. There is a good deal of truth in this. It often happens that when a chief is conspiring against an enemy, he will send some of his female servants to carry messages to those with whom he wishes to hold correspondence, and if they are missed, to say that they have run away. No one in this land of treachery knows who is his friend; consequently all are suspicious and vigilant.

14. An Englishman, named Birch, arrived from Nukulau. He came from New Zealand a few months since, and has been residing at Nukulau with the Consul till the present time. He has come for medical aid, having been afflicted for several weeks with the dysentery.

17. The weather has been too unpleasant for me to venture to Vewa the three past days. Mr. Birch has

remained on board, and is rather better than when he first arrived. He is a bachelor, but, strange as it may appear, is social and agreeable; therefore I have set him down in my book as belonging to the class accidental, or those who remain single from necessity. The bachelor who is one from choice, is never at ease in the company of respectable women; indeed, he affects to believe there are none such. He avoids the company of those who are not betrothed, lest they should have some designs upon his affections, or fortune, or both. He avoids the company of the betrothed and the married, lest they should lead him into sin. Such is his vanity that he believes every lady looks upon him with interest, and would never be convinced to the contrary. If he should happen to attend a party (which he seldom does), one would observe, as he enters the room, that he casts a glance around to see if any lady is present who has no *beau* to attend her home. If he sees this to be the case, he pleads an excuse to the company, and departs an hour before the party breaks up, exulting that he "slipped out of that." On the contrary, the bachelor who is one from necessity, does not appear to believe that every lady he meets is in love with his person, or his fortune, and he fears not to converse with her, neither does he avoid and affect to despise her because she is a woman, but treats her as a woman should be treated—with respect.

18. The fat brother of the King of Bau died last night; the one whom Tanoa called the pig at the time of his restoration. Mr. W. has just returned from the capital, and says that most of the children were minus a finger joint. The men were throwing mud at the ladies, who, in return for the loving messages, were whipping the men in high glee.

Mr. Umbers, of Solavu, gives me the following account

of the late massacre at Ovalau:—"I was in a small schooner lying at anchor about two miles from the island of Ovalau, when we observed fires issuing from eight towns on the coast, and we saw the women and children running in every direction, pursued and killed by their enemies, the mountaineers. Many plunged into the sea, and, by diving, attempted to elude the spears of their adversaries; some reached the vessel, and were saved. The chief of Lavuka, called Tui Lavuka, was one of the victims. His daughter called to him to swim for the reef, which attracted the attention of the savages towards him, and they despatched him immediately. Five white men who were living at Lavuka had their houses burned; one of their wives was killed at the same time. The males belonging to the towns were most of them away, which fact was probably known to the enemy, who chose the favorable opportunity to make their descent and accomplish their designs. About four hundred were killed. One woman swam to our vessel with two children on her back; another came with a basket containing her riches, and had left her children to be destroyed. So sudden and expeditious were the enemy, that, in one hour from the time of the attack, all was quiet."

20. Mr. Birch died, and was buried yesterday. Strangers were brothers and sisters to him during his sickness, and strangers wept over his grave. He received able medical treatment from Rev. Dr. Lyth, while Rev. Mr. Hunt and family attended to his personal comfort, and all were faithful to that immortal part which can never die. Mr. Birch was a gentleman of education and talents, having been bred to the law.

CHAPTER XIV.

The National Dance—The Wedding—Death of the Princess—War with Nakelo—The Lunatic—Evil Spirits—The Alarm—Strangling of a Woman at Bau.

Dec. 24. Hearing that a national dance was to be performed this evening by Retova and a part of the Geer tribe, who have lately arrived at Bau from Mathuata, and being desirous of witnessing it, I repaired to Bau about noon, in company with Mr. J. Reese, an assistant printer in the employ of the mission at Vewa. We first called at the house of the king, and found all the household engaged in preparing for the nuptials of the king's daughter with Navinde, which was to take place on the following day. The bride elect was receiving presents from the people of her tribe, consisting of mats, native cloth, sweet scented oils, baskets, beads, paint, scissors, knives, and many other things which Feejeeans value. Several hundreds of mats and bales of cloth, testified to the lady's rank, and the liberality of her people.

We then called at the house of Tunitonga to see the princess, my little namesake, who, I had been informed, was sick. We found her very ill; indeed, she was probably dying. Her nurse desired me to present some vermillion to paint the little body after death. Two whales' teeth were placed at the feet of the child. When a child of rank dies, it is the custom to strangle one or more of its nurses to accompany it to the spirit land, as all Feejeeans have a great horror of dying alone. The spirits of the whales' teeth go with their spirits, while the teeth themselves are buried with the bodies in the grave. When the souls arrive at the spirit land, the nurse throws the teeth at a big dog, or some huge animal that may be standing in their way, because, if they had nothing to frighten him with, they could not pursue their journey.

From the house of the Tunitonga we went to that of Thakombau. We found him seated near his favorite, Samonunu. A Tonga chief was present, and several other visitors. We had an opportunity, during our stay, of observing the manner in which food is served in the houses of the chiefs. There appear to be cooks employed nearly all the time, as the Feejeeans have no set time for their meals. The chiefs do not eat together, and are always served separately. Two females placed before the party to be served, a wooden tray and some fresh green leaves. A small native pot was then brought, containing boiled fish, which were placed in the tray, and the water in which they were boiled was poured into a cocoa-nut shell, and handed to the chief, who drank it. Cooked tarro was placed on the leaves, and the damsels fanned the chief while he partook of his repast, at the close of which, the servants clapped their hands. The same ceremony was observed when he drank. Samonunu's meal was served in the same manner, and with the same ceremonies as that of the chief. All were served by different cooks, who invariably approached and retired on their knees. The food that was left by the superiors, was devoured by the servants and "*kaises.*" Some messengers arrived while we were there; these entered on their hands and knees, and pronounced the word of respect, "*Ndua whoa.*" After delivering their message, all clapped their hands. The chief answered them, and then all hands were clapped again.

Vatai sent for us to come to the house of Navinde, and we took leave of the royal couple. Samonunu expressed her regret that I did not reside at Bau instead of Vewa, and Thakombau asked if I wore gloves because I was afraid of getting cold in my hands.

On our arrival at the house of the Lasakau chief, we were offered some native puddings, of which I am very fond, and having observed the cleanliness of the natives in preparing their food, I did not hesitate to eat some. We then repaired to a little distance to see a native oven, where food was being prepared for the grand wedding which was to take place on Christmas day. The oven was about ten feet deep, and forty in circumference. Stones were placed in the bottom, on which fire was put, then wood and stones. After the wood was consumed, the stones were sufficiently heated, and pigs were then wrapped in green leaves and laid in the oven, then hot stones, then pigs again, then another layer of stones, and after a sufficient number of pigs, the oven is filled with tarro, yams, or whatever vegetables they may wish to cook, then leaves, hot stones and earth are placed on the top, where they remain until the food is cooked.

Navinde appeared very active and happy, said that he could not go to his house to see me, being so busy in superintending the preparations for the feast; but he had sent some puddings, and asked if I ate any of them. I told him that I did, and thought them very nice.

As it was now time for the dancing to commence, we repaired to the "*rara*." The square was surrounded with spectators, among whom, room was made for us. Soon we observed one of the dancers come from the inn, and squat like a monkey in the centre of the "*rara*." He was followed by one or two others, and they continued to assemble in this manner till they numbered about thirty; when they arose, the chanting commenced, and the dancers performed their evolutions for about fifteen minutes; when they all raced back to the hotel as though an army was pursuing them, and we saw them no more. All appeared disappointed. Mr. Reese said that he supposed a club dance was to be performed, which would be worth witnessing.

Retova appears rather afraid, as he does not exactly understand how he stands with the old king on account of the murder of Tui Mathuata. He has brought the Geer people with him instead of the Mathuata natives. The dancers had painted their faces in a variety of patterns, and wore white turbans on their heads, and white bands around their arms and just below the knees. The other part of their dress was worn as usual.

25. Mr. W. and myself started about nine o'clock, A. M., for Bau, being desirous of witnessing the ceremonies of a Feejeean wedding in high life. We went first to the house of the bride's father, where we saw the marriage portion and the bride. The latter looked quite modest and rather bashful. We remained here but a few moments, and then passed on to the new house that had been prepared for the bride. We found the happy bridegroom seated on the door sill, his face well besmeared with dirt, and his dress not remarkable for its cleanliness. He desired us to walk into the house, and be seated near his mother. We observed in front of the building a wall of roasted fish about ten fathoms in length and five feet in height. We did not see the vegetables, as they were in some other place with pigs and turtles. The floor of the house was spread with four or five layers of the best of Feejeean mats; these had been provided by the Lasakau tribe. In one corner of the house, a basket ten feet long, four wide and three deep, was suspended from the rafters, filled with green leaves, and on these were placed pigs and turtles.

The Lasakau matrons (no maidens are allowed to take

any part in the marriages) were seated in the centre of
the house, leaving a broad space unoccupied near the
door.   On the right hand of the principal entrance, the
mother of Navinde was seated with her "*popalagi*"
guests.   The Lasakau ladies all wore old "*lekus*," and
their persons were oiled with cocoa-nut oil, scented with
sandal-wood.   Each one, the mother excepted, wore a
garland of flowers thrown over one shoulder.   The garlands were made of sweet-scented flowers.   One was offered me, and I threw it over my neck, which seemed to
please the company exceedingly.   Navinde was ordering
the arrangement of the food, and when all was completed,
one old man said to the chief, "The food is now ready.
We hope that the god will be pleased with your marriage,
and that you will live long and happily with your young
wife."   The speech ended with clapping of hands.   The
bridegroom then took seven whales' teeth and sent them
by four old men to Tanoa, with a complimentary message,
and a request that the king would send his daughter to
the house where his people were waiting to receive her.
Navinde then departed, and was seen no more for the
day in that vicinity.

     After this, two old Lasakau men and one old Bau man
came in and seated themselves near the central door on
the left.   In a few moments the grand procession appeared, consisting of the bride and the married ladies of
her tribe.   Her mother was not present.   The procession
came singly, and moved very slowly.   About one hundred preceded the bride, and then the lady herself appeared.   She wore a band of "*bula-leka*" shells around
her head, and bracelets of the same on her arms; a necklace of small whales' teeth on her neck, and in her hands
she carried two large whales' teeth.   She was arrayed
in a new, handsome "*leku*," with a bale of marked na-

tive cloth attached to it, and a train of some forty yards
in length; the latter trailed on the ground, and the former was borne by two women. Oil was dripping from
her person. As she entered the house, she laid the two
large teeth at the feet of the old men, then turned and
seated herself by the mother of Navinde. The rest of
them now followed, and all were seated in the unoccupied
part of the house. The Bau ladies were dressed in
new, handsome " *lekus*," and wore flowers in their hair.
After all were seated, the old Bau messenger presented
whales' teeth to the Lasakau messengers, accompanied
with a long speech, enumerating the names and titles of
the king, his greatness and goodness, and love for Navinde, which he had now shown by the gift of his daugh--
ter, who was of high rank, being his daughter by the
queen, who was a woman of the highest rank in Somosomo. At the conclusion of the speech, the Bau ladies
clapped their hands. The Lasakaus then took the teeth,
and promised for their chief that the young Marama
should ever be treated kindly—that they hoped wars
would cease, in order that he might not be separated
from her—that the winds might be favorable—that she
might have a plenty of fish to eat, and that yams and all
their food might ever be plentiful in their lands, and
ended by complimenting the king upon his greatness and
goodness, and pronouncing him a god whom his enemies
could never kill. At the conclusion of this eloquent
speech the Lasakau ladies clapped their hands, and the
men departed. I inquired if the men were priests, and
was answered that they were not, and that the priests
had nothing to do with marriages.

After the departure of the men, the bridegroom's mother and two other aged matrons proceeded to divest the
bride of her ornaments. The oil was wiped from her per-

16

son, her handsome " *leku* " was exchanged for an old one, and taken, with all the other ornaments, by the mother-in-law of the bride. The Lasakau ladies had been chanting continually, from the time of their assembling till the present, only stopping while the old men made their speeches. The Bau tribe now commenced, and chanted for the space of an hour or more, when they concluded their music. The Lasakau ladies now proceeded to exchange their " *lekus* " with the Bau ladies, and began to chat and frolic as though the minister had departed. The garlands were also presented to the Bau party.

After some little time, quiet was again restored, and the singing recommenced. We inquired if the ceremonies were ended, and were informed that the parties would remain and sing a little longer, and then retire.

The Bau party were to take with them all the mats from the house, and bring the bride's portion in return. Tanoa had given his daughter ten servants, and Navinde had provided five to commence house-keeping with.

Samonunu now came to chat with us, and from her we learned that the bridegroom would not visit at the house of the bride till the next day, or perhaps for a week, or a month. The feast is prepared for the Bau tribe alone, and is divided into portions according to the rank of the family, and sent to them. When the marriage is fully consummated, the Bau people are again feasted, and some of the elderly ladies of the tribe proceed to the house of the young married lady, and cut off the woolly tresses from her head; these had hitherto remained uncut from childhood.

We now prepared to depart, when the mother of the chief desired us to go to a house belonging to him, where another of his wives resided (he had four), and partake of some refreshments, observing that she had some of my favorite puddings in store for me. We complied with her request, and then departed.

On our arrival at the boat, we found a baked pig in it, as a present from the bridegroom, weighing about one hundred pounds.

29. The Charles Wirgman, Capt. Waldron, arrived from America, by whom we received some newspapers and letters from home. We learn from Capt. W. that the Charles Wirgman visited the island of Manicola on the passage from Feejee to Manilla. The natives visited the brig in great numbers. Capt. Osborne used every precaution to prevent surprise, but the natives made an attempt to take the vessel. They did not succeed, however, being repulsed with considerable loss of life, and the destruction of many of their canoes. Their shyness when we called to see them, was probably owing to this circumstance.

Thakombau has sent to the bark seven whales' teeth, a root of yanggona, and a piece of native cloth. The teeth, yanggona and cloth are to be presented to the Natawa people, with orders from the royal city to that people to fish for Mr. W. Two young men of high rank were also sent to accompany Mr. W. to Natawa to collect "beech de mer."

My namesake, the little daughter of Thakombau and Samonunu, died on the Sabbath. My informant inquired if it was good or bad for her to die on that day. No one of her nurses was strangled with her—another glimmer of civilization! Had a princess of her rank died two years ago, as many as two of her nurses would have been murdered to accompany her to the land of souls.

Jan. 1, 1847. Mr. W. having sailed for Natawa, I once more take up my residence in my straw house.

5. A boat called the Blackbird was robbed a few days

since by the natives of Sau Kasa. The boat was stripped of its sails, and every thing belonging to it.

12. The Mathuata chief and his people have left Vewa to-day, for their homes.

Retova has heard that his enemies have burned his town since his absence, and that several places, such as Tavea, Naloa and some others, have joined his enemies; therefore he was afraid to return, as he would be obliged to pass Tavea and Naloa, and Elijah has gone with them for protection.

14. Mrs. Hunt came to my room, followed by six strange natives armed with clubs. She held in her hand a broad leaf that was tied like a native pudding. "Would you like a pudding?" she asked. Having something of a headache, I told her I did not dare to eat it. "I will open the leaf," she said, "you may be tempted." The leaf was untied, and found to contain letters from my husband. The six men who were now my visitors had brought them from Motureke. Having conferred so great an obligation upon me, they appeared to feel that they had earned the privilege of remaining a long time in my house. As two hours would expire before I should be summoned to dinner, I began to contrive to get rid of them. Three of the number asked me if it would be good for them to go and bathe. I told them it was good for them all to bathe. They said they would leave their clubs with their companions, and return again very soon. The other three seemed determined to remain. After the departure of their companions, they said that they were sick for the want of sleep, and asked me if they should lie down upon the floor and sleep. I told them that I was about to visit Mrs. Lyth, and they must wait till my return. They said, "Yes, it is very good; we will go to Mr. Hunt's, and wait, and leave our

clubs at your house." "No," I said. "It is good for
you to take all your clubs outside of the door." This
being done, I went, and remained so long that my visitors were obliged to look for another place of rest.

Mr. Hunt having procured some of the materials from
the two whaling vessels that were destroyed at Ovalau,
the white residents of Solavu, who have received many
kind acts from the mission, offered to raise and board a
house for him at Vewa. They have now completed their
work, having raised and boarded a large building, which,
when finished, will be the most comfortable dwelling in
Feejee. It is situated on a lofty hill, fronting the sea,
and commands a fine prospect of the surrounding bays
and islands.

17. A meeting was held at Bau yesterday, for the
purpose of formally declaring war with Rewa. Messengers were sent to the towns in this vicinity, and the drums
have not ceased to beat during the past night.

21. A party of warriors have gone to attack Nakelo,
whose chief appears to have recommenced hostilities between the two kingdoms or states, on account of the
daughter of Tanoa, who has been given to Navinde.

Feb. 2. The warriors have returned to Bau, having
destroyed Nakelo by fire. We do not learn that any
lives were lost, the inhabitants of the town having fled.
Elijah has returned from Mathuata, accompanied by two
hundred of the Naikoratumba people, who have come to
a " *solavu vaka masi.*"

5. Accompanied by Dr. and Mrs. Lyth, we ascended
the elevation back of the mission premises, to the " *rara,*"
to witness the presentation of the masi brought by the
Naikorotumba people to the chief of Vewa. We found
the Vewa people seated on one side of the "*rara.*" A
company of about one hundred and fifty of the visitors

entered the "*rara*" in single file, each carrying a club
or musket; one carried a large palm-leaf fan. These
had "*masi*" wound around their persons, and laid in
large folds falling from their shoulders. They passed
through the "*rara*," and entered a narrow defile at the
opposite end. Then followed fifty men, so enveloped in
folds of "*masi*" that nothing could be seen but their
faces; they stood on one side of the "*rara*," near the
Vewa people. The natives who had passed into the defile, now came dancing forth to the centre of the "*rara*."
One appeared to be the master of ceremonies, giving directions in a loud voice for the different evolutions which
they performed. Some of their movements were graceful, some ridiculous, but none which the most chaste
might not witness. Every part of the body appeared to
be exercised more than the feet. The figure of the dance
was difficult and pretty. Could the Polka dancers of
civilized lands witness this, they might learn modesty,
at least. After the dance was concluded, the "*masi*"
was left on the "*rara*," and the visitors all retired to the
"*buri*."

6. To-day a feast was spread on the "*rara*" for the
Vewa visitors. It consisted of bread-fruit, bananas,
mandrai, yanggona, and twelve baked pigs. All these
were placed in large piles; eight or ten bushels in a pile.
The men of Vewa with their chiefs were on one side of
the "*rara*," and their visitors on the other. Several
speeches were made, and answered by the spokesman
(as they are here called) of each tribe. After all the
formalities and ceremonies were over, the food was taken
away by the visitors.

8. Last night several of the Naikoratumba people di-
verted themselves by tormenting one of their company
who was partially deranged. They tied his hands behind

him, knocked him about, made him walk over hot coals, and allowed him no rest at night. In the morning he eluded the vigilance of his tormentors, and leaped from a precipice ninety-three feet in height. He was found on the beach below, still alive. Some of his tribe proposed that the sufferer should be clubbed at once; but others said, "If we club him we shall offend the chiefs of Vewa, who are 'lotu;' we had better hasten while it is yet early, and bury him, and we will say that he killed himself by the fall." While they were tying him up in a mat, two men were employed in digging a hole to serve for a grave, that the man might be buried before any of the Christians should become acquainted with the affair, and prevent them from showing their love to their suffering brother. They were prevented, however, by a Christian, named Noah, who was passing near the spot, and inquired what they were doing. They told him they were about to bury a dead man. He disbelieved their statement, and ran to tell Dr. Lyth that he believed the man was alive. The Dr. hastened to the spot, and commanded the men to untie the mat. As they did so, the sufferer raised his hand, and waved it as if for air. He was immediately taken to the "buri," where Dr. Lyth afforded such medical aid as the case required, and Noah was appointed his nurse. In a short time his senses were restored, and two days after, he was able to sit up, and appeared only to have injured his head on one side.

16. At breakfast this morning Mr. Hunt gave some account of the conversion of the principal priest of Nandy. He renounced heathenism in consequence of becoming angry with the gods of the lands because they did not cure him when he was sick. It is not uncommon for Feejeeans to get angry with their gods. Sometimes when they continue sick a long time, or meet with any

other troubles, they will take their clubs and dare them
to come and fight, using the most provoking language to
their godships that is to be found in their vocabulary.
In this case the priest had been ill a long time, and had
presented many offerings to his gods for the restoration
of his health, but all to no purpose; the gods seemed to
have other business to transact. A Tonga Christian
was residing at the place, and advised him to try English medicine. He consented, took medicines prepared
by Mr. Hunt, and recovered. On his recovery he said,
"I will serve the gods of Feejee no longer. I am very
angry with them. I will now serve the "*popalagi's*
God." Accordingly he sought instruction in the Christian religion, and appears to have become a good man.
He states that for some time after he had renounced
heathenism, his shaking, or convulsion fits would come
on involuntarily, and just as they did when he believed
that he held communication with the gods. This alarmed him much, and he inquired of the teacher what he
should do when thus attacked. The teacher told him
that he must pray heartily to God, and the wicked spirit
would depart. He says that he prays now a great deal,
and is not troubled.

12. Intelligence has just been received of the murder
of two white men belonging to Solavu. They stopped at
a town on Vetelavu, about two miles from Vewa, to buy
some fowls. Some trifling dispute arose about the price,
when the natives murdered them. Namosi and some of
his people will visit the place on their return from
Ovalau.

Thakombau has become angry with one of his brothers, and banished him from Bau for the present, ordering him to go to a town on Vetelavu. This he has not
done, but has come to Vewa instead. Elijah came to

ask the advice of Mr. Hunt about allowing him to remain here. He thinks, as he was justly banished, that it would be wrong to harbor him in V. Mr. H. was of the same opinion, and the prince has received orders to proceed.

15. Last night a female servant belonging to Rev. Mr. Jaggar's family was severely attacked with tetanus, accompanied with delirium. This disease is not uncommon in these lands, and usually proves fatal. Natives are often wounded in the feet, which being unprotected, they often take cold in the wound, and tetanus follows, then death. The disease is often accompanied with a partial delirium. When a young, good-looking woman is taken with it, it is said that some god wants her for a wife, and nothing is done for her relief, as they would not excite the anger of the god by trying to detain her. If an ordinary, poor girl is afflicted, the god wishes to obtain her for a servant, and she, too, is left to die. In this case, the servants awoke Mr. J. in the night, and told him that a god had taken possession of Atta. Mr. J. supposing that the girl had been troubled by a dream, answered that they must tell her to go to sleep. In the morning Dr. Lyth and Mr. Hunt were informed of her case. They found her speechless, and her whole body dreadfully convulsed. She was immediately steamed, according to the directions given in a medical work, by Dr. Beech, of America. This process soon relaxed her nerves; her jaws became unfastened, and the violence of the spasms abated. This is the second case of tetanus that has been relieved by steaming during the past week. The first was that of a woman belonging to Namosimalua. When Dr. Lyth entered the house, he found several Christians surrounding the patient, and praying to God that the evil spirit might depart from the woman,

who was shaking and foaming as the priests do, when they pretend that they are inspired. The doctor and Mr. Hunt soon had a tub of hot water ready, and commenced steaming, and the patient, who had been speechless for an hour, soon cried out, "Oh! I am cooked,—I am cooked." She is now recovering.

The native Christians believe that people are possessed by evil spirits (and in this belief they are fully borne out by the Bible, both the Old and New Testament testifying to the same). They believe that some of the priests are really possessed by the devil, at times, while others are thought to be hypocrites. They think that the gods whom they formerly served were evil spirits, and that they are wandering about now, seeking whom they may destroy; but not possessing sufficient knowledge to distinguish a disease of the body, and supposing that a person who is deranged in intellect is possessed by some evil spirit, and reading in the Scriptures that "This kind goeth not out but by fasting and prayer," they commence praying, without making use of any remedies.

16.   During our walk in the afternoon, we met Capt. Bowles, who commands a schooner from Tahiti. He was feeling very indignant against Thakombau. He had just been to inquire when his oil, that he had engaged and paid for, would be ready. The chief told him that it would not be ready for a long time, if ever, and that the Consul had offered him a higher price for the oil, and perhaps he should let him have it. Capt. B. replied that he had received remuneration for the cargo, and that he had no right to dispose of what did not belong to him. Thakombau then said, "Why did you come here? I did not send for you; however, white men make good eating,—they are like a ripe banana." He then ordered

Capt. B. and Mr. J., who was with him, to leave his house.

A party of Bauans have returned from a battle with Rewa, having lost twenty of their number. When they approached Rewa, every thing was so silent that the invaders, supposing the town vacated, approached quite near, when they were suddenly fired upon, and twenty were killed.

20. Received letters from Mr. W. The following is an extract:—

"I sent a boy some days since to Fawn's Harbor in company with a native, with orders for a house to be built, as my schooner was to go there and fish. The place belongs to Somosomo, and its chief went on to see that every thing was in readiness for the business to commence on the arrival of the schooner. On the arrival of the chief, yanggona was prepared, as is their custom on receiving so illustrious a visitor. After the yanggona had been prepared and drank, the chief said that an oven must be prepared and a pig killed. The boy, understanding the language imperfectly, thought that the oven was being prepared to cook himself in, and feeling no disposition to be cooked just at that time, took to the bush. After travelling two days he reached the bark, having eaten nothing since his flight. He stated that the chief had given orders for him to be baked, and he had no doubt but that the schooner would be taken, and all hands murdered.

In a few days after the arrival of the boy, I received a letter from the captain of the schooner, saying that in consequence of the disappearance of the boy Nat, no one knew whether the natives were afraid that the hostage, who is a son of the chief, would be punished or killed, and nothing could be done in the way of business till the fate of Nat was ascertained.

I sent on a messenger immediately, stating that the boy was safe; on the reception of which, the natives commenced fishing."

21. Sabbath. Ratu Luke, a chief who was banished from Bau a short time since, on account of his dislike to heathenism, was married in the chapel at the close of the forenoon services. He had been advised to marry the widow of the late Lasakau chief; but he said that she was of too high a rank for him, and that he should be happier with one of meaner birth. The bride and bridegroom were arrayed in native cloth, which was wound around their bodies to the size of a hogshead. Their costume was any thing but becoming.

23. As Mrs. Hunt and myself were returning from our evening walk, we perceived the old nurse of Vatai seated upon a slight elevation, with her head bending towards her knees. As we approached, we observed that her hair had been nicely oiled, combed, and parted in front, and she had placed herself in that position that we might not fail to see her. She asked us if we would be angry if she wore her hair in that fashion,—if it was becoming for an old woman like her to wear it so,—if the grandmothers in our country wore their hair in that way, or if young people only dressed their hair so. After we had answered all her questions, she asked us if we would give her a comb to keep her hair nice. After this was settled, she kissed our feet, (she had knelt during the conversation,) and we passed on.

Vatai has been married to Namosi, who has dismissed his other wives. During his alarm, when he was expecting daily to be murdered by the chiefs of Bau, he took to praying with all his might, dismissed his concubines, was married, and baptized by the name of Melchisedek. Vatai has been baptized by the name of Lydia.

One or more of the nurses of the women of rank often live with them through all their changes in life, and are buried with them. They are treated kindly, and appear to feel more affection for their charge than the mother.

24. Our schooner arrived from Somosomo and vicinity. Capt. Smith states that a Natawan was killed and brought to Somosomo while he was there. The body was brought in a canoe, and on its arrival strings were attached to its wrists, and it was dragged from the shore, through the dirt, to the house of the chief. The joy of the chief, on seeing the body, was most extravagant, although it presented a most disgusting spectacle, having been killed three days, and being much swollen. The chief gave orders to have the " *lovo* " heated at once.

This morning a messenger came from Navinde, desiring Dr. Lyth to come to Bau immediately, and attend to the Marama-lavu, who is dangerously sick. So great was the anxiety of the chief on her account, that he immediately followed the messenger, and earnestly desired the doctor to cure her, stating that he had presented large offerings to his god, but he supposed that he was angry because she was given to him when she had been promised to the chief of Nakelo. On their passage to Bau, Dr. L. took the opportunity of preaching on the folly of serving false gods. The lady was found to be feverish, but was not considered dangerous by the doctor.

26. Rev. Mr. Hunt returned from Nukulau, where he went to receive letters which had come by the " Auckland." By him I received a large packet of letters, which had been in the charge of J. Chamberlain for some two years past. I feel very much indebted to Mr. Hunt for his kind perseverance in obtaining our let-

ters, which had been so unkindly detained from us for so long a period.

27. We learn that a woman was strangled in Bau yesterday. Her husband had been killed at Rewa. The king sent word that she must live, and take care of her infant child. She declared, however, that she would die and rejoin her husband, for great was her love to him.

March 4. The Lasakau people have returned from a battle with one of the Nakelo towns. They burned the town and killed nineteen of its inhabitants. One of the bodies of the slain was brought to Vewa last night. Whether it was sent as an insult to the Christians, or for a feast to the heathen, is not known. There are about ten families at Vewa that still adhere to heathenism, the men assisting in the wars, &c. The Christians will not allow them to cook and eat the body, and it is to be sent to another place. The schooner Sir John Franklin has been so unfortunate as to strike on one of the numerous reefs in this vicinity, and it is feared that she will be much injured.

6. The schooner Sir John Franklin has escaped injury, and sailed for her destination.

10. The American bark, Pilot, Capt. Hartwell, arrived from Salem, Mass. She belongs to S. Chamberlain & Co., and we expected to receive letters from our friends at home. They supposed, however, that we should leave Feejee before the arrival of the Pilot, and did not write. I find that most people had rather receive letters than write them.

11. The bark Zotoff arrived, having gathered all the " beech de mer " from the reefs of Natawa. The bark sailed to the head of Natawa Bay. The captain states that the bay extends to the distance of 45 miles. It is

fifteen miles in width, and no anchorage is to be found, except at the head of the bay.

14. While the Zotoff lays at Vewa, preaching is held on board on the Sabbath. The missionaries preach alternately. To-day none of our crew attended the services, several being angry on account of being denied visiting Bau and spending the last night.

15. Thakombau visited the missionaries, and said that he had received information from Tahiti, that France was intending to send missionaries to Feejee, and that priests were to be landed on the islands whether the natives were willing to receive them or not. He said that he was not willing to receive them, because by and by they would take possession of the lands of Feejee, as they had done at Tahiti,—that he was quite satisfied with the English "*lotu,*" which he intended to embrace by and by, and that he wished to have nothing to do with France or her religion,—if missionaries came they might starve to death, as he was determined to allow them no food.

He called at my room, said that I was a "*Marama venaka,*" took my large arm chair, and placing it before the looking-glass, sat and viewed himself as long as he chose, and then departed.

16. Considerable excitement seems to prevail at Bau regarding the French. The king has sent to Vewa and commanded English flags to be displayed, in case a French vessel should appear, at Vewa, Bau, and on as many of the other islands as flags can be procured, to be shown.

17. Vewa was honored with a visit from the old king. The Kamba people are engaged in thatching the roof of the new mission house, and the king came, as he said, to tell them to do their work faithfully. The king and

his son appear to improve every opportunity, of late, to show kindness to the mission.

21. Notwithstanding it is said that a " *buri* " is ready to be consecrated with the body of Mr. W., or some of his people, in consequence of the affair with the Salem vessel in 1836, before mentioned, we are now about to visit that place, and shall no doubt become acquainted with the brother of the murdered chief. Some of the white residents appear to think that every possible effort will be made at Ba to take the bark and bake the captain.

———

CHAPTER XV.

Departure for Ba—The Soul Destroyer—The Attack—Account of One Buried Alive.

March 27. All necessary arrangements being completed for our voyage to Ba, we once more took leave of our kind friends at Vewa, and set sail for Motureke. Elijah accompanies us, with several of his people, who are to serve as trading men on shore, that the lives of our people may not be endangered on the barbarous coast to which we are bound. A young chief of Ba, who has been visiting at Vewa of late, also accompanies us with several attendants.

Namosimalua has " *tambued* " the coast for the bark C. to fish at; but Thakombau has sent a large quantity of yanggona by Elijah, and orders for the " *tambu* " to be removed, and for the natives to fish for the Zotoff. Mr. W. has been told that Bau has no influence on the lands to which we go,—that Namosi is acknowledged as their head chief as far as Raverave, and beyond that the chiefs are all independent.

29. We arrived at Naikarotumba. This town is under the dominion of Namosimalua. They have chiefs of their own, but he is their king. Several of this tribe have renounced heathenism, and are supplied with Tonga teachers.

31. We anchored at Raverave. This place is famous as being the residence of the great god, Dengai. The mountains a little back from the shore are called the Kauvandra. It is said that the god inhabits a cave in the side of the mountain.

The following legend of this place has been kindly furnished me by Rev. Mr. Hunt, as it was told him by a native.

An Account of Ravugalo, or the " Soul-Destroyer."

" We do not know the origin of this god, whether he is the son of Dengai or not ; we know, however, that the god of the Kauvandra appointed him to kill souls. He resides at a place called Nembanggatai, where the spirits of men go when they enter the separate state at Kauvandra. The town is inhabited, and a parrot is stationed there, who calls out when a spirit enters it. If one soul comes, it calls once; if two, twice, and so on. The god and his children hear the calls of the parrot, and hasten to prepare their clubs to kill the spirits as they pass their dwelling. They do not succeed, however, in killing all who are passing this dangerous spot; many are strong, and pass safely on to the Kauvandra, while others are killed and eaten by the god and his sons, and are never seen again in this world or any other. Some of my people have heard the noise of the

17

god, as he knocks out the brains of his ghostly victims.

Ravagalo is now dead, and the business is carried on by his sons. A short time since, as he was holding his club, ready to attack a poor soul that was passing, and carelessly sitting on a stump of brushwood, which had been left with a sharp point out of the ground, it penetrated his body and caused his death.

He said to his children, 'I am dead. Take me to the ' buri.' My sons, look well to the souls to be eaten.' A man who is employed as a messenger between the Kauvandra and this world, brought the news of his death here.

The spirits who are so fortunate as to pass safely through the town of the 'Soul-Destroyer,' go to the Kauvandra on the top of the mountain. Many ladies reside there, who often ascend to the highest points of the land to witness the wars of Feejee. On the arrival of the spirits at the Kauvandra, they proceed to a steep precipice, called Naindelinde. On the margin of this precipice two persons sit, father and son, who have been appointed to interrogate the new comers. ' From whence have you come?' they ask. ' From the earth,' is the reply. 'What have you been doing there?' The spirit then recounts his deeds which he performed while in the body on the earth. After he concludes his history, he is invited to take a seat on the broad end of a large steer oar, (which is placed directly over the precipice,) to take the air. From this the soul is suddenly plunged into ' bulu.' Some say that only the bad spirits are sent to ' bulu,' and that the good ones remain at the Kauvandra with Dengai. Others assert that the spirits who have visited ' bulu,' visit this world and the Kauvandra at their pleasure."

I have heard some accounts of punishments that are awarded to the souls of the wicked, but they are scarcely fit to record. One can never get a true idea of heathenism from books, as many of its most revolting characteristics cannot be penned.

April 1. Anchored at Ba and were visited by Touaga, the brother of the murdered chief. He appears friendly, and has promised to employ his people to collect "beech de mer" for the vessel. Some red paint was presented to him with a black silk head dress, and a native comb ornamented with beads. He painted his face red, fixed his head dress on his head, placed his comb in his hair, then seated himself upon the table opposite the looking-glass, and seemed to think that he looked "plenty well enough."

He had never seen a white woman before, and I obtained a share of his attention. After gazing at me intently for some time, he exclaimed, " Sa tha ni lewa ni vete, Venaka ni lewa ni papalagi." "The Feejeean women are bad; white women are good."

There are two chiefs of equal rank at Ba. Vakambua is the name of the other. He seldom visits any vessels that come here. I believe they are not related, and are often at enmity with each other. It is said that when Touaga's brother was killed, he was laying a plan for the murder of Vakambua.

16. We are still at Ba, and have several houses under way for " beech de mer." Touaga often visits us, and, as yet, says nothing about eating us. We think the " buri " must be at the Kauvandra, as we hear nothing about it at this place.

As I have presented Touaga with several articles which he appeared to value highly, he seemed to wish to make me some return, and one day inquired if there was any thing on shore that he should bring me. I told him if he had any "*karwais*," I should like some. He said there was an abundance on the land, and some should be brought. A small quantity was brought the next day. He made a great parade in presenting them. I pronounced them very good, and supposed the affair settled; when, to our surprise, before he left the vessel he asked Mr. W. what he would give him for the vegetables that he had brought for me. He was asked what he wanted. "Beads," he replied; which were given him. This, however, is the only case of the kind. I have witnessed no such meanness from any other chief of Feejee.

The females of this coast are not employed in collecting the "*beech de mer*," consequently, they do not visit the vessels. I have seen but few.

Elijah preaches the gospel wherever he goes, and does not suffer any opportunity to escape without recommending it to his countrymen.

We find that the name of Bau carries an influence with it wherever we go. The manners of the chiefs and people on this coast compare with those of Bau and vicinity, as the manners of our most remote little country villages would with those of the most fashionable cities. The chiefs appear to be treated with but little ceremony, and have but little authority.

29. A boat belonging to some of the white residents of Feejee came alongside of our vessel. From its master we learn the following item of news:—A cutter belonging to the Consul had been sent to a place called Mbaga, for the purpose of obtaining provisions. Three men were on board, and the cutter was anchored near the shore, that is, so near that the natives could swim to it with ease. Six natives went on board, and the men,

feeling no suspicion of evil, were completely off their guard. One was carelessly seated on the deck, another was leaning on the main boom, while the third was stooping to arrange some matters in the cuddy. One native threw the man that was seated on the deck overboard, another sprung to clasp the man at the boom, but clasped the boom, which gave the man a chance to escape; a third native attacked the other man, but he, having the advantage of his situation, being partly in the cuddy, slipped from him, and snatching a loaded pistol, discharged its contents into the arm of one of the assailants, when they all jumped into the water, and swam to the shore.

May 1. Our steward and one of the sailors have been sick for several days; the steward with the dysentery, and the sailor with inflammation of the lungs.

Last evening Touaga came alongside in a canoe well filled with natives. They wished to come on board and sleep, but were refused. Perhaps it might have been safe for them to have come on board; but Mr. W. knew that our safety was more certain for them to be ashore.

Elijah has gone to Raverave.

3. The steward complained to-day of being in great pain. I inquired if he had eaten any thing except what I had sent to him from the cabin. He replied that he had not; but I learned afterwards that he had eaten two small fish, remarking, as he did so, that he could not live on rice, bread and gruel.

George, the sailor, appears to be worse. A blister was applied to the chest, as he complained of difficulty in breathing. He wore it an hour, and then threw it overboard, saying that it did him no good.

4. We are now sailing towards Namula. It is nearly calm, and our progress is very slow. As we pass

along the coast of this part of Vetelavu, the broken hills
gradually slope to the water's edge, where the mangroves seem to form a barrier. Their defiles are filled
with trees and shrubs of dark foliage, which, contrasting
with the lighter verdure of the hills, make the whole
appear increasingly beautiful. In the back ground are
seen the lofty mountains of the interior, with their rugged and irregular peaks towering above the whole, and
imparting a majestic as well as beautiful appearance to
the scenery.

Mr. W. was called at four o'clock this morning to
George, whom they thought to be dying. He was
placed in a warm bath, and other remedies being applied, he was relieved. He suffers much; not being
able to lie down at all. His sickness has been occasioned by sleeping on deck. Mr. W. had often spoken to
him and the steward about it, but they chose to have
their own way, and are now suffering the consequences
of rejecting good advice.

6. Namula. Mr. W. is busy, having a number of
" beech de mer " houses in this vicinity. There are several towns about here, but none of them are visible.
There are some half dozen petty chiefs, but none of
much rank. They go out themselves to collect " beech
de mer " the same as the " kaises."

8. The Perseverance arrived from Vatea with fish,
discharged, and sailed again the same day. The captain brought no news.

The steward and George are no better. Having tried
many remedies for the cure of the steward, and all seeming to fail, salt and vinegar were recommended, but not
liking the taste of it, he threw it away, and expressed a
desire to drink lime water, which one of the crew had
recommended; he said this was too strong, and after

drinking it once, gave it up. Mr. W. or myself now give him his medicines instead of sending them to him.

9. As the crew were raising the anchor, preparatory to our return to Ba, George came upon deck. His face was purple, and he was speechless. Mr. W. ordered them to let go the anchor, and many remedies were tried for the relief of the sufferer; at length he was relieved by bleeding. He was in a fit for the space of two hours. In the evening he desired Mr. W. to write his will for him, which was done. He is very irritable and impatient, cursing and swearing because the Almighty does not cure him, or take his life. His real name is Bernardo H. Bloom. He is a German by birth.

10. We returned to Ba. An awning has been spread on the deck, and the sick sailor remained there during the day. I asked him to-day if he felt prepared to die, knowing that he had given up all hope of life. He said he supposed he was. I asked him if he read his Bible. He replied that he did. I told him if he did, he knew what constituted a Christian character, and asked him if he believed that he was a Bible Christian, and if he was conscious of loving and serving God. His reply was in the affirmative, and he added, "I never sinned much. God is merciful. He will not send me to hell for the few sins that I have committed." "I know nothing of your life," I replied, "except that since you have been on board this vessel you have been exceedingly profane; and even since your sickness, you have uttered oaths enough to sink your soul in everlasting misery." "Oh, I can repent of that easy enough," was his reply. I conversed with him some time longer, but his mind appeared so completely blinded, that he could not be convinced he was a sinner, or needed the pardoning grace of God. Some of the sailors were present, and he

would look at them with a scornful smile, seeming to say, " You will not frighten this fellow."

One of the boys on board, named George ——, is sick with the dysentery. He has been subject to slight attacks of this prevalent disease, but they have generally yielded to medical treatment and careful nursing. Being somewhat frightened when he is unwell, he is unlike the old sailors, and is willing to take proper medicines and food, and thus subdue the disease before it becomes dangerous.

11. Elijah has returned from Raverave, and we are disappointed to learn that Rev. Mr. Hunt, whom we have been expecting would visit this part of the coast, has returned to Vewa. We hoped to receive his advice for our sick ones, as we have studied our medical books through, and exhausted all our knowledge to no purpose. The steward has been taken into the house on deck, where he can be attended by Mr. W. and myself. He is a most valuable man as a steward, and his services have added very much to the comforts of our voyage. We received letters by Elijah from our friends,—the missionaries at Vewa.

14. We anchored off the dominions of Vakambua, Mr. W. having a house at this place for fishing. There is a little schooner anchored here called the Venus, employed by Capt. Osborne, who arrived at the islands a short time since in the brig Tim Pickering, of Salem, Mass.; but the vessel, striking on a reef soon after its arrival, has gone to Sydney for repairs.

15. We received a visit last evening from the supercargo of the Venus, who stated that he had come to get houses built on this coast for " *beech de mer*," and that he was surprised to find that Capt. W. had taken possession of the whole coast. He proposed that this house

should be given up to him, as he must get a hold somewhere, and if this one was not left to him, he should go
down the coast and see what he could do. He wished
to get along peacefully, if possible, but he must have
houses here on some terms. Mr. W. replied that the
opposite coasts were far more extensive, and he thought
he might find room there; however, he had no objection
to giving up the house to him.

16. Elijah and the supercargo visited Vakambua, to
arrange matters relative to giving the house into other
hands. Vakambua said that he would not do it,—that
he was the friend of Elijah, who had given him yanggona to fish for the bark; moreover, the supercargo had
sent to try to buy the house,—that he was a bad man,
and might go away from his lands. The supercargo
hearing this became angry and insulting to Elijah, when
Vakambua gave orders that said supercargo should be
clubbed. Elijah said, "No; let no harm come to him."
After a long conversation, an agreement was made
that another house should be built for the supercargo.
Vakambua said aside to Elijah, " Red fish shall go to
his house, and black to the bark's."

18. Our sick sailor had another distressing fit last
night. Touaga, the chief, inquired if he might not take
him on shore and bury him. Mr. W. told him that he
was still alive, and "*papalagis*" did not bury their people alive. "Oh, but he is dead," he replied; "he has
no spirit in him, and why should you keep him here?
he is a great deal of trouble, and Marama is all the time
preparing food and medicines for the sick that are on
board; she will not have so much to do if this man is
laid in the ground." Mr. W. told the *humane* chief that
the man could not be buried till life had departed, and
that a man lived as long as he breathed.

Elijah said that when he was a heathen, he had many people buried alive. At one time a young woman belonging to his establishment was sick, or rather weak for a long time. He thought she would never recover, and had a grave dug. She was then called out of the house to see some strange monster that had appeared on the waters. When she came out of the house, she was seized and thrown into the grave. She shrieked and cried out, "Do not bury me,—I am well now." Her cries were of no avail. Two men stood upon her body and held her down, while others threw on the earth, and thus she was buried.

22. The boy George has recovered, and the steward is better. Bernardo is very low. I have conversed with him several times upon the importance of repentance, but he still continues to curse God for his afflictions.

We have removed from the dominions of Vakambua to those of Touaga.

A small boat belonging to Solavu has been here, and we learn that Rewa appears to be gaining strength, and Garenggeo exhibits a good deal of warlike ability and courage, while Phillips, being almost constantly supplied with rum, is growing daily more imbecile.

There appears to be some misunderstanding between Touaga and Vakambua. The latter sent to a town belonging to the former for some pigs, which were refused. Vakambua then sent a whale's tooth to a mountain tribe for them to burn the town of the offenders, and kill as many of its inhabitants as possible. Touaga, being made acquainted with the affair, hastened to the aid of his people. A battle was fought, and Touaga lost nine of his warriors, that were taken to Vakambua, who kept as many as he wished for his own use, and sent the rest as presents to his allies.

25. Touaga and the mountaineers are still fighting. We have seen the smoke and flames arise from four different places, and we suppose that towns are burned there.

Our steward is much worse again.

26. Natives have been to the vessel to-day, but different stories are told by them about the difficulties on shore, therefore I do not think it best to record them, except to say that four empty towns were destroyed by the enemy.

28. Touaga has been off, and says that the war is ended; that he has "*soroed*" to Vakambua because he did not wish the fishing to be interrupted; but by and by Vakambua should "*soro*" to him.

When we left Natemba, Mr. W. took away the "*beech de mer*" pot, as Vakambua's people did not get fish enough to pay the way. They sent word to the chief that the pot was wanted at another place, but sometime hence the schooner should be sent there, when they could re-commence fishing. To-day a Vewa man has arrived from Vendoga, where the pot was sent, and says that Vakambua has sent word that all the Vewa men must go on board the bark, as he shall send an armed force to take the "*beech de mer*" pot, and carry it back to Natemba. Elijah has returned to Vewa, but his brother, Korondvarasa is here, and says that he will go and make all straight with Vakambua, who, in reality, does not care to fish for any one, although he likes to have a trade house in his vicinity, so that if he or his people should be in want of any article, they can fish enough to get it; having received large presents, too, from Elijah, he is ashamed not to appear to do something.

29. Ezekiel, a son of Namosimalua, who is at one of our trade houses, has been wounded by the bursting of a

musket. Mr. W. has sent for him to be brought to the vessel.

June 4. Korondvarasa has returned from Natemba, having made arrangements for the schooner to go there, as the people are done fishing where the schooner has been laying the last few weeks.

Ezekiel has arrived, being much burned and badly wounded. His father also arrived in the morning, bringing us letters from Vewa.

The steward complained in the morning of the heat, and wished to have an awning spread on the quarter-deck, which being done, he was removed, and said he felt much cooler. He disposed of his effects, said he had but a few hours to live, thanked us many times for our care of him during his sickness, and expressed a hope that his sins were pardoned. About seven o'clock, as Mr. W. and myself were standing by him, he died.

5. This morning a coffin was prepared for all that remained of our faithful steward. The body was put into it, and it was placed near the gangway, the national flag was raised half mast, and all stood with heads uncovered while prayers and the burial service were read from the English prayer book. The coffin was then lowered into a canoe and taken to the shore, where it was buried near the trade house. Namosimalua went in the canoe, and prayed at the grave. The name of the steward was Thomas Williams, of Baltimore. During his sickness he was always patient and grateful. He prayed a great deal, and appeared to have a good hope in Christ.

9. Bernardo died about eleven o'clock, P. M. He continued irritable and impatient till the last. A few hours before his death some warm tea was offered him, and, finding that he could not swallow it, he spit it from his mouth, and threw the cup from him in the most spite-

ful manner. He was continually angry with God that he
did not end his sufferings, and take him to heaven.
What an awful state in which to leave the world! as
though a man might curse and swear, practise every im-
purity, and then go to heaven at death. What would
heaven be with such spirits, who die blaspheming their
Maker!

After his body was placed in the coffin, the fiftieth
Psalm was read, and the burial service as before, and
the body was taken ashore and buried by the side of the
steward.

Ezekiel's wounds are doing well, but he is not able to
sit up yet.

19. Capt. Waldon has arrived on this coast in the
Charles Wirgman, for the purpose of collecting "*beech
de mer.*" Capt. Hartwell's boat is at Undu, where they
have commenced fishing.

24. Mr. W. left the vessel after tea, to look at a fishing net which he had set at some distance off. He had
scarcely gone, when I heard sounds of quarrelling on
deck. I repaired immediately to the deck, where I saw
our steward, who was an Italian, and one of the sailors
embracing each other with more vigor than love. The
blood was streaming from the face of the sailor, and their
glaring eyes and angry countenances looked any thing
but becoming. William, the pilot, was quietly seated on
the harness-cask, and the second mate had removed to a
situation where he could have a better view of the fight.
Two sailors were seated on the rail, and the cook was
sitting at the door of the caboose smoking his pipe. I
asked if there was no one to part these men. "Mr. S.,"
said the pilot, "why don't you part them?" No answer
being made, I said, "Mr. Smith, why do you not stop
that business?" "Me no stop dem if dey fight till dey

die," was the reply. I stepped up to the combatants and commanded them to stop at once. I then told the steward to collect his dishes, which had been scattered in the affray, and go aft, and not go forward again till the arrival of his captain. The sailor takes every opportunity to insult and provoke the steward. When the captain returned, he demanded an account of the affair from the one that stands in the place of a second mate. He said dat if he did interfere, dey would have pitched right into him. " And so you left your duty to be performed by Mrs. W. What a courageous man you are!" said the captain.

29. Vendogo. The Charles Wirgman has passed us on its way to Undu. The anchor of the Zotoff was soon tripped, and we followed and anchored near. Capt. Waldon passed the afternoon and evening with us.

July 4. We had roast pork, plum puddings and apple pies for dinner fore and aft. The national flag was raised, and big guns were fired at sunrise, noon and sunset.

10. The Bark Pilot arrived to fish on this coast.

Elijah has arrived, bringing us letters from Vewa, from which we learn of the death of J. H. Chamberlain.

27. Elijah held a prayer meeting on shore, and Korondvarasa sent a request that the Christians would pray to God that the people would leave fishing for " beech de mer," as the Vewa people were tired and wished to go home.

Ezekiel has recovered from his wounds.

One of the crew belonging to the bark has gone to Vewa for medical aid, being attacked with dysentery.

Aug. 1. Divine service was performed on board in the native language, by a local preacher from Vewa. Ten of the Vewa Christians were present, and the manner in which they passed the Sabbath should serve as an example to the white men on board this vessel.

2. Since we have been on this coast, I have had no opportunity of learning the customs of the people, but I presume they do not differ much from other portions of these lands. Cannibalism is as prevalent here as at other places. Our time has been spent in visiting from one trade house to another along the coast from Undu to Natimba. The dialect being somewhat different here from that of the other places that I have visited, I cannot understand it as well.

3. Elijah has again left us for Vewa. When Mr. W. commenced fishing on this coast, he promised to each chief who would collect fifty bags of fish, a present of one musket, one keg of powder and one pig of lead, but told them if they did not get that quantity they should have no present. One chief procured twenty, and demanded his present. Mr. W. told him that he promised nothing unless they procured fifty bags, yet he was willing to present him with one musket, considering that a fair proportion. The chief said that if he could not have the whole, he would not have any thing. Mr. W. told him it was very good for him not to take any thing, as he promised him nothing unless he brought him fifty bags. The chief then told the sailors that he should burn the " beech de mer " house as soon as he reached the shore, but they must not inform the captain till he left the bark. As soon as he had left, Mr. W. was informed of his threat. " A Feejeean never informs when he intends mischief. He has said that, in order that I may recall him and give him what he wants," said Mr. W. The chief, on his arrival ashore, took the trade chest from the house and carried it off. There was nothing valuable in it, however, and when Olamba, another chief, came in

from the reefs, he sent for the chest, which was returned, with a request that the musket he had refused should be sent to him.   The request was not obeyed.

6.   The schooner Perseverance has left fishing at Natimba, and the Charles Wirgman also, as the quantity of fish they obtained was too small to pay their way.

———

CHAPTER XVI.

Departure from Ba—Arrival at Bau—Second Destruction of Rewa—Arrival of the Missionaries—Abandonment of the Mission at Somosomo—The Dinner—The Coronation.

Aug. 15.   Having settled the fishing business on this coast, we are now on our way to Vewa.   The bark Catherine and the Charles Wirgman are near.   Mr. W. and myself took tea on board the C., and passed the evening.   Our schooner has sailed for Vewa.   We learn that our cutter, the Star, in which Elijah and some of his people sailed, has been wrecked on one of the reefs.

We observe some few towns as we pass along the coast, which look romantic and pretty in the distance. Should we visit them, however, we should at once be reminded that we are in Feejee.   It is said that the nearer we approach the sun, the plainer we see its spots.   This is true of Feejee.

28.   We have at length arrived off Bau and Vewa, after a passage of three weeks.   The distance is one hundred miles.

On our arrival at the anchorage, we found there was but just water enough to admit of my being landed on that part of the island opposite to the mission.   As I had not stepped on land for four months, I was anxious to go on shore, and unless I went immediately I should be obliged to wait till the next morning; so before the anchor was down, a boat was lowered, and, in company with four Feejeeans, beside the boat's crew, we started, and soon arrived at Vewa. The Feejeeans conducted me across the little isle to the new house occupied by Rev. Mr. Hunt and family, who had previously informed me that my bed had been removed from my little straw house to a room in the new one, which was reserved for my use. I entered the open door very softly, and approached the study. Mrs. Hunt stood with her back to the door, and was saying to Mr. H., "The vessel has anchored. Capt. and Mrs. Wallis will soon be here. Let us go down to the shore and meet them." "No," said I, "you need not go. Mr. W. cannot leave so soon." I need not add that my reception by this affectionate and estimable couple was the same as ever. I soon received a kind greeting from Dr. and Mrs. Lyth, and Mr. and Mrs. Jaggar. I was almost wild with joy at being where I could move about without danger of stepping into the sea, and where I could enjoy good society again.

29. Rev. Mr. Hunt preached on board the bark. None attended the services except the officers and steward.

The sick sailor at Vewa is no better. Mr. W. fears that his disorder is incurable.

Sept. 1. A dense column of smoke has been seen to arise this morning in the direction of Rewa. As Bau and the Lasakaus have gone there for a battle, Rewa may have been burned.

2. Rewa has been destroyed, and several hundred massacred. The place was betrayed, as before, by some enemy within the camp. We do not understand that the

18

cowardly Phillips does much in the fighting way. Bau fights *his* battles, and butchers his kindred, and he boasts of *his* victories. Garenggeo has again retired to the mountains. Word was sent to him the night before the massacre to escape, as they had no wish to kill him. Phillips would prefer that he should be killed, as he would then reign king without fear; but Tanoa, the King of Bau, rather favors him. It is said that when the warriors were at Natawa, several messages of a pacific character passed between the King of Bau and Garenggeo. Thakombau calls this last war the Nakelo war, and says it will not end till that chief is killed.

5. Dr. Lyth preached on board the bark. On Saturday I visited the vessel, and the steward inquired if there was to be preaching on board on the Sabbath. I told him there would be. "Well, ma'am," he said, "I should think that the captain and yourself had better go on shore to meeting, as the crew will not attend the preaching on board." "Very well," I replied, "they will not be compelled to attend. Preaching will be held on board while we remain here, whether they attend or not. The crew are invited, but if they choose to appear so much like heathen as to stay away, they are at liberty to do so." Dr. L. informed me on his return, that all the crew attended the services.

They supposed, probably, that if they did not hear the preaching, it would be given up, the captain would pass the Sabbaths on shore, and they would have the liberty of spending the day as they pleased.

The sailor that was discharged at Manilla, leavened nearly the whole lump. The sick man at Vewa and one of the boys are the only exceptions. The name of the man is Thomas Lloyd, and that of the lad, John Derby.

A few days since, the bark Auckland arrived at Vewa

from Rewa, and the white residents here had a shameful frolic in consequence of it.   It is said that some of them were so furious that murder would undoubtedly have been committed had not the natives interfered, and secured them by tying them fast.

An old native belonging to this place came in this morning looking exceedingly troubled, and said, "It is very bad for rum to be brought here, for it endangers our lives, and our towns are likely to be burned during the drunkenness of the '*papalagis.*'   We have had a sad time since this vessel lay here.   Would it not be good to make a law, banishing from this isle any person who brings rum on shore?"   "Yes," said Mr. Hunt, " it is good for the chiefs to make such a law at once."

15.   The missionary brig John Wesley arrived.   This vessel was lately built in England, at an expense of thirty thousand dollars, for the service of the Wesleyan Mission in the South Pacific.   An example worthy of imitation!   Rev. Walter Lawry, the general superintendent of the South Sea Missions of the Wesleyans, has arrived, being on a tour to visit the mission stations.   Rev. Messrs. Malvern and Ford, with their families, have been sent to reinforce the Mission at Feejee.   Rev. Mr. Watsford and his wife have arrived from Ono, and Rev. Mr. Calvert from Lakemba.   The district meeting is to be held at Vewa.

19.   We learn that six Feejeeans have been murdered on Vetelavu, not far from Vewa, under the following circumstances:—A cask of oil had floated to their shores, and a Manilla man living at Vewa, tried to purchase it. The natives refused to sell it, and he threatened that he would complain of their refusal to Navinde at Bau.   Accordingly, on his return, he presented a musket to the chief, and desired him to send for the oil, which he did,

with orders for his people to kill as many as possible, if the owners of the oil still refused to sell it. They did refuse, and the consequence was the murder of six of their tribe.

20. Sabbath. Rev. Mr. Ford preached on board the Zotoff, and Rev. Mr. Jaggar preached at Bau. The crew of the John Wesley attended the English services on shore, and, unlike the crew of some vessels, they were well dressed, and appeared like civilized beings. Their captain (Buck), is an efficient and pious man.

In the afternoon Rev. Mr. Calvert preached on board the John Wesley. Mr. W. and several of his people attended the services.

22. It was decided at the meeting which was held last week, that the mission station at Somosomo should be given up, for the present, as the chiefs of that people, with their tribes, continue to reject the gospel, while there are many other places in Feejee where they are crying "Come over and help us." The John Wesley has sailed for Somosomo, to bring Rev. Messrs. Williams and Hazlewood with their families, and the property belonging to the mission.

23. Rokotuimbau, one of the princes of Bau, favored the missionaries with a visit. He is considered to be a very bad chief, is much opposed to Christianity, and seldom visits the Christians. A few Sabbaths since, he encouraged the rabble at the city to throw stones at the missionary who was preaching there. He did not succeed, however, as none were willing to throw the first stone. The dinner being served, the chief seated himself next to Mr. Hunt, and called for a plate. He then desired to be helped to a part of every thing on the table. When he began to make his demands upon the castor, I regretted

that its contents were so mild. A little cayenne pepper might have done him good.

25. A visit from Thakombau. He manifested the greatest friendliness towards the "*lotu*," and desired Rev. Messrs Lawry and Hunt to visit Bau, and try to persuade his father to build a house, and have a missionary go to Bau and live. This is certainly very desirable. Bau is the seat of cannibalism, and if a missionary family lived there, it might prevent many of their horrible feasts, as the chiefs are now becoming ashamed of them, and try to conceal them as much as possible.

26. Messrs. Lawry and Hunt visited Bau, and talked with Tanoa about establishing a mission station there. The king said, "Ah, yes, the '*lotu*' is very good, but I am not ready yet. Wait a little, till I have killed off three towns, and then I will build you a house, you may come and live here, and if my people wish to '*lotu*,' they can."

30. The John Wesley arrived from Somosomo, bringing the missionary families. The following is the list of appointments by the district meeting:—Rev. Messrs. Hunt, Lyth and Jaggar, Vewa; Rev. Mr. Williams, Bua; Rev. Mr. Hazlewood, Ono; Rev. Messrs. Watsford and Ford, Nandy; Rev. Messrs. Calvert and Malvern, Lakemba. Rev. Mr. Hunt was re-appointed chairman.

Oct. 4. The mission families, with Mr. W. and myself, were invited to dine on board the John Wesley. We left Vewa in a large double canoe, and our whale boat. On arriving at the vessel after a pleasant sail, Capt. Buck welcomed us on board his very nice brig. Our dinner was excellent—thanks to the art of preserving meats, vegetables and fruits. The green peas and beans, the currant, gooseberry and damson tarts, did not come amiss to those who had been in Feejee some two or three years.

After we had dined, Dr. Lyth politely showed the ladies over the vessel, which seems to be well fitted for its business. Its finish is plain, but good. We returned to Vewa about five, P. M., well pleased with our visit.

5. Mrs. Williams informs me that they have had much to endure at Somosomo. The natives are impudent and intrusive. They could seldom enjoy their food in peace till their doors were guarded by a faithful dog. One day a messenger from the king came to the house. The dog would not let him enter, and he took their little boy, who was playing outside, and threw him at the animal as if he had been a stone.

At one time, while Dr. Lyth and family were stationed there, the king being ill, sent for him to visit him professionally. The doctor, after prescribing the medicines which his case required, began to converse with him upon the all important subject of religion. The king at once became furious, and seizing the doctor by the skirt of his coat, held him fast while he called for some one to bring him a club. The queen rushed between them, telling the doctor to run. He made his escape, leaving the skirt of his coat in the king's hand, fully expecting to be followed and murdered. Fearing to alarm Mrs. Lyth if he appeared before her till he became somewhat composed, he repaired to the house of Mr. Williams. In a short time an old woman appeared. She entered the house on her knees, trembling, and holding the doctor's hat, and the torn skirt on a stick. She said that the anger of the king had passed away, and there was nothing more to fear. The old woman was followed by the Marama, who begged that they would forget what had passed. A chief officer from the king followed the Marama, who begged pardon of the doctor in the Feejeean manner. The king would undoubtedly have murdered the doctor in his passion, if a weapon had been near, but when his anger was over, he was quite alarmed for the consequences. He had never before shown any direct hostility to the missionaries. He died while Mr. and Mrs. W. resided there.

Tuilili, his son, reigns in his stead. He is one of the greatest cannibals of Feejee. His licentiousness is of the very lowest order. He has a brother whose right to the name of king is equal to his own. They are not on good terms, however, and an old man, a brother of the late king, has been sent for and made king. He exerts no authority. Tuilili reigns, but had his uncle crowned, that his brother might not interfere. The following is an account of the manner in which kings are made in Feejee, as furnished me by the kindness of Rev. Mr. Williams.

"On the 19th of May, it was publicly announced that in ten days Tuithekau would be publicly recognized as king. The interval was to be spent in making preparations for the great event. On the 29th, the food which had been prepared for the occasion was taken to the house of Tuilili for inspection, and then placed in large baskets in a house called New Nasema. Tuilili then made his appearance, and was greeted with the words, ' Sa venaka mai,' ' It is good that you have come.' Orders were then given to avoid all sneezing, after which a bale of cloth was given to Tuithekau, and received for him by Na Mata. Tuilili then advanced to the house where Tuithekau sat, with twenty whales' teeth, which he handed to Na Mata, and said that he had come to make Tuithekau king, and that if all Tuithekau's brothers had been there, he only would have been made king—that he must take care of his health, and not be out late, and allow them to continue as a land and a people.

This speech was answered by Na Mata, who, after running over a long list of gods of both genders, concluded by wishing health to the king, and death to his enemies. A root of yanggona was then presented by a chief of a neighboring town, which Na Mata received and prayed over. The chief of the town of Lauthala then approached, and after the word of respect had been uttered, presented ten whales' teeth, requesting that the chiefs of Somosomo would ' be of a good mind ' towards Lauthala. The teeth were received by Na Mata, and another prayer was offered.

Thanks were then given for the food, after which, it was divided into twelve portions for those that were present, and five to be sent to towns that were not represented. The people separated to eat their food, and then assembled on the ' rara.' Two mats were placed under the shade of a large tree, and a musquito curtain laid over them. Tuithekau seated himself on these, arrayed in black ' masi,' two hundred yards in length, holding in his hand a dirty rod. Na Savasava and Korai Ruki (priests) then walked up to Tuilili, who was seated on the ' rara,' holding in their hands a new head-dress. This they unfolded slowly, each holding a side, and standing so that the lighter end would be wafted towards Tuithekau. While they were unfolding the head-dress they muttered something, but in too low a tone to be understood. With the unfolded head-dress the priests advanced slowly towards the king, giving him and the Wailaga chiefs some advice, such as ' You must not rule the people with a high hand. You must be industrious,' &c. The priests then bound one end of the head-dress (which was a piece of native muslin) round the arm of Tuithekau, and relieved him of his rod, saying that it was the business of a king to sit and receive presents, and urged the people to give liberally. The priests, with several old men, then walked four times round a circle with their hands clasped, and looking upwards with a movement of the nose as if smelling for dead men, and then seated themselves before the king 'mid a clapping of hands, which continued till stopped by the master of ceremonies. They then made a sudden turn which brought their backs and sides towards the king, and remained in that position, as still as Quakers, for some moments. They then took the long black 'masi,' and the cloth which had been presented to the king, to Tuilili. A pause of some eight or ten minutes succeeded, and then six women made their appearance, three bearing each a pot of boiled fish, and the other three boiled yams. As they approached the new king, they knelt three times, then presented the food, which His Majesty accepted, and sent a portion to Tuilili, who, not wishing to eat, went to sleep. After His Royal Highness had partaken of the repast, some old men marked him on the shoulders with red paint, and then took him upon their shoulders and carried him to his house. Thus ended the ceremony of the Coronation."

The following account of a priest at Somosmo was given by Rev. Mr. Hazlewood.

"In the town of Nasarata i loma, the leading character of the place is a priest, named Ra Uageawa. He does not owe his preeminence to his rank, neither is he under any obligation to the beauty of his person, the sweetness of his temper, or the high character of his morals. This being, however, has a considerable influence, and numbers in these and other parts of Feejee look upon him with dread. Many believe that he is able to foretell the events of war, and that in his hands are the issues of life and death. He associates with kings, and affects to despise men of low degree. Yet, notwithstanding his great fame, he is very poor, and is obliged sometimes to make use of extraordinary means to procure ordinary supplies. He has several times pretended to have a commission from Jehovah to call upon us for property, in consideration of his having been our defence from war and protection from fire. As he has not, thus far, produced any order or note of hand, we have felt it our duty to tell him that we were quite satisfied that if he had been so commissioned we should have been apprised of it by our God, and that in the absence of such apprisal we must decline his demands.

As Rev. Mr. Williams was employed in his study one afternoon, a domestic entered, and said that a person without desired an interview. The servant was told to wait upon him in, when the priest presented himself. He took a seat and requested Mr. Williams to lay aside his books and pay great attention to him. This solemn request caused him to look with greater attention on his visitor. He observed that his countenance was more repulsive than ever, and his body much agitated. Being encouraged to state his errand, he proceeded in the following manner:—

'Last month your God, Jehovah, and a small Feejean god came for me to go to England with them. I went, and they took me to a large house which they said belonged to the father of Mr. Williams, of Navatu, (Somosomo.) It was guarded by a large dog, with white fore feet. A lady who was in the house saw me, and called to me to come in. I told her that I was afraid of the dog. She told the dog to go away, and I went in.

It was a good house, but I could not see any spars in the roof. I looked out of the windows, but could not see any bread-fruit or banana trees. There were great riches in the house,—calicoes, prints and cloths. The god said to me, 'Do you see these boxes?' I looked and saw three large boxes,—the lids were up, and they were full of riches to take to Feejee. 'These,' said Jehovah to me, 'are the boxes for Mr. Williams, and you, only you must take great care of the fire. Fire burns. Our talk now is not after the manner of this world, so that you cannot now take any of this property. You must wait till the boxes get to Feejee, and then you must tell Mr. Williams that he must give you some of the property. Only mind fire,—be greatly afraid of it. You have kept Navatu safe a long time, and been their defence in war. Remember, it is your business to look after fire ; as that would burn all the houses with all the riches they contain. Look after the fire; for this is apt to destroy riches and scorch men.'

The priest was told that as the boxes had not arrived, he could not expect to receive any thing from them. He then intimated that something was due for the announcement of prospects so fair. He was told in reply that the truth of his statements was strongly suspected. He seemed to be pondering on something to say, when an old man came to say that the medicine which the priest had given to one of his patients seemed to be hastening her end. 'That is the way of it,' muttered the great man, cursing the patient and the messenger.

With so good an excuse Mr. W. opened the door, and as he showed him out, heartily regretted that there was no jail at hand, where the Feejeean protector and doctor might have been placed for a time, that sober reflection in a cool situation might convince him that the course he had pursued was not unattended with inconvenience."

6. After dinner we were informed that a "*Solavu*" was to be held by the natives of Vewa for Rev. Mr. Lawry. We soon heard the chant of the natives, and observed them approaching round the brow of the hill. As the procession appeared, and at intervals was hidden by the intervening foliage as they were approaching the mission house, their appearance was highly picturesque. All were dressed in their Sunday costume, and each could boast of some "*papalagi*" article of dress. Some wore a shirt, some a hat or cap, and some of the females wore a dress, while others wore native cloth around their persons with a "*papalagi*" cape. The queen was decorated with a scarlet blanket, and Elijah with a large, heavy pea-jacket, lined with red flannel, and buttoned close to his throat,—the thermometer standing at 95° in the shade. Our old grandmother, as she calls herself, was arrayed in an old muslin dress, which I had presented to the queen on my first arrival at the islands. The right side had been worn out, and it now figured wrong side out. None of the native gentlemen of Vewa wore pantaloons; therefore, it can be imagined how thoroughly dressed they were with their shirts and jackets. The native "*masi*" was worn as usual. Some were arrayed in cloth, two breadths of which had been sewed together; it was fastened at the waist, and falling to the heels, covered their persons decently. This is a favorite dress of the men who have become Christians. But to return. An old man headed the procession, bearing a club. He was followed by Elijah, (Namosimalua was away,) bearing a club, and his head decorated with scarlet parrot's feathers. The Tonga teacher followed him, bearing a large, beautiful branch of variegated fo-

liage. Then came the rest of the males of Vewa, all bearing clubs, spears, or some Feejeean article, which they deposited on the veranda, where Mr. Lawry, the missionaries with their families, and myself, were standing. After the men had deposited their offerings, they formed themselves into a square on the green opposite the veranda, thus making room for the females to approach with their gifts. First came the queen with a mat. Mary Wallis then came with an enormous club, and was the only female that appeared with so formidable a weapon. The rest of the females presented mats, native cloth, arrow-root, tumeric, and various other articles. After all had been deposited, Elijah remarked that the gifts were the love of the Vewa people to Rev. Mr. Lawry, who had so kindly come to visit them. Mr. Lawry addressed them in his own happy manner, Mr. Hunt acting as interpreter. After this, all repaired to the chapel, where a kind of exhibition was held. The natives recited chapters from the Bible, repeated and chanted portions of the catechism, &c.

The articles which were presented to Mr. Lawry are to be sold to defray the expenses of a house of public worship which is being erected at Auckland, New Zealand.

The Vewa people do not need their clubs and spears now, because the time has come when they shall learn war no more. It was exceedingly affecting to see these, so late relentless cannibals, thus peacefully giving away their implements of war, and laying them at the feet of those who had brought the gospel to them.

The few men belonging to Vewa who still adhere to heathenism are now away, assisting Bau in its war.

CHAPTER XVII.

The Ordeal—Our Departure for Manilla—Arrival—Christmas in Manilla—
Execution—A Procession—Cemetery—Departure for America—St. Helena—Arrival at Home.

Oct. 10.   This morning I heard some native chanting,
and inquired of a servant the meaning of it.   She said
that the heathen men before mentioned had returned the night before from fighting, and the chant was
one that is used when warriors have been successful in
procuring dead bodies.   It was called the song of
Mbokola.   Mrs. Hunt observed that they would scarcely dare to bring a dead body here; perhaps they had
killed some, and were on their way to wash their clubs,
—a ceremony that is always performed after a battle, although it was not common for that song to be chanted
except when they were dragging a dead body.

I went to " *sara sara*," taking two of the servants with
me.   On reaching the footpath, we observed ten men
approaching; seven of them were of Vewa,. and the
others were strangers, who had accompanied them home.
Their clubs were on their shoulders, and they continued
their death song, which was a repetition of half a dozen
words, ending in a sort of yell.   When they saw us
standing in the pathway, they called to us to go back,
and waited till we had retreated.   After they had turned
off into another path, leading to an uninhabited part of
the island, we followed, as I was desirous of witnessing
the ceremonies in which they were about to engage.
The demons, however, soon observed us, and said that
we must return, as it was " *tambu* " for us to follow.

A few days since, Thakombau presented Mr. W. with

a young cow. He dined yesterday on board the bark, and was offered some beef soup. He declined tasting it, saying that the cow was born at Bau,—he had seen her walking about and eating the grass of the island, and he loved her; therefore, he could not eat a portion of her body.

11. A sad and yet a joyful day to me,—sad on account of taking leave of my dear Vewa friends; and joyful that we were about to sail for Manilla on our return to our native land. We had received many kindnesses from the mission families at Vewa, and our hearts were filled with sadness at the thought of parting. The last words of Mr. Hunt were, "I fully believe that we shall see you again in Feejee."

The John Wesley got under way at the same time, and we left the shores of Vewa together. The John Wesley was bound to Lakemba and Ono with the Rev. Mr. Calvert and Mr. Hazlewood and family.

12. Wo arrived at Naikorotumba, where we found the Catharine anchored. Mr. W. and myself passed the evening on board. Our cook is sick, and one of the sailors, who has been under medical treatment at Vewa for two months past.

15. We arrived at Vendoga, and shall remain a few days, as the "beech de mer" house was left when we sailed from here last, and the chief wishes to fish a little longer.

We learn that a canoe from Ba was cast away last week upon one of the Asua Islands;—the crew were eaten. They were not enemies, but such is their custom. If the canoe had arrived in safety, the lives of the visitors would have been spared, and they would have welcomed them; but when a canoe is cast away, the natives say that it is sent them by their gods, and as they are fond of something to relish their vegetables once in awhile, the flesh does not come amiss.

27.   About two o'clock this morning Thomas Loyd died.   He retained his reason to the last, and appeared willing to die.   Mr. Smith, the mate, took the entire care of him during the last days of his sickness, except preparing his medicines and nourishment.   He made his will, leaving his property to Mr. Smith.   He wished me to accept the sum of fifty dollars, but I declined it in favor of Mr. S.   The chief of Vendoga was paid for a spot of land, and promised that the body should remain undisturbed when buried.   Prayers were read, and the body was buried on the land.   His disease was dysentery, which is becoming very prevalent in these lands.

A few days since the bark Pilot arrived here from Ba. The natives of that place stole the trade chest and a " beech de mer " pot from the shore, and fired some muskets, which were answered by two large guns from the Pilot, who then tripped her anchor and came to Vundu.

29.   When we first arrived at this place, Olamba told the captain that ten bags of " beech de mer " had been stolen from him during our absence from Vewa, but he said the thief would surely be found out, as they had buried leaves from a certain tree, and as the leaves decayed, the thief would pine away and die.   The Feejeeans have many trials by ordeal.   Elijah told me that there was one ordeal in which he had formerly the greatest confidence.   The last time he tried it, was about the " lotu," when Rev. Mr. Cross first came to Vewa.   He put some water into the palm of his right hand, and slowly raised his arm to the perpendicular, saying, " If the ' lotu ' is true, let the water run in a straight line to my shoulder."   It did so.   At this he was much provoked, as he loved heathenism at that time.   He then put

water in his hand again, and said, " If the Feejeean gods are true, let the water run in a straight line,—if they are false, let the water run off in a crooked way. The water ran in all directions, and from that time he believed that Jehovah was the true God; but he did not wish to embrace religion for many years after.

30. We got under way for Nandy, intending to buy yams at that place. On arriving there, we were rejoined by the bark Pilot.

There is an old man on board the Pilot,—a resident of Feejee, but not a native. The chief of Namula sold him a woman last week, who, not suiting the fancy of the purchaser, was returned to the chief, who showed no unwillingness to receive her again. He immediately had her killed, cooked and eaten. He observed to Thomson, that she would make very good eating. Query. Which is the worst of the two ?

Nov. 4. To-day a chief came into the cabin, bringing with him a girl about ten years old. He said that he wished her to go to America, where she might learn to cook, read, and make dresses, and when we returned, we could bring her back. I told him I did not expect to return to Feejee again. "No matter," he replied. I have put a dress on to the child and concluded to take her unless she takes it into her head to jump overboard to-night and return to her home. Her dialect is so different from any language we have before heard, that we can neither understand nor be understood.

5. This morning several canoes came off to the bark. No one noticed the girl that was brought here yesterday, nor did she speak to any one. We conclude, therefore, that she is some captive girl. She appears rather sad.

The barks Zotoff and Pilot are now under sail,—the former for Manilla, and the latter to continue her business

19

in the " *beech de mer* " line at some other part of Feejee, having been rather unsuccessful on this coast. Farewell to Feejee! Your green hills are very beautiful, but your inhabitants are dark in every sense of the word. May the gospel increase and dissipate the great moral darkness that now reigns here!

Our second mate was discharged at Bau to return to Solavu, where he owns *a woman*. Mr. Cloutman, late of the bark Catharine, now serves in that capacity.

We have a young man on board who has been a resident in the cannibal city for the year past. He states that dead bodies were brought to Bau as often as twice, and sometimes three times in a week,—that they were taken to a " *buri*," where a chief, named Rotuimbau, divided them, after which they were cooked, and each portion sent to its destination. If they had more than could be devoured in Bau, portions were sent to other towns. The hearts and tongues are considered the choicest parts, and are claimed by the chiefs. The hands are usually given to the children.

10. The morning dawned upon us any thing but pleasant. About nine, A. M., I was quietly seated on the sofa, giving my lap-dog some meat to eat, when, without any premonition of such an event, I was thrown from my seat to the opposite side of the cabin. I thought that the vessel had been thrown on its beam ends. I soon found my way to the deck, to see what was going on, and learn the cause of my being treated so roughly. As I reached the deck, the first thing that attracted my attention was the jib, which was torn into ribbons, and looked like a hundred pennants floating from the bowsprit. Another sail, tired perhaps of its long service, had fled altogether, and was seen bounding over the angry ocean in detached parts, like a flock of frightened

birds. A sudden squall had struck the bark, and all
was confusion. The sailors were trying to furl the sails,
which was no easy matter. The wind made them so obstinate that they seemed determined not to be made captive, but to follow the example of those that had gone
before. They twitched themselves from the hands of
the men, then flapped and banged them, and cut all sorts
of capers. The wind seemed to exert all its power, and
soon caused the sea to foam and rage,—split the mainsail, blew away the fore-top-gallantsail and the jib,—
tore in pieces the fore-topmast staysail and gaff-topsail,
besides doing other damage. The scene was highly exciting, somewhat terrific, and truly sublime. The captain was on the quarter deck, giving orders to the men, and
speaking in no very feminine voice through the trumpet.
Every part of the vessel seemed to feel itself called upon
to make some audible complaint; therefore, it creaked,
and groaned, and howled as if in great distress. The
gale lasted about two hours. I stood, during that time,
holding on by the door of the house. I had been sea-
sick since we left Feejee nearly all the time, but during
the gale the sickness had departed.

18. We arrived at Pleasant Island. The weather
has been favorable since the gale. Several of the white
residents came off. They have increased in numbers
since we visited the island before; about fifteen are now
residing on the isle. The inhabitants are as rude and
boisterous as ever. They brought off hats in great numbers to sell, and some mats also. One of the natives
thought it best to compliment me by saying, " Captain's
woman very good." Another, looking at him very arch-
ly, said, " Captain hear you talk that,—he kill you,—
he shoot you."

The man who deserted the Zotoff, when we were here last, is thriving well on fish, cocoa-nuts and sleep.

There has been no rain on the island for the last eighteen months. The pigs and fowls are literally starving, as the cocoa-nuts are failing. They were brought on board in abundance for sale, the price having fallen, as the conscientious whites saw we were well supplied with the *long-faced gentry*. When we were here last, and they saw that we greatly needed pork, they pretended that pigs were scarce,—that they had but three or four on the island, and sold us a sick one for eleven dollars cash. Now we could have bought them by the dozen for a trifle.

A sailor, who had been cruising about in the Pacific for the last four years, desired to leave the island and go with us. He had been on board several whaling vessels, all of which he left the first opportunity. He brought all the riches which he had accumulated during his voyages and travels on board the bark with him;— they consisted of one shirt, much worn, and one pair of pantaloons. Mr. W. also took a sick Manilla man on board, who was anxious to return to his country. After increasing our company with the abovementioned persons, we again sailed for Manilla.

28. This morning, as I was seated at an early hour on the quarter deck, I heard a feeble cry for help. On looking up, I perceived a sailor hanging by one hand and foot to the mizzen outhauler. The mate and two men hastened to his rescue. His face had become purple, and he could have lived but a short time longer.

Dec. 12. We arrived at Manilla. Mr. Osborne met us at the landing, and welcomed us in his own truly gentlemanly manner, back to the Eastern city. I did not regret leaving for a time the cabin of our bark for the spacious rooms in the house of Peel, Hubbell & Co.

18. Sabbath. At a very early hour in the morning, we started for a drive into the country. Although the sun had not risen, the bazars were all in readiness for their customers, and the streets were filled with people; Chinamen, Malays and Europeans, all appearing to be engaged about the perishable things of earth, presenting a marked contrast to our own quiet streets on this holy day, where another gospel is acknowledged. As we passed the churches, the interior appeared to be crowded, mostly with females. In passing from the towns to the country, we met many peasants on their way to the bazars with the produce of their lands. Some were seated on buffaloes, that do not travel with railroad speed, and many were travelling on "*Mr. Foot's horses*," with baskets of fruits and vegetables on their heads. The baskets were very broad, and their contents were arranged with much taste. Several were ornamented with pretty bunches of flowers. Their dress was coarse, but clean.

On our return, we observed that the shops in the Escolta were closed. The flags were raised from the shipping, and we were almost deafened by the ringing of bells.

In the afternoon we rode again into the country. The Malays were assembled in great numbers. Cockfighting and flying kites seemed to be their principal amusements. We observed many of their Spiritual Fathers assembled with them. A theatre in the evening concludes the amusements of the day.

25. Last night, at twelve o'clock, high mass was celebrated in the churches. I was told that the ceremony was well worth witnessing; but, being a Protestant, I

could not bring myself to bend the knee to the shrines of a Catholic, and declined attending the ceremony.

Christmas is a very merry time in Manilla. The church bells are continually sending forth their merry peals, fairs are held, streets and houses are ornamented, churches are illuminated, and every one looks animated and happy during the Christmas holidays.

As we returned from our ride in the evening, we passed through several streets where booths were erected, and ornamented in the most fanciful manner. Toys, cakes and confectionary were sold in them. Curious ornaments were suspended in the streets, while pigs, turkeys, hens, dogs, &c., made of reeds and fancy paper, and illuminated with a taper, were seen running about in every direction. They were placed on castors, or very small wheels, and cords were attached so that those who set them in motion could remain out of sight. In one street we saw a very beautiful ship under full sail. It was most tastefully ornamented; its ropes were of silken cords; the sails were of white silk; the bows and stern were beautifully gilded, and the little flags waved most gracefully, as they were fanned by the gentle zephyrs of evening.

In the forenoon some small presents were exchanged between the gentlemen of the house and myself, which occasioned some merriment.

26. I received a call from a Malay woman, who came to ask me for a Christmas present. As she wore more golden ornaments than I happened to posssess of the valuable coin at the time, I dismissed her with the observation, that being a stranger, I was wholly unacquainted with the customs of the country.

January 3. Last night we accompanied Mr. Osborne to his house in the country. It is about three miles distant, and is situated on a small elevation which commands an extensive view of mountains, rivers and plains. Our sleeping apartment was delightfully cool, and for the first time for three years we slept without a musquito curtain.

At dawn of day a servant opened the windows, that we might luxuriate in the " first sweet breath of morn." I soon rose and took a stroll round the house. I found the flowering almond, the tamarind, the coffee plant, the lemon tree, and various aromatic shrubs. I gathered some flowers, but was laughed at by Mr. Osborne, for trying, as he said, " To be romantic at my time of life;" but I shall always love flowers.

About seven o'clock we were joined by Mr. Deland, and after taking a cup of chocolate, we returned to town.

16. Two Malays were to-day publicly executed for the crime of murder. One had killed a man about twenty years ago, and recently murdered his wife. The other had also murdered his wife. The execution took place in front of one of the prisons, and the bodies were left exposed through the day, to serve as a terror to evil doers.

17. About eight o'clock in the evening we rode to a church, two miles distant, to witness a grand Catholic pageant. On our arrival in the immediate vicinity of the church, the crowd was so great that we were obliged to leave our carriage and make our way, as best we might, to the church. The houses and streets near the church were illuminated, pictures were shown, flags and banners of every hue and color were displayed, and nothing was left undone to render the scene attractive. In front of the church is a large open space enclosed by a wall. Within this enclosure were stationed large guns, which sent forth peal after peal, each seeming louder

than the last, adding, of course, to the *sublimity* and *so-lemnity* of a religious festival. Fireworks were display-ed at the same place.

We had just arrived at the door of the church when the procession appeared. One hundred little boys, about three or four years of age, first appeared. These were dressed in the native costume, and each carried a lighted wax candle in his hand. Then came a number of little children, decorated in the most fanciful manner, with golden suns and silver moons and stars shining all over them. Some had wings attached to their shoulders, and all wore crowns composed of materials so brilliant, that it made our eyes ache to look at them. They walked two by two, each bearing a lighted candle, as before. Their little swarthy faces formed a contrast to their decorations, and they looked like any thing but seraphs and angels, which they were intended to represent. The angels were followed by fifty young friars, wearing black gowns, and a short white wrought muslin frock over them. Then came a procession of young girls, who wore dresses of a dark gray silk, embroidered with sil-ver, and garlands of artificial flowers around their heads. Friars then followed, as before,—then little angels again, —then more friars, and then one young girl, whose dress was entirely covered with golden embroidery, with a garland of flowers around her head, surmounted by half a dozen white ostrich feathers. I think that she must have been the queen of the ceremony. She was followed by a kind of car borne on the shoulders of men. The floor of the car was covered with a gaily tinselled cloth, and there, under a glass globe about one foot in height, sat the patron saint, or rather a small decorated wax figure, to represent him. He was as quiet as wax figures usually are in such situations, and did not seem to need the heavy guard of soldiers that marched on each side of his saintship. A band of musicians followed, playing their very loudest, the guns sounded their heaviest, and the rockets shone their brightest, as the diminutive saint entered the church. If this is not idolatry,—what is ? The musicians were followed by a long line of mothers, leading a little one by the hand and carrying an infant. These carried no candles, as did the rest.

We made our way, as soon as we could, into the church, and found it nearly dark,—the altar only being lighted. A priest stood before it, dressed in a white gown, embroidered with gold. He was crossing himself, and making courtesies when we entered, but soon disappeared through a side door. The silver gilded girls were seated on steps below the altar. The church was large and dark, and we could not distinguish any more of those who had formed the procession. We had scarcely entered the church, when a choir of infant voices commenced singing, accompanied by soft and appropriate instrumental music. This was natural, simple and beautiful. There was nothing artificial in those infant voices, and I listened to them with delight. When their songs ended, the lights of the altar were extinguished, and we were left to wend our way in the dark. Ah! I thought, I fear this signifies the end of your brilliant religion,—darkness.

As we returned to our carriage, we saw many of the girls who had figured in the procession, threading their way quite unattended among the crowd. The little urchins, too, it appeared, had not ascended to the upper regions, notwithstanding their pinions. The heavy gilding about them might have prevented their rising. I

could not learn the meaning of what we had witnessed, but I presume it was in honor of the patron saint
of infants.

18.   As we happened to ride on the Calsada in a very
beautiful carriage belonging to Peel, Hubbell & Co., we
were honored with bows from the Governor and his lady,
as we passed them and their suite.

19.   We rode through many of the streets of the city
by daylight.   We found them narrow, and not so clean
as those of the towns in the suburbs.   The buildings are
all of stone, and look any thing but cheerful.   In the
evening, when the city is lighted, it looks pleasanter.
The basements of many of the buildings are used for stores,
and from some the grass was growing over the tops of
the windows, entrances, and every niche where a par-
ticle of soil could find a lodgment.

We entered the plaza, in the centre of which stands
a statue of Charles the Fourth, fronting the palace of the
Governor.   In front of the Governor's residence stands
the city prison, which looks far more like a palace than
that occupied by the Governor,—the latter being very
plain in its appearance.   The cathedral stands at the
right of the palace, and its deep-toned bells are heard
for many a mile.   These buildings form three sides of
the plaza or square ;   on the fourth side stand some
buildings remarkable for nothing in particular.   There
are several churches in the city, with monasteries
attached to them.   We passed a convent containing
about five hundred nuns.   Its walls were forty feet in
height from the ground to the windows.   It is said that
there are about fourteen hundred nuns in Manilla.

20.   During our afternoon drive, we stopped on our
way to visit a cemetery.   We entered a broad gateway,
and passed on to the church, where several people were

assembled. As we approached, they left the church, and proceeded to an open grave with the corpse of an old woman. We followed to the grave to witness the interment. The body was borne on a rude bier of bamboos, on the shoulders of men. The corpse was wrapped in a mat. The grave was like the graves of the cannibals of Feejee, scarcely deep enough for the body to be placed in. The men took hold of the four corners of the mat, and laid it with the body in the grave, then retired to a little distance, while the women approached, kissed the shrivelled hands which were folded across the bosom beneath a cross, whined, but shed no tears. Then the men approached and took hold of one of the hands of the corpse, as if to take leave, when all departed. There were eight mourners, mostly young people, who seemed rather glad that their aged friend was dead. After the departure of the relatives, the body was covered with earth.

The cemetery is of a semi-circular form, enclosed with walls. In these are holes where the dead are deposited. I presume these are the places where the bodies of the wealthy are placed. Each aperture is just large enough to contain one body, and when one is deposited, some lime is thrown in upon it, the hole is fastened up, and remains so till some other member of the family dies. The bones are then taken out and thrown into a Golgotha, which they call an " *Osero.*" What a horrible way of disposing of their dead! It is not surprising that there are so many bones of the saints and martyrs; these places can ever furnish a supply. The cemetery is very small, not comprising one quarter of an acre of land. No grave could be dug without disturbing the dead, and the stench from the little spot of earth was almost intolerable. I could not rest on my return till I had changed my clothing.   We never passed this road on our way to San Sebastian, without meeting some funereal company. We often saw a man or boy, running through the street, bearing a tray on his head, on which is placed the corpse of an infant, decorated like a doll, with flowers, tinsel and all sorts of finery.

21.   We took a long ride in the country early in the morning.   This is a luxury I can but seldom enjoy, as Mr. W. devotes his mornings from early dawn, to business.   The birds sung some of their sweetest songs, the tamarinds and wild almonds showed us their best blossoms, the early dew sparkled and trembled on the grass, and all conspired with our happy hearts to render the scenery enchanting.   I observe a marked difference between the foliage of this country and that of Feejee; the latter is broad, deep and full; the former is scant and narrow, and the trunks of the trees are not covered with creeping plants and vines, as in Feejee.   I presume that the heat of this island is greater than that of the Feejeean isles.

30.   All being in readiness, we reëmbarked on board the Zotoff for our distant home.   We were accompanied to the banca by Messrs. Osborne, Towne, Deland and Douglass, where we took leave of them.   We feel much indebted to these gentlemen for many agreeable hours spent in Manilla.   Capt. McKay of Boston and Mr. Dimon of New York accompanied us to the vessel.   As we were bound for the latter port, Mr. D. gave us a letter of introduction to his parents.

31.   After a good night's rest I awoke in the morning congratulating myself that I had thus far escaped my old enemy—sea-sickness.   I attempted to rise, when the monster laid one huge paw on my head, and the other on my chest, declaring at the same time that I should not

start. I felt highly indignant at such oppression, and determined to resist. I succeeded in dressing, and reached the wash stand, where stood three of the monster's imps. *Dizzy* would not let me arrange my hair, but, giving it a terrible twitch, seemed to say it looked well enough; *Push* threw me against the door and sadly bruised my arm, and *Trip* tried her best to make my heels as light as my head. All this I bore with the patience of a martyr, and staggered to the breakfast table, trying to look resigned, but I found that *Bitter*, who, being a child of sea-sickness, could make herself at home in any element, had placed herself in my tea; *Nausea* held the boiled eggs in her hands, and *Hate-food* kept the bread; therefore I gave up my breakfast, and turned to my dear old friend, the sofa, who is always ready to receive me. It is true that it is not free from faults, being occasionally a little unsteady. It has thrown me from its protection sometimes, and we are obliged to confine our wayward friend with strong cords.

Feb. 3. The clouds have gathered themselves together, covered the face of the sun, and completely hidden his beams from our eyes for the last four days. Boreas has been rough but kind, and has blown us along at the rate of eight miles an hour. The bark, which has been for a long time past a resident in a tropical climate, and is not unaffected with its indolence, complains at this rapid travelling, and even weeps. The waves, arrayed in their white bonnets, elevated themselves to a great height, then came dancing up to the cabin windows, and I thought showed an inclination to make me a visit. I mentioned it to Mr. W., but he laughed, and said that it was only a way they had, and that they would not dare to enter the cabin. "They look proud and saucy enough to enter any vessel," I replied. I had scarcely done speaking, when a wave somewhat taller than the rest dashed into the cabin, seeming to say, "See what I dare to do!" The salt water bespattered the eyes of the captain, loosened the scales, and the order was given to close the windows.

4. We passed the island of Pulo Supata, and three days after, the Amanabas Islands. These are inhabited by Malays, who, it is said, are very treacherous. An abundance of tropical fruits are to be obtained from them, and there is good anchorage for vessels.

8. We spoke the ship Vancouver, from Canton, bound to Boston. I never before saw so much canvass spread from a vessel. There was beauty and majesty displayed as the noble ship passed us, seeming to say, in derision, "Do report us if you arrive first."

10. The last two days we have been *favored* with torrents of rain, which renders the cabin exceedingly gloomy, being lighted by a lamp to make the darkness visible. The strong current and the wind having taken opposite sides of a question, seem to have become enemies; which caused the bark to labor so hard that Mr. W. thought it best to anchor, and we passed so *delightful* a night as to increase one's love for a sea life. The night was exceedingly dark, and our situation was somewhat dangerous, as we were quite near the entrance of the Straits of Banka.

11. The storm abated, and the vessel got under way at an early hour in the morning. We soon entered the Straits of Banka. On our right runs the east coast of Sumatra, which is not inhabited, and presents to the eye one vast jungle. The island of Banka is on our left. This land is more elevated. A chain of hills runs through the island, called St. Paul's. There is a Dutch settlement on it, called Mintou.

12. Mr. W. spoke the ship Santiago, of Boston, from Batavia, bound to Singapore. Several ships and brigs were in sight, and a large Dutch steamer passed us.

14. We spoke the Samuel Russell, nine days from Canton, for New York. It passed us with the speed of a steamer; our vessel seemed as though laying at anchor. Some of our sailors threw a rope over the side, that they might take our bark in tow. Hands were stretched out from the S. R. to receive it. We are now in sight of the high lands of Batavia.

16. We are again in sight of Sumatra. The land is more elevated, and in some parts mountainous. The chain of mountains that run through the centre of this large island terminates here.

In the evening we received some visitors from Angier, who brought for sale, pine-apples, cocoa-nuts, bananas, pumpions, corn, parrots and monkeys. All the eatables, and some monkeys were purchased.

17. As we neared Tamarind Island, we could see several houses of thatch on the isle, and canoes on the shore. Our vessel lay resting on the still waters, or floating at a snail's pace, when some of the canoes approached, and one of the strangers called out to the captain, "Come to anchor!" Several Malays came on board. They brought a turtle and some dead shells for sale; the latter they were constantly dipping in the water that it might not be seen that they were dead. The settlement on the island is of recent date.

20. We are now out of sight of land, having crossed a part of the China Sea, passed through the Straits of Banka, crossed a part of the Java Sea, and passed through the Straits of Sunda, and are now once more on the Indian Ocean. The weather is intolerably hot, and every body is lazy except the two young monkeys, who

are as full of mischief as monkeys need be. The eldest
bears marks of old age, and appears very dignified. We
think that he was a "judge" among his tribe. Sometimes he "makes up faces" at us, but he knows probably that he is not now seated on a wool sack, or decorated with a wig.

April 1. We are near the stormy Cape of Good
Hope. The last week we have experienced continual
squally weather, with some thunder and lightning, and
the sea has been angry and rough. Yesterday, Judge
Grey, the monkey, committed suicide by drowning.
The change of life and habits from his own green woods
to the bark was too much for him. He has never been
happy, and has sought relief from a broken heart in a
watery grave.

4. The clouds gathered in one solid mass, and poured
forth torrents of rain. The wind blew with great violence, and there was every appearance of an approaching gale. As we were trying to drink our tea, a sea
struck on the larboard quarter, and poured down the sky
light into the cabin. We received no injury, however,
but the vessel rolled and pitched continually. The gale
continued to increase during the night, and the vessel
lay to; no one had any rest or sleep. The water came
pouring down the sky lights at intervals, and there was
no dry spot to be found except in the berths. About
eight o'clock, P. M., the quarter boat filled and broke.
During the night we lost the lower swinging boom, and
the fore-topmast stay-sail was split. On the fifth, the
gale continued with great violence, but we received no
other damage than the loss of the stern boat. When
that went, it seemed as though the whole stern of the
vessel was going with it. I fully expected to see the sea
pouring in upon us. We passed a most uncomfortable

day. At four, P. M., the gale abated a very little, and
as we were directly in the track of vessels from the east,
bound like ourselves round the Cape, Mr. W. deemed it
best to bear away on our course. On the eighth day we
were again favored with a pleasant sun, and the ocean
looked as blue and as placid as though it had never been
ruffled by a storm. All were loud in their praises of our
vessel, which had so nobly withstood the gale. The day
before it commenced, there were six vessels in sight. I
trust they suffered no more injury than we did. Our
gratitude for our preservation is due to Him who holds
the winds and subdues the storms.

22. We reached the Seamen's Tank, or St. Helena,
and anchored in safety. Although I had read many descriptions of this far famed isle, which the Giver of all
good seems to have placed here on purpose to refresh
the weary mariner after his exposure to the storms of the
Cape, I had formed no adequate idea of the place.
What must have been the emotions of Napoleon as he
approached his rocky prison—a prison that resembled in
magnitude his own ambition!

Our anchor was scarcely down, when the American
Consul, Mr. J. Carroll, the physician, and two other gentlemen came on board. The Consul invited us to go on
shore with him and remain at his residence during our
stay at the place.

We availed ourselves of his invitation, and were
soon at the consulate, where we were welcomed by
Mrs. Carroll. We dined at three o'clock, and at four,
Mrs. C. and myself started for a walk. Jamestown
is situated in a valley not more than four or five hundred
yards in width, and I could scarcely help feeling as I
passed through the street and looked at the mountains of

stone on each side, that they were about to fall and over-
whelm all in one common ruin.   They do not appear to be
of solid granite, but seem to look loose and crumbling, as
though any slight convulsion of the earth or even the elements might easily discompose them.   I need not write
more of this well known island, as much has been said
about it, and I cannot hope to offer any thing new.   We
visited the garden and the store, where we found the useful, the agreeable and the entertaining.   The houses are
two stories high, and on the street look neat and pretty.
I looked in vain for the costumes of different nations, of
which I have read as being worn here.   All the inhabitants or strangers that we met were dressed in the European style.   There are about four thousand inhabitants
on the island; two-thirds of them are colored.

   After returning from our walk, tea was served, and we
spent an agreeable evening at Mr. Wm. Carroll's, the
Ex-Consul.

   23.   Sabbath.   A company of officers and soldiers accompanied by the band, all in full uniform, passed, on
their way to church, at eleven, A. M.   The martial music, however it might accord with the appearance of the
company which it escorted, did not seem to me in keeping with the holy day.   The whole parade savored
strongly of Catholicism.   There are two Episcopal
churches on the island—one in Jamestown, and the other
in the country, near the Governor's residence.   There is
also a small Baptist society.   We attended the services
of the latter in the morning, in company with the elder
Mr. Carroll, and the Episcopal in the evening.

   Mr. W. gave his men liberty to go on shore on the
Sabbath.   Half the number were to go in the forenoon,
and return to the vessel at noon, when the other half

were to leave. No money was allowed, as Mr. W. did not wish to have any drunken frolics on the Sabbath. Accordingly, the respectable part of the crew visited the island in the morning, and returned peaceably to the vessel at noon. The drunkards took their turn in the afternoon. Two of them, called Bob and Tom, soon came to the Consul's and asked Mr. W. for money, but their request was denied. They came again and again; and the third time they used very improper language to their commander. We were greatly annoyed and mortified by their conduct. They had evidently procured rum somewhere.

24. I arose at an early hour, and seated myself at my chamber window in front of the principal street, to see what I could of life in St. Helena. I saw some red-coats pass, then some donkeys from the country, bearing cabbages, turnips, peaches and pears, and then came several poor people who had been to buy their breakfast, consisting of a loaf of bread, large or small according to the number to be served. Some had hot coffee, and a portion of fish or flesh, while others carried a bottle, which may or may not have contained coffee, tea or milk. At length a long procession of liberated Africans passed, who were dressed in white frocks and blue trowsers. They were accompanied by a driver with a whip in his hand. I inquired what became of these liberated captives, and was informed that they were let out in the colonies for the term of five years, which they were required to serve to defray their expenses to government. I could not learn what became of them after this term expired.

The Consul informed us at breakfast that eight vessels had arrived since Saturday morn, all of which had suffered from the late gale off the Cape. One, a Swiss ship, had lost its commander overboard, and was greatly injured. He remarked that none had suffered so little injury as our bark. "Ah!" said I, "the Zotoff,

' With all its faults, I love it still.' "

Contrary to our expectations, Mr. W. was detained till six o'clock in the evening. In the morning we called on Mrs. Leege, the mother of Mrs. Carroll. She seemed to possess a heart overflowing with love. As this lady lived a near neighbor to Napoleon before his removal to Longwood, I had many questions to ask concerning him, and the old lady seemed never to tire of talking about him. She said that he seldom missed a day without visiting their cottage. He was much attached to Mrs. Carroll, who was then an infant, and while caressing and playing with the child he would seem almost cheerful.

After tea we took leave of Mrs. C. and her niece, who had received and entertained us in so agreeable a manner that we left with regret. The ever attentive Consul, with Capt. Grinnell, who had dined at the consulate, accompanied us to the vessel where we took leave of them.

Our anchor was once more raised, and our sails spread for home. Bob had been exchanged for one of Capt. Grinnell's men, but Tom remained on board. After we had got well under way, Tom was ordered to haul tight the main-topmast studding sail tack. The impudence of Tom the day before had been received so mildly on shore by the captain, that he was now disposed to try it again. He had no sooner uttered his speech than Mr. W. caught him by his beard, which was of a most convenient length, and throwing him upon the deck, placed his knee upon his breast, and told him that he was not on shore now, but on board a vessel where impudence was never allowed—that he had not forgotten the insults of yester-

day, and that he would be required to look well to his
conduct the rest of the passage. He then allowed the
sailor to rise, and making him feel the end of a rope a
few times, he sent him forward that he might have an
opportunity for reflection before using any more impudence to one as large as himself.

25. Tom has shaved off his long beard, which got
somewhat twisted last night, and has asked the captain's
pardon for his past conduct, saying that rum caused it.
He also begged me to forgive his behaving so badly when
there was a lady on board, and promised that there should
be no future cause for complaint. He will probably keep
his promise unless Neptune supplies him with rum, which
I believe he is not in the habit of doing.

May 1. The weather is pleasant, and all hands are
employed in scrubbing, painting, tarring, &c., to clean
and improve the appearance of the bark. The spring
cleaning at home is nothing compared to this home cleaning in the spring.

We talk now a great deal about home, and every one
looks cheerful. My Feejeean girl is learning to sew,
and appears quite happy. She hates the stewardess,
however, who is a colored woman, whom we engaged in
Manilla, and who breaks all our dishes, loses the spoons,
knives, &c., and then lays it to the *caravan*, as she calls
Phebe, meaning cannibal.

4. About eleven, A. M., we observed a brig at some
distance steering S. W., but its course was soon changed
to W. N. W., and it seemed intending to make us a visit.
Sometimes, no doubt, it is exceedingly pleasant to receive a visit " while sailing o'er a waste of waters," but
we were in a suspicious place, being somewhat near the
" slavers' track;" moreover, the vessel bore a suspicious appearance, being long, low and black, with raking

masts, and sailing with the speed of a steamer. Again, its conduct was suspicious. Why should it alter its course and hurry towards us in such a manner?—we had showed no signals of distress. Mr. W., after watching its movements, said, "If it is a pirate, we stand no chance of running away from her." He then ordered the four large guns to be loaded, and the course of the bark to be altered, that we might run to meet our visitor, for such it seemed intending to be. The guns were loaded, the ports triced up, the course altered, and the guns looked out saucily from the open ports, all arrayed on the side of the bark where they could be observed from the suspicious vessel, which had advanced most rapidly towards us, but showed no colors. As soon as all was in readiness, and they observed us standing towards them, their course was again altered, and they seemed as anxious to get clear of, as they had been to visit us. It is probable that if the vessel was a pirate, it took us for a man-of-war, as all the show possible was made of heads on our decks, and I believe it is not usual for merchant vessels to run towards a piratical vessel. The mate had filled one of his socks with powder to put in the biggest gun, and it was thought best to fire it after the retreating vessel, which was done, and the sock has never been heard from since.

7. We are now sixty miles north of the Equator. The weather continues pleasant. A shark has followed us for several days past, but the remains of a porpoise were thrown overboard, and the shark has stopped to feast upon it. It is to be supposed that his apparent attention to us was not from love, but like others of his species on land, he followed the sailors for what could be obtained. Our days pass monotonously but hopefully.

Many changes probably await us on our return to our native land.

Mr. W. employs a part of his time in teaching those who were lads when we left Salem, the science of navigation. They have made good progress. George, especially, bids fair to become a thorough and scientific navigator.

10. Joy! joy! the highlands of Neversink are in sight. A New York pilot is on board, and we soon expect to leave our prison home for *terra firma* once more.

12. Last evening our anchor was lowered in the harbor of New York. I knew not that we had a friend in the city to greet us, but it was pleasant to feel that our voyage was ended, that our perils in strange lands and on the deep were over, and that after an absence of three years and eleven months, we had safely reached the happy shores of America.

This morning, Capt. H., a friend who had removed from Charlestown with his family during our absence, came to welcome us to our native land, and I was soon an inmate of his very comfortable dwelling, surrounded by his family, and receiving their warm congratulations.

June 13. The lad, Nat, informed the mate, that, as he was walking through one of the streets of the city, he met Tom, the sailor, who, it will be remembered, behaved himself so unbecomingly at St. Helena; moreover, Tom invited him to walk a little way with him. He complied with the request, and soon found himself in the office of a lawyer, who required him to make a deposition respecting the cruel conduct of Capt. Wallis to Tom when off St. Helena. He said that he told the lawyer he knew nothing about it, and left the office immediately. In the afternoon the three Salem lads and one sailor left the city for their homes.

14. A handsome bill was presented this morning to Mr. W. It had been contracted by the Salem boys for pies and cakes. I did not learn whether confectionary was included; perhaps a separate bill may be forthcoming for that luxury.

Tom, the sailor, came to Mr. W., saying that he had not been sufficiently sober to visit him before, and showed a document in the hand-writing of the lad, Nat. Mr. W. examined the paper, and found that it contained an exaggerated account of his conduct towards Tom on the night we left St. Helena. After perusing the document, Mr. W. returned it to its owner, and quietly asked what he intended to do with it. "Nothing, sir," replied the sailor. "I never thought that you punished me as much as I deserved. Nat and George were at me all the way home about prosecuting you when we arrived here. They said that New York was just the place for it, and George said he should persuade his father to prosecute the captain for punishing him when he insulted the Feejeean chief; finally, Nat drew up the said document, and finding me on shore half drunk, persuaded me to go to a lawyer, and show him the paper." Mr. W. could not believe the whole of this statement, but called the men aft, and, on questioning them, they testified that it was true, adding that the two boys above named had omitted no opportunity of urging Tom to "prosecute the captain."

23. We arrived at Salem. The meetings, greetings and sayings, on that, to us, happy occasion, I will leave for the reader to imagine.

CHAPTER XVIII.

Departure for a Second Voyage to Feejee—Arrival at New Zealand—
Death of Two Missionaries—Departure from New Zealand—Arrival at
Feejee—Trials of the Missionaries—The Gale.

Oct. 12, 1848. After remaining at home for the space
of four months, I was induced to trust myself again on
the mighty waters, and accompany my husband in his
search for the riches of this world. As I left my readers
to imagine our joyous meeting with friends from whom
we had been so long absent, I will leave them to imagine
the parting scene. It is not my purpose to attempt a
description of either.

We embarked on board the bark Zotoff, belonging to
S. Chamberlain & Co., of Salem, bound to New Zealand,
Feejee, &c. Mr. J. F. Lovett serves as first, and Mr.
C. Fornis as second officer. J. Derby, who sailed and
performed the last voyage as a boy, now re-shipped as a
sailor. Mr. W. finding it impossible to furnish his boys
with pies, cakes, and milk for coffee and tea, has carefully avoided engaging any more of the Salem pets, but
has two boys supplied by the city missionary. It was
not his purpose to be troubled with any, but on receiving a promise that he would break no mothers'
hearts, he consented to receive them. One is only
twelve years of age,—a mere child. Phebe, the Feejeean girl, is to serve as stewardess. She was highly delighted with all she saw in America. The cook and two
of the sailors are Salem men; the rest of the crew are
foreigners.

Feb. 19. We arrived at New Zealand. Nothing unusual
occurred during our voyage. The lives and health of all

have been spared, we have crossed the ocean in safety, and our anchor is once more cast near the land.

The town at the Bay of Islands was mostly destroyed in 1844 by the natives of this part of the island; but as we came in sight of it, I observed that several new buildings had been erected, which gave signs that there were civilized people in the place. We also observed that the little Episcopal chapel, and the parsonage belonging to it, had been left standing by the ruthless despoiler; also the church and buildings belonging to the Roman Catholics.

Our anchor was not down when we were visited by Mr. Bateman, the harbor-master, who cordially invited us to make his house our home during our stay. The residence of Mr. B. and lady is situated at about half the distance to the top of Flag-Staff Hill, and looks very pretty and romantic, but we found the way truly toil-some. We were met at the door by Mr. and Mrs. B., and introduced to several ladies and gentlemen. During the evening we were informed by Mr. B. that our esteemed friend, Rev. J. Hunt, died in Feejee sometime during the last October, and that his family had arrived in Auckland, on their return to England.

During our residence in Feejee, I had been in the family of Mr. Hunt for nearly a year, and had an opportunity of becoming well acquainted with the many excellencies of his character, and had become much attached to him and his truly estimable wife. The news of his death filled our hearts with sadness.

21. Capt. Wright called upon us. He invited Mr. W. and myself to spend the morrow with his family at his residence, a little above the Wapoa. I spent most of the day in writing letters to friends at home.

22. Mr. W. and myself started in the boat, to pay our promised visit to Mr. Wright and family. We enjoyed a delightful sail up the river on which the little village of Wapoa is situated. There is a small military force stationed at Wapoa. On our arrival at the residence of Capt. W., we were warmly received by him, and his lady and daughter. We spent a most delightful day, were regaled with pears, apples and grapes, and were presented with apples to take to the vessel. Capt. Wright lost a large amount of property during the rebellion of the natives in 1844.

23. I visited the spot once occupied as the residence of Capt. Clayton, in company with Mrs. B. The pretty cot had been destroyed, our friends had departed, and nothing was left of former days but two centennial plants and a rose geranium. I plucked a slip from the latter, intending to plant it in a strange soil. Capt. C. and family saved nothing but the clothes they wore at the time the natives destroyed the place. We walked over the grounds that were once so prettily decorated and owned by Mr. Caflin. There was now no little basket of strawberries, nor splendid boquet of flowers to be offered; a little, very little hedge of hawthorn was all that was left. We passed on and soon arrived at the parsonage. The garden fence was gone,—the beautiful plants and shrubs were all destroyed,—the pretty lattice, that once supported the honeysuckle and rose,—all,—all were gone. The little building, once occupied by the happy and devoted minister of the gospel, as a study, was now a place of shelter for the goats. We entered the piazza; the wind sounded mournfully through the house, the shutters to the windows were rattling, and every thing spoke of desolation. Here, there seemed to be something left that affected the mind even more sadly than

the places we had previously visited. Where are those happy countenances that once met us at the now closed doors? One has been called from her earthly joys and sorrows to join the saints on high, while her companion is, it is feared, a confirmed lunatic. Such are life's changes!

27. We took leave of our very kind friends, Mr. and Mrs. Bateman, and reëmbarked on board our floating, but hitherto safe home. We were kindly furnished by them with various plants and shrubs from their garden to take with us to Feejee. We shall ever remember their kindness. Should they wander to a strange land, may they ever meet with the kindness they have so liberally bestowed upon us.

March 6. Anchored at Motureke after a passage of ten days from New Zealand. Mr. Whippy, being on his way to Bau, left his canoe and came on board. He informed us that the Salem brig, Tim Pickering, was wrecked at Levuka during a severe gale, which occurred on the 5th of April, 1848. A schooner belonging to some of the white residents of Feejee was lost at the same time. Rev. Dr. Lyth was a passenger, but left the schooner and went on board the Tim Pickering at the commencement of the gale, and thus his life was providentially saved, as were the lives of all those who were on board the brig. The schooner was manned by three, two of whom were drowned; the third was a son of Mr. Whippy. He jumped into the sea before the schooner went to pieces, where he sustained himself by swimming from nine o'clock in the morning till four o'clock the next morning, when he struck his hand against some solid substance, which proved to be the little boat that had belonged to the schooner. He kept hold of it for some time, but it was full of water, and, as

he had no means of freeing it, he let it go, finding it
easier to sustain himself without it. He had now been
one day and night in the sea, and the storm still continued in all its violence; but "Hope on, hope ever"
seemed to be his motto; fear never entered his heart,
nor did his physical strength seem to abate; he merely
kept himself afloat, and the tide drifted him where it
listed. About daylight the waves cast him on a reef,
where he thought he could rest till the tide rose. He
could perceive no land, and his only prospect was to
commit himself again to the watery element, as the coming tide would soon compel him to leave the reef. He
had not been in this situation long, however, before he
perceived a dark object approaching the spot where he
was resting, which proved to be the little boat before
mentioned. On, on it came, and seemed to say, "I will
not forsake thee." David freed it from water with his
hands; there was one thole-pin left, which exactly fitted
for a plug to the hole in the bottom of the little ark.
David embarked, and without sail, oar, or paddle, once
more committed himself to the raging elements, where
he was drifted and driven about for two days and two
nights, when the storm abated, and he found himself
near land.

Here other perils awaited him, and now fear entered
his mind. He knew that it was an invariable custom
for all Feejeeans to murder the shipwrecked, and he had
no reason to believe that he would be spared. He landed, however, and hid himself in the bush, where he was
soon found by a native. David told him who he was,
and the native desired him to remain where he was till
he returned to the town and informed the chief. "No,"
said David, "you intend to bring other men, to kill and
eat me here without the knowledge of the chief. I shall

go with you to the town; if I am killed, it shall be by the orders of the chief, and then my father will know what to do about it."

On their arrival at the town, a scene of confusion ensued. Some were for killing and eating the poor lad at once, others were in favor of deferring the butchery for a time, and the exhausted boy was near being torn in pieces by the contending parties, and he began to feel that it would have been better to have perished in the waters than to fall into the hands of these merciless savages, who were thus thirsting for his emaciated body. He had not, however, been saved from the storm and flood to serve as food for cannibals; here, too, was a way of deliverance appointed by Him who had saved the life of the lad thus far. A chief of another tribe was present during the confusion, and I presume he must have been a "*vasu*" to the place, as he claimed David for his own, and thus put an end to the contention.

After his liberation, the chief inquired his name, &c. David told him that he was the son of the Mata ge Mbau at Solavu. "Then I possess a prize," said the chief; "you shall be restored to your father." The chief soon took him home. The father received him as one restored from death. Great was the rejoicing,—the fatted hog was killed, the deliverer and his followers were feasted, and on their departure were loaded with valuable presents by the grateful parent. David had drifted to the distance of about seventy miles from the place where the unfortunate schooner was anchored, and about ten or twelve from Solavu, where his father resided.

The Levuka people first took possession of the property belonging to the Tim Pickering, but it was eventually claimed and given up to Bau.

We learn that the mission of Feejee has been variously afflicted since we left. Mrs. Hazlewood, wife of Rev. D. Hazlewood, died the last week, of dysentery, leaving an infant two weeks old. Mr. H. is stationed at Nandy. Two little girls are also deprived of a mother's affection and care by this afflicting dispensation.

Another event has occurred which it gives me more pain to record than the death of the righteous. Mr. Jaggar, who has labored so indefatigably and with so much apparent sincerity for the space of ten years in the ministry of the gospel, has committed a most grievous sin, has been deposed from the ministry, and has gone to New Zealand with his family.

7. We arrived off Bau and Vewa, but were obliged to remain several hours on board after the vessel was anchored, before the tide would serve for our landing at Vewa, and it was nearly dark before we reached its shores. Dr. Lyth, with his family, met us on the shore. The tide was not yet full, and we were obliged to step from the boat on to a canoe in order to land. My mind was entirely occupied with the sad changes that had taken place since we parted from the kind friends who had now assembled to greet us on our return. Mr. W. was leading me across the canoe, and cautioning me to be careful of my steps, but I did not hear or attend to the caution, my feet slipped and I fell, receiving a violent blow on my chest from a cross bar of the canoe. When I arose from my muddy bed, I presume I could not have been taken for a Naiad. I was conducted to the house in my *elegant* plight, and made as comfortable as possible; but I continued to suffer from the effects of the severe blow I had received.

Rev. Mr. Calvert has removed to Vewa with his family, and occupies the late residence of Mr. Hunt. Mr.

C. has gone to Nandy to bring the two little motherless girls of Mr. Hazlewood to Vewa. Mrs. C., whom we had not seen before, soon came in.

We learned that Rev. Mr. Watsford and family had removed to Lakemba, and that they had suffered much during the past year. Their little girl had died from the effect of ill-treatment received from a Feejeean girl that had been employed by Mrs. W. to assist her in taking care of the child. As the girl always appeared kind, the parents had no suspicion that any thing was wrong, although their babe became sickly, and would often scream as if in great distress. The parents brought it to Vewa, that it might have the benefit of Dr. Lyth's advice; but no one seemed to understand the disease. The child lingered for some months, when an eruption appeared in its side, and in two weeks after the exposure and fright during a severe gale of February last, the little sufferer died. The girl, who had assisted in its care, confessed that she had often, when displeased about any thing, squeezed the dear babe in her arms with all her strength, thus injuring it internally, and no doubt causing its death.

After spending some time in company with our friends, we returned to the bark. Mr. and Mrs. Lyth and Mrs. Calvert kindly invited me to reside with them while we remained in Feejee. I had decided to accompany my husband to the Ba coast, but accepted their invitation for the time that we should remain in the vicinity.

8. This morning, with a sad heart I revisited my once happy home. No alteration was to be seen in the interior of the house, and the furniture was the same as when I left; but those who had said, "My dear Mrs. W., I think that we shall meet again in this life," were not there. The little girl who had stretched out her

arms and said, "Me kith aunty Wathy," was nowhere to be seen. One had entered his glorious rest,—the others had departed,—all seemed dead to me.

The following account of the last days of our lamented friend, is from the copy of a letter written by Mr. Calvert to Rev. Dr. Hannah of England, who was the theological tutor of Mr. Hunt. The letter is long, giving a summary of the birth, conversion, education, ministry, &c., of Mr. Hunt, which I shall not copy entire.

"On the 6th of September I arrived at Vewa, by the Wesley, from Lakemba. I found brother Hunt able to sit on the sofa, and walk over the room with a stick; but very much shattered by his frequent attacks, and continued disease.

On the 7th I had a long conversation with him. He spoke of his very severe attack of illness. After the removal of his paroxysm, on the 9th of August, he entered into a full consideration of his state. He said,—'I had most humbling views of my own nothingness and uselessness which distressed me, until it came to my mind powerfully, as if the Lord had spoken it to me, 'Are not ye my work in the Lord? If I be not an apostle unto others, yet doubtless I am to you; for the seal of mine apostleship are ye in the Lord.' 'After that the Lord would not allow me to reproach myself, but manifested himself to me in a surprising manner, and I seemed overwhelmed and filled with the love of God. My will was completely lost in God's will.' At the same time, he said, 'I feel my work is done.'

On the 17th, I read, at brother Hunt's request, the 9th and 10th of Hebrews. After prayer he said, 'I never had such views and hold of the Saviour as I have in this illness. I feel him to be a perfect Saviour.'

On the 26th he had been confined to his bed a week,

21

and was very much reduced. I read the 17th of John
and prayed. He was much engaged in devotion during
prayer. Towards the close, he began to weep. After
we rose from our knees, his weeping continued and increased, until at length he burst out crying aloud,
'Lord, bless Feejee! save Feejee! Thou knowest my
soul has loved Feejee. My heart has travailed in pain
for Feejee.' Mrs. Hunt and myself were gratified with
the outburstings of what always filled his heart; but we
knew his weakness would not admit of such great exertion, therefore, we tried to prevent him. I said, 'The
Lord knows you love Feejee. We know, the Feejeean
Christians know, and heathens of Feejee know it too.
You labored hard for Feejee when you were strong.
Now you are so weak you must be silent. God will save
Feejee. He is saving Feejee.' For a short time he
wept aloud; but again, unable to suppress his emotions,
he wept and called aloud, with great vehemency, grasping
me firmly with one hand, and raising the other, exclaimed,
'Oh, let me pray once more for Feejee! Lord, for Christ's
sake, bless Feejee! save Feejee! save thy servants!
save the heathen! save thy people in Feejee!' His full
heart was overpowered, and he would gladly have ago-
nized beyond his strength, as he had labored, in behalf
of Feejee; but we insisted upon his giving up and being
easy.

On the 28th he said, 'For two days I can think only
of Paul's language,—' I am in a strait betwixt two.' If
needful for my family and the church, I shall be raised
up again. I have no choice. I am resigned to the will
of God. I am more,—I love the will of God. He rules.'
I said, 'If we ruled, we should keep you; but He knows
best.' 'Yes,' was his reply. 'He is my ruler, my
protector. He will soon make it up in many ways.'

At daylight, on the 4th of October, we found brother Hunt exceedingly weak. We assembled round his bed. He said, 'How strange! I cannot realize that I am dying; and yet you all look as if I were. If this be dying, praise the Lord.' At his request brother Lyth read the 14th of John. He engaged with his wonted earnestness in prayer. He desired again and again to be left alone. His mind, which retained all its vigor to the last, was fully engaged, his eyes uplifted, and his lips moving. I said, 'The Lord is faithful and keeps you.' 'Yes,' he replied. About one o'clock he said, 'It is a solemn thing to die,—very solemn.' I said, 'Mr. Wesley, in dying, clung to Jesus, and you do.' 'Yes,' he replied, with solemnity. 'I cling to Jesus, and am right. I have nothing else to look to. He is all I have to trust in. If I look from Him, I am in a vortex,—have doubts and condemnation. I have full faith in Him. I have peace and pardon through Him. I have no disturbance at all.' His whole soul was engaged with the Lord. He cried aloud, 'Oh, Lord, my Saviour! Jesus!' More than usual earnestness marked his countenance. Shortly after this wrestling with the God of all grace and consolation, his complacent smile bespoke gratitude and joy. Then he appeared to be engaged in meditation. Again he spoke: —'I want strength to praise Him abundantly!—I am very happy.'

About eight o'clock in the morning, after being informed of the approach of death, he said to Mrs. Hunt, 'Oh, for one more baptism!' She then asked him if he had received a fresh manifestation. His reply was, 'Yes; hallelujah!' and added, 'I do not depend on this (significantly shaking his head). I bless the Lord. I trust in Jesus.' Soon after he said, 'Now He is my joy. I thought I should have entered heaven singing, 'Jesus and salvation.' Now I shall go singing, 'Jesus, salvation and glory,—eternal glory.' He then settled down, saying many times, 'Hallelujah!'

He delivered messages to the chiefs, the people, his brethren and sisters; prayed for his children, desiring them to obey and imitate their mother; affectionately commended his much beloved partner to the guidance of Divine Providence ;, prayed for God's blessing on a faithful servant, who had been with him ever since his arrival in Feejee; and then desired me to pray.

About three o'clock, P. M., he grasped me and turned on his side, and after breathing with difficulty for about twenty minutes, his spirit departed to eternal blessedness.

The natives flocked to see the remains of their beloved minister. A neat coffin was made, and covered with black cloth, on which was inscribed:—

'REV. JOHN HUNT
Slept in Jesus
October 4, 1848.
Aged 36 years.'

Early on the morning of the 5th, the principal chief of Bau arrived, with many attendants. He was impatient to see the remains; and was evidently much affected with brother Hunt's message, and the account we gave of his end."

It seems mysterious to us that so good and faithful a servant in the vineyard of the Lord should be called thus early from his labors. In these he was truly abundant, as I was a witness while an inmate of his happy family. He seldom retired to rest before twelve o'clock at night, and always rose at early dawn. Every department of the mission received a portion of his care. With some assistance, he translated the New Testament into the

Feejeean language, translated hymns, prepared cate-
chisms, instructed a class of young men in theology, and
prepared them for native teachers. He attended to the
erection of two commodious buildings; and the sick received his constant care till Dr. Lyth's removal to Vewa.
The amount of labor which he accomplished was truly
astonishing; but his heart was in his work, and he never
seemed to grow weary or tire. Every one loved him,
for he was the friend of all. Mr. Calvert states with
truth, "That he gained much influence every where,
and with almost every body. In his intercourse with
chiefs, heathen and Christian people, captains of ships,
foreigners, his brethren,—every one,—he was most happy; and was successful in doing good to an immense extent. The effects of his life, voyaging, prayers, preaching, conversation, &c., are on a broad basis, and will
doubtless tell much as long as Feejee exists."

9. Vewa has changed much in its appearance during
the past year. Many of the former houses were blown
down during the severe hurricanes of February and
April, and others have been erected in their stead. The
large house belonging to the chief, and the little "*buri*"
of his son, were destroyed, and smaller houses have, in
part, replaced them. The chapel was also destroyed.

10. Though feeling very unwell, and still suffering
from the effects of the blow which I received on landing,
I attended service in the chapel. The rude pulpit is
covered with black, and every object reminds me of him
who has gone to his rest.

After the conclusion of the services, I visited the grave
of our lamented friend. He lies interred just back of
the chapel. A neat fence surrounds the grave, and
white sea shells cover it. I felt, as I gazed upon the

narrow bed, that I sorrowed more on account of his loss than I rejoiced in his happiness.

Dr. Lyth conducted all the religious services of the day,—both English and native. There was no one to preach on board the Zotoff.

16. It has rained at Vewa some part of every day for the last six months. I can scarcely get an opportunity to go out of doors, as the mud does not get dried from one shower to another. This morning Mr. W. sent for me to come to the bark, if I was able, as Thakombau and lady wished to see me. The man who brought the message had dressed himself in a neat suit of white, to wait upon me to the vessel. He succeeded in handing me safely over the stile, but on going over himself, he slipped, fell into the yellow mud, and decorated his clean suit finely. He looked mortified, but there was no help for it; the tide was fast receding, and he must go with me as he was.

I found our royal visitors in a most gracious humor. They, with their numerous attendants, passed the day on board. The Bauans have rebuilt Rewa, and are ready to crown Phillips king of the place, but he has not the courage to reside there, on account of his brother, Garenggeo, who still resides in the mountains. Thakombau has commenced building a stone house for himself, but as there is only one mason at work, it will not go up as speedily as buildings of that sort are erected in America.

18. Navinde, with his lady, visited us to-day. This visiting of the chiefs, accompanied by their principal wives, is quite a new thing in Feejee. It has never been known till quite lately, and, as yet, has only been done by Thakombau and Navinde. I have had visitors from Bau nearly every day, and some presents. My

namesake, too, and the wife of Elijah are constant visitors. Their words are invariably after the word of salutation. " *Sa mate* Mr. Hunt. Mrs. Hunt *sa lako.*"
" Mr. Hunt is dead. Mrs. Hunt is gone."

19. There were no religious services, as Dr. Lyth is
ill with the dysentery, attended with considerable fever.
Two of their children are also sick. Their residence
can scarcely be healthy in the rainy season, as its locality is low and damp. Mrs. Calvert has invited the
family to spend some time at the Vale Kau, thinking that
the change may prove beneficial to them all.

We have laid out a pretty garden spot in front of
the piazza at the Vale Kau, but I sadly fear that the
plants brought from New Zealand will rot in the ground
before they take root, on account of the quantity of rain
that falls daily.

23. Namosimalua is absent from Vewa the most of
the time, his wife having left him to reside with her
friends in Bau. She endured much from his tyrannical disposition before leaving him. Soon after she left,
Elijah persuaded her to return ; but instead of being
received with kindness by her husband, he met her with
the most severe reproofs and accusations till she became
nearly maddened, fled from the house, and leaped from
the precipice near which the house stands. She was
taken up senseless, and carried back to Bau. She has
not yet recovered from the effects of her fall. She has
been much blamed for leaving her tyrant; but I think
she is more to be pitied than blamed. Obliged to be the
wife of one that she could never love, she has endured
his brutality for years, till endurance could scarcely
be called a virtue. For ten years she has adorned the
religion that she has professed; but in a moment of
temptation she has brought a wound upon the cause by

her attempt at self-destruction.   I have not seen her, as
she does not come to Vewa, and I have not been able to
go to Bau.

24.   Elijah has returned from Ba, where he has been
since our arrival, and arrangements are making for him
to accompany us on that coast, to assist, by his influence with the chiefs, in collecting our cargo.

Of the deep piety and devotion of Elijah, all speak in
the highest terms.   Even the white residents, who formerly spoke of his religion as being "all a humbug,"
are now compelled to acknowledge that he, who was a
most relentless cannibal, is now "a bright and shining
light."

26.   Mrs. Calvert has given me some account of the
sufferings of Mr. and Mrs. Hazlewood at Ono during the
gale of April last.   It appears that the profusion of musquitoes at Ono renders the place at times almost insup-
portable.   No rest is to be had, day or night.   Mr. H.
had built a little house on a very small uninhabited
island, on a reef situated at some distance from Ono, or
far enough from the large island to discourage the musquitoes from undertaking a journey to the place.   Here
the family were in the habit of retiring, to rest a little
from their tormentors.

At the commencement of the gale, Mr. Hazlewood
went to Ono to preach, and the winds became so furious
that he could not return to his family.   He could only
look towards the little island which held his dearest
earthly treasures, with fear that the billows were about
to cover it, and pray to God to save them.   Besides
Mrs. H. and the children, there were two or three native women and one man only on the reef.   About midnight their house was blown down, and they fled to a
little place that had been built to cook in; from this,

however, they were soon driven by the waves of the sea. They then fled to a part of the island that was a little more elevated, the natives made a shelter of leaves, and they remained in this situation for two days, till the storm abated, and the anxious and distressed husband rejoined his suffering family. Mr. H. could perceive from the large island that the house was gone, and for two days he had feared that all his dear ones had been swept away by the flood; his meeting with them again, was like their being restored from the grave. Since then, one of their children has died. At the last District Meeting the family removed to Nandy, where Mrs. H. died.

27. Dr. Lyth and family are now visitors at the Vale Kau. He is very feeble, and we are anxious about him. The children are somewhat better. The faithful man who served the family of Mr. Hunt many years, often calls to see me. He says, "You loved Mr. and Mrs. Hunt greatly, and so did I, and when I look upon you, I feel that I must see them too."

The British man-of-war, Calypso, paid a short visit to this group a few months' since. They burned the town on Vetelavu belonging to the chief who murdered the two white men while we were on our late voyage to Feejee. Being short of provisions, they did not attend to the other cases.

April 1. Mr. Calvert arrived last night from Nandy with two of the little Hazlewoods. There are now ten children at the Vale Kau, all under eight years of age. Mr. and Mrs. Calvert are desirous that Dr. Lyth and family should reside here permanently, while they remove to the Vale Vatu.

CHAPTER XIX.

Departure for Ba—Feejeean Names—Dillon's Rock—Prospect of a Battle
—Visit of a Missionary—A Feejeean Plot—The "*Soro.*"

April 4.   All things being in readiness for our departure to Ba, I took leave of our kind entertainers with
regret, and embarked once more on board the Zotoff.   I
had been quite unwell during my stay at Vewa, and
Mrs. C. had shown me all the kind attention of a sister,
and the more I became acquainted with her the more
admirable her character appeared.

On arriving at the vessel, I found several additions to
our former company.   Elijah and a dozen of his people
were to accompany us to Ba.   There were some curious
names among them, such as Ngone Tha (a bad child);
Nga (a duck); Kalava (a rat); Bona Boaka (a pig's
tail), &c.   Thakombau has presented a large ox to be
given to Touaga, that he may be of " a good mind " towards Mr. Wallis, and procure him a great many fish.
The animal stood gazing about him, apparently astonished at the novelty of his situation.

7.   Ba.   We arrived here this afternoon, after stopping on our way at Buladagaloa and Tabua, to make
arrangements for the erection of " *beech de mer* "
houses.

As we passed Raverave Elijah told us a legend concerning it, but says he does not like to tell such stories
now, although once he believed them all to be true.

The natives of Feejee always have a story on hand.
Every town, place and tribe, has its legendary accounts
of its origin, and concerning all its affairs.   There is
scarcely a rock, island, mountain or river that we pass,

which has not its tale. They must be a most imaginative people. On moonlight nights the natives often sit relating and listening to stories.

24. Buladagaloa. In company with Elijah and the pilot, I visited the town at this place. We sailed up a narrow river, walled on each side by the beautiful mangroves. After landing, we crossed several dykes, and at length arrived at a high fence, and apparently a strong one, being composed of large stones, mud and logs, surmounted by a lighter one of reeds. This fortification is called a "*ba-ni valu*," or a fence of war. We entered an opening, and found a small town of about thirty houses romantically situated in a mud puddle. I stooped and looked in at the doors of a few of them, but had no desire to enter. They were without mats, and looked cheerless enough. We passed out of the town, and took a long walk towards the mountains. Several of the inhabitants followed us, and appeared more curious to see Phebe, who accompanied us, and who they were told had been to America, than they were to see the white woman. Just back of the town are several acres of fine table land, dry, and a much better locality for a town than the site now occupied; but fear of their enemies deters the natives from building upon it.

The people belonging here have for many years been carrying on a warfare with many of the towns of Ba and other places.

26. We crossed from Vetelavu and anchored off Dillon's rock, which is quite a prominent object, considerably elevated, of a dark color, and flat at the top. An event occurred at this place in the year 1813, which I shall relate as Dillon has given it in his voyages.

In order that the story may be properly understood, it is necessary to state that Dillon came to Feejee in the ship Hunter, Capt. Robson, for the purpose of collecting sandal wood at Bua and the vicinity. Capt. R. had been here several times before for the same purpose, when he had assisted the natives in fighting their enemies, and in procuring bodies to satisfy their cannibal appetites.

On his arrival here in 1813, his old friends told him that the enemies he had assisted in conquering had revolted, and it would be difficult for them to cut sandal wood, unless he would first assist them to reconquer their foes, after which they would load his vessel in a short time. Capt. R. again assisted them, and they destroyed a great many people, towns and plantations, but the chiefs and natives did not come up to their agreement. Several months passed, and the vessel remained without its cargo. The chiefs remained away, and the disappointed captain was provoked at the trick played upon him. He vowed vengeance against his old allies, and took fourteen of their canoes at the commencement. Soon after, Capt. R. wished to have a cutter belonging to the Hunter taken on shore for some repairs. Before doing this, however, he wished to possess himself of the rest of the Wailea canoes, that he might repair the cutter in safety. We now proceed to give an account of the expedition and battle in Dillon's own words:—

"On the morning of the 6th of September, the Europeans belonging to the ship, and also the Europeans from Bau were all armed with muskets, and placed under the command of Mr. Norman, the first officer. We landed at a place called the Black Rock, and were soon joined by the Bau chiefs and a hundred of their men. The boats and canoes then put off into deep water, which precaution was used to prevent their getting aground by the tide ebbing. On landing, the Europeans began to disperse into straggling parties of two, three and four in a group. I begged of Mr. Norman to cause them to keep close together in case of a sudden attack from the islanders; but no attention was paid to my remonstrance. We proceeded by a narrow path over a small level plain without interruption, until we arrived at the foot of a hill, which we ascended, and soon gained the level or table land on its top. There a few natives showed themselves, and tried to irritate us by shouts and gestures.

Mr. Norman turned to the right, along a narrow path, which led to a thicket where were some native houses. I followed him with seven other Europeans, the two Bau chiefs and one of their men. Here a few natives tried to dispute our passage; they were fired at, and one was shot dead; the rest retreated. Mr. Norman then directed the chief's house with some others to be set on fire. The order was immediately obeyed, and all were in flames in a few seconds. A few minutes after, we heard dreadful yells and shoutings of the savages proceeding from the road by which we had ascended to the table land. The Bau chiefs understood from the yells that some of their men as well as Europeans were killed by the Wailea people, who were concealed in ambush until they got us on the table land, where they attacked our straggling parties, who, having discharged their muskets, were killed before they had time to reload. Others, I afterwards understood, on seeing themselves nearly surrounded by the savages, threw down their muskets and ran towards the boat; two of them escaped. In Mr. Norman's party there were ten musket men, with the two Bau chiefs, and one of their followers. We determined to keep close together, and fight our way to the boats.

We immediately got out of the thicket on to the table land, where there were not more than three of the island-

ers, who shouted and called out to us that several of our
men were killed, as well as Bau men, and that we should
immediately share a similar fate.   On reaching the brink
of the path by which we were to descend to the plain, we
found Terence Dun lying dead with his brains beaten out
by a native club, and the whole plain between us and the
boats covered with thousands of infuriated savages, all
armed.

Before descending to the plain, a young man named
John Graham separated from us and ran into a thicket
of bushes on the left hand side of the road, where he was
quickly pursued by the three savages above mentioned,
who despatched him.   The remainder of us proceeded
down the precipice.   On getting to the bottom, the savages prepared to receive us.   They stood in thousands
on each side of the path, brandishing their weapons, with
their faces and bodies besmeared with the blood of our
slaughtered companions.   At this moment, a native who
came down the precipice after us, threw a spear at Mr.
Norman, which entered his back and passed out of his
breast.   He ran a few yards and fell down apparently
dead.   I fired at this native, and reloaded my musket as
soon as possible, when, on turning round, I found my
companions had all run by different routes.   Taking advantage of the absence of the natives, who had all quitted
the path and pursued our flying men, I dashed along with
all possible speed, but had not proceeded more than a
few yards when I came on to the dead body of William
Parker, who was prostrated across the path with his musket by him.   I took it up and retreated.

About this time the natives observed me and gave
chase.   One of them came up so close to me that I was
obliged to throw the musket away, and a pistol also
which I had in my belt.   In a moment after this, I

reached the foot of a steep rock that stood on the plain. Finding it impossible to get to the boat through the crowds of natives that intercepted the pathway, I called out to my companions (some of whom were on my right),

Take the hill! take the hill!' We then got to the top of it, where I joined the following persons. Charles Savage, a man named Luis, Martin Bushart, Thomas Dafny and William Wilson. The three former resided at Bau, and joined us at this island; the two latter belonged to the ship. Mic Macabe, Joseph Atkinson, and the two Bau chiefs were killed; these men had joined us here. Dafny fired his musket on the plain, and then broke it off at the end in defending himself. He was wounded in several parts of the body, and had four arrows stuck in his back; the point of a spear had pierced his shoulder, having entered from behind, and came out in the fore part, under the collar bone.

It fortunately happened that the rock to which we had escaped was so steep that few persons could ascend it at a time, and it was too much elevated for the natives to annoy us much with their spears or slings. They, however, shot several arrows at us, which were impeded by a strong gale of wind that blew them off their intended course. Our chief officer having fallen, I now, as next in rank, took command of the party, and stationed them in the best way I could to defend our post. I did not allow more than one or two muskets to be fired at a time, and kept the wounded man loading for us. Several of the natives ascended the hill to within a few yards of us, and were shot by us in self-defence as fast as they approached. After some of them had been killed in this manner, the rest kept off. Having but little ammunition left, we were as sparing of it as possible; besides this, we did not wish to irritate the natives more than they

already were, by firing, except when driven to it by necessity.   From our elevated situation we had a clear
view of the landing place; the boats at anchor, the two
Bau canoes and the ship were waiting our return.   We
had but little prospect of ever rejoining them, though I
had some hopes that Capt. Robson would make an effort
to rescue us by arming six Indian soldiers that were on
board, two or three Europeans, and the Bau people in
the canoes.   These hopes soon vanished when I saw the
Bau canoes set sail, and steer towards their own island
without passing alongside the ship.

The plain which surrounded the rock was covered with
armed savages assembled from all parts of the coast,
amounting to several thousands, who had been in ambush, waiting for us to land.   This assemblage now exhibited a scene revolting to human nature.   Fires were
prepared, and ovens heated for the reception of the
bodies of our ill-fated companions, who, as well as the
Bau chiefs and their slaughtered men, were brought to
the fires in the following manner.   Two of the Wailea
people placed a stick or limb of a tree on their shoulders,
over which were thrown the bodies of their victims, with
their legs hanging down on one side and their heads on
the other.   They were thus carried in triumph to the
ovens prepared to receive them.   Here they were placed
in a sitting posture, while the savages sung and danced
with joy over their prizes, and fired several musket balls
through each of the corpses, all the muskets of the slain
having fallen into their hands.   No sooner was this ceremony over than the priests began to cut up and dissect
these unfortunate men in our presence.   The feet were
cut off at the ancles, the legs from the knees, the thighs
at the hip joints, the hands at the wrists, the arms at the
elbows, the shoulders at the sockets, and lastly, the head

and neck were separated from the body. Each of these divisions of the human frame formed one joint, which was carefully wrapped in green plantain leaves, and placed in the ovens to be baked; meanwhile, we were closely guarded on all sides but one, which fronted the thick mangrove forest on the banks of the river. Savage proposed to Martin Bushart to run for that, and endeavor to escape to the water's side and swim for the ship. This I opposed, threatening to shoot the first man dead who left the hill, and my threat for the present had the desired effect. By this time the fury of the savages was somewhat abated, and they began to listen attentively to our harangues and offers of reconciliation. I reminded them that on the day the fourteen canoes were seized and taken, eight of their men had been made prisoners on board the ship, where they were now confined. One of them was Bete, brother of the chief of Wailea. I represented to the multitude that if we were killed, the eight prisoners would be put to death on board; but that if I, and my five companions, were not sacrificed, we would cause the eight prisoners to be released immediately. The head priest, who is regarded as a deity by these savages, immediately asked if I was speaking truth, and if his brother and the other seven men were alive. I assured him they were, and that I would send a man on board to the captain to order them to be released, if he would convey the man in safety to the boat from among the multitude; this the priest promised to do immediately. As Thomas Dafny was wounded, and had no arms to defend himself, I prevailed on him to venture down the rock with the priest, and thence to the boat. He was to inform Capt. Robson of our horrid situation, which may be more easily imagined than described. I also directed him to tell the captain that it was my particular request

22

he should release one-half of the prisoners, and show them a large chest of iron mongery, whales' teeth, &c., which he might promise to deliver to the remaining four prisoners with their liberty, the moment we returned to the ship. This man proceeded as directed, and I did not lose sight of him from the time he left us until he got on the ship's deck. A cessation of arms took place in the meantime, which might have continued unbroken had it not been for the imprudence of Charles Savage, who put a greater temptation in the way of the natives than they could withstand.

During this interval several native chiefs ascended the hill, and came within a few paces of us with protestations of friendship, and proffered us security if we would go down among them. To these promises I would not accede, nor allow my men to do so, till Charles Savage, who had resided on the islands for more than five years and spoke the native dialect fluently, begged me to allow him to go down among the natives with the chiefs to whom we were speaking, as he had no doubt their promises would be kept, and that if I allowed him to go he would certainly procure a peace, and enable us all to return in safety to the ship. Overcome by his importunities I gave my consent, but reminded him that I did not wish him to do so, and that he must leave his musket and ammunition with me. This he did, and proceeded about two hundred yards from the foot of the rock to the place where Vunisa, the chief of Wailea was seated, surrounded by chiefs who were happy to receive him, their secret determination being to kill and eat him. They conversed with him, however, for some time, and then called out to me in the native dialect, 'Come down, Peter, we will not hurt you; you see we do not hurt Charley.' I replied that I would not go down until the prisoners arrived.

During this discussion, Luis, the Chinaman, stole down the opposite side of the hill unknown to me, with his arms, for the purpose of placing himself under the protection of a chief with whom he was intimately acquainted, and to whom he had rendered important services in former wars. The islanders finding they could not prevail on me to place myself in their power, set up a scream that rent the air. At that moment Charles Savage was seized by the legs, and held in that state by six men, with his head placed in a well of fresh water until he was suffocated; while at the same time a savage got behind the Chinaman, and knocked the upper part of his skull to pieces with his huge club. These wretched men were scarcely lifeless, when they were cut up and put into the ovens already prepared for the purpose.

We, the three defenders of the rock, were then furiously attacked on all sides by the cannibals, whom our muskets, however, kept in great dread, though the chiefs stimulated their men to ascend and bring us down, promising to confer the greatest honors on the man who should kill me, and frequently inquired of their people if they were afraid of three white men when they had killed several that day. Thus encouraged, they pressed close upon us. Having four muskets between three of us, two always remained loaded, for Wilson being a bad marksman, we kept him loading the muskets, while Martin Bushart and I kept firing them off. Bushart had been a rifleman in his own country, and was an excellent marksman. He shot twenty-seven of the cannibals with twenty-eight discharges, only missing once. I also killed and wounded a few of them in self-defence. Finding they could not conquer us without a great sacrifice on their part, they kept off and vowed vengeance.

The human bodies being now prepared, were withdrawn from the ovens and distributed among the different tribes, who devoured them greedily. They frequently invited me to come down and be killed before it was dark, that they might not have the trouble of dissecting and baking me in the night. I was bespoken joint by joint by the different chiefs, who exultingly brandished their weapons in the air, and boasted the number of white men each had killed during the day.

In reply to all this, I informed them that if I was killed, their countrymen confined on board our vessel would be killed also; but that if I was saved, they would be saved. The ruthless savages replied, 'Capt. Robson may kill and eat our countrymen if he chooses, we will kill and eat you. When it is dark you cannot see to shoot us, and you have no more powder.'

My companions and myself, seeing no hope of mercy on earth, turned our eyes towards heaven, and implored the Almighty Ruler of all things to have compassion on our wretched souls. We had not the most distant hope of escaping the savages, and expected to be devoured as our companions had been. The only thing which prevented us from surrendering quietly, was the dread of being taken alive and put to the torture.

These people sometimes, but not very often, torture their prisoners in the following manner:—They skin the soles of the feet, and then torment their victims with firebrands, so as to make them jump about in that wretched state. At other times they cut off the prisoner's eyelids, and turn his face to the sun, at which he is obliged to look with his bare eyes.

Having no more than sixteen or seventeen cartridges

left, we determined as soon as it was dark to place the muzzles of our muskets to our hearts with the ends on the ground, and discharge them into our breasts, thus to avoid the danger of falling alive into the hands of these cannibal monsters.

At this moment the boat put off from the ship, and soon got close to the landing place, where we counted the eight prisoners landing from her. I could not imagine how the captain could have acted in so strange a manner, as the only hope presented of our lives being spared, was by allowing a part of the prisoners to land, who would of course intercede with their friends on shore to save us, that we might in return protect their countrymen when we returned to the ship; but this precaution not being attended to, all hope seemed to have fled, and the only hope of relief left, was the dreadful determination of destroying our own lives in the manner already mentioned.

Shortly after the eight prisoners landed, they were conveyed unarmed up the rock to me, preceded by the priest, who informed me that Capt. Robson had released the eight men, and sent a chest of cutlery, iron-mongery, &c., on shore for the chiefs, with orders that we were to deliver our muskets to them, and that he would see us in safety to the boat.

I replied that as long as I lived I would not part with my musket, which was my own property, as I was certain they would slaughter me and my companions as they had Charles Savage and Luis.

The priest then turned to Martin Bushart, and harangued him on the policy of our complying. At this moment the thought entered my head of making the priest my prisoner, and either to destroy him or to regain my liberty. I tied Charles Savage's musket with my neck-handkerchief to the belt of my cartridge-box, and presenting my own musket to the priest's head, told him that I would shoot him dead if he attempted to run away, or if any of his companions tried to molest me or my companions. I then directed him to proceed before me to the boat, threatening him with instant death in case of non-compliance. The priest proceeded as directed, and as we passed through the multitude, he exhorted them to sit down, and upon no account to molest Peter or his countrymen, because if they attempted to hurt us he would be shot, and they, of course, must be aware that they would consequently incur the wrath of the gods in the clouds, who would be angry at the disobedience of the divine orders, and cause the sea to rise and swallow up the island with all its inhabitants.

The multitude treated their priest's injunctions with profound respect, and sat down on the grass. The priest proceeded towards the boat, with the muzzles of Bushart's and Wilson's muskets at each of his ears, while the muzzle of mine was placed between his shoulders. Finding night approaching, and anxious to prolong life, I had recourse to this dreadful expedient, being aware of the influence and sway which the priests in all barbarous nations have over their votaries.

On getting to the boats the priest made a sudden stop. I ordered him to proceed, but he refused in the most positive manner, declaring that he would go no farther, and that I might shoot him if I chose. I threatened to do so, and asked him why he would not go to the water's edge. He replied, 'You want to take me on board alive, and put me to the torture.' There being no time to spare, I told him to stand still, and turned my face to him with my musket presented, threatening to shoot him if he attempted to move until I got into the boat. We then walked backwards to the water's side, and up to our breasts in water, where we joined the boat, and had no sooner got into it than the islanders came down and saluted us with a shower of arrows and stones from slings.

Being once more out of danger, we returned thanks to Divine Providence for our escape, and proceeded towards the ship.

I expostulated with Capt. Robson on his extraordinary conduct in causing so many human beings to be unnecessarily sacrificed. He offered some absurd apologies, and inquired if we were all that had escaped. I told him we were, but that if the natives could have made a proper use of all the muskets that fell into their hands on that occasion, we must all have been killed."

Thus ends the story of Peter Dillon, who must have been taught by the disastrous events above recorded, that it was not so fine sport after all to go on shore and shoot savages as though they were so many monkeys, to burn their dwellings and destroy their plantations.

The father of Mary Wallis, the Lasakau widow, was one of the Bau chiefs who was killed on that occasion.

April 27. Anchored at Tavea. The Glide, a tender belonging to the bark, was sent to this part of Feejee some weeks since, to get houses under way, and urge the natives on with the fishing against the arrival of the bark. On her return, we met at Buladagaloa, and were informed that nothing could be done here at present, as several of the Tavea people had been murdered at Yanganga, in consequence of which, war would commence immediately.

Namosimalua being at Naikaratumba with his large canoe and many of his people, hastened hither that he might join with Elijah in inducing the natives to give up hostilities, at least for the present, and go on with their fishing, it being deemed of more importance to collect luxuries for the Chinese, than to feed themselves with human flesh.

The Tavea people have hitherto been a very bold, saucy set of natives, provoking their neighbors by their hostile proceedings. Of late, however, Natemba has renounced heathenism, and seems to have become a better, though not a good man. His enemies, however, are not at peace with him, as they have recently shown by the massacre of ten of the warriors of Tavea. The Tavea people have been engaged for some time past in fishing turtle for Bau, which they had placed in a pen on the island of Yanganga. Eleven men who were sent to bring the turtle to Tavea, were all murdered but one, who escaped to tell the tale. Retova and a chief of the island of Naloa are among the most powerful of the enemies of Tavea. They have exerted an influence along the coast and among the adjacent islands in this vicinity, so that now the little island is completely hemmed in on all sides, and its inhabitants imprisoned. We hope, however, that the arrival of the Waqa Vanua, the Langi Lavu, and the influential characters which they have brought, will change the present aspect of affairs for the better.

28. Four canoes have arrived at Naloa from Mathuata, for the purpose of joining that people against Tavea. It is said that they contain a great number of warriors, and intend to attack Tavea to-morrow. Natemba is here, Namosimalua spent the night at Naloa, and Elijah has gone to prevail upon Dumbui, the chief, to come here and meet Natemba, and see if they can come to an amicable settlement.

Elijah, on arriving at Naloa this morning, assembled the chiefs and warriors of the place, with those who had come from Mathuata, and thus addressed them: "Why did you kill the people of Tavea?"

"Because many years ago they killed our people."

"Are you now satisfied ?"

"Yes."

"Do you wish for war ?"

"It is just as you say. If you say war, it shall be war; and if you say peace, it shall be peace."

"I have come in the '*waqa vanua*,' or the big ship," said Elijah, "to assist Capt. Wallis in getting "*beech de mer.*" I wish you to leave fighting and go a fishing. The Tavea people wish to fish, but they are afraid. You have killed ten of their strong men. The "*waqa vanua*" is sent here from Bau with yanggona from its chiefs for you to get "*beech de mer*" for it. If you kill or trouble any who are employed in its service, I shall send word to Bau, and they will come, as they did some-time ago, and make you all run for your lives. My speech is ended."

They replied that his speech was good, and it should be as he said. Elijah then requested Dumbui to accompany him to the bark and meet Natemba; but he probably remembered sundry acts of his own, committed during the latter part of our last voyage, which did not add to his dignity as a chief, and refused to accompany Elijah, saying that Capt. W. would keep him and he dared not to come. Elijah asked him if he had not known Capt. W. for many years. He replied that he had. He then asked him if he had ever known him to confine a Feejeean on board any vessel that he had commanded. He replied that he had not. "Then come with me," said Elijah, "he will not do so now. Do you not know that Mrs. Wallis is on board, and the vessel is a '*waqa ni lotu?*'" Dumbui entered the boat with fear, not daring to refuse to visit the vessel, yet fearing the punishment due to his former transgressions. While on his passage to the bark, however, a capital idea occurred to his mind, and inspired him with confidence. He suddenly cried out, " *Au sa lotu.*" " I am a Christian." He seemed to feel that if he acknowledged himself a Christian, he was safe.

Namosimalu, with his principal chiefs and officers, Natemba and several counsellors of Dumbui arrived, and a great meeting was held on our decks and in the house of the bark. The meeting was opened by Namosimalua, who stated that its object was to consummate a peace between the contending parties present. The parties talked long and sometimes loud when relating their grievances, but they finally concluded to bury all their animosities and unite in their labors for the bark. None of the Mathuata warriors were present, feeling no doubt disappointed at the change of affairs. They came to fight, that they might procure dead men for their ovens and appetites, and do not like to return to their homes as they came.

We have been informed that while Retova was fitting the canoes for the present expedition, he sent whales' teeth to Natemba, with complimentary speeches and protestations of love and friendship, which Natemba, at the time all unsuspicious, received, and returned others in their stead.

After the breaking up of the meeting on deck, Namosimalua, Elijah, Natemba, Dumbui, and two of the attendants of the latter, came into the cabin, where all knelt while Elijah offered a most fervent and appropriate prayer. He prayed that this peace might be permanent, —that the parties might not only be Christian in name, but that they might love God and serve him truly,—that they might give up war, killing and eating each other, till their lands, and live no longer like pigs, but be like men, &c.

Dumbui and Natemba knelt by the side of each other, and I am not certain that Dumbui was not desiring all the time to eat a piece of his neighbor. Natemba appears much altered, and sincerely to desire instruction in the gospel.

29. Sabbath. Elijah preached at Tavea in the morning, and at Naloa in the afternoon. He found Dumbui at Naloa so deeply engaged in some native game of amusement, that it was long before he could leave to attend to the preaching.

May 13. Since my last date nothing of importance has occurred. The natives of Naloa and Tavea have erected "*beech de mer*" houses, and been engaged in collecting the precious article. They seem to regard Elijah as their prophet, priest and king. Dumbui is as much a Christian at heart as he ever was; but having renounced heathenism, he cannot well avoid listening to religious instruction. Elijah says perhaps God will soften his heart by and by.

16. Retova has honored us with a visit, when the chiefs and people held another meeting on board, and had another talk, after which they drank yanggona and became friends.

Yanggona drinking is a great affair in Feejee. No meetings are held and no business is transacted without the drinking of yanggona. It is a part of their religious ceremony.

The Feejeeans give the following account of the origin of this root:—They say that a man and his wife started many years ago from Tonga, in a canoe, for the purpose of trying to catch the sun for a "*tombe*," or neck ornament. They thought they should find the place where it sets, by sailing towards it, and they kept on till they arrived in Feejee. Their child was buried on an island near Bau. From the grave, the first root of yanggona ever known in Feejee sprang up.

17. Elijah preached at Tavea. He had a large and attentive congregation. Natemba and several of his tribe wish to be married and baptized. In accordance with their request, I have written to Rev. J. Williams, at Bua, to request him to visit this place, when convenient, for the purpose of performing such religious ceremonies as he deems expedient.

19. Last night an unusual noise near the windows of the cabin awoke us. Soon after, the watchman entered, and informed Mr. W. that he believed "De devil was hanging by de hook over de stern." It was found to be an enormous shark. He was safely moored till morning, when he was sent ashore to serve as a feast for the natives.

25. Rev. Mr. Williams arrived from Bua, visited Tavea, where he preached, married, and baptized several couples. Natemba is now called Moses.

In the morning, just at the dawn of day, Elijah walked to a retired spot on the island, and knelt among the bushes to pray. He had not been thus engaged long, before he heard a slight rustling among the bushes. Feeling no doubt, in such a land as this, the importance of watching as well as praying, he looked up and saw a man standing over him, with his club raised, just ready to strike. "What! is it you, Elijah?" exclaimed the man, "I thought it was some one who was hiding for a vile purpose, and was just ready to kill him." "The Lord has preserved me from your murderous hand," said Elijah, "as He will ever preserve those that fully trust in

Him." The man walked off, and Elijah finished his prayer, thanking God most heartily for his preservation.

After tea I visited the island of Tavea for the first time. All the boys and girls of the place closely followed our steps, just as the boys run behind a crazy person in our streets at home, and when we turned to look at them, they would run away as if afraid that we should bite them. The island is very small, its inhabitants numerous, and the houses in a dilapidated condition. The house of Moses was large, but nearly in ruins. " Why do you not build better houses?" I asked. " We are afraid that our enemies will come and burn them," was the reply. Formerly, no food was raised here,—the inhabitants depending entirely upon the main land for their subsistence, but, having learned at length how easy a matter it is to be surrounded by enemies, and starved, they have set out bread-fruit and banana trees in abundance. The island of Naloa has been the garden of Tavea till of late. Dumbui has built a town and settled there with his tribe. There are now large plantations on it belonging to the Tavea people; but they have recently been kept from procuring food there by the hostility of Dumbui and his cannibals. On our arrival, the Tavea people had subsisted for some time on green bananas only. We walked to the opposite side of the island, and found that a few rods only separated it from the Vanualavu, or the main land.

Mr. Williams here gave me an account of the manner in which the natives exchange their food. The inhabitants of the small islands bring their fish to the main, and deposit it on the shore in heaps, taking care to keep a good distance from their neighbors, for there seems never to be a time when Feejeans can trust each other. The inhabitants of the main also deposit the veg-

etables which they may have brought, in heaps like the
others.   When all are ready, a rush is made by the parties to procure what they can, and run for their homes.
Of course, the division of food is most unequal.   A poor
old woman has, perhaps, been successful in fishing, and
carries to the shore a larger quantity than the rest; but,
distanced by the strong and more active, she totters
back to her home without any thing in return.   About
dusk we returned to the bark, where Mr. Williams
preached in the evening in English in the house on
deck, and afterwards prayed in native in the cabin.

26.   Mr. Williams left us to return to Bua.   He related the following incident of their life at Bua.   It appears that after the death of Tui Mbua, a son, named
Muchanamu, assumed the title of Turaga-lavu, and
imagined himself a great man.   He had an elder brother, whose rank was equal to his own, but he had been
reared by a relative who had for many years been at
variance with his father.   He renounced heathenism,
became a good man, and cared not to govern the people
belonging to his late father.   Accordingly, there was no
one to dispute the authority of Muchanamu, and he proceeded to lay the following plans for his own aggrandize-
ment and the benefit of posterity.   He assembled all his
warriors, and in secret conclave communicated his plans
of the *great* and *glorious* enterprise in which he wished
them to engage.   First, they were to proceed to Mathuata, kill Retova and as many of his people as possible,
in revenge for an uncle who had been killed long before.
After their conquest of Mathuata, on their return to Bua
they were to destroy all their enemies, burn their towns,
destroy their plantations, and bring the women and
riches to Bua.   After their return from this *glorious*
campaign, they were to attack the mission station, mas-

sacre Mr. Williams and the children, and take the property belonging to the mission for a spoil. After all this was accomplished, the women and the riches were to be divided among the warriors, Mrs. W. falling to the share of Muchanamu. A "*buri*" was to be erected to commemorate the wonderful events, the warriors were to be feasted, and then return to their homes laden with riches and covered with glory. The assembled warriors were delighted with the glowing prospects now set before them, and proceeded at once to cut and erect the posts for the great "*buri*," which was to be finished on their return.

After several days of feasting, the army departed for Mathuata, which was to be the first scene of action. They had not travelled far, when Muchanamu went into a town to order food to be prepared for himself and his warriors. It appears that he went into the town alone, which is an unusual thing for a chief. I know of no instance in Feejee in which a chief ventured abroad unattended. The inhabitants of the town, whom he supposed were his friends, showed their love to him by depriving him of his life and sending his body to Raverave. No reason is known for the act. Many stories are told, but the truth is not to be obtained, at least, at present. The sudden and unexpected death of their chief cooled the courage of the warriors, and they fled in terror to their homes.

27. It will be recollected that Mr. Williams and family were stationed for several years at Somosomo. He related to us some anecdotes of Tuilili, the ruling chief of that place. He describes him as being exceedingly large in size, and possessing a great deal of muscular strength, the expression of his countenance as most wicked, and his general appearance revolting in the ex-

treme.   He is a great tyrant, but tender of his own subjects.

On one occasion a man stole some article from Mr. W.   He complained to the chief, who began to take fire at once.   " Who is the man?" he asked.   The name was mentioned.   " Oh, but he is one of my men. I thought it had been somebody else, that I might have punished him."   " And why is one of your men to be passed by? the loss is the same to me," said Mr. W. Nothing more was said about the affair, and the culprit did not know that his chief knew of the depredation which he had committed.   The chief, however, kept the thing in his mind, and determined to give his people a lesson through the punishment of another.   Soon after the first complaint, a Tonguese stole something, when the chief clubbed him severely, saying that was the way to serve thieves.   His people received the warning, and were benefited by it.   Thus the object of the chief was effected without punishing one of his own people.

Messrs. Lyth and Williams at one time refused him some request that he had made, when he became exceedingly angry, rushed into the house, and catching hold of them, took one in each hand, (both are small men, and he almost a giant,) and threatened to smash them together.   In a few moments, however, he became cool enough to listen to reason, and soon became as loving as he had been angry.   Their tea was about being served.   He seated himself by Mr. W. and would eat from the same plate, and the same piece of bread must serve both; first one taking a bite and then the other. He would sometimes eat half a banana, and thrust the remaining half into the mouth of one of the gentlemen. Sometimes, when his body was well besmeared with black and red paint, he would fall to hugging one of the gentlemen, till the victim would get the greatest portion of the paint transferred to himself.

A few months previous to the death of the king of Somosomo, the father of Tuilili, he went to Bau. Tuilili stood on the shore, his bosom heaving, and the big tears coursing down his cheeks, exclaiming, "Oh! I shall never see my old father again." The gentlemen of the mission called to see him soon after, and found him seated in one corner of his house, with a few of his father's old friends, weeping most bitterly, and talking of his father. Contrary, however, to the fears of Tuilili, the old king lived to return to his home, and be buried alive by his *dutiful* and *affectionate* son. The following story of the death of the king is given as related to us by Mr. W.

As soon as he heard of the sickness of the king, he called to visit him. Tuilili met him with one of his affectionate embraces, and said, "See, the father of us both is dead!" "Dead!" exclaimed Mr. Williams, as he glanced at the heaving breast of the king. "Yes, his spirit is gone,—that is only his body that moves," was the reply. The king raised his hand to his neck, and felt of a necklace of whales' teeth that had been placed there, then coughed, and laid his hand on his side. The loving son would not allow Mr. W. to speak to the king, who, finding that he could not save him from being buried alive, turned his attention to the living. Two women had been strangled already, and they were preparing more for the awful ceremony; but Mr. W. prevailed on Tuilili to promise that no more should be sacrificed. The body of the still living king was wrapped in mats, and with those of the women was taken to a place called Nasima, where he was divested of his ornaments and carried to his grave. The bodies of the women were first placed in the grave, and then that

23

of the king.   He was heard to cough in the grave before the earth was thrown in.

Thirty whales' teeth, twelve muskets, four clubs, and a large quantity of cloth had been presented to the sick man, but he was sent to "*bulu*," to encounter all the dangers of the way without either, and no other protection than that which could be afforded by the women who had accompanied him.   There is one particular family at Somosomo, whose privilege it is on the death of a chief to supply a man, who is strangled and goes on before his superior, to hold a certain large dog, (which is always in the way between this world and "*bulu*,") while the chief passes on his way.   On this occasion, however, the family, from some cause, could not meet the supply, and that part of the ceremony was omitted.

Mr. W. thinks that the indirect influence of Christianity may be observed in the ease with which many important parts of their former ceremonies, on such occasions, have been laid aside.

After the interment of the king, there was a great demand for scissors, razors, knives, &c.   Dandies were despoiled of their well-dressed whiskers, moustaches, &c. A great reduction of fingers also took place, but there were not enough to supply the demand, and many were required from the country.

28.   Mr. Williams while with us also related the following affair, which lately occurred at Nandy, the station occupied by Rev. D. Hazlewood.   Mr. H. was at Bua with his child at the time.

The Saukase people sent a messenger to the chief of Solavu, saying, "The people of Nandy have embraced the '*lotu*' religion.   We will go and kill them, burn their towns, and despoil them of their riches.   Will you join us?"   The chief of Solavu has been for some

time past exceedingly virulent against the Christians of
Nandy. He sent word, therefore, that he would gladly
join in the work of destruction. The hostile tribes lost
no time in joining their forces and marching towards
Nandy. As they approached the place, their courage
entirely forsook them, and instead of clubbing, spearing,
shooting, and then feasting on the bodies of the slain, as
they had boasted, they stopped, looked fearfully at each
other, and, at length sent a messenger into the town,
saying, "What shall we do?" "Do what you choose,"
was the answer. Another messenger came, saying,
"Tell us what we must do." "Do just what you wish,"
was the brief reply. The Nandy people had prepared
themselves for the reception of their enemies, and were
quietly waiting their approach. At length the invaders
came within speaking distance of the assembled warriors
of Nandy, and both parties seated themselves upon the
ground, and stared at each other. After some time, the
commander of the besiegers said to the Christian chief,
"You 'soro' to us, and we will go home." "Why
should we 'soro' to you, having done you no harm?"
was the cool reply. "Ah, no, but you 'soro,' and we
will leave you in peace," said he. "No, we shall not
'soro,'" said the chief. Another pause ensued, and
they continued to look at each other. A warrior then
took a whale's tooth, and holding it on one side, that it
might not be seen by his fellows, walked stealthily to the
Nandy chief, and in a whisper said, "Here, you take
this tooth, and 'soro' to us, that we may go home."
"I shall do no such thing," replied the chief. The dis-
concerted warrior returned to his place, and the parties
still stared at each other. The invaders could not sum-
mon courage to attack the Christians, and they were
ashamed to leave the place without doing any thing. At

last the Solavu, or the Saukase chief, (I have forgotten which,) took a whale's tooth, and, pretending to represent the Nandy people, presented it to his own warriors, or the two hostile tribes, and said, hurriedly, "Here, you take this tooth, you be of ' a good mind' towards us, and we will be of ' a good mind' towards you. After playing " *soro* " in this manner, they departed. I think Mr. W. said that the Saukase people were subject to Nandy.

After the Saukase people returned to their homes they held a council, when a speaker, addressing the assembly, said, " We have acted like fools. We went to fight Nandy; we returned as we went; we were afraid, and now we are ashamed. What shall we do?" "Renounce our gods and join the Christians. It was the Christians' god that made you afraid," was the reply. " *Venaka*" (it is good) was the response. The result was that the whole tribe renounced heathenism, and are receiving religious instruction.

30. Raverave. Retova has become quite impatient with us for remaining so long at Tavea, that "*kaise*" place, as he terms it. He had forbidden the selling of food to that people, and thrown out sundry hints about burning houses, &c. Accordingly Mr. W. made arrangements for the Tavea and Naloa people to go on with their fishing, while he visited Raverave with the bark and made love to the chief.

I notice a marked difference in the dialect of the different parts of this group of islands. For instance, the inhabitants at the windward of Raverave call the name of the chief of Mathuata, Garatova; at the leeward, Retova; while the inhabitants of Geer call him Oratova.

Namosimalua came here from Naloa to present his

large canoe, the Lagi-lavu, to Retova. He was accompanied by some sixty or eighty of his people, who have all remained here for the last five weeks. Namosi is fond of making a great show; but Retova is *not* fond of feeding so many visitors for such a length of time.

June 1. A Vewa man died last night at Raverave. He had formerly renounced heathenism, but on coming to this place to live, he took a couple of wives, and returned to all the *innocent delights* of heathenism again. The widows were anxious to accompany their husband to the other world, and were preparing to do so, when Elijah landed from the boat and forbade their being strangled.

4. Namosimalua and Retova have requested Mr. W. to take the chief of Vewa, with his attendants, pigs, turtles, and all belonging to him, to Naikarotumba, or Vetelavu. Mr. W., not having sufficient supplies for so large a company, as he would be expected to find them food on their way, and not deeming it important for the interests of his voyage, he modestly refused compliance, much to the chagrin of the chiefs.

6. The visitors of Raverave departed this morning, after having, like the locusts of Egypt, eaten down every green thing.

CHAPTER XX.

Visit to Raverave—Feejeean Affection—Visit to Bua—Feejeean Courtesy —District Meeting—Arrival of the Zotoff—Departure from Bua—Arrival at Vetelavu—Thakombau's visit—Cannibalism.

June 7. I accompanied Elijah to Raverave. The town is surrounded by lofty hills, open to the sea only at

the north.   It contains about fifty houses; most of them
are small.   The town of Raverave had been destroyed
some two years since, but was immediately rebuilt.   Two
large " *buris* " were erected on the same spot where the
two destroyed had stood.   On our way I was shown a
ditch where the remains of Tui Mathuata, the murdered
king, were thrown at the time of the massacre.

On arriving at the town, as we passed a little " *buri*, "
we heard the voice of Retova, and were about to enter;
but observing several clubs on the outside, Elijah said
that he was probably engaged with messengers from distant towns, so we passed on to his house.   This we
found to be large and neatly finished.   It is quite new,
and called Garenggeo.   Every house in Feejee has a
name.   There were a dozen women and several children present.   "Where is the Marama ?" I asked.
"We are all Maramas," was the reply.   I observed
several musquito curtains, made of native cloth, thrown
over bamboos.   These are let down at night, and form
distinct sleeping apartments,—an arrangement not to be
found among the civilized natives of Manilla, where fathers, mothers, brothers, sisters, uncles, aunts and
cousins, if they happen to be there, all sleep in one
apartment.

As Retova did not come in, Elijah, Phebe and myself
walked out to " *sara sara*. "   We first went to the grave-
yard.   Here we found some half dozen graves, with
little houses, like beehives, built over them.   Fine cinnet was wrought in the open fronts, in the form of a
spider's web.   A large and beautiful tamarind tree waved over the graves.   This tree and one at Tavea are all
of the kind to be found in Feejee.   They have. grown
from the stones of the fruit, which were presented by
Mr. Wallis in 1826.   Tamarinds were hanging from it

in abundance. It is very uncommon for one to die a natural death in this group, which may account for the small number of graves.

We next visited the spot where Tui Mathuata met his untimely fate. Several men assembled here, and all seemed eager to answer my inquiries respecting the occurrence, pointing out the different positions occupied by the murderers and the murdered. I told them that it was very wicked for them to kill people in that way. "Yes," they said, "it is very wicked. The Feejeeans are a foolish people." "You do not believe what you say," I replied, "or you would follow the good example of Elijah, give up your wicked practices, and become Christians." "Yes, Marama, we intend to do so by and by," they replied. They would have deemed it very uncivil to have differed from me in opinion, or to have said any thing in favor of their own customs.

While we were talking, several women joined us. As I was desirous of entering their sacred edifice, and seeing Elijah look as though he liked not to take the responsibility of such an act, I said to an old man, "Is it 'tambu' for a white woman to go in here?" "No," he replied. "You may go in. It is 'tambu-lavu' for a Feejeean woman to go. If she should enter our god's house we should kill her." Thank heaven! I exclaimed, as I ascended the steps, that I was not born in Feejee. I think one may be allowed to indulge a little of the Pharasaical spirit here, where there is so marked a distinction between God's creatures.

Elijah and the old man followed me, leaving the women astonished at so unheard of a thing, as for a woman to enter the house of a god. The old man showed me where the king was seated when Korovaka-turaga entered,—where hung the murderous weapon,—how he approached the unsuspicious victim,—where Retova sat, &c., &c. The "*buri*" is a lofty edifice, neatly built, but contains no offerings to its god,—no riches whatever. One club hung against the wall, and one breadth of European cloth was suspended from the ridge-pole of the building to the ground. This serves as a veil to hide the god when he descends to communicate with his subjects. I am not certain, however, about his descent. As the veil extends to the ground, it is probable, that, being an inhabitant of the lower regions, he ascends to this part of the world. As the gods, however, do not show themselves, even to the priests, we have no means of ascertaining the exact truth, and must leave the question unsettled.

"Do your priests never go behind the veil to see their god?" I asked the old man. "If he were to see the face of the god, he would die," was the reply. From whence could they have obtained that idea? so perfectly in accordance with the Bible. From whence their offerings of the first fruits of their lands to their gods,—and the rite of circumcision?—of throwing ashes upon the head when they have offended a superior?

We passed out of this and went on to the other large "*buri*," where the body of Muchanamu was taken and divided after it was baked. Some say that no one ate of it, being very much spoiled, as it did not arrive till several days after the murder. Others say that the "*kaises*" devoured it. I inquired where our old friend, the Mbete, was, and was told that he was dead, and that no one succeeded him. Retova says that if a *papalagi* missionary would come here and live, he would "*lotu*," and have no Mbete in Vete. Thus the house seems to be swept and garnished. Who shall take possession?

Shall demons be allowed to enter this broad opening, or shall the gospel light illume the place, teaching men and women to serve God?

The fact that there were no priests, accounts for their being no offerings in the " *buri*." The sacred veil was made of cloth that I had seen in our trade room a short time before. I took hold of it and said, "How dare you use *papalagi* cloth for this purpose? Shall I tear it from its hangings, and take it away?" " *Kagua Marama, kagua Marama, sa venaka ongo.*" "Do not, do not, it is very good."

We now returned to the Vale Garenggeo. Retova was still absent. We were offered some bananas, and informed that when they expected me to come and see them, a few days since, they prepared puddings for me; but as I did not come, they sent them to the vessel, and now they had nothing to offer.

After resting for awhile, we left for the purpose of returning to the vessel. On our way we were joined by the chief, and shown the oven where Muchanamu was baked, and the spot where his head was buried. Human heads are never eaten. Phebe kept close to me, and since we have been in Feejee has shown no disposition, so common in the females, of running away. One of the white residents of Solavu informed me that those of them who had resided for any length of time in this group, had provided themselves with iron chains for the purpose of confining their women who showed a disposition to leave their masters and owners. Thus we see there are slaveholders in this part of the world; but this is not surprising, as many of these slaveholders came from America, that glorious land of liberty, where three millions of the population are held in bondage!

9. Retova came on board this morning, and soon

after a canoe arrived from Kandavu, bringing its chief. Ashes were scattered over his head, and a handful was placed on one shoulder. He approached Retova with an air of the deepest humility, exclaiming " *Au soro, au soro* "—" I ask your pardon, I ask your pardon "—and offered the chief a whale's tooth. It was accepted, thus showing that the offender was pardoned. It appears that the chief of Ngagumu had offered love to one of the swarthy dames of Kandavu. Tomarau-ni-waqa, the chief of Kandavu, was justly indignant at such conduct, and determined to punish the bold offender, which he did by burning his town. He then came, as related above, to ask the pardon of the chief of Mathuata, as the town of the offender belonged to him. The Ngagumu messengers came to settle their part of the affair the day that I visited Raverave. Both parties must ask the forgiveness of Retova, as both were his subjects.

Elijah has gone to Tavea and Naloa, to preach on the coming Sabbath. His preaching costume consists of a plain piece of white or blue cloth fastened around the waist, falling as low as the ancles. Over that is worn a striped shirt, and a gray frock coat completes the suit.

10. Inquired to-day of Retova where his friend Korovaka-turaga was. He said that he was living at Naivu; that after the murder of the king they became afraid of each other; that he was afraid to sleep and Korovakaturaga also ; that one morning all the women and children of his friend were missing, and when another morning came he had also run away; that he had now become his enemy, and sought every means to annoy and injure him since his residence at Naivu, and that a few weeks ago thirteen of his people had been murdered by his orders. " How many of his people have you killed?" I asked. " I have had none killed," he

replied. "It is very bad to kill people in that way." "You are only waiting for an opportunity," I said. "Who killed the king of all these broad lands?" "Korovaka-turaga. He is a very bad man. He ordered Harry and his companions to be murdered," was his answer. "Did you not deceive your uncle, and draw him here to your town by your fair speeches, and then employ your friend to murder him? God is very angry with you for it, and it is He who has caused your friend to become your enemy. Now you have no rest or peace for fear of your enemies. You are losing your flesh. See how poor you are. And what did you gain by your wicked, cruel act? Your friend that was, is a strong man. Your uncle was old and weak. His son has been joined by the strong man and his people, in consequence of which he is strengthened, while you have become weaker." He looked distressed, but made no reply.

11. We received a visit from several of the ladies belonging to the harem of the chief; among the number was a daughter of the late king. She had been demanded by, and given to Tanoa, king of Bau, but while on a visit to her father, as she and several of her women were one day employed in fishing, she was taken to Mathuata by force, to become a wife of her cousin, who was the determined enemy of her father. The affair gave great offence to Tanoa at the time, but when Retova went in the bark to visit Bau on our first voyage, he "soroed" to the king with a musket and some whales' teeth. The offering was accepted, but it is said that the king has not forgotten the insult.

16. I have just concluded the reading of Typee and Omoo, by Melville. The author writes most beautifully. Every word has a meaning. Some of his statements and descriptions, although finely written, are, I think, incor-

rect. For instance, the damsels in the valley of Typee may have blue eyes, but they are to be seen in no other islands of the Pacific, except with a white skin.

His description of the bread-fruit tree reads very prettily, but I do not understand it. Wherever I have seen it, the foliage is perennial. He says the fruit "hangs in golden spheres." The fruit when ripe is green, when unripe is green, and the leaves are green.

Melville should never come to Feejee, for there would be some danger of his readers becoming cannibals. He would present the rites of heathenism and cannibalism in forms so attractive that they would be anxious to enjoy the delicate feasts. I am not sure that many damsels who have read of the "pretty blue-eyed tawny" of Typee, have not tried to hold a raw fish in their delicate fingers.

A word about Omoo. The author has given a faithful and true picture of the lives of deserters from ships. They are to be found in very many of the islands of the Pacific, and many of them are precisely as he has portrayed them—a lazy, lying, thieving set, and would rather steal their food at any time than earn an honest subsistence by even weeding a garden. If missionaries are residents where they are, they will be sure to flee from their presence as the author states, and then blame and ridicule their proceedings.

18. A young woman was strangled in the town. She had suffered for several weeks from some complaint in her head. Mr. Wallis had directed Elijah to let blood from a vein in her arm, to shave her head, and apply blisters. Medicines were also administered, but nothing relieved her, and to-day, as soon as Elijah left the place to visit Bau and Vewa, the Marama said, "Now Elijah has departed, the girl cannot recover, she will be a long

time dying; let us strangle her that we may not be troubled with her any longer." The assembled dames of Raverave pronounced the speech to be very good, and soon ended the sufferings of the girl with the strangling cord.

July 5. Retova has sailed this morning for Namuka, with a numerous retinue, to attend a "*Solavu.*" I told him to see that no people were killed and eaten while on their passages. He replied that he was too good a man for that business.

The wife of the chief Ndury, who is a native of Vewa, and a niece of Elijah, tells me that Retova and Ratanga have given up their cannibalism.

8. We have been honored with a visit from a party of Raverave ladies, all dressed in their best "*lekus*" for the occasion. These seldom visit the shipping. I was on the deck when they arrived, but as they expressed a wish to see the cabin, I invited them down. The great object of attraction was the looking-glass. As they stood before it arranging their hair, &c., I told them that they were "*vinde vinde,*" or proud. "And so are you proud," said one, as she seated herself on the floor, looking very prim, and imitating exactly, I should think, my own manner at the time of my visit to their town. The natives are accomplished imitators.

The ladies composing the harem of the chief are mostly of equal rank. The daughter of the late king ranks the highest, but she seems not to be a favorite. She is childless, too, so that Retova has no benefit from a "*vasu*" to the territories of his enemies. One of his wives is the daughter of a chief of Thakendrove, another of Jekombea, and another of Geer. Her father, a chief of Geer, was murdered a short time since by the order of Retova, on account of some love affair.

16.   Elijah has returned from Vewa, bringing us letters from the ladies of the mission.   We learn from them that the Consulate at Rewa has been destroyed by fire. The fourth of July was being celebrated by the firing of guns, when, by some accident, the buildings took fire and were soon in ashes.

18.   As the natives of Raverave and vicinity appear tired of fishing, Mr. W. thinks best to return to Ba for a season, and let this people rest.   Retova has received a handsome American flag among other things, as a present, with which he appears highly delighted and perfectly satisfied.   It has long been his ambition to possess a large, handsome flag.

19.   Tavea.   As Mr. W. intended to remain at Tavea a few days, I started in the Glide at daylight to visit Bua. The land breeze soon died away, when our craft lay perfectly still upon the glassy bosom of the waters.   Mr. W. seeing our situation, sent the jolly boat and six Feejeeans to row, that we might speed on our way and not be obliged to pass the night on the water.   Elijah and myself took passage in the boat, and were soon on our way, the commander of the Glide observing as we left that they would soon overtake us when the sea breeze arose. Supposing this would be the case, we took no water or provisions on board for our crew.

As we passed Naloa, Elijah said there was a rock near the shore that was visible at ebb tide, which is classed among the gods of Feejee.   It is about three feet high, and is supposed to devour all the musquitoes that would otherwise settle on the island.   It is called the musquito's tooth.   I remarked that they had better remove his godship to the island of Ono.   At ten o'clock a slight breeze arose, which enabled us to endure the scorching rays of the sun.   The breeze did not favor the passage of the Glide, as it was directly ahead; therefore the rowers had the pleasant prospect of rowing a distance of forty miles before resting from their labors. A pint bottle of coffee and a small loaf of cake had been provided for myself, and had found their way to the boat, wrapped in my boat cloak. Finding that all had left the bark fasting, I divided half of the loaf among them, reserving the other half and the coffee for dinner.

At twelve o'clock we had made good progress. Three of the men rowed at a time, relieving each other alternately. I now gave them the rest of the loaf and the coffee; the latter was scarcely enough to wet their lips. As Elijah and myself did not work, we obeyed the apostolic injunction " not to eat."

About four o'clock we passed Nai Thombothombo, the supposed residence of the principal god of this island. His dominions are somewhat extensive, and covered with a dense forest of trees, shrubs and creeping vines. Elijah said that no person would dare to take even a leaf from the place, lest Okuru, the god, should be angry. Elijah had not probably been among the worshippers of Okuru, as he seemed to know but little about him, farther than that it was said he had many wives, and numerous attendants of little gods. As this is an acknowledged fact, I conclude that Okuru is not of the Roman faith.

The coast by which we passed, presented but little variety of scenery; broken hills and rugged defiles being the principal objects. There were on some parts sloping hills nearly covered with a tree called the Ndrala, which bears a bright scarlet blossom; the trunk and limbs were white, and nearly destitute of foliage. The natives plant their yams when this tree is in blossom.

We arrived at Bua bay an hour before the sun set, and Elijah asked if they should land and rest a little, and refresh themselves with some cocoa-nuts, great quantities of which were growing near. I gladly assented, for I had been pained on account of the long day's labor which I had occasioned, and which they had so cheerfully performed. If one seemed to lag, Elijah would say, "Work away, Mr. Wallis will be angry if we do not reach Bua by dark." I said, "What strong men you are! You are not weak. You pull hard and fast. See how the boat flies through the water!" After this they would ply the oars with vigor, saying, "It is our love to Mr. W. and yourself which causes us to be strong men." Now the truth was, they did not feel a bit of love, and I presume they were wishing me any where else than where I was, but a Feejeean will never be outdone in compliments.

I remained alone in the boat, while my crew, with Elijah, repaired to the land. In about half an hour they returned, loaded with young cocoa-nuts. The meat had just begun to form, while the shell was full of cool, delicious milk. With what eagerness I quaffed the delectable beverage, I will leave those to imagine, who, like myself, have been seated in an open boat for the space of twelve hours without once changing their position or breaking their fasting. I did not suffer from hunger or thirst through the day, and I had been sheltered from the rays of the sun by an umbrella. We had not seen a canoe on our way, and our journey seemed likely to terminate without any romantic occurrence whatever.

Having to cross the bay, which is eight miles wide, before we gained the mouth of the river, we now hastened on, and arrived at the entrance of the river a few moments before the sun left us for a time, to illume other climes. As we sailed up the beautiful river, we seemed to have entered some fairy scene. Not a ripple

stirred the waters; the beautiful mangroves which lined
its banks were reflected in them as in a mirror, and even
the untutored natives seemed to feel an influence from
the beauties of nature, for instead of the quick, strong
pull at their oars, they now plied them gently, so gently that they scarcely ruffled the surface of the waters,
as if they feared to disturb the surrounding harmony of
the scene. I shall never forget the happiness of that
hour. It rests upon my mind like some happy dream of
childhood. I had such dreams once, and shall never forget them. They seem to be interwoven with my very
existence, and their memory has accompanied me through
all the varied scenes which I have passed.

About dark we arrived at the mission station, and were
welcomed at the landing by Mr. and Mrs. Williams, who
had received word of our coming by a native of Tavea,
who had performed the journey from Tavea to Bua in
much less time than we had the distance over land, being
only eight miles, while the numerous capes and points to
be rounded by water make the distance about forty miles.

20. Bua is a part of the main land. Fine table land
extends to the distance of six or eight miles. The course
of the river which runs through it has never yet been
traced to its source. The mission house is located on a
bend of the river, and looks exceedingly romantic from
an opening between the cocoa nut and bread fruit trees
at a little distance, where one catches the first view as
he ascends the river, nor is its beauty lessened on a
nearer approach. It is decidedly the prettiest and best
dwelling to be seen in Feejee. It was built under the
superintendence, and with the assistance of Mr. Williams,
who, in addition to his other acquirements, possesses a
good share of architectural knowledge. Order is to be
seen in every department of the mission. Mr. and Mrs.

24

Williams have five children of their own, and one of Mr. Hazlewood's.

22. The town in which the mission is situated is called Televa, and is governed by the eldest son of Tuimbua, the late king, who, as I have before stated, renounced heathenism some time since. He and some of his people appear to be truly converted, while nearly all the inhabitants of his town are nominal Christians. He has been a great warrior in his day, or rather in the early part of it, for it is now only mid-day with him. His countenance is one of the most strongly marked that I have seen. He has received the baptismal name of Hezekiah; appears to feel a great deal for the spiritual welfare of his countrymen, and is receiving instruction from Mr. Williams, for the purpose of becoming a preacher.

On the opposite side of the river stands the town of Vaturua, which was the residence of the late king during the latter part of his life. This people are very much opposed to the Christian religion, or not so much on account of the religion itself, as the insult which they fancy they have received on account of it. It will be remembered that one of the former wives of Elijah was a daughter of Tuimbua. He married another, and returned her to her kindred and tribe. This insult they will not forgive. The old men of the place declare that she shall have no other husband, that the insult may not be forgotten. It is said that these wicked old men were the counsellors of Muchanamu, the chief, and are now trying to pervert his successor, who is called Peter, and who appears friendly to the mission, and inclined to peace. Peter has a younger brother who listens to them, and appears to tread in the steps of Muchanamu to do evil.

Vaturua was formerly the residence of Tuimuru, Tuimbua's cousin, who adopted Hezekiah as his son. For many years the two chiefs lived in amity, but, at length, dissensions arose between them, and they became inveterate enemies. Hezekiah was in favor of his relative, and fought against his father for many years. The warfare, however, was not carried on by the fighting of battles, as few, if any, were fought for several years. If a stray man or woman was found by the hostile tribe, they were caught and devoured. A spear would be thrown across the river, sometimes hitting a person, and sometimes a tree. After several years had passed in this way, the people of Vaturua determined to attack Televa, and have a regular battle. This they did, and drove Tuimbua, with his people, off some distance into the interior, where he lived for several years, each party amusing themselves by destroying occasionally a town or plantation belonging to his enemy. The Vaturueans took up their residence at Televa, which they have continued to occupy till this day.

When the American squadron visited these isles, one of the vessels came to Bua, and its commander invited the two chiefs on board, and advised them then and there to settle their difficulties, and become friends again. The chiefs talked over their affairs, pretended to forgive each other, kissed, exchanged their dresses, and then declared that they would be like brothers, as in days of yore, and that fighting should no longer be known in their lands, but that they would till them, catch their fish, and eat their yams in peace.

Tuimbua now returned to Bua, and settled at Vaturua. The peace was not of long continuance. Tuimbua was not celebrated for his warlike abilities. He seemed rather to love peace, and on the commencement of war again, he sent to Vewa to ask the assistance of Verani, promising him his favorite daughter for a wife, as a reward for his services. Elijah came, both parties fought, but neither conquered, and the chiefs lived at enmity, carrying on a desultory warfare until four years since, when Tuimuru renounced heathenism, made peace with Tuimbua, and died soon after, leaving Hezekiah to reign in his stead.

Tuimbua died about a year afterwards, leaving, besides Hezekiah, three sons of equal rank, Muchanamu, whose fate has been recorded, Peter and Uarambata. Such is a summary of the history of Bua, as given me by Elijah on our late passage to this place.

23. Sabbath. I attended the native service in the chapel in the morning. The congregation was not as large as at Vewa, but the singing was far better. I cannot become habituated to listen with pleasure to the singing where the tune is snapped off at the end of every two lines. It destroys all the harmony of music; however, the custom of *lineing* out the hymns may serve to fix the attention of the worshipper on the words. I think it must serve to cramp rather than elevate the soul, which I believe to be the design of music.

After the native service in the morning, Mr. Williams preached in English. The latter service was held in his study. It was very pleasant to me to unite once more with the people of God in worshipping Him who has bestowed so many blessings upon us, and saved us from so many dangers to which we have been exposed.

24. Mrs. Williams informs me that they were somewhat alarmed, a few nights before my arrival, by the following occurrence: Uarambata, taking advantage of the absence of his brother, sent a man to dig some tarro belonging to the mission grounds, which coming to the

knowledge of one of the servants of the house, he went immediately to Vaturua, and requested that the tarro might be returned. The young chief appeared quite ashamed at being caught in so mischief-like an act, and sent it back with orders to his man to dig the tarro belonging to a native who had just built a new house not far from the mission premises. The owner of the tarro bed resisted the order, and would not let the man dig it. The man departed without it, threatening to burn his house that night. About midnight, Mr. W. and family were awakened by the shouting of natives, and the crackling of bamboos, which resemble in sound the firing of muskets. They arose, and soon perceived the poor man's house in flames. The missionaries did not know for some time how the affair would end; perhaps their own buildings were doomed also. After destroying the house, and making as much noise as possible to add to the terror of the scene, they departed without farther mischief.

On the return of Peter, so anxious were the old men of Vaturua to tell their story, that they did not wait for him to land from his canoe, but met him there, where they related the occurrence just recorded, and begged his permission to go and fight the Televans. Peter sat quietly and listened to their narrative, and then made the following answer: "You wish for war. I desire peace. You wish to fight my brother of Televa. I intend to be of a 'good mind' towards him. He is a strong man. He made my father run. You may go and fight the Christians, while I will return with these, my friends, who have come with me, and live with them. My speech is ended." The war-loving and Christian-hating Vaturuans returned to their town; and quiet seems to be restored for the present.

Peter, with several of his attendants, called to see me the day after my arrival. He appears to be about twenty years of age, his countenance is good, and his appearance preposessing. His mother was a native of Tonga-taboo, which accounts for his good looks.

25. As I was walking along the bank of the river, I perceived a canoe about to sail. It contained only one old man and woman, and I told them that I would go a little way with them. As I stepped upon the frail little bark, the old man shouted, "Now I am the king of Fee-jee!" The natives, of whom there were several on the margin of the river, laughed, and asked where he was going. "*Au sa lako ge papalagi*"—"I am going to the white man's land," he replied. After a pleasant sail, I landed where the foot-path from the town terminated, and returned to the mission-house, having enjoyed a pleasant walk in addition to my excursion on the river.

In the evening Mr. Williams gave me an account of the hurricane experienced by the missionaries in February last at Nandy. At the commencement of the gale, the roof of the house occupied by Rev. Messrs. Watsford and Ford, with their families, was carried away. The rain poured in torrents, and the house tottered in a manner that showed it was unsafe for them to remain in it any longer; neither was there any shelter from the rain. The waves of the angry ocean were rising and threatening to engulf them. They must go somewhere. As they left the slight elevation on which the house stood, they found themselves two feet deep in water. They took refuge in a building near, which, being low, seemed not to be as much affected by the wind as the higher buildings. They were soon driven from this by the water, and they had no sooner left it than it fell to the ground. Their only hope was to gain the native village, but between them and it was a wide sheet of water, formed by the mountain torrents. The ladies and children were obliged to remain exposed to all the violence of the gale, while the gentlemen and servants exerted every nerve to construct a raft for them to cross the water. After this was done, the ladies, with their frightened babes, were placed thereon, and two servants took charge of it while the gentlemen waded on up to their necks nearly in water.

On reaching the central force of the current, the natives cried out, "We cannot manage the craft; we shall all be swept into the sea (as were several natives during a former gale). The gentlemen came to their aid, and with great difficulty succeeded in forcing the raft to stem the current, and they landed at the village. Here they were driven from house to house for some time by the rising of the waters. At length they reached the only house in the village that was not partly under water,—being situated a little on the rise of the mountain. The water soon came in here, and they were preparing to leave to ascend the mountain as their last hope of safety, when a native said, "Stop a moment, I think the water has become stationary." Every eye was fixed intently on one spot which marked the rise of the waters. After a while it became evident that the element had begun to recede, and as the tide ebbed the house became dry. They now began to think of dry clothing, but no well-stored chests are to be found in the houses of the natives; not feeling the importance of clothing themselves, of course they were not prepared to supply visitors. Some Tonga cloth was brought forward, in which they wrapped themselves and slept during the night. On the morrow the storm had abated, and search was made among the wrecked articles for clothing; but nothing could be found that was dry except one trunk containing the wearing apparel of Mr. Watsford, in which the ladies and gentlemen arrayed themselves. I will not attempt to describe their appearance.

The loss to the mission by the wind and flood was considerable. Their books were nearly all spoiled. Mr. Watsford's eldest son was almost suffocated by the kindness of the native who had him in charge. He wrapped a blanket so closely around him, to shield him from the wind and rain, that he became quite purple. Their little girl died in two weeks after. Mrs. W. is still suffering severely in consequence of her exposure.

Mr. Ford and family left in the John Wesley during her last visit to the islands; Mr. F. being afflicted with a disease in his head that is increased by a residence in a tropical climate.

From the different events recorded in this book relating to the mission in Feejee, it may be seen that the life of a missionary is not one of ease and exemption from trials, as some pretend to suppose. There is no exaggeration in what I have recorded. They are the simple facts, and show that these devoted people of God have, in the words of the apostle, suffered by perils of the ocean, by perils of the land, and by perils from false brethren. And what do they gain? Not worldly honor, for the missionary is despised by the world. The next world, however, will show what is gained by those who faithfully serve their Master here.

26.   As Mr. and Mrs. W., with myself, were enjoying an evening walk, a messenger summoned us to return, saying that some "*papalagi*" gentlemen were at the house waiting to see us. We hastened home, and had the pleasure of welcoming Messrs. Calvert, Hazlewood and Malvern.

The District Meeting was to be held at Bua, and the gentlemen had anticipated the coming of the John Wesley by a smaller conveyance.

27. This morning, hearing the most dolorous crying in the town, I inquired its cause, and was informed that some one was dead. Mrs. W. said that all cried on these occasions; some for grief and others from custom. A short time since a child died in the town, and a woman of Vaturua, hearing of the death, said that she would cross the river and join in the cry. She came, but was too late; the cry was over. "Never mind," she said, "I will cry here;" so she sat down in the footpath, where she cried as loud and as long as she chose, and then returned to her home apparently quite satisfied with herself.

28. The John Wesley arrived, bringing Dr. Lyth, the Chairman of the District Meeting. The gentlemen of the mission had now all arrived, with the exception of Mr. Watsford, who was detained by the continued illness of Mrs. W. The children of Mr. Hazlewood go to New Zealand in the mission brig when it returns. The eldest son of Dr. and Mrs. Lyth, with the two eldest boys of Mr. and Mrs. Williams, depart at the same time to attend school at New Zealand. The missionaries of Feejee have adopted the wise plan of sending their children to be educated among civilized beings as soon as practicable. I believe this is the only way in which their children can be trained for future usefulness. It is next to an impossibility to keep children free from the deleterious influences of heathenism; and the sooner they are sent away the better it is for them, though hard is the parting. This is not one of the least of the trials of the missionary.

29. At an early hour in the morning I started in a

canoe, with an old native servant to manage it, and three
of the little sons of the missionaries for companions, for
an excursion up the river. We had not proceeded far,
when I was shown the grave of the late king, which
looked like a little grassy mound. It was a quiet spot,
shaded by a large eva tree. An oven, for cooking the
bodies of dead men, is also to be found under the
shadow of the same tree. Two weeks since, eight
men were cooked in that very oven. It appears that a
party of men belonging to the town where Muchanamu
was murdered, visited another town with whom they
were on friendly terms. The visitors occupied the
" buri," and in the evening after their arrival they were
joined by the chief of the place, with several of his attendants. During the conversation that ensued, the
visitors boasted that they had killed the chief of Bua,
and one said, " I ate a peace of his heart." The chief
listened to the statement, and made no comment. The
next morning men were stationed at the entrance of the
" buri" with clubs, and as the visitors came forth to enjoy " the sweet breath of morn," they were severally
clubbed. The bodies were sent to Bua, where they were
cooked and devoured. This is, probably, but the beginning of murders that will be committed on account of the
death of Muchanamu.

The dead are sometimes cooked whole, and after
being taken from the ovens are painted and ornamented
as for a feast or war. They are thus taken, in a sitting
posture, on the shoulders of men and carried to some
distant town. In passing them, one would not perceive,
till quite near, that they were dead.

We sailed on through several miles of level country.
The tall cocoa-nut trees were very abundant, waving
their crowned heads in the breeze, and seeming to invite

us to admire their graceful beauty. The lemon, the citron, the lime, and the fig trees are also to be observed among others, imparting a variety to the foliage which was truly beautiful. One lemon tree was bending over the margin of the river, so completely loaded with its golden fruit as to appear just ready to fall into the still waters beneath.

My little companions were complete botanists, having a name for every green thing. Having proceeded much farther than I was aware before we turned towards home, it was nearly noon before we arrived, and Mrs. W. was feeling some anxiety on our account. We had not, however, been startled by the report of a musket. The poisoned arrow had not whizzed past us, we had felt no blow from the club, no point of a spear, no bite from cannibal teeth, and had passed a "*lovo mbokalo*" without being baked in it.

30. Sabbath. After divine service in the afternoon, several of the gentlemen, with Mrs. W. and myself, crossed the river, and repaired to a small settlement near its banks, where Mr. Calvert was to preach. We found but eight or ten houses whose inhabitants have renounced heathenism, and are desirous to be instructed in the great truths of the gospel. The buildings were scattered about any where in a thick grove of banana and cocoa-nut trees.

Mrs. W. and myself seated ourselves on a native drum, under the shade of an eva tree, while Mr. C. addressed the assembly. During the sermon, we observed the Mbete of Bua approach and enter the nearest hut, where he must have listened to the greater part of the discourse. At the close of the services, Messrs. C. and W. entered the dwelling, and recommended to him the religion of Jesus. He said that the "*lotu*" was very good, and by and by he would embrace it.

As we left the place, I thought I had never before worshipped in so splendid a sanctuary. The roof was of the purest azure, and the walls were elegantly decorated with verdant ornaments.

From the settlement we visited the town of Vatarua. Peter was absent, but the gentlemen conversed with several respecting the excellency of the true "*lotu*." With the true native courtesy they assented to all that was said, and promised to renounce heathenism by and by, as usual. The posts which had been erected for the great "*buri*," by the warriors of Muchanamu, were still standing as they left them. This "*buri*" was to have been finished on their return, and dedicated with the bodies of Mr. W. and his children. But God, in whom the missionary trusts, did not suffer this to be. He arrested the savage, and brought all his plans to nought. Mr. W. remarked that he hoped to see the building finished, and to preach the gospel in it.

I stood gazing a long time upon the spot on which this terrible scene was to have been enacted, during which my imagination was not inactive; but as there are horrible realities enough to record of this people to satisfy the most horror-loving reader, I forbear to record imaginary ones.

Dr. Lyth preached an excellent sermon in English in the evening.

31. After tea, Mrs. W. being engaged in her maternal duties, and the gentlemen all in the chapel, I wandered out alone, and passing through the town, entered a retired path leading to the "*rara*," a distance of about a quarter of a mile from the town. Engaged in my own solitary musings, I wandered on, forgetting that I was

in a heathen land, or that I might meet some who were
not as good as the Televans.   I had gained about half
the distance to the "*rara*," when I was aroused and reminded of my lonely situation by hearing some one approach.   I thought it might be one of the Christian-
hating cannibals of Vatarua, but my fears were soon
removed by perceiving the figure of a woman, as she
appeared, and was then hidden by the intervening foliage.   On reaching the spot where I stood, she said that
her father, seeing me pass on my way alone, sent her to
accompany me, and see that no harm came to me.
Would a civilized being have done more?

Aug. 2.   At daylight I was informed that the Zotoff
was at anchor in Bua Bay, and we soon had the pleasure of welcoming Mr. Wallis and Elijah at the mission
house.

The members of the District Meeting had closed their
business, and were ready to depart, expecting to sail at
the same time with the Zotoff.

Mr. Calvert has received an appointment to Bau, and
will remove to the city as soon as suitable buildings are
erected.   No other changes are expected to take place
the coming year.   Many more missionaries are needed
in Feejee.   The mission has become sadly weakened by
death and other causes the past year.   The bereaved
Mr. Hazlewood sends his dear babe and the little girls
to New Zealand in the John Wesley.

After dinner we took leave of the good company assembled at Bua, and embarked in the jolly boat to
join the bark, that there might be no hindrance to our
sailing at an early hour in the morning.

My pleasant visit at Bua will be long remembered.   I
found the place like an oasis in the desert, where the
traveller is refreshed and benefited.   Mr. and Mrs. W.

showed the most affectionate attention to my comfort, health and pleasure during my visit.

The weather was rather squally, with occasional showers of rain when we left Bua. The bark had not come into the bay, but was lying at so great a distance off, that its hull could not be seen as we entered the bay from the river. A cutter belonging to Solavu was at anchor near the J. W., and Elijah proposed that, as the sea was rough, and the wind, though fair, was likely to increase, Mr. W. and myself should take passage to the bark in the cutter, while he and the other Feejeeans would go on in the boat, adding that he could not feel comfortable, if we remained in the little boat in such weather. To this arrangement Mr. W. consented, and we removed to the cutter. In the convenient little vessel we reached the bark, after two hours' sailing, with the apparent speed of a steamer.

3. Although the morning seemed to indicate a storm, Mr. W. thought that he would venture to cross to Vetelavu. When half of our passage was accomplished, the sky became very dark, the wind blew half a gale, the heavy thunder rolled, the lightning played, and the rain fell in torrents. Our situation is never very enviable on board the bark in a severe thunder storm. There is too much powder and cutlery on board to render one quite comfortable in such seasons. But there were no rocks and reefs directly in our course, and we anchored at Malaka, on Vetelavu, about 3 o'clock P. M.

4. We sailed to Tabua. The chief, with several attendants, visited the bark, where he received some presents, and promised to fish well for the "Turaga ndena." On his return to his town great lamentation was heard, and sad news awaited his coming.

His principal wife, with some twenty or thirty of his

tribe, mostly women and children, went to an inland town to procure a supply of food. The most friendly intercourse had been held between the inhabitants of the two places for the last four years; therefore, the Tabuans suspected no evil. The chief of the inland town belonged neither to Ba nor Tabua, but has been in the habit, in former years, of joining the strongest party. Believing Tabua to be the strongest, for several years past he has adhered to them, and helped them against their enemies. But the chiefs and people of Ba, having been rather successful of late in catching and eating the Tabuans, the high-minded and honorable chief has become the ally of Ba. The Tabuans knew nothing of this change, and went to exchange their fish for the products of the country, when their former friends received them with their love tokens, called clubs, and soon sent the souls of their terrified victims to another world. The women and children were all massacred, and one man. Two men escaped to tell the tale.

This changing of parties is a common occurrence among independent chiefs. Dumbui, of Naloa, pretends great love for Retova. Whales' teeth and love messages are continually passing between them, yet Dumbui told Mr. Wallis that if Bau should come to fight Mathuata, he should fight on the side of Bau.

5. We anchored at Ba. The inhabitants belonging to the town of Vakambua are engaged in preparing the slaughtered Tabuans for feasting. It is the custom, when natives are murdered in this way, to send the bodies immediately to the town of some superior chief, who was the principal enemy of the slain. More than two thousand of the inhabitants of Feejee have been murdered since we have heen among this group. It is

beyond our power to estimate the number killed in the interior of the large islands and on the smaller ones, as we have had no intercourse with them.

Elijah remarks that the population has rapidly diminished since the introduction of fire-arms. On our passage in the little boat to Bua, he observed that when he was a lad, the whole coast which we passed by was lined with towns, the inhabitants of which had been mostly killed in their wars.

10. Elijah informs me that it is a custom on this coast, and many other parts of Feejee, when one tribe visits another, after they have partaken of the food provided for them, to gather up every thing that is left, and take it away with them. They collect even the smallest crumbs, lest they should fall into the hands of strangers, who, by rubbing poisonous herbs over them after their departure, would cause their death. This was once the universal custom, but of late years it is partially abolished. He farther remarks that his father, who died an old man, used to say, during the last years of his life, that Feejee had changed much since he was a lad. In former days, the intercourse between the different tribes was more restricted. When one clan visited another, they went well armed and in a most formal manner. The women and children never accompanied them, nor even were sent, as now, to exchange food. While they remained at a strange town, no social intercourse took place between the parties, each keeping by themselves, approaching only within speaking distance. Tribes or clans only visited for the purpose of exchanging property. Their meetings for that purpose were held on an open space of ground, which I have already described as the "*rara.*" The different parties entered it from opposite directions. The riches which they brought

were placed in the centre. The natives would then seat themselves, when the chiefs would address each other through their officers, in the most respectful, formal and complimentary manner. After the speeches, dancing commenced, sometimes one party performing, and then the other, taking care to keep at a good distance from each other. At the conclusion of the ceremonies, which were ended by feasting the guests, each party retired to separate habitations. Tribes inhabiting distant parts of the group knew nothing about each other.

Namosimalua appears to have been the first Feejeean traveller of distinction. He seems to be of a restless, active disposition. He has visited and conquered the inhabitants of many places who were not previously known at Bau and the vicinity except by name. For many miles of coast on this side of Vetelavu, the inhabitants acknowledge him as their king. He has depopulated some small islands, and it is said that he had no small share in killing and scattering the inhabitants of the now almost desolate coast of Vanualavu, between Bua and Mathuata.

Elijah was the constant companion of his uncle for many years, and both rendered themselves notorious by their conquests and deep treachery.

12. Lautoke. The schooner William and David arrived. The fish which it brought was taken on board, and the vessel is discharged, as there is not sufficient business on this coast to employ two cutters and a schooner.

13. No farther service being required of Elijah, and his presence being very much needed at Vewa, Mr. W. parted with him to-day with reluctance, and he sailed for his home in the Glide.

As he left, I said to him, " Will you not return to
25

Vewa and accompany us to America?" "It would be difficult," he replied, "for me to visit America. I should see so many beautiful women, and so many other attractive objects, I should be in danger of forgetting the concerns of my soul."

24. Lautoke. The Glide returned from Vewa, bringing us letters from the Consul at Rewa and the missionaries at Vewa. We learn from them that the British frigate, Havanah, has arrived among the group. We hope that Naivu will receive a visit and a lesson before the vessel departs. Mr. Calvert writes, after detailing some items of news, "There is one thing which I must not forget to tell you, though it will make you tremble. While we were absent at Bua, Navinde caught fourteen women and clubbed one man. News came to Vewa that the women were all to be clubbed the next day. Our wives could not rest, and procured a canoe and hastened to Bau with a whale's tooth to present to Tanoa to spare their lives. They were too late to save them all; nine had just been clubbed, but the others were saved at the intercession of the ladies, who approached the king with aching hearts and trembling frames."

27. In the afternoon the mission brig came in sight and anchored near. We soon had the pleasure of receiving a visit from Mr. Calvert. We learned from him the cause of the late capture of the fourteen women by Navinde. It appears that there were visitors at Bau, and food was to be prepared for them; therefore, the king ordered his butchers (whose especial province it is on these occasions) to provide meat for the guests. In compliance with this order, Navinde, with several others of the Lasakau tribe, repaired to the main, and succeeded in obtaining fifteen human beings, ten of whom were slaughtered and five saved. When the ladies offered

the whale's tooth to the king, he said, "Those that are dead, are dead; those that are alive, may live."

Thakombau and Navinde accompanied Mr. C. on board the Havanah, where they were lectured on the horrible custom of cannibalism. Thakombau said, "Oh, in England you have a plenty of beef, therefore you have no need to eat each other, but in Feejee we have no other meat to give our friends." What a horrible feature of cannibalism is thus presented, to kill and eat each other where no enmity exists, merely for the love of the flesh of their own kind. When Mr. Calvert afterwards reproved Thakombau for his speech, he said, "Our fathers did the same years ago, but we are now growing wiser, and if you come to Bau and live, we shall be ashamed to eat so many human bodies." It is said that neither the king nor Thakombau feed, themselves, on human flesh, yet, as the above shows, they do not hesitate to provide it for their friends. If Mr. Calvert resides on the island, it will be in his power to prevent many horrible scenes like those just recorded. If cannibalism should be abolished from Bau, hundreds of lives would be saved annually. If only a canoe load of visitors should arrive at the imperial city, the butchers must hasten to catch one or more persons with which to feast them. None are employed in this business except the Lasakaus. Before the Vewa people embraced Christianity, they were honored by being the butchers for the royal city, and well did they execute their trust.

Mr. Calvert has been endeavoring to bring about a reconciliation between Garenggeo, Bau and Phillips. He has advanced so far as to stop, for the present, all hostilities between the powers that be. He performed a journey to the mountains, and returned accompanied by Garenggeo, and the brothers met. Garenggeo came

unattended, save by the missionary, while the boastful,
cowardly Phillips feared to meet his brother unaccom-
panied by a host of his people.   It appears that the Consul had been engaged in efforts to bring the brothers
into favor with each other, and in conjunction with Phillips had sent for Garenggeo to come to Nukulau, hold a
meeting at the palace of the Consul, and become friends.
But Garenggeo, knowing by sad experience that no faith
could be put in his treacherous brother, had feared to
come.

When the brothers, through the influence of Mr. Calvert, met, Phillips, surrounded by his people, paced to
and fro before Garenggeo, saying, "Why did you not
come when I sent for you?"   "Because I was afraid ;
I could not trust your assurances of friendship, as you
are not a true man; you say one thing and mean another," replied Garenggeo.   "Why did you come then
with the missionary?" he asked.   "Because he is true.
He told me that I should be safe, and I could trust him,"
he replied.   After some more catechising, on the part of
Phillips, he said, "Yes, I am strong.   I conquer my
enemies.   I do not have to run.   I conquered Rewa."
"You are weak were it not for the strength of Bau.
Bau conquered Rewa, but it was through you that our
brother was murdered," returned Garenggeo.   After
some more conversation, of which the above is only a
specimen, Phillips, who had not been very much pleased
with Mr. C.'s interference and presence, desired all the
white people to go out and leave him with his brother.
Mr. Calvert said, "If we go out, your people must go with
us.   Your brother has no one to protect him, and you
must not have all these people around you."   This command was not in accordance with the desires of the *heroic*
cannibal, but he had no alternative, and reluctantly con-

sented. After the departure of the spectators, the brothers talked, cried, kissed each other, and exchanged their "*masis*," and loved each other mightily for some time, and the result is that Garenggeo has returned to the mountains and Phillips to Nuque, both desirous of living on friendly terms, yet neither able to trust the other. I think it probable that each will reside where he is, until the death of one, when the other can safely reign as king of Rewa.

The Havanah sailed to Ovalau, where the trees and bushes were most furiously attacked by those on board, to show the natives the power of their fire-arms. We do not learn that any of the places rendered memorable by the massacre of white men, are to be visited or punished. Experience shows that moral suasion does not always avail in Feejee. The lesson given to the inhabitants of Malolo has been most salutary and lasting. There is no place in the group where white people can visit with more safety, and receive kinder treatment. Mr. Calvert returned to the J. W. in the evening.

28. The J. W. sailed at sunrise for Rotumah.

I accepted the invitation of Mr. Calvert, yesterday, to visit Lautoke, where we enjoyed the luxury of a walk. I need the exercise of walking, as my health suffers from my long residence in so confined a space as the cabin and quarter deck of the bark. Mr. C. urges my going to Vewa; but I have decided, if my health does not improve when we return to the other coast, to accept of the kind invitation of Mr. and Mrs. Williams, and remain awhile with them at Televa, as they are the most lonely, and I can communicate with Mr. W. oftener, by writing, from Bua.

CHAPTER XXI.

The angry chief—Popery in Feejee—Conspiracy—A Letter—Arrival at Bau—Dirge—Our Final Departure from Feejee—The Uncas—Arrival at Manilla — Departure — Small-pox on board — Deaths — St. Helena—Home.

Aug. 29. The Glide, in charge of Mr. Lovett, sailed on the 26th of this month for Mathuata, for the purpose of establishing houses and preparing for our return to that coast.

Last evening one of our hostages, belonging to the tribe of Nasurawalla, came into the cabin in great agitation to ask liberty to go on shore. While he was speaking, a sailor came and said that he had just caught him stealing a fine new musket. He was just about to jump overboard with the musket, to swim to the shore, when he was observed, and his course arrested. He was exceedingly alarmed, but Mr. W. told him that he would receive no other punishment than that awarded by his chief. Nasurawalla came on board to-day and said that he was very angry with Ndausamu for stealing the musket, and he had come to take him into his canoe, where he should kill and then throw him into the sea. Mr. W. smiled, and informed him that the thief was not Ndausamu, but Nga. The chief was silent for a moment, and then said, "I am greatly ashamed. I thought it was Ndausamu, who is a '*kaise*;' I could punish him, but Nga is a chief, and my sister's child." No more was said about clubbing, casting into the sea, or punishment of any kind. He would not have punished the "*kaise*," as he said, but would pretend that such was his intentention, that Mr. W. might present a whale's tooth to spare his life.

Sept. 5. Namula. The second chief of this place, and ten of his people, have renounced heathenism, but there is no one to instruct them in the precepts of the true gospel; and without instruction they are little better than before.

We have been visited by some of the females of this place, none of whom can boast of more personal beauty than *our Phebe*. It is said that the females of this coast engage in more masculine employments than those of many other parts of the group,—that they assist in cultivating the lands, in building the houses, and sometimes follow the warriors to collect the slain of the enemy, and afterwards cook them. They wear grass "*lekus*," braid no cinnet, plat no mats, and manufacture no cloth, and, in short, appear far behind the other portions of Feejee that we have visited, in their *arts* and *sciences*.

12. Veudongo. We learn that the Tabuans are angry because Elijah has prevented the warriors of Bau from coming to fight or to assist them against their enemies. They have left fishing, and will sell no food to the Vewa man who has charge of the "*beech de mer*" house. The truth is, Elijah asked the chiefs of Bau to defer their assistance till Mr. W. had left this coast, as it would interrupt his fishing.

The Glide arrived yesterday from Mathuata, and brings word that such is the anger of its king towards Mr. W., that he will have nothing more to do with him. He is angry because he deems the present that was given to Natemba, of Tavea, more valuable than the one which he received. Some muskets, whale's teeth and gunpowder, will set all right again on our return. The Glide sails for the same place to-day.

13. Nasurawalla declines fishing any more, as he is about to engage in a war with Nandy, on this coast. He states that his anger is great towards the people of that place; that at one time they made peace, and he gave them riches, and in three days afterwards they murdered four of his men, and now he accepts of no "*soro*," but will burn their towns and kill as many as possible.

18. Ba. A Tonga teacher has been stationed at this place for a year past. He is my old friend Wesley. Learning that we are about leaving, he brought a pig and a pair of ducks to present to Mr. W., and some hen's eggs and a valuable shell, from his wife to me. I admire the manner in which a present is offered in Feejee. The simple words are uttered, " This is my love to you." Can civilization offer any thing prettier?

19. Yanganga. We have again crossed the waters which divide the two large islands. As my health is improving, I have given up the idea of visiting Bua for the present.

20. Raverave. The boat was sent ashore on our arrival with an invitation for the angry chief to visit us. He came, but said nothing for a long time. Mr. W. was full of love towards him, &c., and after awhile he softened him enough to say yes and no a few times. I presented him with a white muslin head-dress, and told him that I had commenced embroidering a girdle for him, but if his anger continued, I would finish it and present it to Thakombau.

When I first visited Mathuata, I presented Retova with an embroidered girdle, which pleased his fancy much. He took it with him to Bau, where it was begged from him. He had many times requested me to work him another; but I told him that he would not keep it, and I could not present that kind of work where it was esteemed so lightly. He would say that none but the chiefs of Bau would beg such an article, and if I would give him another they should never see it. Accordingly, when I heard of his anger I thought I might contribute towards restoring his good humor, and commenced the ornament. He desired to see it at once, and, after placing it in every possible point of view, said it would be far more beautiful than the first, and that no chief of Bau must have it. It was evening when he came off, and he soon returned to the town, after saying he would come in the morning and receive his presents.

21. Retova came off in good humor, proposed that the bark should go to Namuka, where he would soon join it, and that "*beech de mer*" houses should be erected at Mali, Nduri, Ndrua-ndrua and Yanganga, and he would see that Mr. W. obtained two hundred bags of fish in two moons. He received his presents, and left while the anchor, which is not allowed to rest long in any one place, was raised, and we departed.

23. Nduri. The Caroline arrived alongside from Vewa. By this conveyance we received letters from our friends, and learn that owing to the continued failure of Mrs. Watsford's health, they will probably leave their station and go to New Zealand the present year. If so, one of the other missionaries must take the place of Mr. Watsford, Lakemba being a most important station, rendered more so perhaps on account of two Jesuit priests, who came to Feejee several years since, and took up their residence near the Protestants.

It appears that the Jesuits have sadly degenerated in these latter days. They were formerly the pioneers, penetrating to the most distant parts of the globe, and enduring almost every kind of misery, braving death in its most terrific forms, and many of them falling martyrs to their zeal. Now, however, they wait for the "Protestant heretics" to pave their way. Such has been the case at the Sandwich, Friendly, Society, and Feejeean groups of islands. There are thousands of islands in the Pacific where no missionary foot has ever been placed. Why do not the Catholics occupy some of those waste places? Perhaps it is not permitted by Divine Providence. Had these priests of Feejee settled on the Ba, or Mathuata coasts, where there are many who are strongly desirous that a missionary should live among them, and are all ready to renounce heathenism, no doubt they would have made many proselytes; whereas, by locating themselves in the immediate vicinity of the Protestants, who had gained a footing and the confidence of the chiefs of the land, they are most effectively hindered from propagating their pernicious tenets.

The following account of the introduction of Popery into Feejee was kindly furnished me by Dr. Lyth: "It was in the month of August, 1844, that the first attempt was made to establish a Roman Catholic mission in Feejee. A bishop, accompanied by two priests, landed in Lakemba. There were already Wesleyan missionaries residing on different islands of the group, and Lakemba was one of our oldest stations. So satisfied were the chiefs with their Protestant missionaries, that the priests received but a cold reception. The bishop first tried to prevail upon Fenau, the Tonguese chief, to embrace Popery, and receive the priests' offering as an inducement to make him king of Vavau, (one of the Friendly Islands,) in the place of king George. The chief absolutely refused. It would seem that their object was to

gain, through Fenau, a footing at Vavau, having failed
with king George.

Not succeeding with the Tonguese residents, they next
turned their attention to the Feejeeans, the proper inhabitants of the land. They applied to Tuinayau, the
principal chief of Lakemba and the windward group.
He said that he had already received his priests, (refer-
ring to us,) and wanted no others. They neglected no
argument to prove that their religion was the only true
one, and that we were false teachers, nay, missionaries
of the devil. But all was of no avail. The chief plainly
told them that they were not wanted in Lakemba, and
positively objected to their remaining. The bishop then
proposed that they should remain in Lakemba till an opportunity should offer for them to go to Somosomo, which
is another of the Protestant stations. To this, neither
Tuinayau nor Fenau would consent. Finding that neither
threats nor promises would influence the chiefs in their favor, they fixed upon another expedient, by which they ulti-
mately succeeded in palming the two priests on Lakemba.
They left Lakemba, and on their way left the two priests
on the island of Namuku. The bishop appears to have
had as little regard to the feelings of the two 'Holy
Fathers' as to the natives in this step. The elder of
the two remonstrated with the bishop on thus throwing
them on the mercy of the natives; but he only replied
by asking if they intended to disobey orders, adding,
that if they did, they must take off their gowns. They,
therefore, submitted, and the bishop left them so scantily
supplied that, from the first, they depended entirely on
the natives for their food. Namuka being but a short
distance from Lakemba, it was not long before the 'Holy
Fathers' returned. Having two or three Tonga converts that came with them, and a French servant, they

took possession of the house of a Tonguese, and commenced their worship and teaching at once, in spite of all that had been said against it by the chiefs. They declared, however, that as soon as a canoe should go to Somosomo they would proceed to their destination. The chief offered them a canoe at once, and told them to go. Finding that they could not cheat the chiefs with lying promises, they told them plainly that it was their intention to remain, that they might kill them if they chose, but that they would remain. The chief, finding his remonstrance vain, at last submitted to that obstinacy he could not remove. He was doubtless influenced, too, by the fear of French frigates, which the 'Holy Fathers' threatened should come and punish them if they opposed the true religion.

The priests commenced their instructions by saying, 'Where are these missionaries from?' Nobody knows them. England is a poor little place, whereas, France is a great country that supplies England with beef, &c.

They exhibited their well known picture representing their church as a large, flourishing tree, and the several Protestant churches as dried, withered branches, broken off, and dropping into the burning gulf beneath. The shrewd heathen said, 'If your country is so large and rich, how is it that you are forced upon us without food, or any riches to buy it? We do not know you. We know the English. They do not come among us like 'kaises,' but bring riches and pay for their food. Your picture is a false one.' The laugh became so strong against them, that it was withdrawn, and has not been publicly exhibited since.

During the five years that they have resided here, they have been joined by some few of the Tonguese and Feejeeans; but of late the priests are teaching them to reverence the Sabbath. This causes dissatisfaction among their followers, who say that they might as well join the English ' *lotu* ' if they are required to keep the Sabbath."

The bishop committed an oversight in leaving his priests so destitute. A Feejeean hates poverty, and charity is as cold here as in civilized lands. The 'Holy Fathers' were near starving in several instances. For months they could procure no food, except the mama apple. The missionaries, hearing of their destitution, sent them a basket of food, which they received with apparent thankfulness; but on the return of the servant who carried it, the basket was found with all its contents on the door steps. It was not long, however, before hunger compelled them to accept food from the 'English heretics.' They have been threatening for some time past to bury an image of the Virgin Mary upon the grounds of the missionaries, which they assert will drive them away. Of course, they will take all the merit of driving Mr. W. and family from the station.

Since the first year, a French vessel has visited La-kemba occasionally, and, learning their error respecting leaving their priests without means of subsistence, repaired it by seasonable supplies.

The priests have learned the fact, that Tuinayau is exceedingly fond of yanggona, (the native grog,) and they have sent to Tonga for a large supply, thus evincing their intention of making a *spiritual* convert of him, if possible. In my opinion, Tuinayau would have been a Christian years ago, could his appetite for yanggona have been subdued, and his supplies have been withheld. He is an old man, and his mind is kept in a continual stupor by this indulgence, and when he is not supplied, he is attacked with what strongly resembles the ' *deli-*

rium tremens,' I should judge, from a scene once witnessed by Mrs. Calvert, which she described to me.

26. Namuka. We have once more reached this far-
off region, where all communication with the world is
ended for the present, so I must give up the pleasure of
receiving the kind and interesting epistles from Vewa
and Bua. My books and newspapers must be re-perused.
I expect to find nothing of interest to record in my journal; therefore, must make up my mind to enjoy a tame
existence in this untamed country.

We do not go to Vesongo, as before, but have anchored off the little island of Namandrua.

30. The principal chief of Vesongo and his affectionate wife have departed this life since our last voyage to
this place. Masella was sick for some little time, and
then the strangling cord put an end to his existence at
his own request. His wife, desiring to accompany him,
was also strangled.

Otima gave me an account of the affair, as one would
relate an amusing incident, although he always appeared
very fond of his parents while living. A chief, called
Ndovo appears to have assumed the authority of the deceased chief.

Oct. 8. Two men started, a few days since, to go a
little distance up the coast and beg a canoe. On their
return they were attacked by an enemy, and one was
killed. One of the murderers was a brother of one of
the two in the other canoe. As the club was raised to
despatch him, the brother leaped upon the canoe, exclaiming, " He is my brother. You must not kill him."
The other still held the club raised, and declared that he
would strike. "Then kill me first," replied the affectionate brother, as he firmly clasped his new-found relative in his embrace. The man was saved, and returned

to Vesongo in the canoe which he had begged. When the affair was related to Ndovo, he said, "Why did you not bring the body of the slain, that I might eat him?"

10. The political state of this part of Feejee is not, I think, to be understood by common minds. Ndovo is chief of Vesongo, and of a place called Raverave, between here and Naivu, up the coast. That people are at enmity with these natives of Vesongo, and yet both tribes are ruled by one chief. I have made many inquiries, but can learn nothing definite upon the subject.

The Raverave people committed the murder recorded above. We learn that Ndovo was angry with the murdered man, on account of his formerly running away and joining an enemy. The man had, however, returned to his lawful chief, "soroed," and been pardoned.

"Time by moments steals away,
First the hour and then the day;
Small the daily loss appears,
Yet it soon amounts to years.
Thus another year has flown,
And is now no more our own
(Though it brought or promised good)
Than the years before the flood."

12. It is one year to-day since we sailed from our native land. How vividly are the scenes of that day brought back to my remembrance! We had been invited to attend the marriage ceremony of a dear friend, but instead of engaging in the festivities of so happy an event, it was our lot to part with our friends.

Retova has arrived with three canoes and men to fish "beech de mer." Several Geer canoes have arrived for the same purpose, and the prospect seems to be brightening.

16. Retova has left for Mathuata, on account of the death of a child. An express came for him this morning. We inquired of what disease the child died, and were told that the god had killed it, being angry because the chief came to Namuka. The chief was on shore when the canoe arrived. On being sent for, he appeared very sad, and said that if he had remained at Raverave, the child would not have died.

20. Retova returned, after having appeased the angry god with a feast and a whale's tooth. He remained on shore last night at Ndrua-ndrua, but when he came on board this morning, he said that fear had prevented him from sleeping.

Namuka is the name of a district of this region, comprising a considerable extent of land, with several towns and tribes. Muta is situated but a little distance to the right of Ndrua-ndrua, where the son of the late Tui Mathuata resides, while Korovaka-turaga resides at Naivu, a few miles on the left of the island. This knowledge of the proximity of Retova's enemies effectually prevented him from enjoying the rest he so much needed.

The natives who have assembled at Ndrua-ndrua are very much afraid that their enemies will burn the " *beech de mer* " house. Three Muta canoes passed this place for Naivu while Retova was absent. One came along side the bark, and its crew of four men came on board. Ndova was here at the time, and conversed with them in the most friendly manner. Several of the Vesongo canoes were on the reefs at the time, yet no collision took place between them.

The Vesongans, however, kept an extra watch for several nights on shore, till they supposed their enemies had returned to Muta.

28. We were amused yesterday with a little instance of native cunning. Several came to the bark and said it was difficult for them to fish, as they had but little food. Mr. W., knowing this to be true, sent the jolly boat to the main, and procured a load of bread-fruit and bananas. When the boat returned, Mr. W. wrote a note to Derby, at the house on shore, directing him to select a part for his own use, and give the remainder to the chief Ndrui, to divide among the natives. The note was given to Ndrui, with verbal instructions to the same effect. Accordingly, he took charge of the food and note, and repaired to the shore, where he divided the whole of the food among the natives, who offered a part of it to Derby for sale. After he had bought and paid for it, the note was delivered, thus showing that they intended to make the most of their present.

29. Retova is again summoned to Raverave, as visitors have arrived from the royal city who require his presence. It is said that Elijah is one of the visitors; if so, we shall probably see him here in a few days.

Nov. 3. In the morning, a messenger came off from Ndrua-ndrua to say that the brother of the chief Ndovo had been killed in battle, and all the chiefs had gone to Vesongo to bury him. As soon as the body was brought to the town, two of his wives were strangled with all possible speed, lest they should not be able to overtake the soul of their departed husband in time.

About noon the cry was raised on deck that the " beech de mer " house was on fire. In ten minutes it was destroyed, with five hundred dollars worth of " beech de mer " in it. Mr. Wallis had been fearing and expecting this disaster, and had the fish brought to the vessel to finish the drying, upon the decks as soon as was practicable, but twenty canoes had brought a large quantity,

26

and some of it was quite unfit to bring off. He had seen the carelessness of those who had charge of the house, and talked to them about it, but it was in vain.

While the house was burning the Caroline arrived from Male and Nduri, bringing eleven bags of fish, and reporting that the two houses they were tending were doing well. At eight o'clock, P. M., the Glide arrived from the houses at Naloa and Yanganga with seventeen bags of fish. Elijah came in the Glide, and brought letters from the Consul, our friends at Vewa and Bua, and one from Thakombau, or Tui Vete, king of Feejee, as he is now called. The purport of the king's letter is to inform Mr. W. that he had sent a special messenger, in company with Elijah from Bau to Retova, Natemba and Dumbui, to desire them to fish well for Mr. W., that his vessel might be filled. To this message from Bau, we are chiefly indebted for the fish received by the Glide, as these houses did but little before the visit of Elijah and the Bau chief. They brought two canoes as a present to Retova. Elijah says, that after they had delivered their message to Retova, he told them to go away as quickly as possible, as he wished to return and assist Mr. W. in collecting his cargo.

The English sloop of war Daphne has visited the group, but I do not learn that any notice is taken of the frequent massacres that have occurred among the islands. Mr. Calvert, Thakombau and Elijah went to Rewa in the vessel for the purpose of meeting Phillips and Garenggeo, but it appears that they were obliged to leave matters as they were. Thakombau desired Garenggo to go to Bau. This he refused to do, saying that he had nothing to do with Bau; that he was willing to make peace with his brother, who might go to Rewa and be its king. Thakombau said if he would not go to Bau, no more could be done about it. Garenggo is well aware of the treachery of his countrymen, and fears to trust himself in Bau. He has not forgotten, probably, the fate of Nalela, the Lasakau chief, nor how, after Rewa was destroyed, his brother gave out word that all who had joined with Rewa during the war, should be pardoned, if they would " *soro* " to him, and that when hundreds came to " *soro*," he had them all murdered, and sent their bodies to Bau. It was said as many were killed in that way as when Rewa was burned. It is not surprising that, knowing all this, he has no confidence in their protestations, and prefers to remain in his mountain home.

4. The Glide sailed this morning for Naloa, Tavea, &c. Elijah returned in it.

We learn that Mr. and Mrs. Watsford have left their station for Auckland, and Dr. Lyth and family have removed to Lakemba; therefore, Bau can have no missionary for the present.

Thakombau says, that sometimes he feels very good in his mind, and means to " *lotu* " at once; then his mind changes, and then he is " *vaka develo* " (like a devil) again. On his return from Rewa, he was informed that a conspiracy was afloat to kill him. It is a custom among the great ones of Feejee to send food to their relatives. In accordance with this usage, Bau was in the habit of sending food to Lasakau, as a compliment to the Marama of Bau, who was the wife of Navinde. While Thakombau was at Rewa, Navinde visited the island of Kandavu. During his absence, his wife went to her father, the old king, and desired him to send no more food to Lasakau, as her husband and several others were gutting up a " *vari* " to kill her brother. One of the principal conspirators is Navinde's half-brother. His father was the rebel chief whose tongue was devoured by Tanoa, on his restoration to Bau, while his victim sat by and witnessed the horrible repast. Ratu-ndamu, the son, was a little boy when this occurred, but he has probably remembered the fact; nor will he forget it until he has had vengeance upon some of the family belonging to the king. Navinde has retired to the island of Ngau, and the other conspirators have fled to different places. Navinde has been rising (in his own estimation) since his marriage with the daughter of the king, and he has supposed, probably, that Thakombau is the only obstacle in the way of his becoming the greatest man in the kingdom.

19. Arrived and anchored at Nai Thombo-thombo on our way to Bua. Being about fourteen miles distant from Bua, I started in the jolly boat, about six o'clock in the evening, for that place. The crew consisted of four Vewa men to row the boat, and old Koru, of the same place, to act as guide and protector. I thought that we should have a bright moon to light us on our way, but in this I was disappointed, as she chose to wear a thick veil of grey, and thus deprive me of the pleasure of viewing the coast and river scenery by moonlight. After a dull passage of five hours, we arrived in safety at the mission station. Messrs. Williams and Hazlewood met me at the landing. I found Mrs. W. quite ill of influenza.

I learned that the heathen party at Bua had been very quiet since my former visit. The young chief is ill of consumption.

The yam season had commenced, and before taking their yams from the ground, it is usual to sacrifice a number of human beings. Five persons have been taken in this vicinity, and sent to as many different towns. As Mrs. Williams was standing on the piazza, a few days

since, she observed a party of the heathen on the opposite bank of the river cutting up a human body, and preparing it for the oven; the head and entrails were soon
after seen floating down the river. Mr. Williams had
them buried.

Mr. Hazlewood related the following horrible occurrence which took place at Nandy: "A native woman
who had ' *lotued* ' was one day returning to her dwelling
from a class meeting which she had been attending,
when her son met her, and at once cleft her skull. He
was immediately surrounded by the Christians and beaten
to within an inch of his life, and then suffered to crawl
away as best he could. He was angry with his mother,
because she was not strangled on the death of her husband, which had happened a short time before."

20. The Zotoff arrived at noon, and Mr. W. came
ashore, when, after remaining a short time, we once
more took leave of our kind friends, and departed, never
expecting to see them again on the shores of time.

25. We anchored at Motureke. On Monday, the
26th, there being no prospect of a breeze to waft our
bark to Bau on that day, I took passage in one of the
small boats for Vewa. The rowers were lazy, and our
passage was rather long. Koru was my protector, as
before. Two of the oarsmen were heathen, and were
very earnest in coaxing the god of the wind to raise a
breeze, promising to feed him with puddings and sugar-
cane if he would save them their labor at the oars. One
hinted that if I would give each of them a piece of cloth,
their god would be propitious. I told them that, as it
was not fashionable for the Feejeean gods to wear cloth,
I thought they would be quite satisfied with what had
been promised.

On our arrival at Vewa, I found the family of Mr.
Calvert all in good health.

27. Several of the towns on the main land are engaged in hostilities. The war drum is beating, and we
have seen the smoke of two burning towns. One or both
belonged to Navinde, who is still at Ngau. No one appears to know whether he is guilty of laying a plan to
kill Thakombau or not. It is reported that Navinde had
engaged to kill Thakombau, and a chief called Vunivalu,
with his son Karoe Sigalavu, was to kill Garenggeo; and
another chief, called Tanoa, was to kill his father, the
king of Naitasere. The truth, however, has not been
ascertained, except in the case of Phillips. The conspirators against his life have fled to the mountains. Thakombau has sent for them to be killed where they are, or
for them to be returned to Phillips; but the mountaineers
refuse to do either.

There is a town situated not far from Bau called
Buretu. It formerly belonged to Bau, but revolted and
joined Garenggeo, the exiled chief. Bau has decreed its
destruction, which makes the difference now between Bau
and Garenggeo. When the two chiefs met on board the
English man-of-war Daphne, for the purpose of settling
their difficulties, Garenggeo stipulated that Buretu should
be saved. Thakombau refused, and thus ended the affair
for the present.

Mr. Williams, the American commercial agent for
Feejee, has left the dominions of Phillips, and lives on
the island of Motureke.

29. A letter, of which the following is a copy, was
sent to Thakombau from Her Britannic Majesty's ship
Daphne, addressed to Tui Vete, (Thakombau,) king of
Feejee:

Her Britannic Majesty's ship Daphne,
At sea, Oct. 10, 1849.

Tui Vete,

Being now about to leave the Feejee Islands, I am led by an earnest desire for their welfare, and also by a sincere esteem for yourself, to address a few lines to you in the language of friendship.

These beautiful islands have been, until now, the scene of the grossest and most degrading impostures that have ever disgraced mankind, leading in their results to practices in which treachery and murder are stepping stones to the gratification of the vilest passions and appetites.

No people ever did, nor ever will become great or honorable while sunk in so profound a depth of ignorance and crime; and it is because I know you to be far too intelligent to be deceived by the flimsy superstitions which surround you, that I entreat you, for the good of your country, to use your powerful influence in stopping those abominable cruelties which disgrace it, and which cannot be thought of without disgust by any enlightened mind. I am confident that you cannot contemplate the kidnapping of unoffending women and children to supply a cannibal feast, nor the murder of a wife on the death of her husband, without shame for the cowardice of the former, and for the folly of the latter, as well as for the cruelty of both.

Depend upon it, such practices cannot last; and great will be the honor acquired by that chief who has the courage to oppose them. There is one man, and only one, who can effectually do this; that man is yourself. I would say to you, therefore, do not leave for another the opportunity which has fallen to your lot, of conferring so great a blessing upon your country. Let it be seen that cowardice and cruelty are no longer to be forced upon your people by a gross and ridiculous superstition.

They are an industrious and intelligent people; let them be protected and encouraged, and they will become great and prosperous. How much greater will be the ruler of such a people!

These few words have been written in the spirit of friendship, and are intended to promote the real welfare of your country, and your own true dignity and honor; therefore, I trust that you will give them your serious attention.

I will conclude with a request, which I make because I think it will, in a very great degree, forward those objects.

We must expect that in a short time your father will be numbered with the dead. According to a horrible practice, to which I have alluded, many women of his household would be murdered in cold blood on this melancholy occasion. Let me ask, as a personal favor, that you will interpose your authority to save these poor women from becoming the victims of such atrocious superstition. I beg their lives at your hands, and I earnestly hope that your compliance with my request will be one step towards the happiness of Feejee.

That Feejee may be blessed, and that you may be truly great, is the sincere wish of your true friend,

E. G. FANSHAW, *Captain.*

Dec. 2. In the afternoon Mrs. Calvert and the children and servants, with myself, embarked in a double canoe, intending to call at the bark and then proceed to Bau. On arriving at the bark, we found Tui Vete on board, and so many other Feejeean visitors that we concluded to keep on our way to the city. The king, hearing of our intention, started at once and reached Bau before us. He passed our canoe in one of a smaller size, and was seated in a large arm chair, which had been lashed to the canoe. When we first arrived in Feejee, he would have ridiculed the idea of a Feejeean sitting in an arm chair on a canoe ; but he is greatly changed since my first acquaintance with him. He appears fond of many of the comforts of civilized life.

Our stay at Bau was very short, as the clouds looked black and we feared a squall of wind before our return to Vewa.

The large house, formerly occupied by Thakombau, was blown down during one of the gales, and we found him living in a smaller one which had been erected on the same spot. Samonunu showed us the beginning of a stone house, but when it would be finished was more than she could tell.

We called on the old king, Tanoa, and found him surrounded by old men, who were drinking yanggona. I found the king much more feeble than when I last saw him. He still retains a fondness for ornamenting his head. He wore a white " *sala*," with several yards of pink ribbon wound about it. The ribbon had been attached to the whales' teeth that were presented to him by the ladies, when they begged for the lives of the victims of the cannibal feast before recorded. He is very deaf, but his general health is good. He presented me a native mat, and we departed for Vewa.

3. Thakombau spent the day at Vewa. He appears very fond of Mr. Calvert and family, frequently coming to pass a day with them, and holding long and sensible conversations with Mr. Calvert.

5. Samonunu, with several of her attendants, visited us. She brought some mats and presented them to me.

Many of my Vewa friends have also presented bread-fruit, mats, baskets and other articles.

7. As Mrs. Calvert and myself were standing on the piazza, a canoe, filled with natives, came in shore singing the following dirge, on the death of our much lamented Mr. Hunt.

Ni Make ko Misisi Uniti.

" Mei Misisi Uniti,
Ka sega ni kana,
E gunuva na una wai katakata
Ai sulu loaloa ka dolava,
Ka culu vata kei na vunai sala
Ai vakaruru toka ni matana. E — —

A vu ni koha,
Misi Uniti sa mate toka ;
A kai Vewa era sa loloma ;
A siga lotu levu me ra laki cola.
Digitaki nai sulu loaloa,
Nai sula ni vakarokaroko,
I vale ni soro sa mai bulu toka—
Ko mata vakaloloma. E — —

Misi Uniti so mate toka
Ko Josefa ka dau loloma
Josuia ko mai lako—e
A vale i Kupa me sa cuvu toka :
Kato balavu ko laki vasota ;
Era vakota ai me ra sa cola—
I na vale—kau me sa tau toka
Duti laki nai sula loaloa—
Ai coco toka ni kato. E — —
Misi Uniti me lave ki loma
E vei ko matai me sogata,
Tukilaki nai vako me ra toka. E — —

" Mrs. Hunt has not eaten,
She only drinks warm water;
The black cloth is opened;
Black is stitched to her bonnet,
And serves as a covering for her face.   A — —

Mr. Hunt is dead;
The people of Vewa mourn;
The preaching day came,—
They wear black dresses,—
Dresses of reverence.
He is carried to the chapel;
His face was lovely.   A — —

Mr. Hunt is dead;
Joseph loved him;
Joshua goes to the house of the carpenter,—
A long box is made; he nails it;
It is carried and put in the wooden house.
The black cloth is torn,
They line the box:
Mr. Hunt is lifted into it;
The carpenter nails it down;
Fasten it down and let it remain.   A — —

The natives sing or chant the above, with many others of their composing, in which they relate his love to them, with his sayings and doings while among them.

11.   I visited the grave of Mr. Hunt, as I expected to leave Vewa the next day, and set out an acacia tree at the head and at the foot of the grave, and then took my leave of the spot forever.

After this I visited the town belonging to Elijah, where, by the desire of Mary Wallis, I planted some tamarinds and transplanted some geraniums. The slips of rose bushes and geraniums, with many other plants that I had taken from New Zealand, had grown most luxuriously. It is very easy to cultivate a garden of flowers in Feejee.

12.   I took leave of my very kind friends, Mr. and Mrs. Calvert, with their interesting little family of children, and once more joined the bark, which had carried me safely over eighty thousand miles.

Navinde, who had been collecting "*beech de mer*" for Mr. W., had come from Ngau, and was on board when I arrived at the bark.   I asked him about the report that had been in circulation respecting him and Thakombau.   He said it was false, and got up by a poor man, to injure him.   "Why should I kill Thakombau? If I kill him, it would be my own death.   We are friends; I feel no enmity to him," said Navinde.   I asked him how many men he had killed while at Ngau.   He replied that three men had been concerned in stealing one of his pigs, and he ordered them to be killed.   "Do they not kill people in America for stealing?" he asked. I told him they did not.   "Well," he said, "it is not many years since people in England were hung for stealing."   I presume he learned it from some of the English sailors, of whom there are many about here.

13.   We arrived at Motureke and anchored.   A few hours after anchoring, we received letters and a basket of fine pine-apples from Lakemba, from Mrs. Lyth.

The king of Lakemba, with many of his principal chiefs, has at length embraced the Christian religion. It is now fourteen years since the Wesleyans first arrived at Lakemba, where, although the king has hitherto refrained from embracing Christianity himself, yet he has not opposed his subjects, and the gospel has advanced rapidly in that region.   Cannibalism has been abolished from that isle ever since the missionaries arrived.

18. Since my last date, we have passed down the coast of Vetelavu, and are now anchored at Nandy, (not where the mission is located ; the place of this name before mentioned as being the scene of the hurricane, is situated on Vanualavu,) buying yams in great abundance. This is the birthplace of Phebe. We have given her liberty to go on shore, but no one as yet appears to notice her, although many natives are visiting the vessel. We have some Vewa men on board, who tell us not to let her go ashore alone.

19. Yesterday Phebe's mother came to see her after I had recorded the above. She kissed (Fecjee fashion) every part of her child's face, and shed some tears. Mr. W. gave her presents, and then she wished to return ashore. She told Phebe that she had better remain where she is, and did not invite her to visit her home. They parted without any emotion, and Phebe says, to-day, that she would like to go to America again.

The Glide, which has been presented to Elijah for his services during our voyage, has just left for Vewa. Eleven Vewa men, who have been in the employ of the bark, and two white men, have also left, and our company is quite reduced. We are now all ready for sea.

24. We have no favoring wind, as yet, to fill our sails and bear us hence. Yesterday the cutter belonging to the mission arrived on its way to Ndronga. Elijah came in it, and we had the pleasure of receiving letters from our friends, Mr. and Mrs. Calvert.

A Sydney cutter, commanded by Capt. Allen, visited us yesterday. He has lately been robbed of nearly all his stores and trade. As his vessel was very small, he bought a little island near the large one, called Vetelavu, where he deposited the most of his trade and stores, leaving two white men and a boy to take care of the same. The chief who sold the land told the purchaser to shoot any natives who should come to molest them. The men, being ignorant of Feejeean courtesy, supposed that they had full liberty to shoot Feejeeans when they chose, than' which nothing was farther from the mind of the chief when he told them to do it. A chief may club and kill his subjects at will, but he never wills that they should be killed by white men; even a blow from a white man is remembered, and no opportunity is lost of avenging it.

Some time after the white men had taken possession of the isle, a native came one day to get some cocoa-nuts, when one of them fired a musket, and the ball made a plain path over the top of the man's head, carrying away the hair and skin. Soon after this affair, several more came to gather cocoa-nuts, when the white men made them prisoners, took away their clubs, spears and canoes, and gave them to other natives. Such is a specimen of their conduct towards the natives. They did not try to conciliate them, nor seemed to remember that their own lives were at the mercy of the natives by whom they were surrounded. They had been told many times that they would be attacked and killed, but the warnings had no effect upon their conduct. At length, about the 6th of the present month, they were attacked by fifty of their enemies. The arm of one of the white men was broken, while the skulls of three others were fractured, and their bodies were beaten with clubs until they were completely black and blue. The natives then took what stores and goods would be valuable to them, and destroyed the rest. They had been induced to spare the lives of the white men, hoping to receive a ransom, and took them, with the spoil, to the mountains.

Capt. Allen arrived four days after the events recorded above, and with the aid of a chief of some note in the vicinity, succeeded in liberating the prisoners, who are likely to recover, and it is hoped that they may learn a lesson of prudence and forbearance, should they have dealings in future with this race of cannibals.

The two vessels have left this morning, and our bark is once more under way. There is no wind, and we are resting quietly upon the glassy bosom of the waters.

26. On the 22d a severe gale commenced, and lasted for three days, during which no injury was experienced except the loss of sails.

Jan. 15, 1850. At sunrise we heard the welcome cry of "Sail oh!" and about 10 o'clock, A. M., the American whale ship, Uncas, came within hailing distance, and the captain came on board and dined; after which Mr. W. and myself accompanied him on board the Uncas, where we were introduced to Mrs. Edwards, the captain's wife. We enjoyed a social chat, took tea, and returned to the bark at dusk. There is something novel as well as delightful in going out to tea on these lone waters, where we never before saw a sail except our own.

16. Capt. Edwards and wife passed the day with us, and we found it quite too short; although but acquaintances of yesterday, our intimacy seems of years.

18. The Uncas still remains in company.

19. We have lost sight of our friends.

22. The Uncas came in sight at daylight, and spoke us at nine o'clock. The captain said, "You are in my debt. I have come for my pay. I shall send my boat for you and Mrs. Wallis to come here and spend the day." Accordingly we went on board and passed a most delightful day. We have had calms and light airs for some time, and our progress is slow. We cannot

find the monsoon. It must have blown away during the gale that we had off Feejee.

23. A fine breeze. The Uncas has outsailed us on her way to Guam. Capt. Edwards has been from New Bedford about six months, and has been quite successful in getting oil.

Feb. 7. Our anchor was cast in Manilla Bay at about six o'clock, P. M. The captain and Mr. Saunders (a passenger from Feejee) went ashore to get our letters from home, to hear the news, &c. We had heard nothing from home since we left, and looked with anxiety and pleasure for our communications. At nine o'clock I heard the paddles of the returning banca, and soon after Mr. W. and Mr. S. came on board, each bearing a little bundle in his hand. I met them at the companion way, and held out my hand to receive the letters. " Here are some cakes that Mr. P. has sent you, with an invitation for you to reside at your old quarters at the house of Peel, Hubbell and Co., during our stay at Manilla," said Mr. W., as he put the bundle into my hand. " But where are the letters?" I asked. I was told that there were none for any of us. We passed into the cabin, ate some cakes, and in due time retired to rest, and to dream of home if we could.

8. We left the bark, and were welcomed at the house of Peel, Hubbell, Co., by Messrs. Edwards and Pierce and Mr. Towne. We learned that some changes had taken place among the managers of the house. Mr. Edwards has received the appointment of American Consul, and Mr. Osborne has left the firm and returned to America. Mr. Pierce, of Salem, is his successor. After dinner we enjoyed a pleasant drive on the Calsada.

9. My girl, Phebe, came on shore and the child of

Mr. Saunders, who, with her father, came as a passenger in our bark from Feejee.

The small-pox is raging fearfully in Manilla. Phebe and Mary Saunders are to be vaccinated at once.

28. The United States sloop of war, St. Mary, arrived. The Consul called on board and invited the Commodore, with his Secretary, to reside here during their stay at this place.

March 1. Commodore Geisenger, with his Secretary, Mr. Sleigh, and several of the officers of the St. Mary, dined here yesterday.

In addition to our usual afternoon drive, the Commodore, Mr. Pierce, my husband and myself, enjoyed a delightful drive about the suburbs of Manilla by moonlight.

2. Our hosts gave a dinner party to the Commodore and his officers, and the house of Russell, Sturgiss & Co. It was a splendid affair. I received an invitation to spend a day with Mrs. Steele, of the ship Anstiss, of Boston, commanded by Capt. Steele, which arrived a few days since from Hongkong.

3. I passed a pleasant day with Mrs. Sturgiss and Mrs. Steele. The house occupied by Mr. and Mrs. Sturgiss is most delightfully situated at a little distance from the road leading to the balsa, surrounded by green fields and flower gardens, and is decidedly the most beautiful country seat to be seen about Manilla. The house of Russell, Sturgiss & Co., gave a dinner to the Commodore and his officers and the house of Peel, Hubbell & Co. About eight in the evening, Mr. Sturgiss, Capt. Steele and Capt. Wallis joined us. We then took tea and returned home.

5. The Commodore and suite left the house, expect-

27

ing to sail in the evening. At 10 o'clock, A. M., the Commodore sent his boat, and an invitation for Mr. W. and myself, with several others, to visit the St. Mary. We were shown over the vessel, partook of an elegant collation, and then returned delighted with our visit.

10. Whatever road we take during our afternoon drives, we meet the dead that are being borne to their graves. They are mostly children, who have died with the small-pox. The bodies are dressed in the most ludicrous manner, and carried through the streets on a tray, or bier, while their faces are horribly disfigured by the disease. Thus they are borne along, spreading infection through the streets and among the numerous inhabitants of the places where they pass.

14. The American ship, Vernon, arrived from Hongkong. Capt. McKay is accompanied by his wife.

20. All being in readiness, we took leave of our truly hospitable hosts, who had so kindly received and entertained us so many times, and rejoined our bark to wend our way homewards.

21. The weather is delightful. A gentle breeze fills our sails and we are homeward bound.

Every precaution has been used to prevent the small-pox from spreading, but Mr. Saunders, one of the passengers, is now sick with it, and we fear he will not have it lightly.

28. The weather continues fine. Mr. S. has recovered, and was dismissed from the hospital this morning. It was purified as soon as he left, and a negro, named John Battis, has taken possession, being sick with the dysentery.

9. We anchored off North Island at sunset. The British bark, Enmore, Capt. Dunsford, anchored near.

She is in rather a leaky condition, her crew being obliged to work at the pumps half an hour once in two hours. Capt. D. spent the evening with us.

14. The poor negro died and was buried in the deep, and there was none to mourn or care for his loss. The flag was raised half mast, the funeral service was read, and although there was no exhibition of grief for the departed, yet all appeared, and no doubt felt, the solemnity of the scene.

May 27. We had a severe gale of wind, which commenced on the 23d and lasted till the 26th. A part of the bulwarks, several of the ports and portions of the head-rail were stove ; the vessel leaked some in her upper works, and we were all sufficiently uncomfortable while the gale lasted.

28. An active, interesting Portuguese lad, whom Mr. Wallis shipped in Manilla, was taken sick, and was carried to the deck cabin that he might have proper attendance, and be made as comfortable as possible. His mind was somewhat wandering during the day, and at night became more so. He constantly imagined that every one wished to kill him. He came into the lower cabin, with tears streaming down his cheeks, and the perspiration standing in large drops on his forehead, his hair disordered, and his body convulsed with an agony of fear, asking, "What for you want to kill me, Capt. Wallis? I no hurt you. I want to go home and see my father." After a time he was prevailed upon to return to the cabin on deck, where he soon became so violent that his hands and feet were bound, and it was sometimes more than two men could do to manage him. His shouts and ravings during the night and the next day were fearful and distressing to hear.

30. Antonio de Roce appears somewhat exhausted from continual and violent raving, but his fever is exceedingly high, and no hopes are entertained of his recovery.

June 2. Antonio breathed his last about six o'clock, P. M. His sufferings during his sickness were truly severe, but his death was as gentle as the slumbers of an infant.

3. Antonio was buried with the usual ceremonies. He was a native of Fayal, and of respectable parentage. He had been absent from home about sixteen months, and was very anxious to return. His promptness in duty, and the kindness of his disposition, had endeared him to his shipmates, and they sorrowed for his loss.

On the first day of the month we experienced another violent gale, although we had doubled the stormy Cape, and thought we were where gales were not prevalent, but we found, to our discomfort, that the winds in this region could raise heavy seas that caused our bark to groan, that washed in upon our decks, that could break in cabin doors, carry off a billet head, split a staysail, carry away halyards, and, in short, could cut up as many pranks as any Cape gale.

14. We anchored off the Island of St. Helena. Here we found the ship Anstiss, which we left at Manilla. She sailed eight days after us, and arrived a few hours before. As soon as the anchor was down, our friend, the American Consul, came on board, and we accompanied him to his residence, where we found Mrs. Carroll, Capt. and Mrs. Steele, of the Anstiss, and Capt. and Mrs. Plummer, of the ship St. Petersburg, of Boston.

The evening passed pleasantly at the Ex-Consul's, with

music and conversation. At one time during the evening
we missed him from our company for a few moments.
On his return, he handed a paper to one of his daughters, who took her seat at the piano, and played off-hand
to the tune of " Yankee Doodle," a song in which the
names of each gentleman were introduced, with an allu-
sion to their business, and also something complimentary
to their wives.   I need not say that this extemporaneous
production produced great applause.

15.   At six o'clock, A. M., I took leave of our American friends, who were to sail for home at ten, and
mounting a one horse carriage in company with Mrs.
Carroll, we started for Longwood.   We saw appearances of rain, but they did not deter us.   We went on
and soon the rain descended in torrents; but being well
sheltered beneath cloaks and umbrellas, we kept dry,
and before we reached Longwood, had fine weather.
So much has been said about the ride to Longwood and
Longwood itself, that I will add nothing farther, except
that we looked down horrible gullies and ravines, and
found the house where Napoleon lived and died, a mis-
erable looking place.   I considered the view from Longwood rather pretty; the new house, too, is beautiful,
and the flowers that surround it still more so.

We returned about twelve; after which we visited the
grave of the excellent Mrs. Judson, about which so
much has been said by those who have visited it, that I
should fail in an attempt to present any thing new.

At three o'clock we went on board.   The Anstiss and
St. Petersburg sailed a few hours before.   The vessel
was soon under way, and we felt that we were bound
home in earnest.

25.   We have had favoring winds since leaving St.

Helena, and to-day have crossed the Equator. All hands are as busy as possible in fitting and cleaning for home.

July 10. We encountered large quantities of the Gulf weed; this is a delightful sight to the homeward bound.

16. Ran into a fog bank, which told us that we were near land.

18. Our anchor was cast in Salem harbor,—we were at HOME.

GENERAL RETURNS OF FEEJEE DISTRICT, 1847.

Chapels 36 ; other Preaching Places 20 ; Missionaries 7—now increased to 9 ; Native Teachers 36 ; Day School Teachers 106 ; Local Preachers 60 ; Class Leaders 90 ; Church Members 1,060 ; On trial for Church Membership 200 ; Day Schools 44 ; Scholars of both sexes 2,000 ; Total number professing Christianity, including all the above and about thirty regular residents from various parts, 3,500. The above is as near as I can state at present. The schedule is not yet made out.

J. HUNT.

ERRATA.

Page 36. Seventh line from the top, for " Bau," read *Bua*.

Page 59. Sixth line from the top, for "the civilized lady continued, read *so says the civilized lady*.

Pag. 61. Ninth line from the bottom, for " Queen of Egypt," read the *wife of Potiphar*.

Page 121. Thirteenth line from the bottom, for "vals," read *valo, valo*.

Page 158. Fourteenth line from the bottom, for " Saka," read *Sanka*.